Contemporary Issues in Global Criminal Justice

Contemporary Issues in Global Criminal Justice

Edited by
Ed Johnston
Sophie Marsh

LEXINGTON BOOKS
Lanham • Boulder • New York • London

Published by Lexington Books
An imprint of The Rowman & Littlefield Publishing Group, Inc.
4501 Forbes Boulevard, Suite 200, Lanham, Maryland 20706
www.rowman.com

86-90 Paul Street, London EC2A 4NE, United Kingdom

British Library Cataloguing in Publication Information Available

Library of Congress Cataloging-in-Publication Data Available
ISBN 978-1-7936-3733-8 (cloth : alk. paper)
ISBN 978-1-7936-3734-5 (electronic)

Contents

Acknowledgments

We would like to thank the contributors for their hard work in helping me bring this idea to fruition. Covid-19 hugely delayed the project and I am grateful for their patience.

Ed would like to thank his partner, Wolfy, for once again giving up their evenings and free time to complete this project. I am thankful you recognize there are not enough bundles or time in the day.

Sophie would like to thank her partner, Charlie, for his unconditional support and encouragement. She also would like to thank her parents, John and Lesley, for their unwavering support and belief.

We would also like to thank Becca Beurer and Carter Moran at Rowman & Littlefield for all their help and guidance along the way.

Ed and Sophie
January 2022

List of Cases

Aksoy v. Turkey 100/1995/606/694 (ECHR, 18 December 1996)

Andonovski v. the former Yugoslav Republic of Macedonia, no. 24312/10 (ECtHR 23 July 2015)

Asenov v. Bulgaria, no. 42026/98 (ECtHR 15 July 2005)

Asllani v. the former Yugoslav Republic of Macedonia, no. 24058/13 (ECtHR 10 December 2015)

Assenov and Others v. Bulgaria (1998) App. No. 24760/94, 28 Eur. H. R. Rep. 652

Blake v. Guatemala, "Judgment" (1998) Inter-Am. Ct. H. R. (Ser. C) no. 36

Boicenco v. Moldova, no. 41088/05 (ECtHR 11 July 2006)

Brown v. Canada (Attorney General)(2017), 136 OR (3d) 497 (S.C.J.).000

Bushel [1670] Vaughn 135, 124 Eng Rep 1006 CP 1670).

Chahal v. the United Kingdom (ECtHR 15 November 1996), Reports of Judgments and Decisions 1996-V

Dodov v. Bulgaria, no. 59548/00 (ECtHR 17 January 2008)

Dvorski v. Croatia ECtHR, App. No. 25703/11

Dzeladinov and Others v. the former Yugoslav Republic of Macedonia, no. 13252/02 (ECtHR 10 April 2008)

El-Masri v. the former Yugoslav Republic of Macedonia (GC), no. 39630/09 (ECHR, 2012)

Ergi v. Turkey (2001) App. No. 23818/94, Eur. H.R. Rep. 18

Gorgiev v. the former Yugoslav Republic of Macedonia, no. 26984/05 (ECtHR, 19 April 2012)

Gül v. Turkey (2000) 34 Eur. H.R. Rep. 28

Hajrulahu v. the former Yugoslav Republic of Macedonia, no. 37537/07 (ECtHR, 29 October 2015)

Ilhan v. Turkey (2000) 34 Eur. H.R. Rep. 36

J.A. v. Switzerland (2020) ECHR, App. No. 6325/15

James and Others v. The United Kingdom (1986) ECHR, App. No. 8793/79

Jasar v. the former Yugoslav Republic of Macedonia, no. 69908/01 (ECtHR, 15 February 2007)

Jordan v. The United Kingdom (2001) ECHR 300

Kelly v. The United Kingdom (2001) ECHR 240

Kolpak v. Russia (2012) ECHR App. No. 41408/04

L.R. v. North Macedonia, no. 38067/15 (ECtHR, 23 January 2020)

Labita v. Italy [GC], no. 26772/95 (ECHR, 2000-IV)

Leander v. Sweden (1987) ECHR, App. No. 9248/81

McCann and Others v. The United Kingdom (1996) App. No. 18984/91, 21 Eur. H.R. Rep.

McKerr v. The United Kingdom (2001) ECHR, App. No. 28883/95

Okkalı v. Turkey, no. 52067/99 (ECHR, 2006-XII) (extracts)

Plokhovy v. Russia (2020) ECHR, App. No. 45024/07

Prosecutor v. Lubanga, Case No. ICC-01/04–01/06 OA 10, Judgment on the Appeals of The Prosecutor and The Defence against Trial Chamber I'2 Decision on Victims' Participation of 18 January 2008, p. 96 (July 11, 2008)

R v. Brusch and Horvat [2012] 1 Cr. App. 47

R v. Massey (2007) EWCA Crim 2664

R. *v.* Ewert (2018] 2 SCR 165

R. v. Gladue (1999) 1 SCR 688

R. v. Ipeelee (2012) 1 SCR 433

R. v. Moses (1992), 11 CR (4th) 357 (YT TerrCt)

R. v. Nur (2015) 1 SCR 774

R. v. Sharma (2020) ONCA 478, leave to appeal granted by the Supreme Court of Canada on 14 January 2021

R. v. Sinclair (2010) 2 SCR 310

R. v. Smith (1987) 1 SCR 1045

R. v. T.M.B. (2011) OJ No. 4836, 2011 ONCJ

R. v. Vandyke (2013) ABPC 347

Salman v. Turkey (2000) 34 Eur. H.R. Rep. 17

Selami and Others v. the former Yugoslav Republic of Macedonia, no. 78241/13, (ECtHR, 1 March 2018)

Selmouni v. France (GC), no. 25803/94, ECHR 1999-V

Situation in the Democratic Republic of the Congo (*Prosecutor v. Lubanga Dyilo*), Case No. ICC-01/04–01/06–119, Decision on Victims' Participation (Jan. 18 2008)

Situation in the Democratic Republic of the Congo (*Prosecutor v. Lubanga Dyilo*), Case No. ICC-01–04–01/06 OA8, Decision of the Appeals Chamber on the Joint Application of Victims a/0001/06 to a/0003/06 and a/0105/06 concerning the "Directions and Decision of the Appeals Chamber" of 2 February 2007 (13 June 2007)

Situation in the Democratic Republic of the Congo (*Prosecutor v. Lubanga Dyilo*), Case No. ICC-01/04–01/06–1136, Application for leave to Appeal Trial Chamber I's January 18 Decision on Victims' Participation (28 January 2008)

Situation in the Democratic Republic of the Congo (*Prosecutor v. Lubanga Dyilo*), Case No. ICC-01/04–01/06 OA 9 OA 10, Judgment on the appeals of The Prosecutor and The Defence against Trial Chamber I's Decision on Victims' Participation of 18 January 2008 (11 July 2008)

Situation in the Democratic Republic of the Congo, Situation No. ICC-01/04–101-tEN-Corr, Decision on the Applications for Participation in the Proceedings of VPRS 1, VPRS 2, VPRS 3, VPRS 4, VPRS 5, and VPRS 6, Public Redacted Version (17 January 2006)

Situation in Uganda (*Prosecutor v. Kony et al.*), Decision on victims' applications for participation a/0010/06, a/0064/06 to a/0070/06, a/0081/06 to a/0104/06 to a/0127/06, ICC-02/04–101 (10 August 2007)

Situation in Uganda, Case No. ICC-02/04–106, Response of Legal Representative of Victims a/0119/06 to the Prosecutor's Application for Leave to Appeal the Decision on Victims' Applications for Participation a/0010/06, a/0064/06 to a/0070/06, a/0081/06 to a/0111/06 to a/0127/06 (31 August 2007)

St Ann's Island Shooting and Fishing Club v. The King, [1950] SCR 211.

Sulejmanov v. the former Yugoslav Republic of Macedonia, no. 69875/01 (ECtHR, 24 April 2008)

Trajkoski v. the former Yugoslav Republic of Macedonia, no. 13191/02 (ECtHR, 7 February 2008)

Usmanov v. Russia (2020) ECHR, App. No. 43936/18

Velásquez-Rodríguez v. Honduras (1988) Inter-Am. Ct. H. R. (Ser. C) No. 4

List of Legislation

American Convention on Human Rights 1969

An Act to amend the Corrections and Conditional Release Act and Another Act, SC 2019, c. 27

An Act to amend the Criminal Code (sentencing) and other Acts in consequence thereof, SC 1995, c. 22

Canadian Charter of Rights and Freedoms, Part 1 of the Constitution Act, 1982

Charter of Fundamental Rights of the European Union [2000]

Constitution Act, 1867 (UK), 30 & 31 Vict., c. 3

Constitution Act, 1982, being Schedule B to the Canada Act 1982 (UK), 1982, c. 11

Corrections and Conditional Release Act, SC 1992, c. 20, as am

Criminal Code, RSC 1985, c. C-46, as am

Declaration of Basic Principles of Justice for Victims of Crime and Abuse of Power, UNGA A/RES/40/34 (29 November 1985)

Directive 2010/64/EU of the European Parliament and of the Council

Directive 2012/29/EU of the European Parliament and of the Council (2012) establishing minimum standards on the rights, support and protection of victims of crime, replacing Council Framework Decision 2001/220/JHA

Directive 2013/48/EU of the European Parliament and of the Council

European Convention on Human Rights and Fundamental Freedoms 1950

European Union (Withdrawal) Act 2018

Indian Act, RSC 1985, c. I-5, as am

International Criminal Court, Rules of Procedure and Evidence, 2013 ICC-ASP/1/3, R. 48

Narcotic Control Act, RSC 1970, c. N-1

Resolution ICC-ASP/18/Res.1, Resolution of the Assembly of States Parties on the proposed programme budget for 2020, the Working Capital for 2020, the scale of assessment for the apportionment of expenses of the International Criminal Court, financing operations for 2020 and the Contingency Fund (6 December 2019)

Rome Statute of the International Criminal Court, 1998 U.N. Doc. A/CONF. 183/9

Safe Streets and Communities Act, SC 2012, c. 1

Sentencing Act 2002, s 25

Sexual Offences Act 2003

Street Offences Act 1959

United Nations Declaration on the Rights of Indigenous Peoples Act, SC 2021, c. 14

Introduction

Ed Johnston and Sophie Marsh

As this book illustrates, there are a vast array of contemporary challenges in global criminal justice. This collection draws from academics from across the globe to proffer analysis of contemporary problems in a number of different jurisdictions and legal systems. Problems in England and Wales, New Zealand, Croatia, Spain, the Netherlands, Canada, and the Republic of North Macedonia are covered throughout this collection. Issues surrounding the use of the International Criminal Court are also examined. The book explores problems at the pre-arrest stage, the investigative stage, the trial, and finally the post-conviction stage.

The book opens with Marsh's chapter, "The Importance of Protecting Sex Workers from Harm." The chapter outlines the risk of harm that sex workers are subjected to and critically analyzes whether they are adequately protected from such harm. There are an estimated 80,000 female sex workers in the UK, and selling sex means managing daily risks from clients and pimps. Those who work on the streets are significantly more susceptible to threats of physical, emotional, and psychological violence than those who operate indoors. Policies lack an unrealistic approach due to their inherently punitive nature, criminalizing already-vulnerable sex workers. Such criminalization may consequently prevent sex workers from reporting violence from pimps and clients because of the barriers that exist between sex workers and police. It is apparent that policies are focused on removing the problem of prostitution, rather than finding wider solutions to tackle the issues. Drug addictions and violence from both pimps and clients are not a focus of such policies. The lack of regard for the safety of sex workers has forced them to adopt their own protection measures, such as working in a pre-determined location or an area with CCTV. Other means of protective measures include telling a fellow sex worker where they are going and taking note of a client's car registrations.

However, with the rise in welfare agencies and police forces working together to criminalize violent pimps and clients, there is a shift toward prioritizing the welfare of sex workers. Nonetheless, the issue of pushing prostitution further underground and leaving sex workers more vulnerable by criminalizing the clients requires further addressing.

In the second chapter, "The Impact of the Judicial Role on Treatment and Punishment in the New Zealand Alcohol & Other Drug Treatment Court," Carr examines the impact of the judicial role on mandated treatment in New Zealand. Drawing from ethnographic research, the chapter illustrates how through a therapeutic mandate, the judicial role blurs the distinction between treatment and punishment. The wide discretion of judges and collaboration with community treatment providers, lauded by proponents of the Alcohol and Other Treatment Court (AODTC) as key to its therapeutic effectiveness, were found to create a number of harms for participants. The chapter suggests that the AODTC functions on legally mandated treatment involving overt expressions of judicial power, dubious decision-making practices, and judicial decision-making that favors unjustifiable punishments under the guise of the treatment. The AODTC threatens to undermine the legitimacy of the New Zealand judiciary through a foreign set of values and standards.

The book moves on to explore issues in policing. James and Hester's chapter examines the stop and search powers in England and Wales. The power is one of the police's most commonly used powers, with more than a thousand stop and searches conducted every day in 2019. Within these stops, there is a high amount of racial disparity, with higher proportions of ethnic minority populations subject to the use of this power. Not only does this chapter examine the trends in racial disparity, it also considers the "political interference" that has been happening with stop and search since the coalition government came to power in 2010. Such interference has seen the introduction of the Best Use of Stop and Search Scheme (BUSS), by the then home secretary Theresa May, only for police forces to be told by subsequent home secretaries to ignore aspects of this relating to section 60 "no suspicion" searches. This chapter also examines the media portrayal of stop and search, with routine debates involving high-ranking police officers and politicians disagreeing over the link between stop and search and an increase in knife crime. Finally, and arguably most importantly, these changes and how they are implemented by the police, are examined in terms of the impact stop and search has on the key foundations of the British policing models of police legitimacy and policing by consent.

The fourth chapter by Karas and Buriĉ adopts an international lens to issues in policing. Their chapter examines concerns in the interrogation stage of the police investigation in Croatia. In 2017, the Croatian Criminal Procedure Act (CPA) underwent one of the biggest reforms of police conduct in relation to criminal proceedings in recent history, a significant change in the way police authorities interrogate a suspect. Now, the police interrogate the suspect in an analogous manner to that of a public prosecutor. This means there is mandatory audio-video recording of every interrogation and strict exclusionary rules should there be a breach of procedure. Prior to the reform, the law vaguely regulated the procedure of police interrogation (which was called "collecting of information"). Such procedure lacked any guarantees for the protection of the rights of the defense of the suspect and the arrested person. Lack of guarantees was compensated by ban to use the protocols of such interrogations as evidence before the court. However, this ban also led to lack of court oversight over police conduct with the suspect and the accused person in the earliest stages of the proceedings. At the same time, this regulation made Croatian police very efficient in resolving cases of most serious crimes. Fear of decline in the efficiency of the police work was one of the biggest obstacles in the introduction of the reform. The chapter presents a holistic overview of the arguments advanced in favor, as well as against the reform.

In chapter 5, Mehzeb Chowdhury explores issues around automation in policing. The chapter suggests that the integration of technology into state security apparatuses has prompted questions about the risks of "big data" and its effects on society. Examining the impact of mechanization, this chapter extrapolates the possible futures of law enforcement in technological societies. Neoliberalism in modern policing, technological determinism, the risk society, abstract systems of trust and legitimacy, and the recent push toward evidence-based practice, is explored to underscore the possible drivers and consequences of modernity. The potential and scope of mechanization, prominently artificial intelligence (AI) is critically evaluated with emphasis on its limitations and vulnerability to abuse by state actors, idealistic expectations surrounding its capacity to reduce or even eliminate human error, racism, sexism, and prejudice from the criminal justice system, as well as the dangers of such technologies augmenting historic and existing fallacies within the same.

Chapter 6 keeps with the theme of technology enhanced policing, and Raquel Borges Blázquez asks "Artificial Intelligence and the Use of Algorithms in the Criminal Judicial System: Chimera or Panacea?" The chapter highlights how artificial intelligence offers countless advantages to our lives. On one hand, the capacity of a computer to store and connect data is far superior to human capacity. On the other, its "intelligence" also involves deep ethical problems to which the law must respond. The chapter uses the term "intelligence" even though nowadays machines are not considered intelligent. Machines only use the input data that a human being has previously considered as true. This truth is relative and the data will have the same biases and prejudices as the human who programmed the machine. In other words, machines can be racist, sexist, and classist if their programmers are.

The United States have been utilizing artificial intelligence for many years to attempt to prevent crime and assist with recidivism forecasts. The chapter suggests we should carefully consider how, when, why, and under what assumptions we can make use of artificial intelligence and especially who is going to program the machine.

Chapters 7 and 8 explore issues at the trial stage. Keane's chapter highlights the range of measures available to protect the vulnerable accused at trial. The chapter argues that the normative principle at the heart of the measures available is the concept of effective participation. The author shows how the scope and requirements of the vulnerable accused's right to effective participation in Scots law is in some important respects, unclear, and that the lack of comprehensive, rational, and authoritative legal guidance on the matter is potentially imperilling the system of legal protection that does exist, which appears badly overreliant on individual and institutional discretion in certain places. Ultimately, this chapter serves as a warning call that political attention requires to be given to the position of the vulnerable accused in Scotland, especially given ongoing changes wrought to criminal justice due to the Covid 19 pandemic.

Chapter 8 provides an account of jury trials in England and Wales. The chapter argues that much of the research carried out on juries and their decision-making, has focused on certain psychosocial characteristics such as confidence, attractiveness, gender, and ethnicity as well as jury size and decision rule. It has also focused on the individual juror rather than the more realistic jury as a group and on verdict outcomes, i.e., guilty or innocent, rather than the processes to reach this decision. This has meant that little is known or understood about the jury as a collective decision-making group. This is important to note, as many factors could influence these decision-making processes and ultimately whether someone receives a fair trial. This chapter briefly discusses the history of the jury in England and Wales, and then explores the role of the jury to discuss the importance of examining the jury as a group alongside their decision-making processes in order to ensure, as far as possible, a fair, informed trial.

Doughty's chapter analyzes victim and witness participation across international courts and tribunals. This is still relatively novel in practice. The International Criminal Court has enshrined victim and witness participation within its Rome Statute and Rules of Procedure and Evidence, and created a dedicated Victims and Witnesses Unit. Despite also ruling upon international atrocities, the European Court of Human Rights and its attached convention do not permit any kind of victim or witness participation. This is particularly unusual given many of the European Court's member states have domestic provisions providing a right for victim standing. The right to participation for impacted victim-witnesses is vital in achieving a just outcome for all parties involved. Should the International Criminal Court's system be viewed as the gold standard for the remaining exclusionary international court systems? Would the European Court benefit from a Victims and Witnesses Unit of its own, and is this feasible? This chapter will respond to these queries through an exploration of international victim participation alterations made as the International Court developed insight through cases, and by examining how the European Court could improve justiciability for victims by learning from the International Criminal Court's experience.

The final chapters of the book examine issues at the post-conviction stage. In chapter 10, Pivaty examines the use of out-of-court disposals in the Netherlands. This chapter describes the history and the nature of this phenomenon in the Netherlands. It observes that in the Netherlands the main relevant trend in the last years has been not the growth of out-of-court disposals as such, as the proportion of criminal cases dealt with out of court has remained relatively stable. Rather, in the Netherlands, there has been a shift toward more coercive use of out-of-court disposals. This trend manifested itself mainly in the introduction of a new, nonconsent based, legal instrument, the so-called penal order (*strafbeschikking*). The chapter reviews the main criticisms of the current system of administrative out-of-court disposals in the Netherlands. Although this system is often criticized for its lack of compliance with fair trial rights, this chapter argues that the fair trial rights framework might be ill-suited to assess whether administrative out-of-court disposals function fairly toward criminal suspects in practice. The chapter concludes by calling for more empirical research into the practice of administrative out-of-court disposals rooted in the theoretical framework of procedural justice.

In chapter 11, Myles traverses the over-representation of Canada's Aboriginals in Canadian correctional facilities. These numbers have increased in recent years, as crime rates have fallen. In 1996, the Royal Commission on Aboriginal Peoples explained the over-representation through Aboriginals' high crime levels and discrimination against them within the criminal justice system. To alleviate the over-representation, the commission proposed that Canadian Aboriginals administer their own criminal justice systems. This chapter explores the over-representation as a complex phenomenon reflecting multiple contributory circumstances. Nevertheless, the current growth in the over-representation correlates with the marked increase in the offenses for which a mandatory minimum is handed down. While the Canadian government has not relinquished control over the criminal justice system, changes expected to lessen the over-representation remain possible. Court processes emphasizing holistic healing of Aboriginal offenders over incarceration have helped to lower recidivism. Canadian courts have declared unconstitutional various mandatory minimum sentencing provisions. All participants in the court process would benefit from further education. Yet, a sustained commitment from the Canadian, provincial, and territorial government is necessary to counter the over-representation. Whether such commitment emerges will depend on Euro-Canadian social attitudes.

The book closes with a chapter from Lažetić and Mujoska–Trpevska, who chart issues with the penal system of the Republic of North Macedonia. The chapter offers a statistical overview of the structure of the prison population in the Republic of North Macedonia between 2007–2020. The chapter analyzes five categories of offenders: women, juvenile prisoners, drug-addicted prisoners, violent prisoners, and prisoners with mental illness. All the categories contribute to the overarching problem of overcrowding. The Republic of North Macedonia has lost several cases before the ECtHR because of breaches to the human rights of the prisoner. These violations include ill-treatment and brutality of prisoners. The chapter contains an overview of the most relevant cases regarding violations of Article 3 of the ECHR in North Macedonia. The chapter suggests points of reform for the prison system and the rights of the prisoner.

We hope you enjoy this multinational volume of concerns. It paints a bleak picture of the current state of criminal justice. This not just limited to one jurisdiction; the issues are very much global. Furthermore, there appears to be a further danger on the horizon in terms of automation of police work and the use of artificial intelligence. We hope this edition inspires further work and exploration in these areas.

Dr. Ed Johnston and Sophie Marsh
January 2022

Chapter 1

The Importance of Protecting Sex Workers from Harm

Sophie Marsh

While selling sex in itself is legal in England and Wales, its quasi-criminalized nature has created disparity between legislation and law enforcement.[1] Thus, the issue of regulating sex work poses barriers for legal framework both nationally and internationally.[2] However, there exists little consensus on how to effectively address the prostitution problem.[3] It is estimated that approximately 11% of British men aged 16–74 have paid for sex on at least one occasion, amounting to 2.3 million individuals.[4] Consequently, for the estimated 80,000 female sex workers in Britain,[5] selling sex means managing daily risks from clients and pimps.[6] Nonetheless, such risks ceased to take an interest from academics and the public prior to the 2000s,[7] despite violence towards sex workers from clients and pimps being regarded a major public health issue.[8] Current policies lack an unrealistic approach to prostitution due to their inherently punitive strategies, criminalising vulnerable sex workers as a result of over-policing.[9] Such responses ignore empirical evidence surrounding sex workers' experiences with police[10] which are often stigmatized.[11] It is this stigmatisation that may subsequently prevent sex workers from reporting violence they suffer due to the chasm between sex workers and police.[12] Subsequently, sex workers have been forced to find their own means of self-protection due to lack of adequate protection from the criminal justice system.[13] While welfare approaches, such as the Nation Ugly Mugs scheme,[14] have had a positive impact on the safety of sex workers, it is evident that policing responses must adapt to support vulnerable sex workers from both violence and exploitation.

The Context of Prostitution in England and Wales

Historically, the purchase of sex was not criminalized, nor was the sale of sex. However, the law sought to criminalize certain Behavior conducted by prostitutes. For example, S.1 of the Street Offences Act 1959[15] stated: "it shall be an offence for a [person] [aged 18 or over] [(whether male or female)] [persistently] to loiter or solicit in a street or public place for the purpose of prostitution." "Persistently" was defined as "takes place on two or more occasions in any period of three months."[16] However, this legislation created issues for criminal justice responses, particularly as evidencing "persistence" proved challenging. To catch just one prostitute soliciting on two or more occasions across a time period of three months requires a vast amount of police resources, notwithstanding that sex work generally lacks visibility.[17]

Selling sex has raised a number of concerns in England and Wales due to is exploitative nature. In 2014, the All-Party Parliamentary Group report on prostitution commented that there are "near pandemic levels of violence experienced by women in prostitution."[18] This comment is highlighted by the 1,080 potential victims of sex trafficking in 2015 alone that were identified by the National Referral Mechanism.[19] Moreover, Kinnell suggested that from 1996–2006, 86 sex workers had been murdered, making them 12 times more likely to be killed while working compared to other women their age.[20] From 2006–2016, this statistic significantly reduced to 34 occupational homicide cases of sex workers.[21] While this statistic has reduced since the 2000s, the likelihood of sex workers being killed while working remains significant, highlighting the vast level of violence sex workers could be subjected to. Consequently, Platt and Sanders labelled sex work as the most dangerous profession.[22] Thus, this chapter will attempt to demonstrate the severe levels of violence that sex workers are subjected to and will subsequently assess whether police and government responses have adequately protected such workers.

While there exists a barrier to data collection due to a lack of visibility of sex work,[23] a Home Affairs Report in 2016 suggested that around 95% of sex workers are female, with an average of 25 clients per week.[24] Around 20–30% of such sex workers are believed to be migrants, with an average age of between 20 and 24 years old.[25] It has been suggested that while the majority of sex workers were female, they have a diverse demographic with regards to characteristics; such as their mental and physical health, national or ethnic background, sexuality, social class, and education level.[26] Such figures therefore demonstrate the complexity and diversity of selling sex in England and Wales and highlights the difficulty faced by the criminal justice system.

The Risks and Violence in Selling Sex

Research has established sex workers are subjected to high levels of violence both nationally and globally.[27] Sex workers that operate on streets are more susceptible to threats of physical, emotional, and psychological violence than those who operate indoors.[28] Nonetheless, in the public space, sex workers fear violence from clients and the public, arrest from police, and harassment from community members protesting against sex work.[29] Church, Henderson, Barnard and Hart found that those 81% of those working on the streets had been subjected to violence while working.[30] In 2019, it was suggested that between 32% and 55% of sex workers operating on the street had been subjected to violence in that year alone.[31] Such violence has been argued to be the result of the criminalisation of sex work as it pushes sex work further underground, leaving sex workers reluctant to report such violence to authorities.[32] Nonetheless, those who work indoors remain susceptible to violence despite the transferal from the street to an indoor setting. Church et al. found that 48% of indoor workers have also been subjected to violence in the commission of sex work.[33] Thus, it is evident that the shift from selling sex on the street to selling sex indoors has not significantly contributed to the harm reduction of sex workers.

Female respondents in a study conducted by Hester, Mulvihill, Matolcsi, Sanchez, and Walker in 2018 reported both fear of and subjection to physical violence and sexual violence. In addition to physical and sexual violence, such harm amounted to stalking, psychological harm and self-harm as a direct result of selling sex. Moreover, while potential perpetrators were identified as clients both police and civilians were recognized as perpetrators of violence towards sex workers. Examples include police raids on indoor premises and the stigma received from the general public.[34] Furthermore, Sanders' study in 2004 provided an insight to the type of violence women are subjected to on the street by interviewing 15 sex workers.[35] The majority had been physical beaten, 7 had been raped, 5 had been held at knifepoint and 3 had even been kidnapped, highlighting the extreme levels of violence that women working on the street are subjected to by clients. This is demonstrated in a global context by Prior, Hubbard, and Birch, who maintained that sex workers "experience relatively high levels of victimization including assault, rape, drugging, verbal abuse, theft, abduction, kidnapping, blackmail, harassment and persecution" in New South Wales, Australia.[36] Thus, it is evident that physical, sexual and emotional violence toward sex workers is not an issue exclusive to England and Wales. However, Day and Ward maintained that it is difficult to predict violence against sex workers as "occupational studies of, and service for, prostitutes cannot be confined to the risks posed directly by exchanges with customers."[37] Thus, this demonstrates the implications of managing risks and violence sex workers are subjected to, limiting the effectiveness of criminal justice responses, which will be further discussed throughout this chapter.

PROSTITUTION POLICY

Debate regarding prostitution policy typically surrounds questions of morality and societal values.[38] For example, sex work is generally regarded as either "morally repugnant, an outcome of patriarchal oppression, an inevitable result of social inequalities, or as work freely chosen."[39] Benoit, Smith, Jansson, Healey, and Magnuson maintain that policy regulating sex work is motivated by two different perspectives on social inequality; hierarchal gender relations and multiple social inequalities (including class, gender, and race).[40] In order to overcome the impact that such oppressive have on the protection of sex workers, restrictive or integrative policies have been implemented across the globe which aim to reduce the inequalities subjected to those working in the sex industry. Restrictive policies entail understanding that sex work will exist despite its criminalization and thus seek to "protect society, protect prostitutes and protect social order."[41] Examples of restrictive policies in practice include licensing sex work in particular areas and mandating health testing for sex workers which have been implemented in the Netherlands.[42] Moreover, integrative policy refers to an understanding that while prostitution can be regarded as an autonomous consensual economic activity, it entails vulnerability and exploitation for some. This involves a multi-level government response, such as anti-stigma campaigns, employment and education support, and community initiatives.[43] Such policies seek to adequately protect sex workers from harm, yet there exists little literature which attempts to evaluate their success.

In addition to restrictive and integrative policies, there are 5 different models implemented across the globe in order to manage, control or regulate prostitution.[44] The first model surrounds the full criminalisation of prostitution, including all aspects of selling and buying sex. The second amounts to partial criminalisation, whereby some elements, such as a third-party involvement or running a brothel, are criminalized. The third refers to the criminalisation of the purchase of sex alone (also known as the sex-buyer model). The fourth model, encompasses the sale of sex in a licensed zone. Finally, the fifth model surrounds full decriminalisation of the sale and purchase of sex.[45] The United Kingdom currently operates the partial criminalisation models, while countries such as New Zealand have implemented full decriminalisation.[46] As a consequence, a global debate exists regarding how to regulate sex work. While some maintain that sex work encompasses gender-based violence which should therefore be repressed,[47] others suggest that the need for protection from violence must be balanced with the right to the autonomous and consensual selling of sex.[48]

In 2016, the Home Affairs Select Committee made six recommendations in their report in prostitution. Such recommendations were: decriminalising soliciting; amending brothel-keeping legislation; deleting previous offences relating to prostitution; developing guidance for police and local authorities; policy changes to prevent trafficking and exploitation; and strengthening the evidence base on prostitution.[49] The Government agreed that research must be conducted in order to better-inform future policy changed and legislation. In 2018, the Home Office commissioned the University of Bristol to examine the prevalence and nature of sex work in England and Wales.[50] The findings suggested that it is difficult to comment on the prevalence and nature due to the lack of visibility and the pervasiveness of stigma within the sex industry.[51] Thus, it was concluded that selling sex in England and Wales is an incredibly complex and diverse industry, posing barriers to protection from exploitation.[52]

Legislation Governing Prostitution

England and Wales have adopted a partial criminalisation model to influence legislation governing the sex industry. While it is not an offence to be a prostitute, S.54(2) of the Sexual Offences Act 2003[53] became the first piece of legislation to define what is meant by a "prostitute." It defines a "prostitute" as: "a person (a) who, on at least one occasion and whether or not compelled to do so, offers or provides sexual services to another person in return for payment or a promise of payment to (a) or a third person; and 'prostitution' is to be interpreted accordingly."[54] The legal framework criminalizes Behavior surrounding prostitution. In particular, current legislation seeks to punish those who use and exploit sex workers. In 2003, the legal framework which governed the selling of sexual services began to focus on the purchase of sexual service. S.51(a) of the Sexual Offences Act 2003[55] was introduced, which reads: "(1) it is an offence for a person in a street or public place to solicit another (b) for the purpose of obtaining b's sexual services as a prostitute. (2) . . . includes a person in a vehicle in a street or public place."[56]

In addition to criminalising those who provide sexual services, the legislation attempted to criminalize those who control prostitution for personal gain, e.g., pimps and madams. Subsequently, legislation was able to adapt in response to new challenges arising as a result of the sex work industry. S.53 of the Sexual Offences Act 2003 illegalized the act of pimping. The act reads: "(1) a person commits an offence if—(a) he intentionally controls any of the activities of another person relating to that person's prostitution in any part of the world, and (b) he does so for or in expectation of gain for himself or a third person."[57] Thus, exploitative conduct of sex workers in pursuit of financial gain became criminalized.

The ruling in *R v Massey*[58] further outlined that the courts are not willing to provide a comprehensive definition of "control" under the offence of controlling prostitution for gain to enable it to remain more flexible. Following this, coercing, bullying and forcing a person into selling sex can all be caught within the meaning of "control." Social isolation from others leaves sex workers particularly dependent on their pimp, particularly if their pimp is feeding their drug addiction. Moreover, the level of coercion is outlined in the case of *R v Brusch and Horvat*,[59] where two vulnerable women with drug addictions were coerced into the UK from the Czech Republic on the promise of a visa and were forced into prostitution. As well use the threat and use of violence, the women's phones were either removed or monitored as a means of further isolating them from society. While the courts held that the women were not kidnapped and detained, the courts ruled "they were, if not detained, at least their liberty had [been] removed to such an extent that the distinction becomes largely illusory."[60]

Consequently, any customer who paid for sexual intercourse with a sex worker who had been exploited would be committing an offence under S.53 Sexual Offences Act 2003. Thus, it is evident that the current approach to prostitution has extended beyond sex workers and seeks to target those who exploit them.

Moreover, the Policing and Crime Act 2009[61] subsequently amended the Sexual Offences Act 2003[62] and made it an offence to purchase sexual services if the sex worker has been exploited. It reads: "a person ('A') commits an offence if: (a) 'A' makes or promises payment for the sexual services of a prostitute ('B'), (b) a third person ('C') has engage in exploitative conduct of a kind likely to induce or encourage 'B' to provide the sexual services for which 'A' has made of promised payment, and (c) 'C' engaged in that conduct for or in the expectation of gain for 'C' or another person (apart from 'A' or 'B')." This legislation primarily sought to tackle sex trafficking. However, it is applied much more widely as it attempts to criminalize any purchase of sex from a sex worker that has been exploited by removing the requirement of the client possessing knowledge of such exploitation. In addition, this legal provision is applied globally. For example, if a man purchases sex from a local prostitute abroad, and the prostitute has been subjected to exploitative conduct, the man can be prosecuted under S.14 of the Policing and Crime Act 2009.[63] Thus, this criminalizes those who seek to purchase sexual services in an attempt to reduce the demand for which sex workers are exploited.

Support for this new legislation was outlined by an American study which established that arresting a male for purchasing sex is likely to reduce the demand for prostitution by 70%.[64] However, obtaining a criminal conviction was only the biggest concern for just 28% of men, which indicates that the criminalisation of purchasing sex may act as a deterrent.[65] Nonetheless, Graham[66] remains critical of the criminalisation of sex work. While the purchase of sex has been criminalized to an extent, there is a growing interest surrounding the total decriminalisation of sex work which will be further explored in this chapter. Subsequently, it appears that legislation alone does not suffice in attempting to protect sex workers from harm.

POLICING RESPONSES TO PROSTITUTION

The 1990s were pivotal in the development of police responses to prostitution as a result of approaches to street prostitution shifting the focus towards the client and the kerb-crawler. Police gained greater powers to deter clients from seeking the purchase of sex, including arresting those that kerb-crawl in pursuit of soliciting sex workers.[67] In addition, approaches developed to feature a multi-agency response, including specialist agencies designed to support sex workers who operated on the streets.[68] Despite such police enforcement approaches, the public became dissatisfied, resulting in protests, lobbying and even vigilante Behavior directly towards sex workers, their clients and their pimps.[69] This supports the notion that society regards sex work as "morally repugnant,"[70] hindering criminal justice responses from police.

In 2000, specialist vice units which specifically police prostitution with a more comprehensive approach by developing clear "ownership" of the issue of pimping were implemented across Britain. The Home Office Report outlined the team in Area 4 where each team member would have an area of expertise, from male sex workers to parlours to intelligence gathering.[71] It was found that vice teams were more successful in prosecuting pimps but were dissatisfied with the pimping legislation as it is too reliant on the evidence of sex workers to secure a conviction. In comparison, non-specialist teams, which often have a tolerance to parlours, are more pro-active in the policing of street prostitution. The team in Area 1 designated women officers who undertook responsibility such as liaising with sex workers and offering them support while processing them through the criminal justice system. However, the team felt that they were ill-equipped to deal with cases that required a significant amount of expertise and sensitivity.[72] Thus, this further demonstrates that police responses to sex work have ceased to adapt in order to adequately protect sex workers from violence.

In 2005, Matthews sought to identify developments in police responses to prostitution.[73] His findings illustrated that the number of vice squads which responded to prostitution-related matters had decreased from 30 in 1994 to 15 in 2004. This was concluded to be a result of more community-based responses. In fact, respondents indicated that such changes were a result of government targets—prostitution was not a concern. Despite the reduction in size of specialist vice squads, there was an increase in the number of prostitution-based support agencies across England and Wales. These centred around health and medical services in response to concerns of HIV and AIDS in the late 1980s, subsequently increasing public health.[74] Nonetheless, while this appears to be a proactive response to regulating prostitution, sex workers remain susceptible to punitive policing.[75]

Platt, Grenfell, Meiksin, Elmes, Sherman, Sanders, Mwangi, and Crago contducted a meta-analysis which reviewed a number of outcomes correlated with repressive policing practice.[76] One study in 2018 featured 5204 participants across nine different studies and concluded that hostile police responses directly correlated with increased risks of sexual and physical violence from clients or other partners. In particular, another study, comprised of 12,506 participants, discovered that sex workers who had been subjected to repressive policing were at a higher risk of infection of STIs. Consequently, their qualitative research suggested that the criminalisation of sex work subsequently disrupted their work environments, support networks, safety, and access to health and justice.[77]

Moreover, Sanders' 2004 study suggested that sex workers have been forced to use of geographical space as a means of protection from violent clients as a result of punitive policing, thus creating a dangerous environment.[78] She discovered that sex workers will operate in a pre-determined location, planning out an escape route and making sure that they are able to call for help. These locations will usually have CCTV which acts as a deterrent to the client. Other means of protective used include telling a fellow sex worker where they are going and taking note of the client's car registrations.[79] Moreover, Maher and Dixon argue that policing "crackdowns" have created an unsafe environment for sex workers as they are not performing preliminary checks due to trying to escape the attention of police.[80] Sanctioning sex workers with ASBOs prohibits them from operating in a specific area and therefore heightens the level of danger for sex workers by displacing the issue into an environment that they are unfamiliar with. Maher and Dixon therefore maintain that "intensive policing may also produce harmful forms of social displacement."[81] Such self-protection and displacement exacerbates sex workers' lack of trust in the police and demonstrates the absence of protection from the criminal justice system.[82]

Consequently, it is evident that previous attempts to adopt a partial decriminalisation approach have ceased to be effective.[83] While subjected to law enforcement approaches, literature suggests that stigmatisation towards sex workers is a result of gender dynamics, eroticization, and social class dynamics.[84] For example, an article in *The Guardian* reads " . . . street sex workers from going out to earn enough money for their next fix of drugs."[85] Such comments ignore the exploitative nature of sex work, stigmatising sex workers as drug addicts and further oppressing them. However, Krusi, Kerr, Taylor, Rhodes, and Shannon's study uncovered that despite increased support for sex workers through policing, some sex workers remain critical of such responses. While this created a shift in attitude towards sex workers as victims rather than deviants, one participant argued "they haven't really been harassing as much lately, but that attitude is still there. I don't think they'll change it back in their heads that we're trash."[86] It is therefore possible that police responses are influenced by stigma, thus hindering effective criminal justice responses to support sex workers.

A Comparative Approach: The Nordic Model

On 1 January 1999, Sweden attempted to abolish prostitution by tackling its demand—it completely criminalized the purchase of sex. Radical feminism influenced the introduction of the Nordic model, also known as the "sexköpslagen" (the "sex purchase law").[87] Through its understanding, prostitution is one of the ultimate forms of male violence against women,[88] particularly as sex workers are assumed to be female and clients are assumed to be male.[89] It viewed sex workers as victims of gender-based violence and so legislation sought to criminalize the "masculinized" client while protecting the "feminized" sex worker from legal action.[90] To achieve its goal of tackling the demand for the purchase of sex, its aim was to target those "deemed to possess power and choice: the clients as well as those profiting from the sex industry."[91] Consequently, the Nordic Model made the purchase of sex a criminal offence punishable by a fine or up to one year in custody. In addition, Sweden not only decriminalized sex workers but offered them support and advice on how to leave the sex industry. Cities such as Stockholm, Malmö, and Gothenburg offered "prostitution units," funded by local councils, providing welfare, employment, and health services for sex workers.[92] Thus, it not only criminalized those who buy sex but decriminalized those who sell it in a bid to protect sex workers from physical and sexual violence.[93]

The Nordic model has been praised by jurisdictions across Europe for its response to tackling prostitution with regard to supporting gender equality.[94] Ireland considered the approach when debating their bill on prostitution,[95] Canada discussed the model before criminalising the purchase of sex,[96] and England and Wales identified the model as a possible approach to adopt.[97] In particular, an Irish democrat, Maurice Morrow, maintained: "[T]he evidence clearly suggests that the approach modelled by Sweden is the best available. It recognizes the abuses involved in the prostitution industry and seeks to reduce the core driver for prostitution—the demand for paid sex."[98] Thus, the

Nordic model has been highly influential in approaches to tackling violence against sex workers across the globe.

Nonetheless, while appealing across the globe in theory, evidence suggests that the law which seeks to criminalize the purchase of sexual services has failed to be implemented effectively in practice. In fact, Norway, Finland, and Iceland confronted obstacles when adopting the Swedish approach as law enforcement agencies did not enforce the amended law.[99] Moreover, Levy and Jakobsson have criticized the Nordic model approach to prostitution as there is no reliable data which suggests a decline in the amount of prostitution.[100] Swedish government members have argued that there has been a "success" since the 1999 amendment,[101] however, such success refers to levels of prostitution have "at least" not increased.[102] In addition, it has been difficult to establish the effect of such legislation on the lives of sex workers.[103] While Sweden attempts to encourage other countries to adopt the sexköpslagen, the lack of empirical evidence to support its success suggests its exportation ought be considered with caution. In addition, the Nordic model may not be enforceable in England and Wales, as there is a much larger network of prostitution compared to Sweden.[104] Subsequently, the final section of this chapter seeks to critically analyse current approaches to prostitution in England and Wales despite its reluctance to adopt the decriminalisation model.

Current Approaches to Prostitution in England and Wales

Despite punitive policing, there are a number of multi-agency responses across England and Wales. The Red Umbrella Project, in collaboration with Changing Lives and run by the Merseyside Police, recognizes violence against sex workers as a hate crime.[105] Thus, it encourages sex workers to report these incidents. It has become the first police force to assign a dedicated Police Sex Worker Liaison Officer who is focused on the victim. The officer aims to protect them from violence, trafficking, and exploitation and improves gathering intelligence on violent clients and pimps. The scheme also provides additional support to sex workers such as mental health referrals and providing education and training in order to help them escape prostitution. However, there exists no research that examines the success of this project.

Moreover, welfare approaches have also sought to target those who purchase sexual services. Ugly Mug schemes were first used at a local level in Victoria, Australia, in 1986 which sought to protect prostitutes from violent clients by sharing information with prostitutes about violent clients through emails and texts. In 2012, the National Ugly Mugs scheme in the UK became the first scheme of its kind to be rolled out nationally, with funding from the Home Office. It pays particular focus to the rights to live free from violence, intimidation, coercion, and exploitation. Although the scheme does not require police involvement, it helps to gather intelligence for the police without the need for sex workers to have a direct involvement with the criminal justice system.[106] The Impact Report 2016/17 suggested that 96% of sex workers surveyed across the UK reported feeling safer as a result of the scheme. In addition, 32% recounted avoiding a particular client as a result of the information available. However, despite its success in aiding the safety of sex workers, only 25% of participants were willing to report violence from clients or pimps to the police.[107] Thus, such findings suggest that while this welfare approach is adequately protecting sex workers from harm, there remains a reluctance from sex workers to engage with the criminal justice system.

In addition, The Merseyside Police introduced the Merseyside Model which places an emphasis on the protection of sex workers from harm and also treats all violence against them as a hate crime.[108] Its aim is to build trust and relationships with sex workers, while providing healthcare checks and medical care to help treat against disease and addictions. One sex worker believed she was going to die during an attack from a client and has praised both Merseyside Police and the NHS for helping her to testify against the perpetrator.[109] This model has received much approval, particularly as the Home Affairs Committee reported that the model led to high levels of police intelligence on dangerous offenders as a result of participation from sex workers.[110] Consequently, it is evidence that multi-agency responses are more effective than punitive policing when attempting to regulate sex work and protecting sex workers from violence and exploitation.

Finally, in November 2020, new criminal records rules came into force which enforced that provided a sex worker has not served a custodial sentence and that their conviction is more than 11 years old, this offence will no longer automatically disclosed to employers.[111] This is monumental in the fight toward reintegrating sex workers into society, particularly with regards to them finding alternative employment, in order to reduce the likelihood of them returning to the violent nature of sex work.[112] However, due to its recency, no data exists on the impact of this measure and whether it has had a positive receival from sex workers and academics alike.

CONCLUSION

It is evident that while sex work is rife in England and Wales, many sex workers are subjected to violence and exploitative conduct.[113] This is not exclusive to sex workers who operate on the street and can include threats of physical violence and the commission of physical, emotional, and psychological violence.[114] Though policies have sought to regulate sex work in a number of ways, they often surround questions of morality and social values.[115] Policies attempt to decriminalize sex workers, aiding sex workers with support services, but it is clear that such policies fail to eliminate the demand for sex work and thus its violent nature. Though England and Wales have adopted a partial criminalization model, excessive and punitive measures persist, which ultimately limit sex workers' trust in the justice system.[116] Moreover, it is unclear whether adopting a full decriminalisation model will thus eliminate the demand for sex work and its violent nature as literature suggests that the Nordic Model has had limited success.[117] It is apparent that policies are focused on removing the problem of prostitution, rather than finding wider solutions to tackle the issues.[118] Nonetheless, with more and more welfare agencies and police forces working together to criminalize violent pimps and clients, it is clear that there is a shift towards prioritising the welfare of the sex workers.[119] However, the issue of pushing prostitution further underground and leaving sex workers more vulnerable by criminalising the clients requires addressing.

BIBLIOGRAPHY

Abel, G., "The Problem with Sex Work Policies" [2019] 48 *Archives of Sexual Behavior* 1925.

APPG on Prostitution and the Global Sex Trade, *Shifting the Burden* (2014).

Benoit, C., M. Smith, M. Jansson, P. Healey, and D. Magnuson. "'The Prostitution Problem': Claims, Evidence, and Policy Outcomes" [2019] 48 *Archives of Sexual Behavior* 1905.

Benson, C., and R. Matthews. "Street Prostitution: Ten Facts in Search of a Policy" [1995] 23 *International Journal of Sociology and Law* 395.

Benson, C., and R. Matthews. *Police and Prostitution: Vice Squads in Britain* in R. Weitzer (ed.) *Sex for Sale* (Routledge, 2000).

Changing Lives, *Red Umbrella Build on Partnership with Merseyside Police* (2019). Available at: https://www.changing-lives.org.uk/general/red-umbrella-build-on-partnership-with-merseyside-police/.

Church, S., H. Henderson, M. Barnard, and G. Hart. "Violence by Clients Towards Female Prostitutes in Difference Work Settings: Questionnaire Survey" [2001] 322 *British Medical Journal* 524.

Cunningham, S., T. Sanders, R. Platt, P. Grenfell, and P. G. Macioti. "Sex Work and Occupational Homicide: Analysis of a U.K. Murder Database" [2018] 22 *Homicide Studies* 321.

Day, S., and H. Ward. "Violence Towards Female Prostitutes" [2001] 232 *British Medical Journal* 230.

Department of Justice and Equality Republic of Ireland, *Turn Off the Red Light* (2017). Available at: http://www.turnofftheredlight.ie/.

Disclosure and Barring Service, *New Filtering Rules for DBS Certificates (From 28 November 2020 Onwards)* (2020).

Doezema, J. *Sex Slaves and Discourse Masters: The Construction of Trafficking* (Zed Books, 2010).
Ekberg, G. "The Swedish Law That Prohibits the Purchase of Sexual Services: Best Practices for Prevention of Prostitution and Trafficking in Human Beings" [2004] 10 *Violence Against Women1187*.
Giobbe, E. "A Comparison of Pimps and Batterers" [1993] 1 *Journal of Gender and Law* 33.
Hayes-Smith, R. and Z. Shekarkhar. "Why is Prostitution Criminalized? An Alternative Viewpoint on the Construction of Sex Work" [2010] 43 *Contemporary Justice Review* 43.
Home Affairs Select Committee, *The Government Response to the Third Report from the Home Affairs Select Committee Session 2016–17 HC 26: Prostitution* (2016).
Home Office, May, T., A. Haracopos, and M. Hough. *For Love or Money: Pimps and the Management of Sex Work* (2000).
House of Commons, Home Affairs Committee, *Prostitution: Third Report of Session 2016–17* (2016).
Jeffreys, S. *The Idea of Prostitution* (Spinifex Press, 1997).
Kingston, S., and T. Thomas. "No Model in Practice: A 'Nordic Model' to Respond to Prostitution?" [2018] 71 *Crime, Law and Social Change* 423.
Kinnell, H. *Demonizing Clients: How Not to Promote Sex Workers' Safety* in O'Neill M and Campbell R (ed.) *Sex Work Now* (Willan, 2006).
Klambauer, E. "Policing Roulette: Sex Worker's Perception of Encounters with Police Officers in the Indoor and Outdoor Sector in England" [2018] 18 *Criminology and Criminal Justice* 255.
Krüsi, A., T. Kerr, C. Taylor, T. Rhodes, and K. Shannon. "'They Won't Change It Back in Their Heads That We're Trash': The Intersection of Sex Work-Related Stigma and Evolving Policing Strategies" [2016] 38 *Sociology of Health and Illness* 1137.
Levy, J. *Criminalising the Purchase of Sex: Lessons from Sweden* (Routledge, 2015).
Levy, J., and P. Jakobsson. "Sweden's Abolitionist Discourse and Law: Effects on the Dynamics of Swedish Sex Work and on the Lives of Sweden's Sex Workers" [2014] 14 *Criminology and* Criminal 593.
London School of Hygiene and Tropical Medicine, Platt L and Sanders T, *Is Sex Work Still the Most Dangerous Profession? The Data Suggests So* (2017). Available at: https://www.lshtm.ac.uk/newsevents/expert-opinion/sex-work-still-most-dangerous-profession-data-suggests-so.
Lowman, J., and L. Fraser, *Violence Against Persons Who Prostitute: The Experience in British Columbia. Vancouver*. (Simon Fraser University, 1995).
Matthews, M. "Policing Prostitution: Ten Years On" [2005] 45 *British Journal of Criminology* 877.
McMenzie, L., I. Cook, and M. Laing. "Criminological Policy Mobilities and Sex Work: Understanding the Movement of the 'Swedish Model' to Northern Ireland" [2019] 59 *British Journal of Criminology* 1199.

Ministry of Industry, Employment and Education, *Prostitution and Trafficking in Human Beings* (2008). Available at: http://www.sweden.gov.se/content/1/c6/04/28/96/88110928.pdf (no longer available).

National Institute of Justice, US Department of Justice, Brewer, D., S. Muth, J. Roberts, K. Duduck, and D. Woodhouse. *Clients of Prostitute Women: Deterence, Prevalence, Characteristics and Violence* (2007).

National Ugly Mugs, *About* (2020). Available at: https://uglymugs.org/um/about/.

National Ugly Mugs, *National Ugly Mugs Impact Report 2016/17* (2017). Available at: https://uglymugs.org/um/about/impact-report-201617/.

Northern Ireland Assembly, *Official Report (12 September)* (2014).

Open Parliament Canada, *Bill C-36: Protection of Communities and Exploited Persons Act* (2014). Available at: http://openparliament.ca/bills/41-2/C-36/.

Ostergren, P., and S. Dodillet. *The Swedish Sex Purchase Act: Claimed success and documented effects. Presented at the International Workshop: Decriminalizing Prostitution and Beyond: Practical Experiences and Challenges,* The Hague, 3–4 March (2001).

Phoenix, J. *Regulating Sex for Sale: Prostitution Policy Reform in the UK* (Policy Press, 2009).

Platt, L., P. Grenfell, R. Meiskin, J. Elmes, S. Sherman, T. Sanders, P. Mwangi, and A. Crago. "Associations Between Sex Work Laws and Sex Workers' Health: A Systematic Review and Meta-Analysis of Quantitative and Qualitative Studies" [2018] 15 *PLOS Medicine* 1.

Prior, J., P. Hubbard, and P. Birch. "Sex Worker Victimization, Modes of Working, and Location in New South Wales, Australia: A Geography of Victimization" [2013] 50 *Journal of Sex Research* 574, 574.

R v Brusch and Horvat [2012] 1 Cr. App. 47.

R v Massey [2007] EWCA Crim 2664.

Sanders, T. "The Risks of Street Prostitution: Punters, Police and Protesters" [2004] 41 *Urban Studies* 1703.

Sexual Offences Act 2003.

SOU, *Forbud mot kop av sexuell tjiinst: En utviirdering 1999–2008. 2010:49. Stockholm: Regeringskansliets Farvaltningsavdelning* (2010). Extract available at: https://www.government.se/contentassets/8f0c2ccaa84e455f8bd2b7e9c557ff3e/english-translation-of-chapter-4-and-5-in-sou-2010-49.pdf.

Street Offences Act 1959.

Taylor, D. "Merseyside Police: 'Sex Workers Are Vulnerable. We Want to Protect Them,'" *The Guardian* (2010). Available at: https://www.theguardian.com/society/2010/dec/22/merseyside-police-sex-workers-protect.

University of Bristol, Hester, M., N. Mulvihill, A. Matolcsi, A. Sanchez, and S. Walker. *The Nature and Prevalence of Prostitution and Sex Work in England and Wales Today* (2019).

Weitzer, R. *Legalising Prostitution From Illicit Vice to Lawful Business* (New York University Press, 2012).

NOTES

1. Cunningham, S., T. Sanders, R. Platt, P. Grenfell, and P. G. Macioti, "Sex Work and Occupational Homicide: Analysis of a U.K. Murder Database" (2018) 22 *Homicide Studies* 321, 321.
2. Klambauer, E. "Policing Roulette: Sex Worker's Perception of Encounters with Police Officers in the Indoor and Outdoor Sector in England" (2018) 18 *Criminology and Criminal Justice* 255, 255.
3. Benoit, C., M. Smith, M. Jansson, P. Healey, and D. Magnuson. "'The Prostitution Problem': Claims, Evidence, and Policy Outcomes" (2019) 48 *Archives of Sexual Behaviour* 1905, 1905.
4. House of Commons, Home Affairs Committee, *Prostitution: Third Report of Session 2016–17* (2016) 4.
5. House of Commons, Home Affairs Committee, *Prostitution: Third Report of Session 2016–17* (2016) 4.
6. Church, S., H. Henderson, M. Barnard, and G. Hart. "Violence by Clients Towards Female Prostitutes in Difference Work Settings: Questionnaire Survey" (2001) 322 *British Medical Journal* 524. 524.s
7. Church, S., H. Henderson, M. Barnard, and G. Hart. "Violence by Clients Towards Female Prostitutes in Difference Work Settings: Questionnaire Survey" (2001) 322 *British Medical Journal* 524. 524.
8. Lowman, J., and L. Fraser. *Violence Against Persons Who Prostitute: The Experience in British Columbia. Vancouver*. (Simon Fraser University, 1995), 40.
9. Sanders, T. "The Risks of Street Prostitution: Punters, Police and Protesters" (2004) 41 *Urban Studies* 1703, 1709.
10. Klambauer, E. 'Policing Roulette: Sex Worker's Perception of Encounters with Police Officers in the Indoor and Outdoor Sector in England' (2017) 14 *Criminology and Criminal Justice* 255, 255.
11. Krüsi, A., T. Kerr, C. Taylor, T. Rhodes, and K. Shannon. "'They Won't Change It Back in Their Heads That We're Trash': The Intersection of Sex Work-Related Stigma and Evolving Policing Strategies" (2016) 38 *Sociology of Health and Illness* 1137, 1137.
12. Klambauer, E. "Policing Roulette: Sex Worker's Perception of Encounters with Police Officers in the Indoor and Outdoor Sector in England" (2017) 14 *Criminology and Criminal Justice* 255, 256.
13. Sanders, T. "The Risks of Street Prostitution: Punters, Police and Protesters" (2004) 41 *Urban Studies* 1703, 1710.
14. National Ugly Mugs, *National Ugly Mugs Impact Report 2016/17* (2017). Available at: https://uglymugs.org/um/about/impact-report-201617/ (accessed 9th December 2020).
15. Street Offences Act 1959, S.1.
16. Street Offences Act 1959, S.1(4)(a).
17. Klambauer, E. "Policing Roulette: Sex Worker's Perception of Encounters with Police Officers in the Indoor and Outdoor Sector in England" (2017) 14 *Criminology and Criminal Justice* 255, 256.

18. APPG on Prostitution and the Global Sex Trade, "Shifting the Burden" (2014), 5.

19. Home Affairs Select Committee, The Government Response to the Third Report from the Home Affairs Select Committee Session 2016–17 HC 26: Prostitution (2016) 4.

20. Kinnell, H. "Demonizing Clients: How Not to Promote Sex Workers' Safety" in O'Neill M and Campbell R (ed.) *Sex Work Now* (Willan, 2006), 142.

21. Cunningham, S., T. Sanders, R. Platt, P. Grenfell, and P. G. Macioti. "Sex Work and Occupational Homicide: Analysis of a U.K. Murder Database" (2018) 22 *Homicide Studies* 321, 321.

22. Platt, L. and T. Sanders. "Is Sex Work Still the Most Dangerous Profession? The Data Suggests So." *London School of Hygiene and Tropical Medicine* (2017). Available at: https://www.lshtm.ac.uk/newsevents/expert-opinion/sex-work-still-most-dangerous-profession-data-suggests-so (accessed 8th December 2020).

23. Hester, M., N. Mulvihill, A. Matolcsi, A. Sanchez, and S. Walker. *The Nature and Prevalence of Prostitution and Sex Work in England and Wales Today* (University of Bristol, 2019), 3.

24. House of Commons, Home Affairs Committee, *Prostitution: Third Report of Session 2016–17* (2016) 9.

25. House of Commons, Home Affairs Committee, *Prostitution: Third Report of Session 2016–17* (2016) 9.

26. University of Bristol, M. Hester, N. Mulvihill, A. Matolcsi, A. Sanchez, and S. Walker. *The Nature and Prevalence of Prostitution and Sex Work in England and Wales Today* (2019), 11–12.

27. Sanders, T., "The Risks of Street Prostitution: Punters, Police and Protesters" (2004) 41 *Urban Studies* 1703, 1705.

28. O'Neill, M. *Prostitution and Feminism* (Polity Press, 2001), 7.

29. Sanders, T. "The Risks of Street Prostitution: Punters, Police and Protesters" (2004) 41 *Urban Studies* 1703, 1705.

30. Church, S., H. Henderson, M. Barnard, and G. Hart. "Violence by Clients Towards Female Prostitutes in Difference Work Settings: Questionnaire Survey' (2001) 322 *British Medical Journal* 524. 524.

31. Deering K, Amin A, Shoveller K, Nesbitt A, Garcia-Moreno C, Duff P, Argento A and Shannon K, 'A Systematic Review of the Correlates of Violence Against Sex Workers' (2014) 104 *American Journal of Public Health* 42, 42.

32. Platt, L., P. Grenfell, R. Meiskin, J. Elmes, S. Sherman, T. Sanders, P. Mwangi, and A. Crago. "'Associations Between Sex Work Laws and Sex Workers' Health: A Systematic Review and Meta-Analysis of Quantitative and Qualitative Studies" (2018) 15 *PLOS Medicine* 1, 1.

33. Church, S., H. Henderson, M. Barnard, and G. Hart. "Violence by Clients Towards Female Prostitutes in Difference Work Settings: Questionnaire Survey' (2001) 322 *British Medical Journal* 524. 524.

34. Hester, M., N. Mulvihill, A. Matolcsi, A. Sanchez, and S. Walker. *The Nature and Prevalence of Prostitution and Sex Work in England and Wales Today* (University of Bristol, 2019), 18–21.

35. Sanders, T. "The Risks of Street Prostitution: Punters, Police and Protesters" (2004) 41 *Urban Studies* 1703, 1709.

36. Prior, J., P. Hubbard, and P. Birch. "Sex Worker Victimization, Modes of Working, and Location in New South Wales, Australia: A Geography of Victimization" (2013) 50 *Journal of Sex Research* 574, 574.

37. Day, S., and H. Ward. "Violence Towards Female Prostitutes" (2001) 232 *British Medical Journal* 230, 230.

38. Benson, C., and R. Matthews. "Street Prostitution: Ten Facts in Search of a Policy" (1995) 23 *International Journal of Sociology and Law* 395, 395.

39. Abel, G. 'The Problem with Sex Work Policies" (2019) 48 *Archives of Sexual Behaviour* 1925, 1925.

40. Benoit, C., M. Smith, M. Jansson, P. Healey, and D. Magnuson. "'The Prostitution Problem': Claims, Evidence, and Policy Outcomes" (2019) 48 *Archives of Sexual Behaviour* 1905, 1914.

41. Hayes-Smith, R., and Z. Shekarkhar. "Why Is Prostitution Criminalized? An Alternative Viewpoint on the Construction of Sex Work" (2010) 43 *Contemporary Justice Review* 43, 44.

42. Weitzer, R. *Legalising Prostitution: From Illicit Vice to Lawful Business* (New York University Press, 2012), 39.

43. Benoit, C., M. Smith, M. Jansson, P. Healey, and D. Magnuson. "'The Prostitution Problem': Claims, Evidence, and Policy Outcomes" (2019) 48 *Archives of Sexual Behaviour* 1905, 1916.

44. Platt, L., P. Grenfell, R. Meiskin, J. Elmes, S. Sherman, T. Sanders, P. Mwangi, and A. Crago. "'Associations Between Sex Work Laws and Sex Workers' Health: A Systematic Review and Meta-Analysis of Quantitative and Qualitative Studies" (2018) 15 *PLOS Medicine* 1, 2.

45. Phoenix, J., *Regulating Sex for Sale: Prostitution Policy Reform in the UK* (Policy Press, 2009) 73.

46. Benoit, C., M. Smith, M. Jansson, P. Healey, and D. Magnuson. "'The Prostitution Problem': Claims, Evidence, and Policy Outcomes" (2019) 48 *Archives of Sexual Behaviour* 1905, 1916.

47. Doezema, J. *Sex Slaves and Discourse Masters: The Construction of Trafficking* (Zed Books, 2010), 109.

48. Ekberg, G. "The Swedish Law That Prohibits the Purchase of Sexual Services: Best Practices for Prevention of Prostitution and Trafficking in Human Beings" (2004) 10 *Violence Against Women 1187*, 1187.

49. Home Affairs Select Committee, *The Government Response to the Third Report from the Home Affairs Select Committee Session 2016–17 HC 26: Prostitution* (2016) 2–5.

50. Hester, M., N. Mulvihill, A. Matolcsi, A. Sanchez, and S. Walker. *The Nature and Prevalence of Prostitution and Sex Work in England and Wales Today* (University of Bristol, 2019), 2.

51. Hester, M., N. Mulvihill, A. Matolcsi, A. Sanchez, and S. Walker. *The Nature and Prevalence of Prostitution and Sex Work in England and Wales Today* (University of Bristol, 2019), 3.

52. Hester, M., N. Mulvihill, A. Matolcsi, A. Sanchez, and S. Walker. *The Nature and Prevalence of Prostitution and Sex Work in England and Wales Today* (University of Bristol, 2019), 4.
53. Sexual Offences Act 2003, S.54(2).
54. Sexual Offences Act 2003, S.54(2).
55. S.51(a) of the Sexual Offences Act 2003.
56. Sexual Offences Act 2003, S.54(a).
57. Sexual Offences Act 2003, S.53.
58. *R v Massey* (2007) EWCA Crim 2664.
59. *R v Brusch and Horvat* (2012) 1 Cr. App. 47.
60. *R v Brusch and Horvat* (2012) 1 Cr. App. 47.
61. Policing and Crime Act 2009.
62. Sexual Offences Act 2003.
63. Policing and Crime Act 2009, S.14.
64. National Institute of Justice, US Department of Justice, Brewer, D., S. Muth, J. Roberts, K. Duduck, and D. Woodhouse. *Clients of Prostitute Women: Deterence, Prevalence, Characteristics and Violence* (2007) 1–13.
65. House of Commons, Home Affairs Committee, *Prostitution: Third Report of Session 2016–17* (2016) 25.
66. Graham, L. "Governing Sex Work Through Crime: Creating the Context for Violence and Exploitation" (2016) 81 *Journal of Criminal Law* 201, 201.
67. Sexual Offences Act 1985, S.1(1).
68. Matthews, M. "Policing Prostitution: Ten Years On" (2005) 45 *British Journal of Criminology* 877–882.
69. Benson, C., and R. Matthews. "Street Prostitution: Ten Facts in Search of a Policy" (1995) 23 *International Journal of Sociology and Law* 395, 395.
70. Abel, G. "The Problem with Sex Work Policies" (2019) 48 *Archives of Sexual Behaviour* 1925, 1925.
71. Home Office, May, T., A. Haracopos, and M. Hough. "For Love or Money: Pimps and the Management of Sex Work" (2000).
72. Home Office, May, T., A. Haracopos, and M. Hough. "For Love or Money: Pimps and the Management of Sex Work" (2000) 30.
73. Matthews, M. "Policing Prostitution: Ten Years On" (2005) 45 *British Journal of Criminology* 877, 877.
74. Matthews, M. "Policing Prostitution: Ten Years On" (2005) 45 *British Journal of Criminology* 877, 878–880.
75. Klambauer, E. "Policing Roulette: Sex Worker's Perception of Encounters with Police Officers in the Indoor and Outdoor Sector in England" (2018) 18 *Criminology and Criminal Justice* 255, 225
76. Platt, L., P. Grenfell, R. Meiskin, J. Elmes, S. Sherman, T. Sanders, P. Mwangi, and A. Crago. "'Associations Between Sex Work Laws and Sex Workers' Health: A Systematic Review and Meta-Analysis of Quantitative and Qualitative Studies" (2018) 15 *PLOS Medicine* 1, 3.
77. Platt, L., P. Grenfell, R. Meiskin, J. Elmes, S. Sherman, T. Sanders, P. Mwangi, and A. Crago. "'Associations Between Sex Work Laws and Sex Workers' Health:

A Systematic Review and Meta-Analysis of Quantitative and Qualitative Studies" (2018) 15 *PLOS Medicine* 1, 3.

78. Sanders, T. "The Risks of Street Prostitution: Punters, Police and Protesters" (2004) 41 *Urban Studies* 1703, 1703.

79. Sanders, T. "The Risks of Street Prostitution: Punters, Police and Protesters" (2004) 41 *Urban Studies* 1703, 1703.

80. Maher, L., and D. Dixon. "Policing and Public Health: Law Enforcement and Harm Minimization in a Street-Level Drug Market" (1999) 39 *British Journal of Criminology* 488, 503.

81. Maher, L., and D. Dixon. "Policing and Public Health: Law Enforcement and Harm Minimization in a Street-Level Drug Market" (1999) 39 *British Journal of Criminology* 488, 504.

82. Sanders, T. "The Risks of Street Prostitution: Punters, Police and Protesters" (2004) 41 *Urban Studies* 1703, 1710.

83. Krüsi, A., T. Kerr, C. Taylor, T. Rhodes, and K. Shannon. "'They Won't Change It Back in Their Heads That We're Trash': The Intersection of Sex Work-Related Stigma and Evolving Policing Strategies" (2016) 38 *Sociology of Health and Illness* 1137, 1137.

84. Krüsi, A., T. Kerr, C. Taylor, T. Rhodes, and K. Shannon. "'They Won't Change It Back in Their Heads That We're Trash': The Intersection of Sex Work-Related Stigma and Evolving Policing Strategies" (2016) 38 *Sociology of Health and Illness* 1137, 1139.

85. Taylor, D. "Merseyside Police: 'Sex Workers Are Vulnerable. We Want to Protect Them.'" *The Guardian* (2010). Available at: https://www.theguardian.com/society/2010/dec/22/merseyside-police-sex-workers-protect (accessed 9th December 2020).

86. Krüsi, A., T. Kerr, C. Taylor, T. Rhodes, and K. Shannon. "'They Won't Change It Back in Their Heads That We're Trash': The Intersection of Sex Work-Related Stigma and Evolving Policing Strategies" (2016) 38 *Sociology of Health and Illness* 1137, 1142.

87. Kingston, S., and T. Thomas. "No Model in Practice: A 'Nordic Model' to Respond to Prostitution?" (2018) 71 *Crime, Law and Social Change* 423, 423.

88. Jeffreys, S. *The Idea of Prostitution* (Spinifex Press, 1997), 78.

89. Kingston, S., and T. Thomas. "No Model in Practice: A 'Nordic Model' to Respond to Prostitution?" (2018) 71 *Crime, Law and Social Change* 423, 423.

90. Ministry of Industry, Employment and Education, "Prostitution and Trafficking in Human Beings" (2008) available at: http://www.sweden.gov.se/content/1/c6/04/28/96/88110928.pdf (no longer available).

91. McMenzie, L., I. Cook, and M. Laing. "Criminological Policy Mobilities and Sex Work: Understanding the Movement of the 'Swedish Model' to Northern Ireland" (2019) 59 *British Journal of Criminology* 1199, 1204.

92. Levy, J. *Criminalising the Purchase of Sex: Lessons from Sweden* (Routledge, 2015), 63.

93. Levy, J., and P. Jakobsson. "Sweden's Abolitionist Discourse and Law: Effects on the Dynamics of Swedish Sex Work and on the Lives of Sweden's Sex Workers" (2014) 14 *Criminology and Criminal Justice* 593, 593.

94. Kingston, S., and T. Thomas. "No Model in Practice: A 'Nordic Model' To Respond to Prostitution?" (2018) 71 *Crime, Law and Social Change* 423, 423.

95. Department of Justice and Equality Republic of Ireland, *Turn Off the Red Light* (2017). Available at: http://www.turnofftheredlight.ie/ (accessed 25th November 2020).

96. Open Parliament Canada, *Bill C-36: Protection of Communities and Exploited Persons Act* (2014). Available at: http://openparliament.ca/bills/41-2/C-36/ (accessed 25th November 2020).

97. House of Commons, Home Affairs Committee, *Prostitution: Third Report of Session 2016–17* (2016) 25.

98. Northern Ireland Assembly, *Official Report (12 September)* (2014).

99. Kingston, S., and T. Thomas. "No Model in Practice: A 'Nordic Model' To Respond To Prostitution?" (2018) 71 *Crime, Law and Social Change* 423, 424.

100. Levy, J., and P. Jakobsson. "Sweden's Abolitionist Discourse and Law: Effects on the Dynamics of Swedish Sex Work and on the Lives of Sweden's Sex Workers" (2014) 14 *Criminology and Criminal Justice* 593, 593.

101. Levy, J., and P. Jakobsson. "Sweden's Abolitionist Discourse and Law: Effects on the Dynamics of Swedish Sex Work and on the Lives of Sweden's Sex Workers" (2014) 14 *Criminology and Criminal Justice* 593, 593

102. SOU, *Forbud mot kop av sexuell tjiinst: En utviirdering 1999–2008. 2010:49. Stockholm: Regeringskansliets Farvaltningsavdelning* (2010). Extract available at: https://www.government.se/contentassets/8f0c2ccaa84e455f8bd2b7e9c557ff3e/english-translation-of-chapter-4-and-5-in-sou-2010-49.pdf, 28 (accessed on 25th November 2020).

103. Ostergren, P., and S. Dodillet. The Swedish Sex Purchase Act: Claimed Success and Documented Effects. Presented at the International Workshop: Decriminalizing Prostitution and Beyond: Practical Experiences and Challenges, The Hague, 3–4 March (2001), 25.

104. House of Commons, Home Affairs Committee, *Prostitution: Third Report of Session 2016–17* (2016), 20.

105. Changing Lives, *Red Umbrella Build on Partnership with Merseyside Police* (2019). Available at: https://www.changing-lives.org.uk/general/red-umbrella-build-on-partnership-with-merseyside-police/ (accessed 9th December 2020).

106. National Ugly Mugs, *About* (2020). Available at: https://uglymugs.org/um/about/ (accessed 9th December 2020).

107. National Ugly Mugs, *National Ugly Mugs Impact Report 2016/17* (2017). Available at: https://uglymugs.org/um/about/impact-report-201617/ (accessed 9th December 2020).

108. House of Commons, Home Affairs Committee, *Prostitution: Third Report of Session 2016–17* (2016), 17.

109. Taylor, D. "Merseyside Police: 'Sex Workers Are Vulnerable. We Want to Protect Them.'" *The Guardian* (2010). Available at: https://www.theguardian.com/

society/2010/dec/22/merseyside-police-sex-workers-protect (accessed 9th December 2020).

110. House of Commons, Home Affairs Committee, *Prostitution: Third Report of Session 2016–17* (2016), 17.

111. Disclosure and Barring Service, *New Filtering Rules for DBS Certificates (From 28 November 2020 Onwards)* (2020).

112. Benoit, C., M. Smith, M. Jansson, P. Healey, and D. Magnuson. "'The Prostitution Problem': Claims, Evidence, and Policy Outcomes" (2019) 48 *Archives of Sexual Behaviour* 1905, 1916.

113. Church, S., H. Henderson, M. Barnard, and G. Hart. "Violence by Clients Towards Female Prostitutes in Difference Work Settings: Questionnaire Survey' (2001) 322 *British Medical Journal* 524. 524.

114. O'Neill, M. *Prostitution and Feminism* (Polity Press, 2001), 47.

115. Benson, C., and R. Matthews. "Street Prostitution: Ten Facts in Search of a Policy" (1995) 23 *International Journal of Sociology and Law* 395, 395.

116. Platt, L., P. Grenfell, R. Meiskin, J. Elmes, S. Sherman, T. Sanders, P. Mwangi, and A. Crago. "'Associations Between Sex Work Laws and Sex Workers' Health: A Systematic Review and Meta-Analysis of Quantitative and Qualitative Studies" (2018) 15 *PLOS Medicine* 1, 3.

117. Ostergren, P., and S. Dodillet. The Swedish Sex Purchase Act: Claimed Success and Documented Effects. Presented at the International Workshop: Decriminalizing Prostitution and Beyond: Practical Experiences and Challenges, The Hague, 3–4 March (2001), 25.

118. Abel, G. 'The Problem with Sex Work Policies' (2019) 48 *Archives of Sexual Behaviour* 1925, 1925.

119. National Ugly Mugs, *National Ugly Mugs Impact Report 2016/17* (2017). Available at: https://uglymugs.org/um/about/impact-report-201617/

Chapter 2

The Impact of the Judicial Role on Treatment and Punishment in the New Zealand Alcohol & Other Drug Treatment Court

Toni Carr

Established in 2012, the New Zealand Alcohol and other Drug Treatment Court (AODTC) is a therapeutic court set up to address the underlying causes of addiction-related offending. Informed by the US DTC model and key components and best practice standards, the claimed benefits of the AODTC are to "reduce" alcohol and other drug (AOD) reoffending, "reduce" AOD consumption, and "reduce" imprisonment, thus positively affecting offenders' health and well being.[1] The AODTC endeavors to do this by transforming the role of the judge from an independent arbiter to that of treatment team leader, whose purpose it is to hold offenders accountable through treatment. However, treatment is based on "absolute abstinence" and the court's willingness to subjectively treat AOD offending as both a disease and a choice that carries a responsibility. Left in the hands of the judges to manage, treatment is not judged to be fair, nor is punishment for program violations judged to be proportionate to the crime. Rather, treatment and punishment are deemed necessary to overcome addiction-related offending.

The implications are that there is nothing to stop the judges from rationalizing treatment as "justice" on the basis that addiction is a chronic and relapsing disease. Or, to make an argument for punishment for relapsing on the basis that it is treatment. In justifying the legitimacy of the program, AODTC founding Judge Tremewan rationalizes treatment as "a smarter system of justice," a "fitting criminal justice response" to offending, even if it means "coercing" treatment, pointing out that:

> Although we talk of coercing or enforcing treatment, offenders have always had a choice as to whether they enter these courts: if offered a place, and can voluntarily leave the court, too, at any time. . . . [because] it is exhausting to suffer from the disease of addiction—where the whole day can be spent committing offences. . . . Abstinence which will require nothing short of them becoming a wholly different person. . . . Using a 'carrot and stick' approach to the proceedings, to hang the charges over the offender's head . . . the court closely monitors progress . . . remembering that addiction relates to a chronic often relapsing disease."[2]

Ultimately, the authority, or the illegitimacy of the AODTC, rests upon ubiquitous therapeutic justice comprising coerced and enforced treatment. To achieve this mandate, the AODTC operates between plea and sentence, which is not currently regulated by legislation or the common law. Section 25 of the Sentencing Act 2002 is the governing provision of the court that allows the judge to adjourn sentencing so that the offender can complete treatment. In the context of AODTC, s25 permits wide judicial discretion to problematize treatment and punishment according to individual accountability for the requirement of absolute abstinence.[3] So, while the AODTC operates in the period between plea and sentence, the judge has ultimate decision-making power with respect to what treatment should be.

Effectively, the judges have unlimited discretion to expand their authority to frame the participants as responsible for their addiction and recovery but, at the same time, as irresponsible. In this framework, the judges deploy the authority and coercive power of criminal justice when monitoring recovery, in ways more conducive to retribution and punishment than treatment.

METHOD

The chapter is based on my seven-month critical ethnographic study of two AODTCs, located in Auckland and Waitakere, between September 2013 to December 2013 and August 2014 to December 2014. Data was collected from four different sources: (i) participant observations, including 246 hours of "in-court" observations, and 290 hours of "out-of-court" observations; (ii) informal conversations; (iii) semi-structured in-depth interviews with 18 participants, 10 involved AODTC participants, including one who had graduated. Eight were conducted with people who had either been declined, exited, or self-exited from the AODTC and, (iv) extensive analysis of US DTC and AODTC documents.

The chapter demonstrates how the AODTC disease-abstinence-accountability mandate invites judicial subjectivity, coercion, oppression, and punitive interventions under the guise of treatment. While the main message is that the judges are doing something innovative and therapeutic, the court therapeutic mandate not only has practical importance for participants' rights to treatment it also raises questions regarding the provision of "treatment." Overall, the chapter contributes to the wider debate on the role of judges as problem solvers in DTCs.

DTCS AND THERAPEUTIC JURISPRUDENCE

Therapeutic jurisprudence (TJ) is a perspective developed to address the anti-therapeutic effects of legal rules and procedures, bringing a focus onto the law's therapeutic effects on offenders' health and well-being.[4] The principle underlying TJ is that the law and legal process can "enhance the psychological and/or physical well-being of individuals without subordinating other core values of the justice system."[5] While DTCs developed independently to TJ, proponents claim they represent "a significant step in the evolution of therapeutic jurisprudence—the evolutionary step from theory to application."[6]

Nolan argued that DTCs adopt TJ through procedural informality, making it possible to speak of "justice" as "treatment."[7] That is, through the "cultural practice of TJ," which in short involves closed court meetings, the judges becoming problem solvers though their power and wide discretion, lawyers supporting the aims of the court, and case managers advancing to the forefront of legal and treatment authority.[8] In this framework, court procedure intersects with TJ in the cultural production of law as a therapeutic process. However, these processes have been found to not only comprise "a dangerous mix for court participants" but have been criticized for undermining procedural safeguards through judicial power and inconsistency, producing a coercive form of justice based on treatment, rather than by reference to formal justice.[9]

Ultimately, the informality of the DTC process, coupled with the therapeutic mandate, has practical importance for treatment. Here a problem-solving mandate replaces due process with judicially mandated enforced therapy on the basis that offending is the result of a disease.[10] This is a significant issue in the AODTC.

In terms of the judicial role, retired US Judge Hora claimed that to apply TJ in the DTC requires judges to "accept their changing role from neutral, uninvolved arbiter to "problem solvers who look at cases holistically."[11] Hoffman argued, "these ideas emanate from the idea that the judiciary can be a powerful force for social change" not by just applying the law in the traditional sense, but by "pushing the existing law to new enlightened boundaries" in a variety of "non-traditional ways," leading judges to believe that "they can play amateur psychiatrist" in treatment.[12] The dangers are that the distinction between punishment and treatment is blurred, leading to the assertion that the DTC represents "rehabilitative punishment."[13] In part, this is the danger of the DTC therapeutic justice process as it subjects participants to coercion and disproportionately severe treatment.[14]

The AODTC accountability policy creates numerous opportunities for the judges to exercise their individual beliefs, to make crucial treatment decisions, and to make normative assessments hanging addiction as a disease onto choice and responsibility, in punitive ways. Because of their wide discretion, there is a disconnect between court procedure and participants' rights to treatment.

The data presented in this chapter reveals how tensions underlying the AODTC's therapeutic mandate and procedural informality mean that, in most cases, the program is not protecting the participants from bias, coercion, and punishment practices under the guise of treatment. In such instances, the power and informal values that constitute the judicial role influence eligibility and progress and promote confusion over the requirements of the treatment program. This casts doubt on the judicial role in managing treatment.

THE AODTC PROCESS

Each AODTC has its own team consisting of a judge, case manager, court coordinator, police prosecutor, and defense counsel. To be eligible, the person must have been charged with offending that is driven by: (i) a moderate to severe AOD dependency, (ii) be aged over 17 years, (iii) including recidivist drunk drivers, (iv) be at high risk of reoffending and facing charges for which the sentencing starting point is imprisonment up to three years.[15] However, it is the judge who makes the final referral decision.

Once a person is identified as being eligible, a determination hearing is held, and the judge sets out various commitments required. If the individual decides to enter the program, he or she enters a plea of guilty. Once accepted into the program, participants enter a contract whereby they agree to abstain from alcohol and other drugs through bail conditions targeting honesty and responsibility on the basis that there will always be a consequence for a breach of rules and compliance. To encourage accountability for abstinence, participants are required to attend weekly court sessions, attend 12 steps AA and NA meetings, and are subjected to regular and random testing throughout the program, residential treatment, and day programs.

Program participation is generally 12–18 months, yet in some cases it might last up to 24 months. Progress is determined by judicial monitoring of three Phase milestones (consisting of 4–6 months each), which are not necessarily linked to treatment time frames, and judicial interpretation of treatment compliance and abstinence time.[16] To graduate, participants are required to be abstinent for 180 days. Participants can exit the court either through a self-exit, termination, or graduation, at which point they are sentenced in accordance with the New Zealand Sentencing Act 2002. Still, beyond these more formal criteria, and due to the procedural informality of the therapeutic court, other more subjective tools are available to the judge when deciding whether an offender is a candidate, or whether a participant is be exited from the program. These include the judge's individual values, beliefs, and understanding of the participant's ability to be honest and responsible with the abstinence policy, all of which invite subjectivity and bias in decision-making.

THE AODTC AS A THERAPEUTIC COURT

> Openness and honesty help the court team to ensure that we are tailoring individualised treatment programmes to the best effect . . . encouraging participants towards new behavioral responses from those previously well-worn neural pathways of deceit and manipulation.[17]

The AODTC handbook makes clear that the judicial role involves "presiding over the court sitting" to deliver a coordinated response to the participant "in a manner that demonstrates appropriate therapeutic techniques."[18] Even though the judges are not health professionals, the conflation of "therapeutic techniques" with the criminal justice process creates tensions between the court's "therapeutic paradigm" that envisions AOD offending driven by a "moderate to severe addiction" and the understanding of responsibility.

During observations, it became obvious to me that within each AODTC, the understanding of the eligibility criteria was often based on the judges being convinced of a participant's motivation and inclination to become responsible for the goal of abstinence. The judges tended to search for, and focus on, participants' individual character traits, leading them to inappropriately construct honesty and personal responsibility as a measure of eligibility:

> Judge: For me however, the motivating factors of honesty are very important in accepting him.[19]
>
> Judge: Let's focus on personal responsibility and seeking to know why he might want to participate in the AODTC.[20]

Informal conversations with legal counsel about declined applicants uncovered evidence of numerous challenges to the court over the eligibility process, and on the grounds of whether the judges understood what addiction is and how it should be treated. Their accounts revealed how the judges and teams regularly *"pick up on a small aspect of an individual's file and reframe it"* . . . "*on poorly justified grounds.*"[21] This includes not recognizing the health needs of participants by the reframing of methamphetamine withdrawal symptoms as a mental health issue. For example, defense counsel conveyed frustration that the judge declined his applicant on the basis that his hallucinations were not addiction related:

> My client was declined on the basis of hallucinations, which were symptomatic of methamphetamine withdrawal, even in the face of corroborating evidence from my client's G.P. of his addiction and withdrawal treatment. [22]

Correspondingly, AODTC treatment provider representatives confirmed similar concerns to me. They saw the judges as being *"out of touch when it comes to identifying participants' needs"* and expressed doubt and concerns as to the judges' capacity to preside over the program.[23]

Complicated by the abstinence policy, and subjective understandings of honesty and responsibility, the judges utilize the voluntary nature of the program to frame participants as choosing to opt into the program on the basis that they choose to take responsibility for the disease of addiction. Here, the AODTC relies heavily on the idea that addiction is a weakness of the will and individual responsibility.

> Judge: I can assume you choose to come into this court; therefore, you choose to confront your addiction . . . then you need a lasting commitment to abstain from alcohol and drugs, you are signing up for intensive supervision and regular testing.[24]

However, AODTC constituted "choice" generates criminal responsibility for addiction, because when participants relapse, they are sent to custody to think about their choices, laying bare the court's authoritarian and hypocritical approach to treatment.

> Judge: Your addiction has been driving this, we know that you can have a better future so; I am sending you back into custody to think about your choices.[25]

Beyond the uncertainty of attributing addiction to choices, the judges engage their power in punitive decision-making practices, indicating that they have not fully understood the implications of targeting abstinence compliance.

> Morris: They require total abstinence. They abuse it with power; they abuse it with telling you what to do instead of letting you feel comfortable where you

> know you can succeed at something. Instead, they put you in a position where they can overwhelm you and stretch you to the point to see how far you can take it. Like it's a game . . . but they're adding to it with more, and more complications and technicalities, they say it's better than jail you know, but if you can't comply with these rules you're off.

As a central ambiguity of the AODTC, the therapeutic mandate permits the judges an uncritical acceptance of the disease-choice-responsibility dichotomy to make the participants governable in treatment. The issue with these approaches is that, if addiction is a disease, then why is it that addiction is framed as a choice and a responsibility, and why are participants punished for a relapse. According to Bowers, the cause of this contradiction is "the lack of theoretical coherence in drug courts."[26] Certainly, these contradictions have been a common finding of other research.[27]

Judicial Monitoring

Reinforcing the extent to which the judicial role is predicated on its US equivalent and the archaic idea of AOD offending as driven by a disease, the AODTC receives the regular guidance of retired US DTC judge Peggy Hora. During observations, I witnessed Judge Hora use the court proceedings to further advance the US DTC model, the moral language associated with the accountability mandate, and the idea that the participants crimes are a symptom of their illness. Leading to the reinforcement of dubious legal beliefs that pathologize offending to disease.[28] This was demonstrated during my observation of Judge Hora's fifth visit:

> AODTC Judge: Judge Hora is there anything you would like to add?
>
> Judge Hora: There are some universal truths you are only as sick as your secrets.
>
> AODTC Judge: Perfect, thank you Judge Hora you are only as sick as your secret.[29]

On another occasion, I observed Judge Hora's involvement change the way the court perceives the threshold for addiction related offending:

> Judge Hora: I see before me a nice family guy, but what I see in the booking photo, I see whoa a mass murderer . . .[30]

In addition to Judge Hora's visits, the judges extend their knowledge of US best practices and principles through regular guidance involving Skype and email contact with the leading doyens of the US National Association of Drug Court Professionals, Douglas Marlowe and Shannon Carey. In those instances when the judges are challenged on the grounds of proportionality and fairmindedness, they justify their decisions on the basis that they operate in accordance with the US best practices and principles. Many of the participants felt humiliated because there was no opportunity for them to seek redress over court procedures. The quote below, confirms how the AODTC justifies its legitimacy on an oversimplified defense that US DTCs are effective:

> Makareta: I wanted a defended hearing over the SCRAM because it was spiking when I wasn't actually drinking . . . but they were saying, we've had people over in America doing all these things so if you're going to go ahead with it then well, all the drug court professionals are going to come over from America for the hearing.

Essentially, the power afforded to the judges has allowed them to take on the might of the criminal justice system to impose punishments for acts that would not normally be punishable in a court, when potentially no criminal offence has been committed.

When it comes to following procedure, a little knowledge of addiction and treatment is a dangerous thing in the hands of the judiciary.[31] Based on the data, the judges use their discretion to make normative assessments hanging addiction onto choice and responsibility. They constitute "honesty" and "commitment" as "tools" of the court to coerce recovery. As such, participants are told that "honesty" is the "most important tool":

> Judge: What is the most important tool?
>
> Mattie: Just be completely honest with what's going on.
>
> Judge: Because it is important to be honest about mixing with people that are in recovery.[32]

However, the participants interviewed saw these tools as an opportunity for the court to intervene with punishment:

> Mahaka: It's just the tools that they use. If you choose not to use those tools, then you choose no. They're flaky, they're extremely flaky on a lot of things, but not punishment.

These interviewees confirmed how threats of prison are regularly utilized by the court for various retributive and deterrent ends:

> Matiu: If you can't comply with these rules, you're off so that's a threat you're always threatened.

> Myles: They use all these big words; the main word and they minimize it and twist and turn it into a word that means something totally different is a threat. If you don't do it, if you don't comply, you're off to jail sweet and simple.

The monitoring process also provided the judges with added opportunities to apply their subjective knowledge of a participant's moral character when targeting motivation. I witnessed the judges translate negative "treatment" reports such as *"his attitude comes over as gangster like"* or *"he's charming but manipulative"* as participants not taking responsibility for their recovery. Poor attitudes were heavily reprimanded, with participants remanded in custody. For example, "Mac" who has been held in custody for a relapse.

> Judge: Are you wanting to make a bail application now, because my recollection is what happened last time is that we held you in custody until your weekend out promise to go to activities, we thought this looks good. . . . Well, you just went out and used, it was the opposite. . . . I'm not trying to rub your face in it. . . . I respect the way you took it when we gave it to you. . . . I'm actually feeling really positive . . . it's not actually about Mac it's about Mac's addiction . . . so in terms of the application what's your bail proposal?
>
> Mac: I'm happy to go on 24 hrs bail.
>
> Judge: I can tell you without any shadow of doubt that there is absolutely no way that I am going to bail you.[33]

The effects are that there is no ambiguity about the role of punishment, at least not from the judges. Rather there is ambiguity over what role treatment has beyond the abstinence-accountability mandate.

Moreover, there are no formal rules to restrain the judges from perpetuating gendered stereotypes of female offending and bias that women require closer monitoring or from creating barriers to treatment, as conveyed by legal counsel:

> Women in the court have a big battle . . . women in violent relationships are not for the court, they're considered too hard. Male participants don't get treated like this, there's a different standard for men in the court and I get bullied when I identify these issues. Women with a history of a number of partners are scrutinized, their relationship history is seen as a significant barrier to treatment, it doesn't happen to men.[34]

Thus, through their authority, the judges actively transform their role through individual values, beliefs, likes, and dislikes.[35]

Bias can also be triggered by previous history with an offender or through knowledge of an offender's personal details.[36] That is, the court problem-solving mandate can provoke an unconscious desire to punish or to control behaviors that otherwise would not require censorship, resulting in disproportionately severe punishment.[37] During observations, there was nothing to stop the judges from promoting confusion over the process of fact-finding. For example, during a precourt meeting the judge deliberates on a female participant's progress based on the judge's previous history with the same participant in a different court:

> Judge: Marama appeared before me at the Manukau District court for drunk driving—she has a history of dishonesty, and she gave me a flat out lie about driving drunk. She is a liar; she cannot be trusted. . . . [38]

Ultimately, the judicial monitoring practices supported by the "therapeutic" mandate have changed the judicial role in a way that is unprecedented in the adult criminal courts. In such instances, the informal values that constitute the AODTC structure and the judicial role influence eligibility and progress and promote confusion over the requirements of the treatment program. As a result, the judges become self-styled therapists perceiving AOD related offending as a symptom of disease while targeting offender accountability, casting doubt on the judicial role in monitoring addiction treatment.

INCONSISTENT JUDICIAL INTERVENTION

The largely unchecked authority given to the judges has created a court that exerts substantial power over the participants to hold them accountable for their offending through treatment and recovery. These processes have given the judges extensive discretion to engage in a profound mix of well-intentioned treatment and disparaging punitive punishment. One effect is that the focus on participant risk to program success often takes precedence over treatment. When I asked the participants how they had perceived their treatment in the AODTC, they conveyed how they received punishment for taking responsibility, were confused with the court's focus on "choices," and were frustrated that the court places unrealistic demands on them that they have difficulty complying with. Their accounts confirm that what determines the treatment provisions appears to be judicial inflexibility and capricious decision-making.

> Miro: When they said [the judge and team] to me that I needed to start changing my behaviors and my way of thinking, I said that it's pretty hard to do that overnight you know. I've only been in the court for 7 or 8 months and they reckon that's plenty of time. But I don't know, I find it really hard to just change and

> that people who do change like that are probably faking it, that's the way I see it. . . . I know we do make bad choices under the influence, but I mean when I've been off the shit, I've still made some bad choices you know. . . .
>
> Morris: The judge punished me for saying that I couldn't drive because I was unwell, and they say any decision you make for yourself; they don't respect you know. At the end of the day, you are meant to make decisions every day of your life for you, for your family, and whatever you know, so yeah, I just don't get it. It's like it doesn't matter what you do, you get punished for making the right decisions for your family and yourself you know, that's how I see it.

The interviews reveal how the judges frequently made up the program requirements depending on their understanding of honesty and compliance, leading to unpredictability, which in turn means that it is hard for the participants to predict what might happen. This despite the AODTC handbook specification that "an appropriate treatment plan is created based on the individual's assessed treatment needs and requirements."[39] All of which points to lack of due process and procedural safeguards.

The judges' preoccupation with compliance is illustrated well in the treatment of people with a traumatic brain injury TBI and mental health needs, despite a strong correlation between AOD related offending and mental health disorders.[40] Considering this correlation, and despite the stated availability of a "psychologist, two alcohol and drug specialists and a clinical supervisor/coordinator"[41] my findings raise a concern that the judicial handling of participants with a TBI and depression is undermining treatment. What follows is an extended discussion of the judicial role in the management of the treatment of participants with a TBI and coexisting needs.

Managing Participants with a TBI and Coexisting Needs

While the AODTC is designed to treat offenders, the procedural informality underpinning the court's therapeutic mandate provides the judges with added opportunities to apply their subjective knowledge of a participant's risk. There is research that establishes how people with an addiction tend to be more susceptible to a TBI, cognitive disabilities, and coexisting needs.[42] Therefore, responding to the needs of this population is important if they are to be treated humanely and appropriately in the criminal justice setting.[43]

My research found that the judges did not discuss with counsel or the other team members whether a sanction is proportionate to the level of risk posed, is punitive, unfair, or disproportionate. Rather, the treatment of these people involved dubious legal decision-making and punitive treatment standards. Even when there was documented evidence of a participant suffering from a coexisting condition and an associated cognitive impairment, the judges persisted with pursuing accountability. For example, "Mike" has a TBI, and is struggling to comply with the abstinence requirement. Rather than recognizing the impact of a TBI upon his cognitive ability to be compliant, the judge leverages the goal of surveillance according to her subjective knowledge of accountability:

> Judge: He is extremely trying.
>
> Counsel: It's his head injury, he's a concrete thinker.
>
> Judge: Well, he is wearing a SCRAM bracelet, however, there are ongoing difficulties around testing, so he cannot be excused. If he fails, then he isn't doing what he should be doing, there is no reason why he can't change his behaviors.[44]

Even though these practices are supported by the US DTC key components and best practice standards, such judicial authority is antitherapeutic, because it generates further misunderstanding around the eligibility criteria, and the knowledge that addiction is a chronic relapsing condition that is denied.

Moreover, the responsibility mandate means that the court renders depression and anxiety as situational and that it does not require the intervention of Community Alcohol and Drug Services. The participants suffering from trauma and depression indicated how they were not receiving evidence based clinical support, and they expressed doubt, frustration, and confusion with the court-mandated treatment and support:

> Morris: I got diagnosed with trauma. That came from being in the drug court, but there is no support. What I'm saying is, you know, they're only dealing with the drug and the alcohol, they don't help with the counseling, with that you got to go and find it yourself. They only deal with a little square you know, but that little square could be coming off something else and they do not acknowledge that, they don't want to know about that.
>
> Monty: There's a lot of people that have underlying problems like me from a serious accident which had death in it, and dealing with guilt and whatever, but they don't want to know . . . they're not helping our problems and that's costly, it's really costly.

While the AODTC legitimizes the authority of the judges to exercise their discretion to make participants accountable, a judicial focus on compliance and the prioritization of risk and responsibility over health and psychological well-being, have undermined the intention "to positively impact on health and well-being."[45] This is because the judges appear to have lost sight of creating "the best chance" for participants' health, well-being, and success in treatment.[46]

Therapeutic Punishment: Punishment Under the Guise of Treatment in the AODTC

Murphy refers to therapeutic punishment as involving a broader set of practices that DTCs employ to quell program violations.[47] Therapeutic punishment in the AODTC begins with the court's construction of the dishonest but treatable addict in need of treatment, reinforced through the accountability mandate. This leaves little distinction between treatment and punishment. Therapeutic punishment is a set of AODTC practices that include the denial of treatment though therapeutic surveillance (including AOD testing and SCRAM electronic alcohol monitoring device); therapeutic sanctions [built on judicially prescribed teachable moments]; and therapeutic remands (comprising judicial intervention and the administering of punishment). Each practice has several different objectives that are informed by the court's values of establishing honesty and accountability during treatment. All have punitive effects through the widening of control, the elimination of participant protections, and by concealing irregularities in treatment.

Therapeutic Surveillance

AODTC therapeutic surveillance requires the judges to assess compliance according to the court abstinence-honesty-responsibility mandate. However, through the combination of testing and SCRAM electronic monitoring, the sole power of the judges to engage in the punitive responsibilizing process is laid bare, leaving little recognition for the rights of participants to treatment as an alternative to punishment:

> Judge: I'm interested in the carrot and stick; the SCRAM is a demonstration of trust and can go a long way. . . . I'll look at strict conditions and curfews, if you put a foot wrong its back into custody.[48]

Complicated by the expectation the participants will engage in a reciprocal relationship with the program, the judges have unwarranted control over participants, blurring treatment with the burden of unjustifiable punishment:

> Morgan: I've been here almost 2 years and missed one piss test. I was supposed to graduate today, but now they're not going to let me graduate because I missed one piss test. . . . I told them that they're turning into a pack of Nazis, you know that's one hell of a punishment because you miss one piss test.

At times, mandated testing culminated in a court failure to protect historically disadvantaged Māori.[49] Māori women conveyed how testing underpinned feelings of futility and shame, culminating in suicidal thoughts:

Marama: They said that they're going to do random testing from now on and we just got to accept it and if we have any resentments against it, we can't challenge it, we cannot challenge anything in this court. I tried to challenge it, but the human rights commissioner told me don't talk to the judge, do not talk to your lawyers, do not talk to anybody on the team this is how you go about doing these things, it's just a letter to the judge jurisdiction thing. . . . I felt unjustified, unjustified, and disrespected as a Māori woman. I felt my dignity had been taken away, and then the very next day, they expected me to go to testing again and face those same people. I didn't go, I got excused, in the end they said you know, you have to go and get a doctor's certificate and I said oh well that's going to be hard because I want to kill myself.

The emphasis on responsibility and compliance left many of the participants characterizing the testing process as the court shirking their responsibility to support them in recovery:

Mel: Testing is a major commitment 'cause you got to be clean before you go into residential, it's meant to takes a few weeks before you can go in there, but they expect you to be abstinent off drugs on your own you know.

Compounded by the misguided notion that participants will be receptive to coerced and enforced treatment, the merging of testing as a regulatory mechanism with the justice process masks the realities faced by the participants. It was clear that the way testing is administered, and the ramifications of a missed or failed test, affected participants' abilities to address their recovery. Added to this is the SCRAM (bracelet) electronic monitoring device a profoundly punitive mechanism of surveillance, utilized by the judges to monitor, coerce, and enforce compliance.

As with mandated testing, SCRAM is dependent more on judicial and team decision-making centred on establishing honesty than on care and support. The participants drew similarities between the courts punitive values, powerlessness, and unjustifiable punishment, even when they were not using:

Maru: My SCRAM would spike . . . it almost pushed me over the edge 'cause I couldn't keep always being in the firing line, always having to explain myself every week you know. Having meetings with my case manager every week, and I was trying to find reasons as to what I was doing you know, what am I using.

Matiu: Even when I wasn't using, it still came up with a use and tampers, I mean how do you explain that?

In the event of a SCRAM result revealing a spike, the judge and team consider acting according to their understanding of dishonesty and program success. However, this process is particularly problematic for those participants with a partner, as the judges crudely translate participants' relationships as a risk to program success. For example:

> Judge: Milo has slept on the sofa for 2 weeks and has a flat line, do we accept that?
>
> Case Manager: Totally accept it . . . the spikes have been extremely low level, not a large wave.
>
> Judge: I think his partner [Dawn] is utterly dodgy, she said that he had taken a sip of wine when they were cooking.
>
> Case Manager: He's a naïve man.
>
> Judge: Well, do we proceed as a team; are the spikes are a result of Dawn's drinking? Or do we accept what the SCRAM people are saying? We want to keep this quiet too team from the other participants. Remember Martha and her SCRAM spiking every 15 minutes, it is just not helpful for participants to know that if their partners are drinking the SCRAM will spike. I am going to ask him to go to ALANON because Dawn is an alcoholic.
>
> Case Manager: Well, the fact that he slept on the couch means that she could not go two weeks without a drink.
>
> Judge: I am not going to encourage him to sleep apart but encourage him to affirm, and to go to ALANON. . . . I have to say that I notice this SCRAM has actually clouded my engagement with him.[50]

One of the consequences of the justification of the responsibility-honesty dichotomy is that it embeds a punitive focus on the control of participants. This conveys a type of moral order, whereby the judges have the authority to use their discretion to label people as failures, and to coerce and enforce compliance with culturally insensitive testing. Therefore, there is inflexibility and uncertainty in the court. For these reasons, rather than acting as an alternative to punishment, the AODTC transforms treatment into punishment.

Therapeutic Sanctions: Creating Opportunities for a Teachable Moment

> Judge: You seriously need to step this up, what I'm hearing overall is that you're not putting first things first, start being responsible and stop wasting time. You need to be more respectful. This is a court of honesty; you need to be open and honest, . . . Because I can tell you without a shadow of doubt, if you do not do something meaningful, I will imprison you.[51]

AODTC sanctions have been referred to as "opportunities for learning, by the judge as a teachable moment."[52] One of the strongest points to emerge from this part of my research was that the sanctioning process involves substantial discretion when identifying a particular behavior as a relapse or violation of treatment. The judges often extended their power by way of a vindictive logic, whereby for those that do not "learn" from their "mistakes" or do not meet the many requirements are sanctioned. Reasons include turning up to court late, being perceived as unmotivated or dishonest, failing to take responsibility for treatment, relapsing, and not satisfying the residential providers' expectations. Here we can see the full effect of the judges problematizing participants behaviors on their intuitive understanding of what leads to program success.

During observations, on average 70 percent of the court day is spent by the judges calculating the level of severity of the sanctions according to the honesty-responsibility mandate. Sanctions ranged from an open admonishment to a loss of clean time, being put back a phase, being left until the end of the court day, written "reflections," time spent on remand in custody, and expulsion. Each sanction is defined as a "teachable moment," aimed at forcing participants to reflect upon their irresponsibility. Despite the acknowledged availability of evidence-based treatment through the court's and treatment providers' reciprocal agreement, essential components of the program are interpreted widely to make participants punishable. The interviews reveal that the written sanction is unjustifiably founded on the behavior modification aspect of the program, often leading to a lack of recognition of participants individual needs and well-being:

> Morgan: Higher Ground gave me a sanction of a 10,000-word essay for pretty much having a bad attitude, when I told my lawyer he just laughed and said that is what they write in a thesis. I had a significant brain injury last year you know and for me to write 10,000 words well I was in no state to do that so I negotiated it down to 5000 words, . . . I opted for that because I would have had to leave with a therapeutic discharge.

Thus, regardless of how participants negotiate the sanction of written work, the process is subject to discretion, and the requirement to teach the participants a lesson about accountability. For those participants considered therapeutically nonresponsive, the most punitive sanction is the use of remand.

Therapeutic Remands

The full effect of judicial power is shown in the use of therapeutic remand in custody as a treatment sanction, also known as "therapeutic remands."[53] The justification for AODTC remand is that "deceit" and "dishonesty" are part of the disease of addiction. As such, remand in custody is defended as a form of "shock" treatment aimed at helping to motivate openness and honesty. This generates an ethical issue regarding the purpose of remand in treatment, and whether and when remand in custody is appropriate as a form of shock treatment.[54]

I found the use of "therapeutic remand" is administered for retributive and vexatious ends, creating new standards for the judges to draw upon the criminal justice process to punish relapse and dishonesty when no criminal act has occurred, to coerce compliance and deter unwanted behaviors:

> Judge: We say honesty in this court involves turning up on time, doing all the things you're meant to be doing, the biggest issue for us is you're lying about use so I'm going to send you to custody to think about your choices.[55]
>
> Judge: I don't want to see you rot in custody. . . . But we know that last time you were out on a weekend it wasn't flash, we need to be in the driving seat not the addiction, so we will revisit this in 1 week [remand to custody].[56]

The interviews reveal how a relapse is regularly punished with time on remand in custody:

> Monty: I had about three relapses and in each I went into remand, the first time was two weeks, the second time was a month, the third time I just finished my jail sentence instead of going back to rehab.
>
> Mel: When I relapsed, I went to prison 3 times in the last 3 months. The first relapse was within the first month, I went to prison for the weekend, got out, the other month of relapsing I went to prison for a week got out, I had a few uses, they went haywire, I went into prison again, this time it was for 2 weeks.

During observations, AODTC participants held on remand are held alongside prisoners awaiting sentence, leaving the AODTC participants vulnerable to prison violence. For example, "Melanie's" time in custody involved violence resulting in a broken arm. Considering this, the case manager forewarns the court that, if Melanie is exited from Higher Ground, she runs the risk of encountering further violence in custody:

> Case Manager: The gang girls got to her in custody before she went to Higher Ground, so we need to take one step at a time—she's received several warnings for rolling her eyes in Higher Ground and is on her final warning.[57]

Three weeks later, I observed the team discuss how Melanie had been exited from Higher Ground and is again on remand in custody as the team seeks to locate suitable mandated housing. Faced with a potential disaster, the judge considers extending her authority to keep another AODTC participant, "Mona," on remand in custody for Melanie's protection:

> Judge: Melanie has been blacklisted, . . . I am concerned for her safety in custody now that Mona is being released on bail today.
>
> Case Manager: Mona and Melanie share a cell in remand, they're seen as narks by the gang girls because of their involvement in the AODTC.
>
> Judge: She is going to be vulnerable when Mona leaves, the gang girls chopped her hair off in custody prior to the drug court . . . then the broken arm in custody and we don't have anywhere for her to live . . . we could keep Mona in custody till we find a place for Melanie.[58]

The above observation is typical of the tensions involved in AODTC decision-making and exposes the paradoxical purpose of using custody and bail conditions as part of treatment. It further magnifies the dangers associated with the use of remanding participants into custody, revealing a lack of judicial investment in the participants' health and well-being. Participants conveyed how an apparent lack of judicial investment in their well-being led to harmful experiences of prison violence, a disregard for their safety:

> Morris: I go in for two weeks and get stabbed in the neck and they quickly rip me out, then put me back in and say, Morris can you handle two days, can you handle it. It's not two days, that's Friday, Saturday, Sunday, Monday on the 5th day I'm out which is Tuesday. She [the judge] means the weekend, not counting the weekend you got two days it's no bloody holiday, each day is counted when you're in prison.

Fundamentally, the court's reliance on remand leaves little room for decision-making based on what is best for participants, and what is required to protect them from harm. During observations, the judges repeatedly mandated inappropriate therapeutic practices to the detriment of participants' safety, health, and well-being. The participants' accounts bear evidence to this.

CONCLUSION

The AODTC operates on the dichotomy that addiction is a chronic relapsing disease and a responsibility, requiring judicial discretion and coercion to enforce compliance. While the judges' discretion is accommodated by the new roles that they occupy, their focus on the disease-abstinence-accountability mandate, and evident disregard for participants' health and well-being, is of concern. There are intended and unintended consequences.[59] The judges have unrestrained power to enforce the monitoring of participants' compliance. This presents with significant harm for participants. The expanded jurisdiction of the judges permits them unfettered discretion to coerce treatment through punishment. Guided by the US DTC best practice components, the disease-crime dichotomy, and the requirement to enforce recovery, the judges' interpretation of "appropriate therapeutic techniques"[60] involves various ambiguous tools aimed at assessing, deterring, and changing the participants through nonclinical inhumane interventions, to the detriment of participants' treatment, health, and well-being.

Considering the tensions underpinning AODTC treatment, the UN Special Rapporteur on the right of everyone to the enjoyment of the highest attainable standard of physical and mental health noted how tensions underpinning criminal justice policy "fuel the perception that people who use drugs are unproductive criminals or moral degenerates, which in turn allows disciplinary treatment approaches to proliferate."[61] Returning to the concepts of judicial power, therapeutic justice, and the cultural production of law, we can see several ways in which the impact of the judicial understanding of AOD related offending and the disease-responsibility mandate underpins the harms generated in the AODTC.

The evidence demonstrates that the legitimacy of AODTC functions on overt expressions of judicial power under the guise of the therapeutic paradigm. In this way, mandated "treatment" has involved dubious legal decision-making practices targeting accountability for addiction and treatment compliance. To make matters worse, the observations and interviews illustrate that the judicial approach to monitoring treatment favors punishment imposed as part of treatment when no wrongdoing has been done, generally associated with a failure to protect participants' rights.[62]

With no template other than the US DTC model and the guidance of a retired US judge and US DTC doyens, the AODTC threatens to undermine the legitimacy of the New Zealand judiciary through a foreign set of judicial values and standards.

BIBLIOGRAPHY

Boldt, R. (2009). *A Circumspect Look at Problem-Solving Courts, Problem-Solving Courts: Justice for the Twenty-first Century*? In P. Higgins and M. Mackinem, Santa Barbara, CA, ABC-CLIO, 13–32.

Bowers, J. (2007). Contraindicated Drug Courts. Public Law Paper Series and Legal Theory Working Paper Series: Retrieved: http://www.law.uchicago.edu/academics/publiclaw/index.html

Brookbanks, W. (2015). *Therapeutic Jurisprudence: New Zealand Perspectives*. Thomson Reuters.

Carr, T. (2020). *Governing Addiction: The Alcohol and other Drug Treatment Court in New Zealand.* PhD thesis. Victoria University of Wellington, New Zealand.

Castellano, U. (2011). Courting Compliance: Case Managers as "Double Agents" in the Mental Health Courts, *Law & Social Inquiry, 36* (2): 484–514.

Colyer, C. J. (2007). Innovation and Discretion: The Drug Court as a People-Processing Institution. *Criminal Justice Policy Review*, 18: 313–328. DOI: 10.1177/0887403407303199.

Hoffman, M. (2000). The Drug Court Scandal, *North Carolina Law Review*, *78*, 1437–1534.

Hoffman, M. (2002). Therapeutic Jurisprudence, Neo-Rehabilitationism, and Judicial Collectivism: The Least Dangerous Branch Becomes Most Dangerous. *Fordham Urban Law Journal*, 29, 2063–2098.

Hora, P., G. Schma, and J. Rosenthal. (1999). Therapeutic Jurisprudence and the Drug Treatment Court Movement: Revolutionizing the Criminal Justice System's Response to Drug Abuse and Crime in America. *Notre Dame Law Review* 74(2): 439–537.

Hora, P. (2002). A Dozen Years of Drug Treatment Courts: Uncovering Our Theoretical Foundation and the Construction of a Mainstream Paradigm. *Substance Use & Misuse* 37(12 & 13): 1469–1488.

Indig, D., Gear, C., and Wilhelm K., (2016). Comorbid Substance Use Disorders and Mental Health Disorders among New Zealand Prisoners. New Zealand: Department of Corrections, Wellington.

Litmus (2014). *Formative Evaluation for the Alcohol and other Drug Treatment Court Pilot*, 31 March 2014.

Litmus (2016). *Final Process Evaluation for the Alcohol and Other Drug Treatment Court, Te Whare Whakapiki Wairua*, 17 August 2016.

McKinlay, A., J. Corrigan, L. J. Horwood, and D. M. Fergusson (2014). Substance Abuse and Criminal Activities Following Traumatic Brain Injury in Childhood, Adolescence, and Early Adulthood. *Journal of Head Trauma and Rehabilitation,* 29 (6), 498–506.

McIntosh, T. and K. Workman (2017). *Māori and Prison*. In A. Deckert and R. Sarre (eds) *The Palgrave Handbook of Australian and New Zealand Criminology, Crime and Justice*: 725–735. New York: Palgrave Macmillan.

Miller, E. J. (2009). Drugs, Courts, and the New Penology. *Stanford Law & Policy Review* 20(2): 417–461.

Ministry of Justice (2014). *Alcohol and Other Drug Treatment Court, Te Whare Whakapiki Wairua, Handbook*, version 2. Wellington, New Zealand: Ministry of Justice.

Moore, D., (2007). Translating Justice and Therapy: The Drug Treatment Court Networks. *British Journal of Criminology* 47, 42–60. DOI:10.1093/bjc/azl028.

Moore, D., and Hirai, H. (2014). Outcasts, Performers, and True Believers: Responsibilized Subjects of Criminal Justice, *Theoretical Criminology,* 18(1) 5–19. DOI: 10.1177/1362480613519287.

Murphy, J. (2015). *Illness or Deviance, Drug Courts, Drug Treatment and the Ambiguity of Addiction.* Philadelphia: Temple University Press.

Nolan, J. (2003). Redefining Criminal Courts: Problem-Solving and the Meaning of Justice. *American Criminal Law Review*, 40, 1541.

Smith, M. (2007). *Report on issues involving the criminal justice sector*. Office of the Ombudsman, Wellington: New Zealand. Retrieved: http://www.ombudsman.parliament.nz/resources-and-publications/latest-reports May 2014.

Tiger, R. (2011). Drug Courts and the Logic of Coerced Treatment, *Sociological Forum*, 26 (1):169–182. DOI: 10.1111/j.1573-7861.2010.01229.x.

Tremewan, Judge L. (2013). What Are the Hallmarks of Such a Court and Why Have We Introduced Them? Leopards Changing Spots. *Address for the NZLS CLE Criminal Law Symposium*, 22 February 2013.

von Hirsch, A., and Ashworth (2005). *A Proportionate Sentencing: Exploring the Principles*, Oxford University Press, Oxford.

United Nations (2013). *Report of the Special Rapporteur on the Right of Everyone to the Enjoyment of the Highest Attainable Standard of Physical and Mental Health.* Anand Grover A/65/255. Retrieved: https://www.ohchr.org/en/issues/health/pages/srrighthealthindex.asp.

United Nations of Drugs and Crime & WHO (2017*). International Standards for the Treatment of Drug Use Disorders*. Retrieved: https://www.who.int/substance_abuse/activities/msb_treatment_standards.pdf.

Winick, B., and D. Wexler (2015). Drug Treatment Court: Therapeutic Jurisprudence Applied, 18 *Touro Law Review*, 479.

Woolhouse, R., A. McKinlay, & R. Grace (2017). Women in Prison with Traumatic Brain Injury: Prevalence, Mechanism, and Impact on Mental Health. *International Journal of Offender Therapy and Comparative Criminology*, 1–16.

NOTES

1. Ministry of Justice. "Alcohol and Other Drug Treatment Court, Te Whare Whakapiki Wairua, Handbook," v 2. Wellington (2014).

2. Lisa Tremewan. "What are the Hallmarks of Such a Court and Why Have We Introduced Them? Leopards Changing Spots." NZLS CLE (2013).

3. Litmus. "Final Process Evaluation for the Alcohol and Other Drug Treatment Court, Te Whare Whakapiki Wairua" (2016).

4. Bruce Winick and David Wexler. "Drug Treatment Court: Therapeutic Jurisprudence Applied" (2015), 18 *Touro Law Review*, 479.

5. Peggy Hora. "A Dozen Years of Drug Treatment Courts: Uncovering Our Theoretical Foundation and the Construction of a Mainstream Paradigm" (2002) *Substance Use & Misuse* 37 at 1472.

6. Peggy Fulton Hora, William Schma and John Rosenthal. "Therapeutic Jurisprudence and the Drug Court Movement: Revolutionizing the Criminal Justice System's Response to Drug Abuse and Crime in America" (1999) 74 *Notre Dame L Rev* 439 at 448.

7. James Nolan. "Redefining Criminal Courts: Problem-Solving and the Meaning of Justice" (2003) 40 *Am Crim L Rev* 1553.

8. Corey Colyer. "Innovation and Discretion: The Drug Court as a People-Processing Institution" (2007) *Criminal Justice Policy Review* 18.

9. Richard Boldt. "A Circumspect Look at Problem-Solving Courts, Problem-Solving Courts: Justice for the Twenty-first Century?" (Higgins and Mackinem, 2009) at 26.
10. Warren Brookbanks. "Therapeutic Jurisprudence: New Zealand Perspectives" (Thomson Reuters, 2017).
11. Hora n 5 at 1481.
12. Morris Hoffman. "Therapeutic Jurisprudence, Neo-Rehabilitationism, and Judicial Collectivism: The Least Dangerous Branch Becomes Most Dangerous" (2002) 29 *Fordham Urb LJ* 2063 at 1479, 2088.
13. Boldt n 9.
14. Rebecca Tiger. "Drug Courts and the Logic of Coerced Treatment" (2011) *Sociological Forum* 26.
15. Ministry of Justice n 1.
16.Ministry of Justice n 1.
17. n 2 at 9.
18. n 1 at 6.
19. AODTC observation, September 2013.
20. AODTC observation, November 2013.
21. Informal conversation, December 2014.
22. Informal conversation, September 2014.
23. Informal conversation, November 2014.
24. AODTC observation, November 2013.
25. AODTC observation, September 2013.
26. Josh Bowers. "Contraindicated Drug Courts" (2007) Paper Series no180 at 6.
27. Jennifer Murphy. "Illness or Deviance, Drug Courts, Drug Treatment and the Ambiguity of Addiction" (Temple University Press, 2015).
28. Andrew von Hirsch and Andrew Ashworth. "Proportionate Sentencing: Exploring the Principles" (Oxford University Press, Oxford, 2005).
29. AODTC observation, December 2013.
30. AODTC observation, December 2013.
31. n 12 at 2067.
32. AODTC observation, December 2013.
33. AODTC observation, September 2013.
34. Informal conversation, December 2014.
35. n 12.
36. n 9.
37. n 9.
38. AODTC observation December 2013.
39. Ministry of Justice at 8.
40. Devon Indig, Craig Gear, and Kay Wilhelm. "Comorbid substance use disorders and mental health disorders among New Zealand prisoners" (2016) New Zealand Department of Corrections.
41. Litmus. "Formative Evaluation for the Alcohol and other Drug Treatment Court Pilot" (2014) at 31.
42. Rachel Woolhouse, Audrey McKinlay, and Randolph Grace. "Women in Prison with Traumatic Brain Injury: Prevalence, Mechanism, and Impact on Mental Health"

(2018) *International Journal of Offender Therapy and Comparative Criminology* 62(10).

43. n 40.

44. AODTC observation, November 2013.

45. Ministry of Justice, n 6.

46. Ministry of Justice, n 6.

47. Murphy, n 26.

48. AODTC observation, September 2013.

49. Tracy McIntosh and Kim Workman. "Māori and prison" in Deckert and Sarre (eds) *Palgrave Handbook of Australian and New Zealand Criminology, Crime and Justice* (2017).

50. AODTC observation, November 2013.

51. AODTC observation, September 2013.

52. Litmus, n 40 at 58.

53. Dawn Moore. "Translating Justice and Therapy: The Drug Treatment Court Networks." *British Journal of Criminology* 47 (2007).

54. Mel Smith. "Report on Issues Involving the Criminal Justice Sector." Office of the Ombudsman, Wellington, (2007).

55. AODTC observation, October 2013.

56. AODTC observation, November 2013.

57. AODTC observation, October 2013.

58. AODTC observation, November 2013.

59. n 12.

60. n 1, at 6.

61. n 9.

62. Von Hirsch and Ashworth, n 28.

Chapter 3

Stop and Search Powers in England & Wales

The Commissioner, the Home Secretary, the Media, and the Public

Jack James and Richard Hester

This chapter considers the continual controversy surrounding the use of stop and search powers in England and Wales. As authors, we have approached this chapter from a hybrid position as current or previous police practitioners (see author notes page) as well as academics with a keen interest in studying stop and search. This allows us to understand the wealth of literature, as well as the implications for and nuances of police practice, which is something we have tried to convey in the chapter without prejudice. In England and Wales, stop and search is one of the police's most frequently used powers, with 1,029 stop and searches conducted every day in 2019.[1] There is still a high amount of racial disparity in stop and search figures, with black people being nine times more likely to be stopped and search than white people (ibid). For the police service, getting stop and search right is fundamental to building and maintaining effective community relationships, but as this chapter explores, that is a far from straightforward process.

This chapter is split into three sections. The first section charts the *historical development of stop and search powers*, from the Vagrancy Act 1824, to the Police and Criminal Evidence Act 1984 and new proposed Serious Violence Reduction Orders (SVROs). We examine how and why these powers have developed as well as how they are used by the police. The section also explores how watershed events such as the Brixton riots of 1981, the murder of Stephen Lawrence in 1993, and the police shooting of Mark Duggan in

2011 have impacted stop and search practices and ultimately police and community relationships. The second section considers the *media portrayal and political involvement relating to stop and search*, with a key examination of how the media can influence public opinion and ultimately affect police and community relations. Particular attention is paid to the use of social media sites, such as Facebook and YouTube, as this presents a relatively new challenge for policing. The "political interference" that has happened with stop and search since the coalition government came to power in 2010, is examined in detail. This comprizes the introduction of the "Best Use of Stop and Search Scheme" (BUSS) by then Home Secretary Theresa May, only for police forces to be told by subsequent home secretaries to ignore aspects of this relating to section 60 "no suspicion" searches. The third section considers *how police application of stop and search powers impacts public perceptions of police legitimacy*, with a detailed examination of key literature and research into the impact stop and search has on the key foundations of the British policing models of police legitimacy and policing by consent. Finally, we consider the position of the police and how they can effectively process the vast amount of conflicting information that is present regarding stop and search in order to improve police and community relationships.

HISTORICAL DEVELOPMENT OF STOP AND SEARCH POWERS

Stop and Search Pre-PACE

It is widely recognized within academic discourse that stop and search powers, or forms thereof, have held a place in British policing since the 1800s.[2] The history of stop and search powers is long and controversial, with keystone events inspiring reform and refinement of stop and search legislation, as well as policing practice, over the last four decades in particular.[3] As a result of legislative change, including the development of the Police and Criminal Evidence Act (PACE) in 1984, stop and search powers have evolved to manifest as a widely practiced contemporary policing power, that maintains an ability to generate both significant praise and criticism.[4]

Prior to the introduction of PACE, the Vagrancy Act of 1824 was the primary legislation utilized by officers for the purpose of a search, with more contemporary stop and search powers introduced under PACE 140 years later in 1984.[5] Regarded as "sus laws," notably sections 4, 6, and 8 of the Vagrancy Act 1824, alongside other local and national legislative powers, provided officers with the legal capacity to search and arrest those who they suspected as being a "suspicious person," "a rogue or a vagabond," or "disorderly."[6]

While the Vagrancy Act was brought into force as a response to incidents of disorder linked to the aftermath of the Napoleonic War in the early 19th century, it fundamentally shaped the way in which formal stop and search powers would evolve and be used into the 20th century, importantly, introducing the notion of suspicion into the new, formal anatomy of policing.[7] In addition to preexisting search powers stemming from the Vagrancy Act 1824 in relation to suspicious and disorderly individuals, section 66 of the Metropolitan Police Act 1839 provided supplementary search powers to officers inside of London. Section 66 of the Metropolitan Police Act enabled officers to stop and search any individual, of whom they held a "reasonable suspicion" to be in possession of stolen or unlawfully obtained items.[8] "Sus laws," alongside legislation such as section 66, maintained positions as being prominent policing tools throughout the early and mid-20th century, with search powers and legislation remaining particularly undiverse and increasingly recognized as being open to abuse.[9]

The use of 19th century "sus laws" as a legal grounding for officers to perform searches throughout the latter half of the 20th century began to fundamentally alter relationships between police and communities, with the aforementioned powers increasingly seen as being ancient and discriminatory.[10] Throughout the 1970s, a growing number of complaints and concerns began to materialize, particularly surrounding the disproportionate application of outdated "sus laws" toward those of black or ethnic minority backgrounds[11] as "poor, young black youths in deprived inner-city locations began to be seen as troublesome and potentially criminal."[12] This unjust representation, accompanied by a moral panic surrounding inner-city street robberies, or "muggings," saw a heavy-handed and disproportionate use of search powers against young black men, particularly in London. As communities of ethnic minority backgrounds felt increasingly marginalized, the "scrap the sus" movement gained traction as a popular, and soon to be successful, political campaign,[13] calling for increased police accountability, greater regulation for search powers, or their complete abolition. Tensions and concerns soon climaxed following the controversial "Operation Swamp" in Brixton by the Metropolitan Police in April 1981,[14] which saw 150 plainclothes officers perform over 1,000 searches and make 150 arrests over a 10-day period in the London borough.[15] This large operation, which relied on the use of "sus laws" to perform searches, is widely recognized as the flash point leading to the Brixton Riots from April 10 to 12, 1981, an event that "signalled the loss of hard-earned legitimacy"[16] for the police and effectively triggered significant legislative reform relating to stop and search.

The Scarman Report, PACE, and Macpherson

The three days of rioting in Brixton in April 1981 manifested from an accumulation of social and economic disparities affecting those from minority ethnic groups in particular, with it being widely recognized that rioters had specific grievances relating to police actions.[17] During the 1970s, "Youngsters were faced with the toxic combination of unemployment, racism, a society which marginalized their political voice and which addressed the symptoms of urban decay with systematic over-policing."[18] Such challenging circumstances resulted in feelings of exclusion, disempowerment, and frustration, which eventually turned to visible anger. The disproportionate use of "sus law" search powers on young black males in London had caused a significant rift between the police and ethnic minority communities, with the breaking point leading to the Brixton Riots being "exasperation at oppressive use of stop and search, in particular the massive Operation Swamp 81."[19] The rioting highlighted the link between the disproportionate use of stop and search on those from ethnic minority communities and profound community resentment toward the police. This feeling of resentment toward the police resonated across other major cities, including Manchester, Liverpool, and Leeds. While labeled as "wanton lawlessness"[20] by then Prime Minister Margaret Thatcher, the Brixton Riots would lead to significant legislative change that sought to "balance the powers of the police with the rights of the public."[21]

Following the disorder in Brixton, Lord Scarman conducted an enquiry into the riots, which "acknowledged that stop and search was necessary to combat street crime but expressed concerns over the extent to which the 'sus laws' were used."[22] The report that followed concluded the riots were primarily a result of an eruption of underlying frustrations and anger, felt largely by young black men, regarding the way in which they were treated by police at the time.[23] Lord Scarman's report recommended that "sus laws" be replaced by new, national legislation, incorporating stop and search powers, which would allow for greater accountability, transparency, and introduce safeguards to standardize approaches to stop and search; such recommendations resulted in the creation of PACE in 1984.[24] The newly established Police and Criminal Evidence Act introduced procedural safeguards for stop and search within an accompanying code of practice,[25] including the development of a uniform approach to defining "reasonable grounds" for suspicion, as well as "requiring officers to provide an explanation of the reasons for a search and to complete a written record detailing reasons and outcomes that would be made available to the person searched if requested."[26] PACE, however, did not prove to be a permanent fix and stop and search was soon to return to the spotlight following the Macpherson Report in 1999.

The long, controversial history and debate surrounding the application of stop and search powers reached "new heights of intensity"[27] in 1999 following a series of highly significant, influential findings stemming from the inquiry into the handling of the investigation into the murder of Stephen Lawrence. The Stephen Lawrence Inquiry, and subsequent report published by Sir William Macpherson in 1999, highlighted a series of concerns surrounding the application of stop and search by forces across England and Wales. Perhaps one of the most significant conclusions to arise from within the Macpherson Report was the notion of the existence of institutional racism within the Metropolitan Police and forces nationwide, with the report defining the concept as being:

> The collective failure of an organisation to provide an appropriate and professional service to people because of their colour, culture, or ethnic origin. It can be seen or detected in processes, attitudes and behaviour which amount to discrimination through unwitting prejudice, ignorance, thoughtlessness and racist stereotyping which disadvantage minority ethnic people.[28]

Macpherson made specific reference to stop and search figures, with the report claiming that overrepresentation of those from ethnic minority communities amounted to a "clear core conclusion of racist stereotyping"[29] by officers. For example, in 1999, the year the Macpherson Report was published, the Metropolitan Police Authority identified that stop searches on Black people accounted for almost 30% of all stop searches within the Met's force area. Furthermore, when Section 60 CJPOA (Criminal Justice and Public Order Act) searches between 1990 and 1999 were analyzed, it was reported that searches on Black people accounted for over 50% of all Section 60 searches.[30] In order to implement essential changes, and to address issues highlighted, the report included three fundamental recommendations required for the improvement of police accountability and transparency in relation to stop and search best practice. The recommendations, numbered 61, 62, and 63, began by outlining a necessity for any stop, regardless of use of legislative provision, to be recorded with the inclusion of a detailed reason for the stop, the outcome, and the individuals self-defined ethnicity. Recommendation 61 also proposed a requirement on officers to provide a copy of the search record to the individual. Furthermore, Macpherson recommended that stop and search figures should be analyzed by forces and published and reviewed by HMIC, allowing for greater transparency, accountability, and scrutiny of stop and search. The report's final requirement highlighted the necessity for forces to engage in campaigns to educate the public on stop and search powers and their legal rights with these amendments, specifically to Code A of PACE, collectively seeking to address highlighted issues surrounding disproportionality in figures, accountability, and transparency.

In the 20 years following the Macpherson Report, stop and search has continued to generate controversy and attract the attention of media outlets and governments alike. The application of stop and search powers were thrust into the public arena once more following the summer riots of 2011, as well as in recent years as Section 60 of the Criminal Justice and Public Order Act (CJPOA) has been increasingly employed as a short-term targeted strategy by forces to help combat the rise in knife and violent crime. Introduced as a core component of the CJPOA in 1994, Section 60 was originally intended to be utilized in order to "tackle football hooliganism and the threat of serious violence at football games, but it is now used for a wider range of purposes."[31] The perceived extension of search powers for the police has reignited debate in 2020, as the government announced the introduction of Serious Violence Reduction Orders, which will allow for officers to search based on previous convictions for knife or weapons related offences. The media portrayal and the extent of government involvement in shaping stop and search use since the publication of the Macpherson Report is explored and discussed in the next section.

MEDIA PORTRAYAL AND POLITICAL INVOLVEMENT RELATING TO STOP AND SEARCH

Media Portrayal of Stop and Search

Stop and search is a topic that continually attracts media attention, and police encounters are readily available to the media due to the widespread prevalence of mobile video recording devices and websites such as YouTube.[32] Certain media outlets have a strong emphasis on police accountability, with stop and search being a particular focus. For example, the online version of *The Guardian* has a section dedicated to stop and search with over 330 news stories dating back to 2000.[33] Police officers behaving in a justifiable and normative way are considered as key elements in procedural justice.[34] This is reflected in the latest College of Policing guidance on engagement and communication[35] where the importance of perception of police fairness is emphasized. This public perception of policing will typically be drawn from two types of encounters: either reporting a crime or being approached by the police.[36]

Not every citizen will have encounters with the police of this nature, though some people will hear anecdotally about police stop and search, but many members of the public will perceive policing through a media lens. We must then consider the accuracy of this media portrayal of policing, and with particular attention to the type of stop and search encounters that are abundant in the media. A simple typing of the phrase "stop and search" into YouTube reveals a range of videos, some are promotional, or training videos uploaded by police forces, but often these videos are public recorded encounters of stop and search incidents. Many of the public recorded encounters can be regarded as having a negative perception of the police, with descriptors of "bullies," "intimidation," "harassment," or "racist" being prevalent.[37] Given that the internet and social media are the second and third most commonly used platforms, respectively, for consumption of news,[38] the impact of negative perceptions of policing in online videos is of great importance to police legitimacy. Taken in isolation, these videos often do not provide any context to the rationale for police-initiated contact leading to the stop and search encounter, as the video recording may start minutes after the encounter has begun. This leaves the viewer to speculate, and with platforms such as Facebook and YouTube, this often leads to negative comments about the police being made, further eroding trust and police legitimacy. Routine sharing with the media of police body worn video (BWV) from stop and search encounters may help to negate this issue and demonstrate that the police are acting proportionately, but current College of Policing guidance[39] does not allow BWV to be shared with the media for this purpose.

Stories about stop and search that are in the mainstream media potentially offer more balance than social media, as the police forces concerned are invited to comment on any story. On Saturday July 4, 2020, two Olympic athletes, Bianca Williams and Ricardo dos Santos, were stopped and searched under section 1 of the PACE.[40] The Metropolitan police reported that the vehicle had been driving suspiciously, on the wrong side of the road, and had initially failed to stop when requested by the police.[41] Bianca Williams publicly disputed the police's version of events and raised concerns that they had been racially profiled as they were both handcuffed during the search with their 3-year-old child in the car.[42] The Metropolitan Police directorate of professional standards initially concluded that there had been no misconduct, but subsequently referred itself to the Independent Office for Police Conduct (IOPC) who initiated a misconduct investigation on October 9, 2020 after reviewing the evidence.[43] This incident was reported in a wide range of news media, most of which also reported comments from the Metropolitan Police that allows a balance, but a major theme among the headlines used was racial profiling. Despite balance in the reporting of this incident, the public are left to draw their own conclusions on whether the stop was lawful or not. Transparency over the full grounds recorded for this stop and search are required for the public to be able to judge this incident. Either the media are not reporting it, or the police are not providing it. The latter seems more likely to be the case, despite College of Policing guidance stating that "police use of stop and search powers must be transparent and accountable."[44] It seems that in order for the police to be portrayed accurately in the media over stop and search, there needs to be a greater release of information held by the police such as BWV and recorded search grounds so that, ultimately, the public can judge the incidents—instead of conjecture filling the information void.

Political Involvement in Stop and Search

There was significant political involvement in the creation of stop and search powers under PACE,[45] and recently there has been a significant contribution from politicians in the debate surrounding stop and search. Major pieces of work by the Equality and Human Rights Commission highlight disproportionality in searches of black and minority ethnic communities. The *Stop and Think* report threatened legal action under the Equality Act 2010 against several police forces,[46] and *Stop and Think Again* sought to highlight the limited progress made by police forces in reducing disproportionality in their stop and search practices.[47] This prompted the HMIC to review police practices over stop and search, finding that 27% of stop and searches they examined did not justify lawful use of the power, leading to several recommendations for reform.[48] This was further emphasized by the then home secretary, Theresa May, making the following comments in a speech to the House of Commons in April 2014:

> I want to make myself absolutely clear: if the numbers do not come down, if stop and search does not become more targeted, if those stop-to-arrest ratios do not improve considerably, the government will return with primary legislation to make those things happen.[49]

This comment can be construed as dictatorial from the government to the police, and the impact of this cannot be understated. Following this, the *Best Use of Stop and Search Scheme* was created in August 2014,[50] with the aims such as ensuring better recording, allowing lay observations of encounters, and crucially increasing the authorization level for section 60 no suspicious searches to above chief superintendent. Although not legally binding, all 43 police forces in England and Wales signed up to the scheme and were monitored by HMIC with findings being reported back to the Home Secretary. In July 2016, the home secretary changed from Theresa May to Amber Rudd. Despite recommendations from HMIC in September 2016 for the level of authorization for a section 60 be lowered to the rank of inspector for exceptional circumstances,[51] the rhetoric from the home secretary remained the same as her predecessor with Amber Rudd maintaining that any increased stop and search powers would be a "backward step."[52]

With a change in home secretary seemingly came a change in position on stop and search, with Sajid Javid announcing in March 2019 that the level of authorization for section 60 will be lowered to inspector, as well as the required threshold of certainty of violence occurring being lowered.[53] The government is now proposing changes to stop and search powers through Serious Violence Reduction Orders (SVROs), arguably influenced by recommendation 14 of the *It Can Be Stopped*[54] report from The Centre for Social Justice thinktank. SVRO proposals would drastically increase police powers to stop and search, by allowing no suspicion searches under section 1 of PACE of people previously convicted of a knife crime (while still serving their sentence) or a court power allowing such people to be stopped and searched without suspicion.[55]

Across a period of around 6 years, the government has told the police that they are doing too much stop and search and have limited their powers. They changed policy, increased the powers, and suggested more stop and search is needed to reduce crime. The police do not always conduct stop and search correctly, but their job is being made harder by this pendulum government policy. The effect of this is that officers across all ranks of the police service will be confused by what they are being asked to do over stop and search, which will filter to frontline officers being cautious about how to use their powers. The current evidence base on stop and search suggests that it has little impact on crime rates and results in marginalized communities.[56] The police service and public require clarity and consistency over stop and search with further longitudinal studies to review the effectiveness and community impact, and not necessarily a range of new proposals to increase stop and search powers. The government appears to be ignoring this evidence base. If these proposals develop into new stop and search laws, it could increase the amount of stop and searches that occur with by-products of minimal crime reduction and negative ramifications for police and community relations.

This ongoing political involvement in stop and search powers seems to be hindering and not helping stop and search. Despite this, the police application of the powers is crucial, as eloquently stated by Neil Parpworth: "the controversy relating to stop and search powers is essentially concerned with their exercize rather than their existence,"[57] as discussed in the next section.

HOW POLICE APPLICATION OF STOP AND SEARCH POWERS IMPACTS PUBLIC PERCEPTIONS OF POLICE LEGITIMACY

While the contentious history of stop and search has been highlighted in this chapter, it is also important to further explore the potential impacts that the use of stop and search powers have on public opinions of the police, as well as the subsequent effect on perceptions of police legitimacy. The term "legitimacy" can, on a rudimentary level, be understood as "the right to exercize power,"[58] a well-recognized and highly important concept, particularly when applied to policing and the powers of the state relating to the maintenance of social order. Empirical evidence stemming from research conducted by Justice Tankebe in 2012, a year after the summer riots in cities across England, highlighted the important relationship between police legitimacy and the preservation of lawful behavior by the wider population. Tankebe's research in London concluded that "legitimacy was found to exhibit both a direct influence on cooperation that is independent of obligation and an indirect influence that flows through people's felt obligations to obey the police."[59] Legitimacy, therefore, is essential in allowing for effective policing and the continuation of public support and cooperation with the police.[60]

In the context of policing, it is well recognized that "personal contacts between police and citizens are important moments in which public trust and the legitimacy of the police is tested, reproduced or undermined."[61] Research has supported the notion that an interaction with a member of the public that is initiated by the police, such as a stop and account or stop and search, is more likely to have a detrimental impact on that individual's ability or willingness to trust the police than if the role of the initiator was reversed.[62] Trust is a fundamental component in the maintenance of police legitimacy.[63] However, with research indicating those stopped by police are less likely to trust them in the future, it appears to be a natural progression for the same individual to indicate they do not view the police as being legitimate in the application of their powers.[64] Stop and search therefore, given its contentious history, presents as being a specific challenge for officers, balancing the necessity to "fight crime" with the maintenance of public trust and perceptions of legitimacy.

The police are arguably in a precarious position. Firstly, attempting to fulfil the expectation placed upon them to be visibly "fighting crime," an expectation resonating from both public and political pressure to be providing a proactive, assertive, reassuring approach.[65] Such an approach may manifest as a stop and account or, providing the existence of reasonable grounds to do so, a stop and search. Secondly, the police must attempt to do this while addressing concerns raised by those who object to encounters such as stop and search, which can have a profound impact on those on the receiving end of such practices,[66] damaging trust and legitimacy between individuals, communities, and the police. Stop and search brings the relationship between trust and police legitimacy to the forefront.[67] The application of stop and search can significantly impact public opinion, either enhancing or undermining trust and perceptions of police legitimacy, not only for those who have experienced the exercise of this policing power, but also for those observing.

Research from the London Assembly Police and Crime Committee in 2014, indicated that "the Met is at another crossroad in its relationship with some Londoners . . . for some parts of the community, distrust with the police is entrenched."[68] The report highlights the importance of building trust to enhance community confidence in policing, particularly among those from ethnic minority backgrounds, citing stop and search as being a powerful symbol of the tension that exists between the Met and many Londoners."[69] A cumulation of academic research surrounding stop and search and police legitimacy indicates that it is not necessarily the of stop and search powers that has the most significant impact on trust and community confidence in policing, but rather the way in which these powers are used.[70] This theme resonates throughout various reports, including a year-long qualitative study by the Criminal Justice Alliance in 2016. After interviewing over 500 black, Asian, and minority ethnic males between 15 and 26 years old, the report concluded that perceptions and feelings following a stop and search are the most important factors likely to result in corrosive feelings of mistrust and confidence in the police.[71] The committee concluded that "the quality of encounters with the police is the most important driver of police legitimacy; this affects people's willingness to cooperate with the police and the police's ability to do their job."[72] The quality of stop and search encounters, alongside the disproportionate representation of those from ethnic minority communities and the resulting feelings of mistrust and contempt for the police that have followed, have undoubtedly significantly contributed to the loss of perceived legitimacy in the past, manifesting as the 1981 Brixton and 2011 summer riots.

As previously explored in this chapter, the 1981 Brixton riots have been found to be rooted in mistrust and anger toward the police, primarily from young black males in London, who felt they were being targeted by officers using outdated "sus laws" for the purpose of a search, derived from the Vagrancy Act of 1824.[73] The Scarman Report made specific reference to the overuse of "sus laws," particularly during "Operation Swamp" in April 1981, a widely agreed flash point for the riots, stating:

> They provoked the hostility of young black people, who felt they were being hunted irrespective of their innocence or guilt. And their hostility infected older members of the community who, hearing the stories of many innocent young people who had been stopped and searched, began themselves to lose confidence in, and respect for, the police. However well-intentioned, these operations precipitated a crisis of confidence between the police and certain community leaders.[74]

This "crisis of confidence" significantly impacted perceptions of police legitimacy and following "Operation Swamp," Brixton saw three days of rioting as frustrations and feelings of victimization turned into visible acts of anger. Brixton is recognized as a very real example of the possible consequences following a significant loss of police legitimacy, which is arguably linked to and caused by the initial diminishment of trust and community confidence in policing.[75] Although the Scarman Report highlighted these concerns and issues with stop and search, leading to the implementation of PACE in 1984 exactly 30 years later, feelings of mistrust and contempt towards the police as a result of perceived inequalities in the treatment of ethnic minority community members would once again see rioting in the streets of the capital. The riots, which started on August 4, 2011, following the police shooting of Mark Duggan resulted in 5 deaths, £3 million worth of damage, and 5,100 offenses across 10 force areas in just four days.[76] Although the death of Mark Duggan is seen as the "flash point" for the disorder, research that has followed the summer of 2011 has since highlighted the importance of the preexisting feelings of mistrust toward police, stemming from perceived "persistent, oppressive, over-policing," particularly of communities with high ethnic minority populations through the use of stop and search.[77] Although the riots of 1981 and 2011 differ in context, the significant community reactions following a particular "flash point" make them important events in highlighting the possible consequences of when community trust and confidence in policing result in a perceived loss of legitimacy. Stop and search, while viewed by some as an important policing power in the prevention and detection of crime, when seen as being applied disproportionately or used ineffectively, can have detrimental impacts on an individual or a community's confidence and trust, which in turn can result in the loss of perceived police legitimacy.

CONCLUSION

Stop and search is a powerful tool that is granted upon police officers in order to keep the public safe. There have been a number of key events that have led to reflection on how stop and search should be conducted, most notably the

Brixton riots in 1981, which resulted in the creation of PACE that is still the defining piece of legislation on stop and search today. PACE, with particular reference to Code A of the codes of practice, is quite clear in terms of how the police should be conducting stop and search. However, policing and stop and search do not occur in a vacuum; other factors influence and shape policing practice. The media have a strong influence over the reporting of stop and search, with outlets such as *The Guardian* having an entire section dedicated to it on their website. A video of a negative stop and search encounter has the tendency to proliferate rapidly on media outlets, particularly with social media platforms increasing their reach. This can have adverse consequences for police and community relations, not just in the location where the search occurred but nationally as well. Even though video footage on social media may not show the full event, damage is easily done with a short clip that reflects negatively on the police. The police service needs to consider increasing transparency through not only more routine use of body-worn video, but considering how that footage can be shared with the public more broadly to allow for a fair judgment of these encounters so sensationalist media does not fill the gaps.

There is a key question of whether politics and politicians are a hindrance or a help to the police in terms of stop and search, with the former seeming the case recently. In the last six years politicians have gone from telling the police that they are doing too much stop and search and that legislation will be restricted, through to relaxing legislation to increase stop and search and proposing new legislation that will increase police powers. The new powers of Serious Violence Reduction Orders will provide the police greater powers to search previous offenders, and there will be strong opposition to not only the powers but their implementation too. This constant flux in political position on stop and search is understandably leaving the police in a state of confusion over how to implement stop and search. This will manifest in continually changing internal police policy, which may filter down to front-line officers who are conducting stop and search being left in a challenging position of not having confidence in their powers or being supported in their actions. The ultimate result of this is that the current state of affairs regarding stop and search is not conducive to building effective relationships between the police and communities, and in particular people from black and ethnic minority backgrounds. All of which is undermining police legitimacy and public confidence in the police, and an honest public debate is required to readdress the balance with fundamental questions around what stop and search powers we want the police to have and how and when we expect them to be used.

BIBLIOGRAPHY

BBC News, "Bianca Williams stop: Police 'want to discuss sprinter's concerns'" (*BBC News*, 6 July 2020), https://www.bbc.co.uk/news/uk-england-london-53307555, accessed 12 October 2020.

BBC News, "Bianca Williams stop-and-search: Met PCs face probe" (*BBC News*, 9 October 2020), https://www.bbc.co.uk/news/uk-england-london-54466254, accessed 12 October 2020.

Benyon, J. "England's Urban Disorder: The 2011 Riots" (2012) 3 *Political Insight* 12.

Bradford, B. *Stop and Search and Police Legitimacy* (Routledge, 2017).

Briggs, D. *The English Riots of 2011: A Summer of Discontent* (Waterside Press, 2012).

Brown, J. "Police Powers: Stop and Search" (House of Commons Library Briefing Paper 3878, 17 June 2020), https://commonslibrary.parliament.uk/research-briefings/sn03878/ accessed 27 October 2020.

Clayton, E. "Stop and Search and Police Legitimacy" (2017) 27 *Policing and Society* 813.

College of Policing. "Engagement and communication" (*College of Policing Authorized Professional Practice*, 2013), https://www.app.college.police.uk/app-content/engagement-and-communication/, accessed 12 October 2020.

College of Policing, "Body-Worn Video" (*College of Policing*, 2014), http://library.college.police.uk/docs/college-of-policing/Body-worn-video-guidance-2014.pdf, accessed 12 October 2020.

College of Policing, "Stop and Search" (*College of Policing Authorized Professional Practice*, 2017), https://www.app.college.police.uk/app-content/stop-and-search/, accessed 12 October 2020.

Delsol, R., and M. Shiner. "Regulating Stop and Search: A Challenge for Police and Community Relations in England and Wales" (2006) 14 *Critical Criminology* 241.

Delsol, R., and M. Shiner. *Stop and Search: The Anatomy of a Police Power* (Palgrave Macmillan, 2015).

Equality and Human Rights Commission. "Race Disproportionality in Stops and Searches under Section 60 of the Criminal Justice and Public Order Act 1994" (*Equality and Human Rights Commission*, 2012), https://www.equalityhumanrights.com/sites/default/files/briefing-paper-5-race-disproportionality-in-stops-and-searches-under-s60-of-criminal-justice-and-public-order-act-1994.pdf, accessed 3 October 2020.

Equality and Human Rights Commission, "Stop and Think: A Critical Review of the Use of Stop and Search Powers in England and Wales" (*Equality and Human Rights Commission,* 2010), https://www.equalityhumanrights.com/sites/default/files/ehrc_stop_and_search_report.pdf, accessed 12 October 2020.

Equality and Human Rights Commission, "Stop and Think Again: Towards Race Equality in Plice PACE Stop and Search" (*Equality and Human Rights Commission*, 2013), https://www.equalityhumanrights.com/sites/default/files/stop_and_think_again.pdf, accessed 12 October 2020.

Grierson, J. "Why Did Police Stop and Search Bianca Williams and Ricardo Dos Santos" (*The Guardian*, 6 July 2020), https://www.theguardian.com/law/2020/jul/06/why-did-police-stop-and-search-bianca-williams-and-ricardo-dos-santos, accessed 12 October 2020.

HM Government, "Stop & Search" (Gov.UK, 2020), https://www.ethnicity-facts-figures.service.gov.uk/crime-justice-and-the-law/policing/stop-and-search/latest, accessed 20 November 2020.

HMIC, "Stop and Search Powers: Are the Police Using Them Fairly and Effectively?" (*Her Majesty's Inspectorate of Constabulary and Fire and Rescue Services*, 2013), https://www.justiceinspectorates.gov.uk/hmicfrs/publications/stop-and-search-powers-20130709/ accessed 12 October 2020.

HMIC, "Best Use of Stop and Search (BUSS) Scheme: The Findings of an HMIC Revisit of the 13 Forces That Were Not Complying with Three or More Features of the Scheme in 2015" (*Her Majesty's Inspectorate of Constabulary and Fire and Rescue Services*, 2016), https://www.justiceinspectorates.gov.uk/hmicfrs/publications/best-use-of-stop-and-search-second-revisits/, accessed 14 October 2020.

Home Office and Theresa May MP, "Oral Statement to Parliament. Stop and Search: Comprehensive Package of Reform for Police Stop and Search Powers" (*HM Government*, 2014), https://www.gov.uk/government/speeches/stop-and-search-comprehensive-package-of-reform-for-police-stop-and-search-powers, accessed 12 October 2020.

Home Office, "Best Use of Stop and Search Scheme" (*HM Government*, 2014), https://www.gov.uk/government/publications/best-use-of-stop-and-search-scheme, accessed 14 October 2020.

Home Office, "Amber Rudd Writes about Stop and Search in *The Times*" (*HM Government*, 2017), https://homeofficemedia.blog.gov.uk/2017/08/09/amber-rudd-writes-about-stop-and-search-in-the-times/, accessed 14 October 2020.

Home Office, "Greater Powers for Police to Use Stop and Search to Tackle Violent Crime" (*HM Government*, 2019), https://www.gov.uk/government/news/greater-powers-for-police-to-use-stop-and-search-to-tackle-violent-crime, accessed 14 October 2020.

Home Office, "Serious Violence Reduction Orders: A New Court Order to Target Known Knife Carriers. Government Consultation" (*HM Government,* 2020), https://assets.publishing.service.gov.uk/government/uploads/system/uploads/attachment_data/file/917277/SVRO_consultation.pdf, accessed 14 October 2020.

Jackson, J., B. Bradford, B. Stanko, and K. Hohl. *Just Authority? Trust in the Police in England and Wales* (Routledge, 2013).

Jackson, N. M. "A Nigger in the New England: Sus, the Brixton Riot and Citizenship" (2015) 8 *African and Black Diaspora: An International Journal*, 158.

Jefferson, T. "Policing the Riots: From Bristol and Brixton to Tottenham, via Toxteth, Handsworth, etc." (2012) 87 *Criminal Justice Matters*, 8.

Keeling, P. "No Respect: Young BAME Men, the Police and Stop and Search" (*Criminal Justice Alliance*, 2017), http://criminaljusticealliance.org/wp-content/uploads/2017/06/No-Respect-290617.pdf, accessed 3 October 2020.

Lawrence, P. "Vagrancy Act 1824 and the Persistence of Pre-emptive Policing in England since 1750" (2017) 57 *The British Journal of Criminology*, 513.
Lea, J., and S. Hallsworth. "Understanding the Riots" (2012) 87 *Criminal Justice Matters*, 30.
Lea, J. "Institutional Racism in Policing: The Macpherson Report and Its Consequences" in Roger Matthews and Jock Young (eds), *The New Politics of Crime and Punishment* (Routledge 2011).
London Assembly Police and Crime Committee, "Police and Crime Committee Response to the Draft Police and Crime Plan for 2013–2017" (*London Assembly*, 2013), https://www.london.gov.uk/about-us/londonassembly/meetings/documents/s26909/Research%20into%20Young%20Peoples%20Views%20of%20Stop%20and%20Search%20for%20Police%20and%20Crime%20Committee%20Investigation%20-.pdf, accessed 7 October 2020.
London Assembly Police and Crime Committee, "Stop and Search: An Investigation into the Met's New Approach to Stop and Search" (*London Assembly*, 2014), https://www.london.gov.uk/sites/default/files/14-02-06-Stop%20and%20search%20FINAL_1.pdf, accessed 7 October 2020.
Metropolitan Police Authority, "A Report of the MPA Scrutiny on MPS Stop and Search Practice" (*Police Authority*, 2005), http://policeauthority.org/metropolitan/downloads/committees/previous/eodb/eodb-040520-05-appendix01.pdf, accessed 2 December 2021.
Miller, J. "Stop and Search in England: A Reformed Tactic or Business as Usual?" (2010) 50 *The British Journal of Criminology*, 954.
Neyroud P, "Past, Present and Future Performance: Prospects for the Measurement of Police Performance" (2008) 2 *Policing*, 340.
Ofcom, "New Consumption Report 2020" (*Ofcom*, 2020), https://www.ofcom.org.uk/research-and-data/tv-radio-and-on-demand/news-media/news-consumption, accessed 12 October 2020.
Parpworth, N. "Reforming Police Powers of Stop and Search: Voluntary Action" (2014) 87 *Police Journal: Theory, Practice and Principles*, 234.
Police and Criminal Evidence Act 1984
Tankebe, J. "Viewing Things Differently: The Dimensions of Public Perceptions of Police Legitimacy" (2012) 51 *Criminology*, 103.
The Centre for Social Justice, "It Can Be Stopped. A Proven Blueprint to Stop Violence and Tackle Gang and Related Offending in London and Beyond" (*The Centre for Social Justice*, 2018), https://www.centreforsocialjustice.org.uk/core/wp-content/uploads/2018/09/CSJJ6499-Gangs-Report-180911-FINAL-WEB.pdf, accessed 14 October 2020.
The Guardian, "Stop and Search" (*The Guardian*, 2020), https://www.theguardian.com/law/stop-and-search, accessed 9 October 2020.
The Police Foundation, "Stop and Search" (2012), *The Briefing*, 3, http://www.police-foundation.org.uk/2017/wp-content/uploads/2017/08/stop_and_search_briefing.pdf, accessed 20 October 2020.

Tiratelli, M., P. Quinton,and B. Bradford. "Does Stop and Search Deter Crime? Evidence from Ten Years of London-Wide Data" (2018) 58 *The British Journal of Criminology*, 1212.

Waddington, P. A. J., K. Stenson, and D. Don. "In Proportion: Race, and Police Stop and Search" (2004) 44 *The British Journal of Criminology*, 889.

Waddington, P. A. J., K. Williams, M. Wright, and T. Newburn. *How People Judge Policing* (OUP, 2017).

YouTube, "Stop and Search" (YouTube, 26 November 2021), https://www.youtube.com/results?search_query=stop+and+search, accessed 26 November 2021.

NOTES

1. HM Government, "Stop & search" (Gov.UK, 2020), https://www.ethnicity-facts-figures.service.gov.uk/crime-justice-and-the-law/policing/stop-and-search/latest, accessed 20 November 2020.

2. Jennifer Brown, "Police Powers: Stop and Search" (House of Commons Library Briefing Paper 3878, 17 June 2020), https://commonslibrary.parliament.uk/research-briefings/sn03878/, accessed 27 October 2020.

3. Joel Miller, "Stop and Search in England: A Reformed Tactic or Business as Usual?" (2010) 50 *British Journal of Criminology*, 954.

4. The Police Foundation, "Stop and Search" (2012), The Briefing, 3, http://www.police-foundation.org.uk/2017/wp-content/uploads/2017/08/stop_and_search_briefing.pdf, accessed 20 October 2020.

5. Rebekah Delsol and Michael Shiner, "Regulating Stop and Search: A Challenge for Police and Community Relations in England and Wales" (2006), 14 *Critical Criminology*, 241.

6. Jennifer Brown, "Police Powers: Stop and Search" (House of Commons Library Briefing Paper 3878, 17 June 2020), https://commonslibrary.parliament.uk/research-briefings/sn03878/, accessed 27 October 2020.

7. Paul Lawrence, "Vagrancy Act 1824 and the Persistence of Pre-emptive Policing in England Since 1750" (2017), 57 *British Journal of Criminology*, 513.

8. Rebekah Delsol and Michael Shiner, "Regulating Stop and Search: A Challenge for Police and Community Relations in England and Wales" (2006), 14 *Critical Criminology*, 241.

9. Nicole M. Jackson, "A Nigger in the New England: Sus, the Brixton Riot and Citizenship" (2015), 8 *African and Black Diaspora: An International Journal*, 158.

10. Tony Jefferson, "Policing the Riots: from Bristol and Brixton to Tottenham, via Toxteth, Handsworth, etc." (2012), 87 *Criminal Justice Matters*, 8.

11. Nicole M. Jackson, "A Nigger in the New England: Sus, the Brixton Riot and Citizenship" (2015), 8 *African and Black Diaspora: An International Journal*, 158.

12. Tony Jefferson, "Policing the Riots: from Bristol and Brixton to Tottenham, via Toxteth, Handsworth, etc." (2012), 87 *Criminal Justice Matters*, 8.

13. Tony Jefferson, "Policing the Riots: from Bristol and Brixton to Tottenham, via Toxteth, Handsworth, etc." (2012), 87 *Criminal Justice Matters*, 8.

14. John Lea, "Institutional Racism in Policing: The Macpherson Report and Its Consequences" in Roger Matthews and Jock Young (eds), *The New Politics of Crime and Punishment* (Routledge, 2011).

15. Tony Jefferson, "Policing the Riots: from Bristol and Brixton to Tottenham, via Toxteth, Handsworth, etc." (2012), 87 *Criminal Justice Matters*, 8.

16. Rebekah Delsol and Michael Shiner, *Stop and Search: The Anatomy of a Police Power* (Palgrave Macmillan, 2015).

17. John Lea and Simon Hallsworth, "Understanding the Riots" (2012), 87 *Criminal Justice Matters*, 30.

18. John Lea and Simon Hallsworth, "Understanding the Riots" (2012), 87 *Criminal Justice Matters*, 30.

19. John Lea and Simon Hallsworth, "Understanding the Riots" (2012), 87 *Criminal Justice Matters*, 30.

20. Nicole M. Jackson, "A Nigger in the New England: Sus, the Brixton Riot and Citizenship" (2015) 8 *African and Black Diaspora: An International Journal* 158.

21. Joel Miller, "Stop and Search in England: A Reformed Tactic or Business as Usual?" (2010), 50 *British Journal of Criminology*, 954.

22. The Police Foundation, "Stop and Search" (2012), The Briefing, 3, http://www.police-foundation.org.uk/2017/wp-content/uploads/2017/08/stop_and_search_briefing.pdf, accessed 20 October 2020.

23. Jennifer Brown, "Police Powers: Stop and Search" (House of Commons Library Briefing Paper 3878, 17 June 2020), https://commonslibrary.parliament.uk/research-briefings/sn03878/, accessed 27 October 2020.

24. Joel Miller, "Stop and Search in England: A Reformed Tactic or Business as Usual?" (2010), 50 *British Journal of Criminology*, 954.

25. Rebekah Delsol and Michael Shiner, *Stop and Search: The Anatomy of a Police Power* (Palgrave Macmillan, 2015).

26. Joel Miller, "Stop and Search in England: A Reformed Tactic or Business as Usual?" (2010), 50 *British Journal of Criminology*, 954.

27. P. A. J. Waddington, Kevin Stenson, and David Don, "In Proportion: Race, and Police Stop and Search" (2004), 44 *British Journal of Criminology*, 889.

28. Sir William Macpherson, *The Stephen Lawrence Inquiry* (Cm 4262-I, 1999).

29. Sir William Macpherson, *The Stephen Lawrence Inquiry* (Cm 4262-I, 1999).

30. Metropolitan Police Authority, "Report of the MPA Scrutiny on MPS Stop and Search Practice" (*Police Authority*, 2005), http://policeauthority.org/metropolitan/downloads/committees/previous/eodb/eodb-040520–05-appendix01.pdf, accessed 2 December 2021.

31. Equality and Human Rights Commission, "Race Disproportionality in Stops and Searches under Section 60 of the Criminal Justice and Public Order Act 1994" (*Equality and Human Rights Commission*, 2012), https://www.equalityhumanrights.com/sites/default/files/briefing-paper-5-race-disproportionality-in-stops-and-searches-under-s60-of-criminal-justice-and-public-order-act-1994.pdf, accessed 3 October 2020.

32. PAJ Waddington, Kate Williams, Martin Wright, and Tim Newburn, *How People Judge Policing* (OUP, 2017), 13.

33. The Guardian, "Stop and Search" (*The Guardian*, 2020), https://www .theguardian.com/law/stop-and-search, accessed 9 October 2020.

34. Ben Bradford, *Stop and Search and Police Legitimacy* (Routledge, 2017), 144. Jonathan Jackson, Ben Bradford, Betsy Stanko, and Katrin Hohl, *Just Authority? Trust in the Police in England and Wales* (Routledge, 2013). 175.

35. College of Policing, "Engagement and Communication" (*College of Policing Authorized Professional Practice*, 2013), https://www.app.college.police.uk/app -content/engagement-and-communication/, accessed 12 October 2020.

36. Jonathan Jackson, Ben Bradford, Betsy Stanko, and Katrin Hohl, *Just Authority? Trust in the Police in England and Wales* (Routledge, 2013). 62.

37. YouTube, "Stop and Search" (*YouTube*, 26 November 2021), https://www .youtube.com/results?search_query=stop+and+search, accessed 26 November 2021.

38. Ofcom, "New Consumption Report 2020" (*Ofcom*, 2020), https://www.ofcom .org.uk/research-and-data/tv-radio-and-on-demand/news-media/news-consumption, accessed 12 October 2020.

39. College of Policing, "Body-Worn Video" (*College of Policing*, 2014), http:// library.college.police.uk/docs/college-of-policing/Body-worn-video-guidance-2014 .pdf, accessed 12 October 2020.

40. Police and Criminal Evidence Act 1984, s. 1.

41. Jamie Grierson, "Why Did Police Stop and Search Bianca Williams and Ricardo Dos Santos" (*The Guardian*, 6 July 2020), https://www.theguardian.com /law/2020/jul/06/why-did-police-stop-and-search-bianca-williams-and-ricardo-dos -santos, accessed 12 October 2020.

42. BBC News, "Bianca Williams stop: Police "Want to Discuss Sprinter's Concerns" (*BBC News*, 6 July 2020), https://www.bbc.co.uk/news/uk-england-london -53307555, accessed 12 October 2020.

43. BBC News, "Bianca Williams Stop-and-Search: Met PCs Face Probe" (*BBC News*, 9 October 2020), https://www.bbc.co.uk/news/uk-england-london-54466254, accessed 12 October 2020.

44. College of Policing, "Stop and Search" (*College of Policing Authorized Professional Practice*, 2017), https://www.app.college.police.uk/app-content/stop-and -search/, accessed 12 October 2020.

45. Ben Bradford, *Stop and Search and Police Legitimacy* (Routledge, 2017). 19.

46. Equality and Human Rights Commission, "Stop and Think. A Critical Review of the Use of Stop and Search Powers in England and Wales" (*Equality and Human Rights Commission*, 2010), https://www.equalityhumanrights.com/sites/default/files/ ehrc_stop_and_search_report.pdf, accessed 12 October 2020.

47. Equality and Human Rights Commission, "Stop and Think Again: Towards Race Equality in Police PACE Stop and Search" (*Equality and Human Rights Commission*, 2013), https://www.equalityhumanrights.com/sites/default/files/stop_and _think_again.pdf, accessed 12 October 2020.

48. HMIC, "Stop and Search Powers: Are the Police Using Them Fairly and Effectively?" (*Her Majesty's Inspectorate of Constabulary and Fire and Rescue Services*, 2013), https://www.justiceinspectorates.gov.uk/hmicfrs/publications/stop-and-search -powers-20130709/, accessed 12 October 2020.

49. Home Office and Theresa May MP, "Oral Statement to Parliament. Stop And Search: Comprehensive Package of Reform for Police Stop and Search Powers" (*HM Government*, 2014), https://www.gov.uk/government/speeches/stop-and-search-comprehensive-package-of-reform-for-police-stop-and-search-powers, accessed 12 October 2020.

50. Home Office, "Best Use of Stop and Search Scheme" (*HM Government*, 2014), https://www.gov.uk/government/publications/best-use-of-stop-and-search-scheme, accessed 14 October 2020.

51. HMIC, "Best Use of Stop and Search (BUSS) Scheme: The Findings of an HMIC Revisit of the 13 Forces That Were Not Complying with Three or More Features of the Scheme in 2015" (*Her Majesty's Inspectorate of Constabulary and Fire and Rescue Services*, 2016), https://www.justiceinspectorates.gov.uk/hmicfrs/publications/best-use-of-stop-and-search-second-revisits/, accessed 14 October 2020.

52. Home Office, "Amber Rudd writes about stop and search in *The Times*" (*HM Government*, 2017), https://homeofficemedia.blog.gov.uk/2017/08/09/amber-rudd-writes-about-stop-and-search-in-the-times/, accessed 14 October 2020.

53. Home Office, "Greater Powers for Police to Use Stop and Search to Tackle Violent Crime" (*HM Government*, 2019), https://www.gov.uk/government/news/greater-powers-for-police-to-use-stop-and-search-to-tackle-violent-crime, accessed 14 October 2020.

54. The Centre for Social Justice, "It Can Be Stopped. A Proven Blueprint to Stop Violence and Tackle Gang and Related Offending in London and Beyond" (*The Centre for Social Justice*, 2018), https://www.centreforsocialjustice.org.uk/core/wp-content/uploads/2018/09/CSJJ6499-Gangs-Report-180911-FINAL-WEB.pdf, accessed 14 October 2020.

55. Home Office, "Serious Violence Reduction Orders: A New Court Order To Target Known Knife Carriers. Government Consultation" (*HM Government*, 2020), https://assets.publishing.service.gov.uk/government/uploads/system/uploads/attachment_data/file/917277/SVRO_consultation.pdf, accessed 14 October 2020.

56. Matteo Tiratelli, Paul Quinton and Ben Bradford, "Does Stop and Search Deter Crime? Evidence from Ten Years of London-Wide Data" (2018), 58 *British Journal of Criminology*, 1212.

57. Neil Parpworth, "Reforming Police Powers of Stop and Search: Voluntary Action" (2014), 87 *Police Journal: Theory, Practice, and Principles*, 234.

58. Justice Tankebe, "Viewing Things Differently: The Dimensions of Public Perceptions of Police Legitimacy" (2012), 51 *Criminology*, 103.

59. Justice Tankebe, "Viewing Things Differently: The Dimensions of Public Perceptions of Police Legitimacy" (2012), 51 *Criminology*, 103.

60. Peter Neyroud, "Past, Present and Future Performance: Prospects for the Measurement of Police Performance" (2008), 2 *Policing*, 340.

61. Ben Bradford, *Stop and Search and Police Legitimacy* (Routledge, 2017).

62. Ben Bradford, *Stop and Search and Police Legitimacy* (Routledge, 2017).

63. London Assembly Police and Crime Committee, "Stop and Search: An Investigation into the Met's New Approach to Stop and Search" (*London Assembly*, 2014),

https://www.london.gov.uk/sites/default/files/14-02-06-Stop%20and%20search%20FINAL_1.pdf, accessed 7 October 2020.

64. Ben Bradford, *Stop and Search and Police Legitimacy* (Routledge, 2017).

65. Ben Bradford, *Stop and Search and Police Legitimacy* (Routledge, 2017).

66. Estelle Clayton, "Stop and Search and Police Legitimacy" (2017), 27 *Policing and Society*, 813.

64 Estelle Clayton, "Stop and Search and Police Legitimacy" (2017), 27 *Policing and Society*, 813.

67. London Assembly Police and Crime Committee, "Stop and Search: An Investigation into the Met's New Approach to Stop and Search" (*London Assembly*, 2014), https://www.london.gov.uk/sites/default/files/14-02-06-Stop%20and%20search%20FINAL_1.pdf, accessed 7 October 2020.

68. London Assembly Police and Crime Committee, "Stop and Search: An Investigation into the Met's New Approach to Stop and Search" (*London Assembly*, 2014), https://www.london.gov.uk/sites/default/files/14-02-06-Stop%20and%20search%20FINAL_1.pdf, accessed 7 October 2020.

69. Neil Parpworth, "Reforming Police Powers of Stop and Search: Voluntary Action" (2014), 87 *Police Journal: Theory, Practice and Principles*, 234.

70. Peter Keeling, "No Respect: Young BAME Men, the Police and Stop and Search" (*Criminal Justice Alliance*, 2017), http://criminaljusticealliance.org/wp-content/uploads/2017/06/No-Respect-290617.pdf, accessed 3 October 2020.

71. London Assembly Police and Crime Committee, "Police and Crime Committee Response to the Draft Police and Crime Plan for 2013–2017" (*London Assembly*, 2013), https://www.london.gov.uk/about-us/londonassembly/meetings/documents/s26909/Research%20into%20Young%20Peoples%20Views%20of%20Stop%20and%20Search%20for%20Police%20and%20Crime%20Committee%20Investigation%20-.pdf, accessed 7 October 2020.

72. John Lea and Simon Hallsworth, "Understanding the Riots" (2012), 87 *Criminal Justice Matters*, 30.

73. Lord L. G. Scarman, *The Scarman Report: The Brixton Disorders 10–12 April 1981* (Penguin, 1982).

74. Rebekah Delsol and Michael Shiner, *Stop and Search: The Anatomy of a Police Power* (Palgrave Macmillan, 2015).

75. John Benyon, "England's Urban Disorder: The 2011 Riots" (2012), 3 *Political Insight*, 12.

76. Daniel Briggs, *The English Riots of 2011: A Summer of Discontent* (Waterside Press Ltd., 2012).

Chapter 4

Reform of Police Interrogations in Croatia

Endangering the Efficiency of the Criminal Justice System

Elizabeta Ivičević Karas and Zoran Burić

After independence, Croatia adopted its first Criminal Procedure Act (*Zakon o kaznenom postupku*) in 1997 (further in text: CPA/97).[1] This statute overtook the model of criminal procedure that existed in Yugoslavia, which was in its main constructive elements built upon the foundations of the Austrian *Strafprozessordnung* from 1873.[2] The latter was a typical example of a reformed or mixed criminal procedure, the prototype of which was laid in the French *Code d'instruction criminelle* from 1808.[3] Croatian criminal procedure, as it was regulated by the CPA/97, presupposed that, in principle, the police were the first authority that acted upon the grounds for suspicion (*osnove sumnje*) that a criminal offense prosecuted ex officio has been committed. Results of police work, which were formally not a part of criminal procedure, were then handed over to the state attorney who had to decide whether to prosecute the suspect or not. If the state attorney considered that there is a reasonable suspicion (*osnovana sumnja*) that a suspect has committed a criminal offense, he/she needed to address the investigating judge who decided about opening the investigation against the suspect.[4] With the opening of the investigation, criminal proceedings against the suspect (who then became the defendant) formally started. The investigating judge conducted the investigation. At its end, the results of the investigation were handed to the state attorney who decided about filing an indictment against the defendant before the court that was competent to conduct the trial.

New Croatian CPA, which is currently in force, was adopted in 2008 (further in text: CPA/08 or CPA).[5] The biggest novelty introduced by the CPA/08 is the abolishment of the investigating judge. The state attorney now conducts the investigation. His/her decision to open the investigation is, in principle, based on the results of police work which is still formally not a part of criminal procedure. CPA/08 did not introduce any major reforms with regard to police work in relation to criminal procedure. Since the adoption of CPA/08, Croatian criminal procedure has been in a state of constant change and has been amended eight times. There are three major forces behind these changes. The first one was the decision of the Constitutional Court of the Republic of Croatia, which declared more than 40 provisions of the CPA/08 unconstitutional.[6] Pursuant to the Constitutional Court, the new CPA/08 did not strike an adequate balance between the interest of effective prosecution of crime and the interest of protection of rights and freedoms of individuals.[7] The balance was disturbed in favor of the former. The second one is the process of harmonization of Croatian criminal procedure with European standards.[8] This presupposes transposition of EU directives on rights of suspects, accused persons, and victims of crime into Croatian criminal procedure legislation, but also its alignment with standards established in the jurisprudence of the European Court for Human Rights. The third one is the endeavor to make the criminal procedure more efficient. The Croatian justice system in general, criminal justice system included, is overburdened with distrust constantly expressed by Croatian citizens in all public opinion polls.[9] With regard to criminal justice, making criminal procedure more efficient, primarily through legislative reforms, has often been offered by politics as a panacea for this problem.

Reform undertaken in 2017 has brought important and far-reaching changes with regard to police work in relation to criminal procedure. The reform has fundamentally changed the legal regulation of police interrogations of suspects and arrested persons. Other aspects of police work in relation to criminal procedure have fundamentally remained the same. This contribution follows by an overview of police interrogations of suspects and arrested persons before the reform (II). Thereafter, drivers of change shall be presented (III). The fourth chapter deals with police interrogations of suspects and arrested persons after the reform and it is divided into three subparagraphs: arguments *pro* et *contra* the reform (1), normative framework (2), and challenges in its practical application (3). In the closing fifth chapter a conclusion is given.

POLICE INTERROGATIONS OF SUSPECTS BEFORE THE REFORM

As explained previously, police are normally the first authority that deals with the suspicion that a criminal offense has been committed. These police actions and measures are formally not a part of criminal procedure and take place during the inquiries (*izvidi*) into the criminal offense. Actions that the police undertake during the inquiries are undertaken in the form of inquires or urgent evidence-gathering actions. The major difference between the two is that the inquiries are normally regulated by police legislation,[10] while the CPA regulates evidence-gathering actions.

Before the reform, interrogations of suspects and arrested persons by the police were not regulated as an evidence-gathering action. Rather, they were regulated as an inquiry into the criminal offense (collecting of information, *prikupljanje obavijesti*). This meant that the way that police interrogations of the suspect and the arrested persons take place were not regulated by the rules of the CPA but were only vaguely regulated by the rules of police legislation. As a consequence of this, the results of these interrogations could not be used as evidence at the trial.[11] The inadmissibility of the protocols of police interrogations at the trial was considered as an adequate legal remedy for the fact that these actions were not conducted following the rules of the CPA. Although this might, at the first sight, seem like a good solution from the position of the suspect or the arrested person, it had far-reaching negative consequences for their position in the ensuing proceedings, as well as for the level of trust between different state actors that participate in criminal procedure.

First, there was a widespread opinion among criminal justice actors that, since results of police interrogations of suspects and accused persons cannot be used as evidence at the trial, these interrogations were not important and that, therefore, it was not necessary for defense attorneys to attend these actions. This opinion was in stark contrast with the fact that has repeatedly been highlighted in the jurisprudence of the European Court for Human Rights. At the earliest stages of criminal proceedings, and especially in the case of arrest, the suspect finds him/herself in a particularly vulnerable position, not only in relation to possible violations of his/her defense rights, but also with regard to the possible risk of being exposed to treatment prohibited by Art. 3 of the Convention.[12] However, this opinion among Croatian criminal justice actors resulted in the fact that Croatian defense attorneys rarely attended police stations.[13]

Second, the fact that the protocol of police interrogations of the suspect and the arrested person could not be used as evidence at the trial did not mean that these protocols were completely inadmissible in the criminal procedure. On the contrary, they were forwarded to the state attorney with the police criminal report and were used as a factual basis for all decisions that were rendered against the suspect in the pretrial phase of the proceedings.[14] Not only that, even more important than this was the fact that the police were, through these informal interrogations, in a position to acquire a number of very valuable information arising out of the self-incriminating statement of the suspect or the arrested person, which could easily be transformed to evidence admissible at the trial (through material evidence or witness statements).[15] A self-incriminating statement of the suspect or the arrested person could very easily be used as a foundation for the whole case against him/her, without the need for the statement itself to be used as evidence at all.

Third, such regulation of police interrogations of suspects and accused persons meant that the trial court was not in a position to examine how was the suspect or the arrested person was treated during his/her stay at the police station, as there were no records in the case file of the informal interrogation undertaken by the police. This meant that the trial court was not able to execute one of its fundamental tasks in a democratic society, and that is to supervise the way that the state authorities, which are given repressive powers in criminal procedure, are using these powers against the citizens.[16]

Fourth, the fact that there was no court oversight over police interrogations of the suspect and the arrested person during the earliest stages of criminal proceedings did not mean that there were no abuses of police powers at this stage of proceedings. Quite the contrary. It is not without good foundations to argue that the fact that there were many abuses of police powers during interrogations of the suspect and the arrested person resulted in the absence of court oversight (see judgments of the European Court of Human Rights against Croatia, *infra* 3.1.). Instead of trying to remedy the problematic aspects of police work in relation to criminal proceedings there was a tendency to exclude these problematic aspects from the criminal proceedings. This indicates that there was a low level of trust of judicial authorities, i. e., state attorneys and courts, in the work of police in relation to criminal proceedings. This attitude toward police and its role in criminal procedure has its historical roots, which go way back to the socialist era. The distrust toward police resulted in an endeavor to exclude the police from the criminal procedure.[17] Of course, this was impossible in reality. Therefore, it was limited to a fiction that police authorities are not criminal procedure authorities and that what the police do in relation to criminal proceedings is not a part of a formal criminal procedure.

How untenable this position was can be clearly shown with the comparison of police and state attorney's interrogation of the arrested person right before the reform. As already explained, police interrogation was not precisely regulated by law (it was not regulated by the CPA at all, and it was only rudimentarily regulated by police legislation). It was considered unimportant for criminal procedure. Due to this, the level of protection of arrested person's rights was low (especially in practice) and there was no trial court's oversight over this action. On the other hand, state attorney's interrogation of the arrested person, which normally took place a couple of hours after police interrogation, was regulated by highly complex and precise rules of the CPA, which prescribed very high standards of protection of the rights of the arrested person, including audio-video recording of interrogation. Moreover, failures of the state attorney to follow the formal procedure, even some technical aspects of it, were sanctioned with the strongest procedural sanction—inadmissibility of the results of interrogation and all other evidence deriving from it. From these differences, a person unfamiliar with Croatian criminal procedure might conclude that there were many abuses of the state attorney's powers against the arrested person and that it was therefore necessary to protect the arrested person with such elaborate procedural safeguards. This was, of course, not the case.

Although there were many arguments why this regulation of police interrogation of suspects and arrested persons was untenable, it was so deeply rooted into the minds of criminal justice actors in Croatia that it was very difficult for them to recognize its illogicality. Even after the judgments of the European Court for Human Rights in which some of the mentioned problems were identified started appearing, it was still not enough to undertake the necessary reforms. Finally, the need to transpose the provisions of the EU Directive on the right of access to a lawyer was used as a cause for the long due reform.

DRIVERS OF CHANGE

As it normally happens with all the big systems, the incentive for change came not from within, but from outside. In the case of police interrogations, there were two external sources for the change: the European Court for Human Rights and the EU legislation harmonizing the rights of suspects and accused persons in national criminal procedural laws.

European Court for Human Rights

In the second section of this chapter, it was said that the protocol of police interrogations of the suspect and the arrested person could not be used as evidence at the trial. However, there was a period from 2002 to 2008, during which this statement does not completely correspond to legal reality at the time. During that period, it was possible to use the protocol of police interrogation of the suspect and the arrested person as evidence at the trial if there was a defense attorney present at the interrogation. The suspect and the arrested person had the right to engage the services of a defense attorney. If he/she wanted to engage the services of a defense attorney, but did not know whom to choose, the police officers were obliged to help him/her in choosing and contacting a defense attorney. If a defense attorney came to the police station and was present during the interrogation of the suspect or the arrested person, the interrogation protocol could be used as evidence at the trial. It was considered that the presence of a defense attorney is such a strong procedural safeguard in the presence of which all reasons to distrust the police vanish.[18] However, in practice, something completely different started happening. This development might be best shown at the example of three judgments of the European Court for Human Rights in which it was identified.

The first case, which appeared before the European Court for Human Rights dealing with police interrogations of suspects and accused persons in Croatia, was *Mađer v. Croatia*.[19] The case concerned a police investigation into murder. A person disappeared and the police suspected that the disappearance was the result of murder. However, the police were unable to direct the investigation into any meaningful way, despite the fact that there was a person whom they suspected was involved in the incident. The police finally came to the house of the potential suspect, Mr. Mađer, and took him to the police station. Mr. Mađer allegedly voluntarily stayed at the police station for a whole day before being arrested. During his stay at the police station, including time before and after the arrest, he was systematically interrogated by the police. These interrogations took the form of informal police interrogations (collecting of information) and there was no defense attorney present. They resulted in his confession and the finding of the body of the victim, whose location Mr. Mađer disclosed. On the third day of his stay at the police station, Mr. Mađer was formally interrogated by the police. The protocol of his interrogation indicated that there was a defense attorney present during the interrogation. The fact that there was a defense attorney present enabled the protocol of Mr. Mađer's interrogation, during which he again confessed to the crime, to be used as evidence before the court. Following his stay at the police station, the arrestee was taken to the judge and a new defense attorney was appointed to him. He immediately complained that he was mistreated by the police and that he did not know who the person indicated in the protocol of his police interrogation as his defense attorney was. In the ensuing criminal proceedings against Mr. Mađer, his defense attorney unsuccessfully attempted to have the protocol of his police interrogation excluded from the file as inadmissible evidence. His arguments were that Mr. Mađer was mistreated by the police (deprivation of sleep, food, and medicine) and that the defense attorney who was allegedly present at his police interrogation was in fact not present at the interrogation. Moreover, he was invited to come to the police station by the police only to sign the protocol of Mr. Mađer's formal interrogation, thereby helping the police to use the confession of Mr. Mađer as evidence against him in the ensuing proceedings. National courts did not accept the arguments of the defense and convicted Mr. Mađer to a long-term sentence of imprisonment after finding him guilty of aggravated murder. The conviction was to a large degree founded on his confession given to the police.[20]

In the proceedings before the European Court for Human Rights, the court found that Mr. Mađer had sustained, during his stay at the police station, a violation of his rights guaranteed by Arts. 3 and 6 of the Convention. In relation to Art. 3, the court found that he had been subjected to inhuman treatment[21] and that there was a failure to undertake an adequate investigation on the basis of his complaints about police mistreatment.[22] In relation to Art. 6 the court found that Mr. Mađer had been systematically interrogated by the police without the presence of a defense attorney and that he had not renounced the services of a defense attorney because he had asked for one on a number of occasions during his stay at the police station. Since his confession given to the police had been used as evidence against him and had formed the basis of his conviction, there had been a violation of Art. 6 of the Convention.[23]

The second case before the court that dealt with police interrogations in Croatia was *Šebalj v. Croatia*.[24] The case concerned a police investigation into more than 30 criminal offenses of theft and aggravated theft. Mr. Šebalj was convicted for all these cases and his conviction was based on the confessions he gave at the police station on two occasions (first time he confessed to 7 offenses, and second time he confessed to 25 offenses). Both confessions were acquired through formal police interrogation, which means that the protocols of interrogations indicated that there was a defense attorney present on both occasions. In national criminal proceedings Mr. Šebalj complained that a defense attorney had not been present during the interrogations and that he was invited to come to the police station by the police after the interrogations have already finished, only to formalize the protocol of police interrogations by signing it. His arguments were rejected by domestic courts and his conviction had been based on his confessions given to the police.[25] The European Court for Human Rights had come to a different conclusion—that the applicant had been denied access to a lawyer during his stay at the police station and that the confession given to the police had formed a basis for his conviction, which constituted a violation of Art. 6 of the Convention.[26]

The third and final case in which the European Court dealt with police interrogations in Croatia was *Dvorski v. Croatia*.[27] The case concerned a police investigation into murder of three persons, robbery, and arson. On the day on which the offenses were committed, various persons, including Mr.

Dvorski were taken to the police station for informal police interrogations. On the second day of his stay at the police station, Mr. Dvorski was arrested. As soon as he was arrested, his mother engaged the services of a defense attorney in his interest. However, the defense attorney chosen by his mother was denied access to the police station and to Mr. Dvorski. Instead of him, another defense attorney was contacted by the police and came to the police station to represent the interests of Mr. Dvorski. This attorney was a former chief of police in the town where the events took place. In the presence of this defense attorney, Mr. Dvorski confessed to the crime and his confession was used as a basis for his later conviction for the criminal offenses in question. During the proceedings before national courts, Mr. Dvorski complained that the lawyer who was chosen by his mother was denied access to him at the police station and that this affected the quality of his defense, but his arguments were rejected by national courts.[28] The case was then referred to the European Court for Human Rights, which found a violation of Art. 6 of the Convention because the applicant was denied access to a lawyer of his own choosing while being interrogated at the police station.[29]

Despite their factual and legal differences, all three judgments follow the same pattern. Suspects are taken to the police station where they are systematically interrogated for hours within the framework of informal police interrogations, without having access to a lawyer and the possibility to effectively use all other rights of the defense (including the right to remain silent). When the police have gathered enough incriminatory information against them (on the basis of their self-incriminatory statements), they are arrested and formally interrogated. However, their formal interrogation does not take place in the presence of a defense attorney of their own choosing, who is there to serve as a guarantee that the suspect will not be mistreated by the police and that his/her defense rights shall be respected. It is taking place in the presence of a defense attorney chosen by the police, who is there to make sure that the confession the suspect gave to the police will be used as evidence against him/her at the trial. An institute that was designed to effectively guarantee the rights of the defense served an opposite purpose in practice. This practice, which was recognized in the jurisprudence of the European Court for Human Rights, was not uncommon to Croatian criminal justice in those days. It was known that there are defense attorneys who act in the interest of the police, and not in the interest of suspects and arrested persons.[30] However, because this problem was not adequately addressed at national level, both in legislation and in practice, it was brought to attention at the international level, in the jurisprudence of the European Court for Human Rights.

These judgments made it clear that there are a lot of problems in relation to what is happening at police stations with the suspect and the arrested person. And all these problems came to the fore only due to the fact that the confession given at the police station in the presence of a defense attorney could be used as evidence at the trial. If it was not for that, what was happening at the police station would still remain an issue, which is not dealt with at the trial. It was reasonable to expect that something will be done, in legislation and in practice, to remedy these problems. However, life took a different turn. Instead of dealing with the issue, the new CPA from 2008 took a step back. Its provisions made it impossible to use the statement given by the suspect or the arrested person to the police as evidence at the trial. This meant that CPA/08 went back to the legal solutions that existed before 2002 and that what was happening at the police station will no further be a matter that should be examined at the trial.

As usually in life, when one door closes, another one opens. A new opportunity for change was offered when reform of CPA/08 was back on the horizon due to the need to harmonize Croatian criminal procedural law with EU directives.

EU HARMONIZATION DIRECTIVES

First, two directives on the rights of suspects and accused persons in criminal proceedings that were transposed into Croatian law dealt with the right to interpretation and translation[31] and the right to information.[32] Their transposition took place with the amendments of the CPA, which were adopted in November 2013.[33] However, these changes did not significantly improve the position of the suspect or the arrested person nor did they reform police interrogations of these persons. The main obstacle for any major reform was the understanding that police interrogations, which take the form of informal police actions, cannot be used as evidence at the trial and that it is therefore not necessary to ensure that the rights of the suspect and the arrested person are effectively guaranteed during these actions. The decisive incentive for the reform came with the directive on the right of access to a lawyer.[34] It was the first among harmonizing directives that clearly indicated that it is necessary to ensure effective access to a lawyer from the fist questioning of the suspect by the police or by another law enforcement or judicial authority.[35] From the wording of the directive, it became clear that it is necessary to ensure the effective exercise of the right of access to a lawyer from the first interrogation by the police, regardless in which form this interrogation takes place and whether it can or cannot be used as evidence at the trial.

When that was accepted, other aspects of the reform logically derived from it. If it is necessary to ensure effective access to a lawyer, then it is also necessary to ensure effective access to all the other defense rights, especially the right to information and the right to remain silent. If it is necessary to ensure effective access to all the rights, that further means that there is a need to adopt adequate legal rules that will enable the achievement of this goal in practice. That further meant that interrogation of the suspect or the arrested person by the police may no longer take the form of an informal police action but must be regulated as a formal procedural action with precise rules embedded in the CPA. If all of this is done, then there is no reason not to accept the results of police interrogation of the suspect or the arrested person as evidence in criminal proceedings. Although a reform of police interrogation seemed necessary from the point of view of EU law and logical from the point of view of national law, almost all criminal justice actors in Croatia were rather skeptical of the proposed reform, for different reasons and with different arguments.

Police Interrogation of Suspects after the Reform

Arguments Pro et Contra the Reform

The main goal of the proposed reform was to ensure the effective exercise of the rights of the defense to the suspect and the arrested person from the earliest stages of criminal proceedings, that is from the moment they are interrogated by the police in relation to the suspicion that they have committed a criminal offense. This meant that legal rules needed to be adopted that are going to ensure the effective exercise of these rights. It also presupposed that the law needed to establish supervisory mechanisms within the framework of criminal procedure that are going to make sure that the enacted legal rules are respected. This required that the results of police interrogations are treated as evidence in criminal proceedings and are supervised by the trial court. Main arguments in favor of the reform may be summarized to the following two: improvement of the position of the suspect and the arrested person and better regulation and oversight over police work in relation to criminal proceedings.

However, there were a lot of reasons to oppose the reform. Some members of the police force were not in favor of it. Their main fear was that the proposed reform was going to significantly affect, in a negative way, the efficiency of police work in relation to criminal proceedings.[36] According to some comparative studies, there are a number of criminal cases, especially the most severe ones, that cannot be resolved without information—the source of which is the suspect or the arrested person.[37] It was possible to conclude, from the absence of their objections, that state attorneys were generally in favour of the reform, at least for practical reason: their workload will be smaller if the police were given the power to formally interrogate the suspect and the arrested person. Judges might have feared that, once what was happening at the police station became an object of examination at trial, it would significantly prolong the trial and make it more complex. Finally, defense attorneys obviously thought that the reform gives too much power to the police. According to some discussions at conferences, they feared that it would be impossible to ensure the effective exercise of the rights of the defense at the police station, but that the results of the police interrogation will nevertheless be used as evidence at the trial.

Despite all the arguments against it, the reform was adopted, and it came to life with the amendments of the CPA from 2017.[38] The main characteristics of the reform at the normative level shall be presented in the following section.

Normative Framework

After the reform, it is no longer possible for the police to informally interrogate the suspect and the arrested person. After a person gained the status of a suspect,[39] he/she can only be interrogated in a formal way, after being notified about his/her rights and in a procedure elaborately regulated by the CPA. The procedure for the police interrogation of the suspect is regulated in Art. 208a of the CPA. With regard to the police interrogation of the arrested person, the rules on the interrogation of the suspect apply accordingly (Art. 108c CPA). The police still have the power to informally interrogate, or gather information from citizens, but not from the suspect. If in the process of gathering information, a citizen (who is then in a position of a presumed witness) acquires the status of a suspect, the informal interrogation needs to be suspended and the suspect (who was initially a witness) may only be interrogated in accordance with the rules on the police interrogation of the suspect (Art. 208, para 5 CPA).[40]

A suspect may be summoned to the police station for interrogation. A suspect who had not answered the summons, or who evades the receipt of summons may be brought to the police station by force (Art. 208a, para 1). The summons needs to contain the information on the grounds for suspicion and an instruction on the rights of the suspect: the right of access to a lawyer, the right to interpretation and translation, the right to remain silent, and the right to leave the police station at any time, unless he/she was arrested (Art 208a, para 2). Before the interrogation, the police need to check whether the suspect received a written instruction on rights and whether he/she understands his/her rights. If the suspect states that he/she does not understand his/her rights, the police need to instruct him/her about his/her rights in an understandable manner (Art. 208a, para 3). If the suspect states that he/she wants to engage the services of a defense attorney, he/she shall be enabled to do so, and the interrogation shall be resumed up to three hours for the defense attorney to come to the police station. If the suspect wants to engage the services of a defense attorney but does not know whom to choose or the chosen lawyer cannot come to the police station, the suspect shall be enabled to retain a defense counsel from a list of lawyers on duty (Art. 208a, para 5). If the suspect states that he/she does not want to engage the services of a defense attorney, a police officer shall instruct him/her in a simple and understandable manner about the meaning of a defense attorney and the consequences of a renouncement of that right. If, following that instruction, the suspect still does not want to engage the services of a defense attorney, his/her interrogation may be resumed without the assistance of a defense attorney, unless the suspect falls into one of the cases of mandatory defense (Art. 208a, para 4). The interrogation of the suspect needs to be audio-video recorded (Art. 208a, para 6). If the police have not instructed the suspect about his/her rights and if the instruction and suspect's attitude toward the exercise of his/her rights have not been audio-video taped, the results of the suspect's interrogation, as well as all other evidence deriving from it, may not be used as evidence in criminal proceedings (inadmissible evidence) (Art. 208a, para 8). A suspect who uses the right to remain silent shall be immediately released by the police (Art. 208a, para 9). To all other issues relating to the interrogation of the suspect by the police, the rules of state attorney's interrogation of the defendant apply (Art 208a, para 7).

As can be seen from these rules, Croatian criminal procedure has gone from deregulated to very strictly regulated police interrogations of the suspect and the arrested person. All interrogations of the suspect and the arrested person need to be audio-video recorded, and any failure of the police to abide by the rules of the CPA is sanctioned with the strictest possible procedural sanction—inadmissibility of the statement that the suspect and the arrested person gave to the police and inadmissibility of all other evidence deriving from it. Although this Copernican turn in the regulation of police interrogations might seem strange, it was a natural consequence of the application of the rules of the state attorney's interrogation of the defendant to police interrogations of the suspect and the arrested person. All the elements of a strict procedural form, as well as harsh procedural sanctions, have been overtaken from the rules of state attorney's interrogation of the defendant. These rules, which are guarantees that all the rights of the suspect and the arrested person shall be respected and that state authorities shall abide to the law and there will be no abuse of repressive powers against the citizen, seem much more needed in the context of interrogations taking place at the police station than in the context of interrogations taking place at the state attorney's office.

Challenges in the Practical Application

As already indicated, it was expected that the reform of police interrogations shall represent a big challenge, not only to police work, but also to the work of other actors in the criminal justice system. However, these fears have so far not proven themselves as justified in practice. Practical application of new rules on police interrogations in Croatia did not hit a strong blow to the efficiency of police work in Croatia, did not make the position of suspects and arrested persons more difficult than before, and did not overburden trials with tiresome examinations of what was taking place at the police station a couple of months prior. In fact, the impression is that nothing major took place at the police station. The criminal justice system quite easily and without any major difficulties adapted itself to the legislative changes. Did the system follow the legislative changes, or did it find ways to trick them? Of course, there are limits of what the legislative change can do. There are also limits to what audio-video recording of interrogations can tell us about what was going on in the street, in the car, or at the police station before the interrogation and audio-video recording began.[41] Changing the law is much easier than changing the institutional culture or institutionally established ways of doing business. However, in relation to police interrogations in Croatia, talking about any abuse of police powers today is just a speculation, because there are no judgments and there is no research the results of which could be used to substantiate that claim.

Despite such a smooth transition from a legally deregulated and judicially unsupervised to legally super-regulated and evidence-producing police interrogations, there were some problems in practice, but the most controversial issue was one that had nothing to do with the substance and the goal of the reform. It was the question whether there is a need for the state attorney to interrogate the defendant before filing an indictment if the police have already interrogated the defendant, in the status of the suspect or the arrested person.[42]

In addition, other questions present a problem in police work. Maybe the most important one is the question of when a person acquires the status of the suspect. As we have seen, from that moment on, the way that the police need to treat this person completely changes. From that moment on, any police action in relation to this person must be preceded by an instruction about the rights of the suspect. These questions are now being resolved in the jurisprudence of the Supreme Court of the Republic of Croatia.[43]

CONCLUSION

This chapter shows how difficult it is to change well-established ways the job is done in everyday life of criminal justice practitioners. At a certain moment in history, due mostly to the distrust in the work of police in relation to criminal proceedings, police interrogations of persons, including the suspect and the arrested person, have been excluded from the evidentiary material that can form the basis of a conviction in criminal proceedings in Croatia. This exclusion, whose intention was to improve the position of the suspect and the arrested person, developed into a very strong instrument for the denial of the rights of defense, which were legally guaranteed to the suspect and the arrested person. Furthermore, it also developed into a very efficient instrument for police investigations into criminal offense, the center of which was the informal interrogation of the suspect and the arrested person, which was the source of all other evidence in criminal proceedings against the defendant. Even when the problems with what was happening at the police stations became evident, the reaction of the legislator and the system was to turn their head further away from those problems. The primary reason for this was fear that the reform wass such a big challenge and would fundamentally change the way the police need to undertake their investigations into criminal offenses and would significantly affect, in a negative way, the efficiency of their investigations into criminal offenses. After the reform was initiated, it was finally accepted that, although it is reasonable to expect problems in police work, especially at the beginning of application of new rules in practice, this is a risk which is worth taken. The reform harmonized Croatian criminal procedure with European standards, thereby effectively guaranteeing the rights of defense to the suspect and the arrested person from the earliest stages of criminal proceedings, but also legally regulating repressive powers of police and putting them under judicial scrutiny. These were goals that made the reform worth instituting.

However, the fear that the reform is going to significantly decrease the efficiency of police investigations into criminal offenses showed itself as unsubstantiated in practice. There were no major issues identified with regard to the application of new rules in practice. At this moment, it is only possible to speculate about the reasons for this. The judicial practice has still not developed to a degree that is necessary to draw any definitive conclusions from it, nor is there any research conducted that could offer credible answer to this question.

BIBLIOGRAPHY

Bayer, V. *Kazneno procesno pravo—odabrana poglavlja, Knjiga I. Uvod u teoriju kaznenog procesnog prava*, Ministarstvo unutarnjih poslova Republike Hrvatske, Zagreb, 1995

Burić. *Qualitative Report for Croatia*, in Stefan Schumann et al. (eds.), *Pre-trial Emergency Defence*, Intersentia, 2012

Burić, Z., and Z. Karas. *Prilog raspravi o dvojbama vezanim uz novu definiciju osumnjičenika i radnju njegova ispitivanja*, Hrvatski ljetopis za kaznene znanosti i praksu, vol. 24, no. 2/2017

Burić, Z. *Re-assessing the Jurisprudence of the European Court for Human Rights on Police Interrogation: Case of Ibrahim and Others v. the United Kingdom*, EU and Comparative Law Issues and Challenges Series, vol. 2 (2018).

Đurđević, Z., and E. I. Karas (eds.). *Presude Europskog suda za ljudska prava Republike Hrvatske u kaznenim predmetima*, Pravni fakultet Sveučilišta u Zagrebu, 2013.

Đurđević, Z. *Odluka Ustavnog suda RH o suglasnosti Zakona o kaznenom postupku s Ustavom*, Hrvatski ljetopis za kazneno pravo i praksu, vol. 19, no. 2/2012.

Đurđević, Z. *Uvodna riječ*, Hrvatski ljetopis za kaznene znanosti i praksu, vol. 24, no. 2/2017.

Karas, E. I., and L. Valković. *Pravno na branitelja u policiji—pravna i stvarna ograničenja*, Hrvatski ljetopis za kaznene znanosti i praksu, vol. 24, no. 2/2017.

Karas, E. I., M. Bonačić, and Z. Burić. *Pre-Trial Procedure in Croatia* in E. Johnston, R. Erbaş, and D. Jasinski (eds.), *A Comparative Analysis of Pre-Trial Procedure in Europe: The Search for an Ideal Model*, Istanbul University Press, 2020.

Karas, E. I., Z. Burić, and M. Bonačić. *Neka pitanja usklađenosti hrvatskoga kaznenog procesnog prava s direktivama o pravima obrane—analiza sudske prakse*, Hrvatski ljetopis za kaznene znanosti i praksu, vol. 27, no. 2/2020.

Karas, E. I., Z. Burić, and M. Bonačić. *Prava obrane u različitim stadijima hrvatskog kaznenog postupka: rezultati istraživanja prakse*, Hrvatski ljetopis za kaznene znanosti i praksu, vol. 23, no. 2/2016.

Karas, E. I., Z. Burić, and M. Bonačić. *Unapređenje procesnih prava osumnjičenika i okrivljenika u kaznenom postupku: Pogled kroz prizmu europskih pravnih standarda*, Hrvatski ljetopis za kaznene znanosti i praksu, vol. 23, no 1/2016.

Karas, E. I. *Pomicanje granica prava na branitelja pod utjecajem europskog kaznenog prava*, Hrvatski ljetopis za kazneno pravo i praksu, vol. 22, no. 2/2015.

Karas, Z. *Dokazni položaj općih izvidnih radnji redarstvenih vlasti*, Hrvatski ljetopis za kazneno pravo i praksu, vol. 13, no. 1/2006.

Karas, Z. *Kriminalistički značaj pribavljanja osumnjičenikovog iskaza prije početka kaznenog postupka*, Policija i sigurnost, vol. 24, no. 2/2015.

Klier, D., M. Kondor-Langer, and S. Glušćić. *Policijska i državnoodvjetnička praksa u ispitivanju osumnjičenika*, Hrvatski ljetopis za kaznene znanosti i praksu vol. 25, no. 2/2018.

Krapac, D. *Kazneno procesno pravo, Knjiga prva: Institucije*, Narodne novine, Zagreb, 2020

Krapac, D. *Zakon o kaznenom postupku i drugi izvori hrvatskog kaznenog postupovnog prava*, VII. izmijenjeno i dopunjeno izdanje, Narodne novine, Zagreb, 2008.

Novokmet, A., and Z. Vinković. *Police Interrogation of the Suspect in Croatia after the Implementation of the Directive 2013/48/EU: State of Play and Open Questions*, EU and Comparative Law Issues and Challenges Series, vol. 2/2018).

Ratkaj, R., *Policijski izvidi kaznenih djela s posebnim osvrtom na ispitivanje osumnjičenika de lege ferenda*, Paragraf: časopis za pravna i društvena pitanja Pravnog fakulteta Sveučilišta Josipa Jurja Strossmayera u Osijeku, vol. 2, no. 1/2018.

Valković, L., and Z. Burić. *Primjena izabranih elemenata prava na formalnu obranu iz prakse Europskog suda za ljudska prava u hrvatskom kaznenom postupku*, Hrvatski ljetopis za kazneno pravo i praksu, vol. 18, no. 2/2011.

Valković, L. *Pravo na pristup branitelju u svjetlu presude Dvorski protiv Hrvatske*, Hrvatski ljetopis za kaznene znanosti i praksu, vol. 23, no. 2/2016.

NOTES

1. Official Gazette (*Narodne novine*), No. 110/1997.

2. Elizabeta Ivičević Karas, Marin Bonačić, and Zoran Burić, *Pre-Trial Procedure in Croatia* in Edward Johnston, Rahime Erbaş, and Daniel Jasinski (eds.), *A Comparative Analysis of Pre-Trial Procedure in Europe: The Search for an Ideal Model* (Istanbul University Press, 2020), 20.

3. Davor Krapac, *Zakon o kaznenom postupku i drugi izvori hrvatskog kaznenog postupovnog prava*, VII. izmijenjeno i dopunjeno izdanje, Narodne novine, Zagreb, 2008, 6.

4. In Croatian criminal procedure, the principle of mandatory prosecution applies, pursuant to which the state attorney is legally obliged to start criminal proceedings if there is reasonable suspicion (*osnovana sumnja*) that a person has committed a criminal offense prosecuted ex officio and there are no statutory obstacles to it. On the principle of mandatory prosecution and (the rising number of) its exceptions in Croatian law, see Davor Krapac, *Kazneno procesno pravo, Knjiga prva: Institucije*, Narodne novine, Zagreb, 2020, 99–108.

5. Official Gazette (*Narodne novine*), No. 152/08.

6. Constitutional Court of the Republic of Croatia, U-I-448/2009, 19 July 2012.

7. For an in-depth analysis of the decision, see Zlata Đurđević, *Odluka Ustavnog suda RH o suglasnosti Zakona o kaznenom postupku s Ustavom* (2012) 19 Hrvatski ljetopis za kazneno pravo i praksu 409–38.

8. Elizabeta Ivičević Karas, Zoran Burić, and Marin Bonačić, *Unapređenje procesnih prava osumnjičenika i okrivljenika u kaznenom postupku: Pogled kroz prizmu europskih pravnih standarda* (2016), 23 Hrvatski ljetopis za kaznene znanosti i praksu, 12–5.

9. See Zlata Đurđević, *Uvodna riječ* (2017), 24 Hrvatski ljetopis za kaznene znanosti i praksu, 265.

10. On police inquiries into criminal offenses, see Robert Ratkaj, *Policijski izvidi kaznenih djela s posebnim osvrtom na ispitivanje osumnjičenika de lege ferenda* (2018) 2 Paragraf: časopis za pravna i društvena pitanja Pravnog fakulteta Sveučilišta Josipa Jurja Strossmayera u Osijeku, 195–200.

11. Vladimir Bayer, *Kazneno procesno pravo—odabrana poglavlja, Knjiga I. Uvod u teoriju kaznenog procesnog prava*, Ministarstvo unutarnjih poslova Republike

Hrvatske, Zagreb, 1995, 286, Zoran Burić and Željko Karas, *Prilog raspravi o dvojbama vezanim uz novu definiciju osumnjičenika i radnju njegova ispitivanja* (2017), 24 Hrvatski ljetopis za kaznene znanosti i praksu, 445–54.

12. For the contemporary development of the jurisprudence of the European Court for Human Rights on police interrogations of the suspect and the arrested person, see Zoran Burić, *Re-assessing the Jurisprudence of the European Court for Human Rights on Police Interrogation—Case of Ibrahim and Others v. the United Kingdom* (2018), 2 EU and Comparative Law Issues and Challenges Series, 342–344.

13. See Elizabeta Ivičević Karas, Zoran Burić, and Marin Bonačić, *Prava obrane u različitim stadijima hrvatskog kaznenog postupka: rezultati istraživanja prakse*, Hrvatski ljetopis za kaznene znanosti i praksu (2016), 23 520.

14. Željko Karas, *Dokazni položaj općih izvidnih radnji redarstvenih vlasti* (2006), 13 Hrvatski ljetopis za kazneno pravo i praksu, 59–86.

15. Zoran Burić and Željko Karas, *Prilog raspravi* (n 11) 454.

16. See Elizabeta Ivičević Karas, *Pomicanje granica prava na branitelja pod utjecajem europskog kaznenog prava* (2015), 22 Hrvatski ljetopis za kazneno pravo i praksu, 378–79.

17. Zoran Burić and Željko Karas, *Prilog raspravi* (n 11), 446–48.

18. Davor Krapac, *Zakon o kaznenom postupku* (n 3) 28–29.

19. ECtHR, app. no. 56185/07, 21 June 2011.

20. More in detail about the facts of the case, see Zlata Đurđević and Elizabeta Ivičević Karas (eds), *Presude Europskog suda za ljudska prava Republike Hrvatske u kaznenim predmetima* (Pravni fakultet Sveučilišta u Zagrebu, 2013), 135–37.

21. The court found that he was deprived of sleep and was forced to sit continuously in a chair for 2 days and 19 hours. Such treatment caused him physical and mental suffering. The court did not find that police officers had beaten him during the interrogation. *Cf.* Laura Valković and Zoran Burić, *Primjena izabranih elemenata prava na formalnu obranu iz prakse Europskog suda za ljudska prava u hrvatskom kaznenom postupku* (2011), 18 Hrvatski ljetopis za kazneno pravo i praksu, 530.

22. The court noted that the allegations that he had made during criminal proceedings that he had been subjected to ill-treatment during his stay at the police station have constituted an obligation for the competent domestic authorities to adequately investigate these allegations. Because an official investigation into these allegations had not been conducted, and the evidence that the trial court heard also did not shed light on the circumstances of the police conduct toward him, there had been a violation of Article 3 of the Convention also in its procedural aspect. *Cf.* Lauta Valković and Zoran Burić, *Primjena izabranih elemenata* (n 21), 530.

23. Ibid, 534.

24. ECtHR, app. no. 4429/09, 28 June 2011.

25. More in detail about the facts of the case, see Zlata Đurđević and Elizabeta Ivičević Karas, *Presude Europskog suda* (n 20), 146.

26. *Cf.* Laura Valković and Zoran Burić, *Primjena izabranih elemenata* (n 21), 537.

27. ECtHR, app. no. 25703/11, 20 October 2015.

28. More in detail about the facts of the case, see Laura Valković, *Pravo na pristup branitelju u svjetlu presude Dvorski protiv Hrvatske* (2016), 23 Hrvatski ljetopis za kaznene znanosti i praksu, 350–53.

29. Ibid, 356–57.

30. Zoran Burić, *Qualitative Report for Croatia*, in Stefan Schumann et al. (eds), *Pre-trial Emergency Defence* (Intersentia 2012) 302–3.

31. Directive 2010/64/EU of the European Parliament and of the Council of 20 October 2010 on the right to interpretation and translation in criminal proceedings, *OJ L* 280, 26.10.2010, 1–7.

32. Directive 2012/13/EU of the European Parliament and of the Council of 22 May 2012 on the right to information in criminal proceedings, *OJ L* 142, 1.6.2012, 1–10.

33. Zakon o izmjenama i dopunama Zakona o kaznenom postupku, *Official Gazette* (*Narodne novine*), No. 145/13.

34. Directive 2013/48/EU of the European Parliament and of the Council of 22 October 2013 on the right of access to a lawyer in criminal proceedings and in European arrest warrant proceedings, and on the right to have a third party informed upon deprivation of liberty and to communicate with third persons and with consular authorities while deprived of liberty, *OJ L* 294, 6.11.2013, 1–12.

35. Article 3(2)(a) of the Directive.

36. Željko Karas, *Kriminalistički značaj pribavljanja osumnjičenikovog iskaza prije početka kaznenog postupka* (2015) Policija i sigurnost 102 *et seq.*

37. Ibid., 106–11.

38. Zakon o izmjenama i dopunama Zakona o kaznenom postupku, *Official Gazette* (*Narodne novine*), No. 70/17.

39. A suspect is a person against whom there are grounds for suspicion (*osnove sumnje*) that he/she had committed a criminal offense and against whom the police or the state attorney are undertaking actions to resolve that suspicion, Art. 202. para. 2, point 1 CPA.

40. This provision was inspired by Art. 1(3) of the Directive on the right of access to a lawyer.

41. See Elizabeta Ivičević Karas and Laura Valković, *Pravno na branitelja u policiji—pravna i stvarna ograničenja* (2017), 24 Hrvatski ljetopis za kaznene znanosti i praksu, 435.

42. See Ante Novokmet and Zoran Vinković, *Police Interrogation of the Suspect in Croatia After the Implementation of the Directive 2013/48/EU—State of Play and Open Questions* (2018) 2 EU and Comparative Law Issues and Challenges Series 436–40. See also Darko Klier, Mirjana Kondor-Langer, and Stjepan Gluščić, *Policijska i državnoodvjetnička praksa u ispitivanju osumnjičenika* (2018), 25 Hrvatski ljetopis za kaznene znanosti i praksu, 454–55.

43. See Elizabeta Ivičević Karas, Zoran Burić, and Marin Bonačić, *Neka pitanja usklađenosti hrvatskoga kaznenog procesnog prava s direktivama o pravima obrane—analiza sudske prakse* (2020), 27 Hrvatski ljetopis za kaznene znanosti i praksu, 546–60.

Chapter 5

The Risks of Risk Aversion

Trajectories of Automation in Policing

Mehzeb Chowdhury

In modern societies, risk has become a dominant preoccupation, attributed to constructing contemporary institutions and contemporary consciousness.[1] Law, order, and ideals of justice have acted as a driving force for modern democracies both as a goal-setting attribute, as well as a legitimizing component.[2] However, structural reorganization, budget cuts, and pushbacks against traditional approaches to maintaining law and order have introduced new challenges to policing in the twenty-first century.[3] Evidence-based, intelligence-led, professional approaches for the modernization of policing have led to policy changes.[4] Previously well-established functions in society have also shifted due to private sector involvement, and emergence of new security and safety providers, collaborative arrangements, and partnerships.[5] Previously established mechanisms of bureaucratic, centralized governance[6] have seen replacement by new forms of networks, nodal governance, and pluralistic systems,[7] considered to be more mobile, cost-effective, and responsive solutions to maintaining society's security.

This postmillennium shift toward a more technological workforce persisted with middle-skill occupations suffering the most.[8] Studies found a decline in such occupations in favor of high-skill white-collar jobs and low-skill operations.[9] Automation slowly incorporated itself into law enforcement, with an increasing reliance on technology in forensic practice.[10] These developments have been touted as being an effective means toward the achievement of organizational objectives but possess equal potential to create and expose stakeholders to risks. The motivations for a move toward technology-focused workforces can also be indicative of society's reassessment of human workers and their limitations, including a newfound need for organizations to maintain a public image of trust and competence.

POSSIBLE DRIVERS OF TECHNOLOGICAL CHANGE

Risk of Losing Legitimacy and Public Trust

From forensic science to frontline police work, consumerism has embodied the restructuring of roles for an objective-driven, service-oriented future.[11] Trust and confidence have become important precursors to resource allocation and growth, with police organizations branding themselves as service providers delivering to its many customers (e.g., the criminal justice system, victims, and the wider society) an essential service.[12] In fact, public confidence has been held to be the principal indicator of police performance by the Home Office.[13] It follows trust and confidence being part of popular discourse, especially in medical, legal, and criminal justice practice for decades.[14]

Trust is understood to be an expectation placed on organizations, individuals, and their discretion.[15] Trusting individuals concerns has been referred to as "face-work" commitments, where another's honesty and probity are sought after.[16] Professionalism in policing requires personnel to be worthy of this trust, to maintain confidentiality, and conceal knowledge by not exploiting it for malign purposes.[17] The quality of police work is thus a matter of reputation and determiner of public confidence in state apparatuses of law and order.[18] Competence of police personnel in fulfilling their duties is also strongly related to public confidence in social institutions as well as trust in individual practitioners.[19]

As a result, trust in police, policing, and state security mechanisms have been points of reflexion for decades.[20] Research from Ipsos MORI found that 31% of Britons stated they would generally not trust the police to tell the truth.[21] In another study, IPCC determined that 74% of its survey participants would make an official complaint if officers failed to properly investigate volume crimes (which includes robbery, burglary, shoplifting, vehicle crime, criminal damage, drugs, and assaults), that trust was higher among the young than the old (73% of 18–34s said that they trusted police to tell the truth, compared to 59% of those aged 55+) and by women more than men (68% to 62%).[22] The figures reflect how past organizational and individual indiscretions (e.g., officer misconduct and allegations of institutional racism)[23] may have played a role among older respondents in how trust and confidence in the police service was conceptualized and held.

Five years later, market research firm BMG found that public confidence in law enforcement effectively dealing with an emergency was at 52%, while one-third of respondents stated that their local police force would not treat them fairly if they needed to contact them.[24] Only a slight majority thought that the local constabulary had a good reputation (52%). Approachability and perceived access to the police was down by 10% from the previous year, as over two-fifths of respondents felt that they were unsatisfied with service. Notably, the survey report admitted that survey questions, reframed from the previous year, may have accounted for a more positive response. Such rewording in data collection and presentation of results to increase public confidence and improve perception are indicative of a wider move by organizations to improve their standing with the public.

While technological change in policing can be driven by social, political, cultural, and legal developments, technology itself can only progress and reach its potential if negotiations between these various factors overlap with a common goal.[25] Often these will be driven by a response to rising crime levels[26] but more recently, implementations such as body-worn and dashboard cameras have seen introduction as a response to ensuring accountability, due to historical and persistent poor judgment and decision-making.[27] It ties in with an evolving proposition that thinking machines, given the right tools, can make better decisions than humans,[28] and evidence that suggests that on-the-job decision-making in law enforcement is subject to a myriad of personal and organizational biases.[29]

In conjunction with the evolution of policing into a vocation, where consumeristic classifications of the public as customers, such notions as "the customer is always right" has been become a central facet of the practice.[30] Service efficacy and performance have also been elevated to essential precursors of end-user satisfaction.[31] It is therefore a possibility that in pursuit of legitimacy,[32] forces could incorporate every available instrument (prominently technology) to elevate their operational efficacy and provide quality service.[33] Public support has been prevalent in technical innovations such as adoption of body-worn cameras[34] as well as CCTV and vehicle dash cams,[35] and going forward, public backing could shape the form and functions of the organizations, as it has in the past.[36]

Modernization and the Risk of Being Left Behind

Technology has been cited as a means of ensuring modernizations overriding objectives, such as increasing efficiency and compensating for decreasing numbers of human workers.[37] The connexion between scientific progress and its effects on societal development are useful indicators of their relationship and symbiosis.[38] In the United Kingdom (UK), the modernization rhetoric consistently focused on a move toward computerized data management and automation of working practices.[39] It overlapped with the broader process of scientification of police work,[40] and the rationalization of scientific provision.[41]

Law enforcement all over the world have also adapted to a plethora of new threats in a rapidly changing world. It coincides with society's overriding need to adapt to technical innovations and their associated terraforming, or risk of being left behind.[42] The proliferation of the internet brought with it a new class of crimes[43] and the need for the police to adapt to them.[44] The rapid nature of change has also prompted shifts in law enforcement culture with a newfound urgency to respond to the demands of modern-day police work.[45]

CCTV and remote monitoring technologies have had a profound effect,[46] complementing modern algorithmic systems that have become adept at taking in and analyzing such data to inform and remotely control environs, making better management decisions, and reaching more efficient outcomes.[47] A demonstration of the vast power of computational policing can be seen in number-plate recognition and tracking for traffic offenses[48] and facial-recognition algorithms tied in with CCTV systems shadowing suspects and aiding manhunts.[49] AI has been adopted for the identification of counterfeit currency,[50] and in the Middle East, for street patrolling.[51]

However, the risks resulting from this expanding technological, mechanized society could be extrapolated to be of a considerable magnitude as well, with the need to avert these risks a driver in itself for greater technology adoption.[52]

Management of Forensic Science-Specific Risks

The use of scientific techniques in crime detection and prosecution opened new avenues of risk management,[53] with human error underlining crime scene-related risks,[54] which include contamination, evidence tampering, planting of evidential artifacts, and missing or undetected evidence.[55] Efficiency and reliability in crime scene work have significant flow-on effects in the forensic and justice outcomes[56] with substantial risks materializing due to misjudging and/or misidentifying a potential scene.[57] Additionally, junk/pseudo-science (such as hair and bite-mark matching), unvalidated analysis techniques, sample contamination, accidental destruction, willful tampering, or erroneous conclusions reached, are laboratory-specific risks that forensic science has introduced into the criminal justice system.[58] The wider effect of these risks could be wrongful convictions, unjust exonerations, which have the potential to affect the reputation of law enforcement and the justice system leading to less public confidence.[59] With the substantial scope of automation and AI in forensic science,[60] policymakers could be interested in minimizing these risks and their potential wider consequences by minimizing human contact with the evidence in both collection and processing—from crime scene to court.[61]

As a Response to Police Culture-Related Risks

On the other end of the spectrum rests continuous pushback from society on the values and culture within frontline law enforcement personnel. A continuing concern of modern society has been the apprehensive attitude toward law enforcement organizations deferring their responsibilities of fairness and due process in favor of hard-line policies to crack down on target groups and furthering executive agenda.[62] Questions concerning often uncomfortable subjects of racism, sexism, and institutional prejudice embodied discourse across jurisdictions since the 1990s culminating in a pronounced movement in the years that followed.[63] Introduction of body cameras worn by frontline police personnel were phased in to combat the risk of prejudicial conduct, while the advent of social media and the internet magnified any misconduct.[64] Increased coverage of CCTV, satellite imaging, and reconstructions of misconduct instances using citizen-captured footage were consequences of this degradation of confidence in police and policing, as well as a need to quell fears of poor service and potential miscarriages of justice.

Police deviance encapsulates conduct that permeates the police profession to weaken or rid it of integrity.[65] Examples can include bribery,[66] excessive force,[67] abuse of authority/misuse of discretion,[68] involvement with criminal enterprizes,[69] active or passive participation in acts of crime,[70] and rewarding or being rewarded for actions unbecoming of a police professional.[71]

Technologies such as automation have been seen in recent times as a means of ensuring efficiency and reliability, leading to a philosophical supposition pertaining to its appropriateness to fight crime. The notion that intelligent systems could make decisions free of errors, biases, and malice is an intriguing one. However, machines taking over from humans can result in widescale unintended consequences. Technical innovations often bring with them concerns of deskilling, workers becoming redundant, anxiety, unrest, and distrust within workforces.[72] Fears over the scope and effects of computing in advancing political and economic goals of the powerful have also given rise to questions about the potential dangers of using artificial intelligence (AI) in critical state apparatuses such as policing.[73]

Potential Unwanted Consequences

Deskilling, Devaluation, and Redundancy

Over the past century, machines have consistently been developed to be more powerful, cheaper, and easier to use.[74] As a result, an estimated 800 million jobs could be lost worldwide to automation by 2030, with five percent of current occupations completely automated if cutting-edge technology is widely adopted, while in 60 percent of jobs, one-third of activities will be automated.[75] It coincides with employment in Western economies growing in both low- and high-skill occupations but falling in middle-skill ones.[76] Middle-skill, middle-class occupations are also those that can be most easily replaced by technology[77]—such as law enforcement.[78]

Police sketch artists, employing forensic techniques to ascertain the likely appearance of a suspect, are losing their livelihood due to many police departments producing digital composite sketches on computers that use software that any officer can be trained to operate.[79] Robots and rovers have been used for the purposes of bomb disposal for decades.[80] An overreliance on CCTV over traditional police patrols have also sparked questions on the future[81] with stakeholders expressing fears of replacement by the machines.[82] They accompany society's broader concerns that technological advancements would negatively impact labor markets and make human workers redundant.[83]

In the UK, there has been increased attention on the role of the police after the postausterity era under the 2010 Coalition government.[84] The police had experienced sustained growth until austerity measures reduced numbers and stunted expansion in England and Wales by an estimated 20 percent leading up to 2015.[85] The number and roles of frontline operational support workforce, of which scientific support are a part, faced planned reductions of 27% from 2010 to 2015.[86] Cuts to police numbers and resources were a constant, until a 2019 revision in recruitment strategy,[87] overlapping with an observable upward trend of violent crime figures.[88]

Job uncertainty,[89] along with the potential threat of replacement by automation, serve as stark reminders that reassessment of traditional policing may be necessary for the reinforcement of the vocation. For years, law enforcement personnel were thought to be professionals, providing staff with a sense of security, due to the understanding that professions are somewhat fortified from redundancy.[90] However, with the introduction of schemes such as the Police Constable Degree Apprenticeship,[91] and a move toward evidence-based policing,[92] new queries about the compatibilities of such dynamic shifts in police practice[93] and the overall professional standing of law enforcement have come to the forefront.[94]

Division and Unrest within the Ranks

Change is inevitable in law enforcement contexts, be it a shift in culture,[95] working practices,[96] or functions.[97] Change is also a precursor to anxiety and fear,[98] especially when instigated by automation.[99] Any shift from the base state, be it in law[100] or technology,[101] invokes a reaction in law enforcement.

Chan[102] found that survey participants in an Australian police force intimated these to include anything from increased strain on personnel burdened with new compliance and accountability requirements, losing autonomy and discretion due to a data-driven decision system, and setting boundaries and requirements that would keep staff from performing their duties in a timely and effective manner. These tie in with concerns that changes in law enforcement may not be sufficiently contextualized to take into account the complexities of policing culture and the role of the police in society.[103]

Technology adoption could also not only be hampered, but actively resisted by organizations that have traditionally been subject to financial constraint and staff shortages.[104] There is a concern that occupational practices already ingrained in policing could be exasperated by the introduction of technology.[105] This is largely in part due to a myriad of reasoning behind past decisions to adopt technology based not on any unified strategy or philosophy, but ad hoc reactions to executive-level intervention, perceived needs, community demands, and available funding.[106]

Racism, Sexism Caused by Biased Training Data

In the manner that forensic analysis had for long been incorrectly considered to be infallible,[107] the misconception that artificial intelligence cannot fail or make mistakes is also prevalent in stakeholder circles.[108] The efficiency and accuracy of intelligence systems are critically dependent on the quantity and quality of the data it is provided.[109] Faulty information or data without context can have potentially disastrous consequences, particularly with strategies that aim to predict crime.[110]

Policies such as predictive policing base their approaches on several precepts, including the digital mapping of individuals, their networks, and building subpopulations, which specific algorithms can be programmed to track and identify as being potentially risky.[111] The concept alludes to the notion that public safety demands the identification of problem groups, keeping them under surveillance, and preventing the commission or even conspiracy of crime.[112]

There are studies that indicate the usefulness of ascertaining and surveilling high risk groups who are more susceptible to violence and criminal conduct.[113] In Chicago, researchers found that networks of only 3,100 people (about four percent of the studied area's population) were responsible for more than 40 percent of gun-related homicides, and that being part of that four percent elevated a person's chances of a gun-related death by approximately 900 percent.[114] The principal factors for this were determined to be gang associations, geographical proximity to gang bases and/or operations, and being involved in drug-related criminal conduct. A telling finding was that the majority of those involved were men of color.

Insights from research of similar target groups have been adapted to develop person-based predictive targeting strategies.[115] Creation of watch lists are a natural consequence of complex systems that guide police and policing to watch, intervene, and prosecute where necessary.[116] However, the selection process of persons and the lists they become part of remain a matter of contention. Generally, police activity directly affects a relatively confined group at the foot of the social hierarchy who are lopsidedly the complainants, victims, and/or offenders.[117] The disproportionate contact between minorities and law enforcement, in fact the criminal justice system has also been documented,[118] with such factors as stops and searches, detainments, arrests, and convictions forming the basis for the determination of future propensity to commit crimes.[119]

These algorithmic mechanisms run the danger of bias and discrimination much like human criminal justice actors.[120] A reliance on targeting data without the contextualization of socioeconomic factors and their intersection with race can lead to racial discrimination, despite the algorithm's marketed inability to be prejudiced. Gendered media coverage and societies' often archaic and reductionist construction of the sexes[121] can have a significant effect on AI training data, leading to biased outcomes.[122]

In a utopian society, AI has the potential to be used for the apprehension of fugitives by predicting their next move, tracking terrorists, pinpointing, and foiling terror plots, and in time, even predict crime. Dick[123] postulated on his fictional canvas, the benefits of being able to predict crime before it happened. Using advanced technology, a fictional police department "PreCrime" was able to fast-forward, and rewind predicted realities in order to apprehend criminals.[124]

However, in the real world, these principles were adopted in an AI-driven predictive policing project in the U.S. with disastrous results.[125] The Sheriff's office in Tampa, Florida, generated lists of people it considered likely to break the law based on arrest histories, unspecified intelligence, and arbitrary decisions by police analysts. Deputies were then dispatched to interrogate them often without probable cause, a search warrant, or evidence of a specific crime.

While the idea of predicting crime may have been enticing to its enforcers, the resultant harassment of citizens served as a stark reminder of the dangers big data and AI pose when improperly handled.[126] Similar predictive technology was operationalized in the UK in 2019 as a risk-assessment and management tool in line their American counterparts.[127] Technology also spilled over to sentencing, with one UK police force attempting to drive bail decision-making with AI, despite widespread concerns of bias and targeting.[128] Notwithstanding the fallacies of these systems, a technology-driven, seemingly objective but all-powerful mechanism of crime control, could also encroach on citizen freedoms and democratic ideals of governance.[129]

MISAPPROPRIATION AND THE POLICE STATE

The move from a surveillance state to a police state would require a minimal shift in technological advancement, given the society attempting such a transition already possesses or has access to machines capable of monitoring and predicting the actions and inactions of its citizens. Concern has been prevalent that equipping an organization already seen to be increasingly militaristic could lead to further abuses in the line of duty.[130]

Justificatory arguments for such shifts are tied in with a myriad of national and international threats becoming commonplace in a globalized postmodern world.[131] Terrorism, civil unrest, social justice upheaval, and the rise of new categories of crime are but a few excuses a state could invoke to mandate a system of tighter control—albeit under the guise of protection of the citizen and for the greater good of the community.[132]

Information holds the greatest potential to be weaponized, with private individuals increasingly likely to voluntarily surrender their rights in the name of convenience.[133] From health trackers, smartwatches, augmented reality glasses, fashion accessories, and even smart contact lenses, the prospect of tracking a person's every move, see and hear what they experience, and to extrapolate patterns from that data, point to the real possibility of a future state leveraging the information to monitor and even control.[134]

In the instance of draconian directives and their implementation through the ranks, a common barrier to many iron-fisted regimes tends to be dissenters and rebels within the state apparatus. Calculated thinking machines would have no conscience-block[135] resulting in application of measures that would hold the potential to aid prospective totalitarian governments to remain in power indefinitely, as movements to overthrow them by the unequipped masses would be practically impossible.[136]

Harvested data, fed through neural networks and deep learning algorithms could analyze, contextualize, and synthesize, identifying suspect behavior, eliminating outliers, and extinguishing rebellions.[137] Thus, the risk of potential artificial intelligence and automation technologies spilling over to politics and political gain, the implementation and enactment of such systems for societal control could predictably be met with pushback from private citizens and interest groups. Orwell[138] expressed these fears by warning of the rise of dictatorships as a direct consequence of technological advancement. The collective anxiety around the possibility of such a future has been seen to manifest in public dissent in overbearing governments and their tendencies to embrace big data for governance.[139]

CONTEXTUALIZING RISKS AND TRAJECTORIES

Notwithstanding such cautionary cases, the overriding objectives of modernization and a prominent neoliberal agenda suggests that transformation of policing by leveraging big data is almost inevitable. Technology's deterministic tendencies[140] coupled with executive decision-making to appease service customers and maintain public image can lead to a pronounced utilization of mechanization and artificial intelligence for criminal justice objectives. The vast potential of emerging technologies, such as quantum computing, also open doors for previously unheard-of possibilities in a range of disciplines.[141]

For example, in forensic blood spatter analysis, a quantum computer could leverage the power of AI to determine, in previously unimaginable timeframes, the exact circumstances or chain of events leading to a spatter pattern. The system could undertake a series of simultaneous simulations, taking into consideration every known type of weapon, height of the shooter, whether they are right- or left-handed, distance from the victim, any environmental factors that may have affected trajectory of projectile, or final spatter pattern, etc. to ascertain the exact events leading up to its formation. Given enough time, it could match the exact dimensions of the spatter pattern and create incredibly accurate models. The question of accuracy in AI-driven policing has been a longstanding concern,[142] and if upcoming technology can assist in quelling such reservations,[143] then an uptick in adoption could logically follow.

However, the risks originating from technical innovations require careful examination of policies so as to avoid outcomes such as redundancy and deskilling, along with issues pertaining to morale and personnel working practices. More importantly miscarriages of justice driven by AI's misguided decision-making due to faulty or incomplete data and state misuse and abuse of technology are likely possibilities given the current heading of the technological present. The great promise of technology is its potential to assist in overcoming humanity's frailties, however AI and mechanization is unlikely to succeed if the same frailties are not identified and extinguished, particularly with respect to law enforcement's struggles to remain impartial with particular groups within society.

CONCLUSION

Mechanization of working practices in both the manufacturing and service industries have prompted debates about the possible futures of occupations where the human element is considered to be nonessential. The lure of a technological society where machines minimize human error has led to mechanization and automation of occupations, some even leading to human intervention becoming obsolete. Mistakes in investigation, institutional racism, officer prejudice, and misinformed judgments have come into focus with damning body and dash camera footage, DNA exonerations, and more robust means of forensic evidence collection and analysis. Faith in machines as less error-prone than humans have driven measures to use artificial intelligence as a means of projecting objectivity and maintain public trust. The aversion of risks, such as evidence tampering, contamination, and manipulation are possible motivators in this move. The solution is not as simple as just handing over the reins to a machine, though. Artificial intelligence and mechanization create exorbitant risks pertaining to redundancy, deskilling, and unrest, notwithstanding the greater threat of insulating police and state misconduct through its seemingly legitimizing power. The solution could be building fail-safe measures into intelligent systems to prevent misuse and create robust datasets of criminological analysis to add context to raw police data. Neoliberalism's move into governance and technological determinism manifesting true serves as an indication of the future of law enforcement. It is a prospect that cannot be prevented in principle but can perhaps be remodeled to prevent a dystopian future.

BIBLIOGRAPHY

Acemoglu, Daron, and David Autor. "Skills, Tasks and Technologies: Implications for Employment and Earnings." In *Handbook of Labor Economics*, vol. 4 (2011): 1043–1171.

Ariel, Barak. "Police Body Cameras in Large Police Departments." *Journal of Criminal Law and Criminology* (2016): 729–768.

Asaro, Peter M. "AI Ethics in Predictive Policing: From Models of Threat to an Ethics of Care." *IEEE Technology and Society Magazine* 38, no. 2 (2019): 40–53.

Autor, David H., and David Dorn. "The Growth of Low-Skill Service Jobs and the Polarization of the US Labor Market." *American Economic Review* 103, no. 5 (2013): 1553–1597.

Barry, Andrew. *Political Machines: Governing a Technological Society*. A&C Black (2001).

Beck, Ulrich, Anthony Giddens, and Scott Lash. *Reflexive Modernization: Politics, Tradition and Aesthetics in the Modern Social Order.* Stanford University Press (1994).

Beck, Ulrich, Scott Lash, and Brian Wynne. *Risk Society: Towards a New Modernity*. Vol. 17. Sage (1992).

Berk, Richard A. "Artificial Intelligence, Predictive Policing, and Risk Assessment for Law Enforcement." *Annual Review of Criminology* 4 (2020).

BMG Research Ltd. "Public Perceptions of Policing in England and Wales 2018." Birmingham: BMG (2019).

Bowling, Ben, and Coretta Phillips. "Disproportionate and Discriminatory: Reviewing the Evidence on Police Stop and Search." *Modern Law Review* 70, no. 6 (2007): 936–961.

Braithwaite, John. "Restorative Justice: Assessing Optimistic and Pessimistic Accounts." *Crime and Justice* 25 (1999): 1–127.

Brayne, Sarah. "Big Data Surveillance: The Case of Policing." *American Sociological Review* 82, no. 5 (2017): 977–1008.

British Broadcasting Corporation "Robot Police Officer Goes on Duty in Dubai" (2017).

British Broadcasting Corporation. "Met Police Technology 'Ineffective and Outdated,' report claims" (2013).

Bromberg, Daniel E., Étienne Charbonneau, and Andrew Smith. "Public Support for Facial Recognition Via Police Body-Worn Cameras: Findings from a List Experiment." *Government Information Quarterly* 37, no. 1 (2020): 101415.

Carney, Nikita. "All lives matter, but so does race: Black lives matter and the evolving role of social media." *Humanity & Society* 40, no. 2 (2016): 180–199.

Carter, David L. "Drug-Related Corruption of Police Officers: A Contemporary Typology." *Journal of Criminal Justice* 18, no. 2 (1990): 85–98.

Cascriani, Dominic. "Covid: Police Watchdog Says Officers Confused by Unclear Pandemic Laws." BBC (2021).

Chan, Janet B. L. "The Technological Game: How Information Technology Is Transforming Police Practice." *Criminal Justice* 1, no. 2 (2001): 139–159.

Chan, Janet B. L. *Changing Police Culture: Policing in a Multicultural Society*. Cambridge University Press (1997).

Chan, Janet, David Brereton, Margot Legosz, and Sally Doran. "E-policing: The Impact of Information Technology on Police Practices." Brisbane: Criminal Justice Commission (2001).

Chan, Janet. "Changing Police Culture." *British Journal of Criminology* 36, no. 1 (1996): 109–134.

Christensen, Angi M., Christian M. Crowder, Stephen D. Ousley, and Max M. Houck. "Error and Its Meaning in Forensic Science." *Journal of Forensic Sciences* 59, no. 1 (2014): 123–126.

Clancy, Anna, Mike Hough, Rebbecca Aust, and Chris Kershaw. "Crime, Policing and Justice: The Experience of Ethnic Minorities." London, England: Home Office Research Development and Statistics Directorate (2001).

Clarke, John. "Citizen-Consumers and Public Service Reform: At the Limits of Neoliberalism?" *Policy Futures in Education* 5, no. 2 (2007): 239–248.

Cockcroft, Tom. *Police Culture: Themes and Concepts*. Routledge (2012).

Coglianese, Cary, and David Lehr. "Regulating by Robot: Administrative Decision Making in the Machine-Learning Era." *Georgetown Law Journal* 105 (2016): 1147.

Coleman, Roy, and Michael McCahill. *Surveillance and Crime*. Sage (2010).

Cook, James, and Hannah Boland. "Cummings' Plan to Create a UK Trillionaire Tech Giant Is Admirable—But Is it Realistic?." *The Telegraph* (2020).

Daugherty, Paul R., and H. James Wilson. *Human+ Machine: Reimagining Work in the Age of AI*. Harvard Business Press (2018).

Davis, Josh P., Charlotte Forrest, Felicia Treml, and Ashok Jansari. "Identification from CCTV: Assessing Police Super□Recogniser Ability to Spot Faces in a Crowd and Susceptibility to Change Blindness." *Applied Cognitive Psychology* 32, no. 3 (2018): 337–353.

Dearden, Lizzie. "Police Testing Technology to 'Assess the Risk of Someone Committing a Crime' in UK." *The Independent* (2019).

den Boer, Monica. "9 Intelligence-Led Policing in Europe." *The Future of Intelligence: Challenges in the 21st Century* (2014): 113.

Dick, Philip K. *The Philip K. Dick Reader*. Citadel Press (1997).

Dutelle, Aric W. "Fingerprint Evidence." *An Introduction to Crime Scene Investigation*. Burlington, VT: Jones and Bartlett Learning (2014): 169–202.

Ericson, Richard V., and Clifford D. Shearing. "The Scientification of Police Work." In *The Knowledge Society*, pp. 129–159. Dordrecht: Springer (1986).

Eubanks, Virginia. *Automating Inequality: How High-Tech Tools Profile, Police, and Punish the Poor*. St. Martin's Press (2018).

Evetts, Julia. "Introduction: Trust and Professionalism: Challenges and Occupational Changes." (2006): 515–531.

Evetts, Julia. "The Construction of Professionalism in New and Existing Occupational Contexts: Promoting and Facilitating Occupational Change." *International Journal of Sociology and Social Policy* (2003).

Featherstone, Mike, and Roger Burrows, eds. *Cyberspace/Cyberbodies/Cyberpunk: Cultures of Technological Embodiment*. Sage (1996).

Feldman, Leonard. "Neoliberalism and Police Reform." In *Rethinking Neoliberalism: Resisting the Disciplinary Regime*, edited by Marianna Pavlovskaya and Sanford Schram. New York, NY: Routledge (2018).

Feldstein, Steven. *The Global Expansion of AI Surveillance*. Vol. 17. Washington, DC: Carnegie Endowment for International Peace (2019).

Ferguson, Andrew G. "The Exclusionary Rule in the Age of Blue Data." *Vanderbilt Law Review* 72 (2019): 561.

Findley, Keith A. "Innocents at Risk: Adversary Imbalance, Forensic Science, and the Search for Truth." *Seton Hall Law Review* 38 (2008): 893.

Fischer, Claude S. *America Calling: A Social History of the Telephone to 1940*. University of California Press (1992).

Freeman, Daniel, Felicity Waite, Laina Rosebrock, Ariane Petit, Chiara Causier, Anna East, Lucy Jenner, et al. "Coronavirus conspiracy beliefs, mistrust, and compliance with government guidelines in England." *Psychological Medicine* (2020): 1–13.

Frey, Carl Benedikt, and Michael A. Osborne. "The Future of Employment: How Susceptible Are Jobs to Computerisation?." *Technological Forecasting and Social Change* 114 (2017): 254–280.

Fyfe, Nicholas R., J. B. Terpstra, and Pieter Tops. "Centralizing Forces? Comparative Perspectives on Contemporary Police Reform in Northern and Western Europe." (2013).

Galloway, Robert A. "Quality Management in Police Services." *TQM Magazine* (1994).

Gardner, Ross M., and Donna Krouskup. *Practical Crime Scene Processing and Investigation*. CRC Press (2018).

Giddens, Anthony. *The Consequences of Modernity*. Cambridge, UK: Polity (1990).

Giroux, Henry A. "Totalitarian Paranoia in the Post-Orwellian Surveillance State." *Cultural Studies* 29, no. 2 (2015): 108–140.

Goold, Benjamin J. *CCTV and Policing: Public Area Surveillance and Police Practices in Britain*. Oxford University Press on Demand (2004).

Grace, Katja, John Salvatier, Allan Dafoe, Baobao Zhang, and Owain Evans. "When Will AI Exceed Human Performance? Evidence from AI experts." *Journal of Artificial Intelligence Research* 62 (2018): 729–754.

Haggerty, Kevin D., and Richard V. Ericson. "The Surveillant Assemblage." *British Journal of Sociology* 51, no. 4 (2000): 605–622.

Heilbroner, Robert L. "Do Machines Make History?" *Technology and Culture* 8, no. 3 (1967): 335–345.

Helbing, Dirk, Bruno S. Frey, Gerd Gigerenzer, Ernst Hafen, Michael Hagner, Yvonne Hofstetter, Jeroen Van Den Hoven, Roberto V. Zicari, and Andrej Zwitter. "Will Democracy Survive Big Data and Artificial Intelligence?" In *Towards Digital Enlightenment*, pp. 73–98. Springer, Cham (2019).

Her Majesty's Inspectorate of Constabulary. Policing in Austerity: Meeting the Challenge. London: Her Majesty's Inspectorate of Constabulary and Fire and Rescue Services (2014).

Hoggett, James, and Cli□ord Stott. "Post G20: The Challenge of Change, Implementing Evidence-Based Public Order Policing." *Crowds in the 21st Century* (2015): 64–74.

Holdaway, Simon. "The Re-professionalization of the Police in England and Wales." *Criminology & Criminal Justice* 17, no. 5 (2017): 588–604.

Holzer, Harry J., and Robert I. Lerman. The Future of Middle-Skill Jobs. Vol. 41. Brookings, Center on Children and Families (2009).

Home Affairs Committee. The Macpherson Report: Twenty-Two Years On (2021).

Home Office. "Home Office Announces First Wave of 20,000 Police Officer Uplift" (2019).

Home Office. "Market Exploration: Future Policing." Defence and Security Accelerator, Defence Science and Technology Laboratory, and Home Office (2020).

Home Office. "New Technology to Detect Knives in Public Places" (2019).

Hoogenboom, Bob. "The Governance of Policing and Security." In *The Governance of Policing and Security*, pp. 73–81. Palgrave Macmillan, London (2010).

Hough, Mike, B. Stanko, W. Agnew-Pauley, J. Belur, J. Brown, David Gamblin, Gillian Hunter et al. "Developing an Evidence Based Police Degree-Holder Entry Programme" (2018).

Hough, Mike. "Researching Trust in the Police and Trust in Justice: A UK Perspective." *Policing and Society* 22, no. 3 (2012): 332–345.

Hudson, Barbara. Justice in the Risk Society: Challenging and Re-affirming "Justice" in Late Modernity. Sage (2003).

Hummer, Don, and James Byrne. "Technology, Innovation and Twenty-First-Century Policing." In *The Routledge Handbook of Technology, Crime and Justice*, pp. 375–389. Taylor and Francis 2017.

Independent Police Complaints Commission. Public Confidence in the Police Complaints System (2014).

IPSOS Mori. "Two in Three Britons Say They Generally Trust the Police to Tell the Truth" (2014).

Jackson, Jonathan, and Ben Bradford. "Crime, Policing and Social Order: On the Expressive Nature of Public Confidence in Policing." *British Journal of Sociology* 60, no. 3 (2009): 493–521.

Jang, Hyunseok, Hee-Jong Joo, and Jihong Solomon Zhao. "Determinants of Public Confidence in Police: An International Perspective." *Journal of Criminal Justice* 38, no. 1 (2010): 57–68.

Jawad, Rana. "Coronavirus: Tunisia Deploys Police Robot on Lockdown Patrol." *BBC News* 3 (2020).

Johnson, Derek, Erin Faulkner, Georgia Meredith, and Tim J. Wilson. "Police Functional Adaptation to the Digital or Post Digital Age: Discussions with Cybercrime Experts." *Journal of Criminal Law* 84, no. 5 (2020): 427–450.

Johnson, Roberta Ann. "Whistleblowing and the Police." *Rutgers JL & Urb. Pol'y* 3 (2006): 74.

Julian, Roberta D., Sally F. Kelty, Claude Roux, Peter Woodman, James Robertson, Anna Davey, Robert Hayes et al. "What is the Value of Forensic Science? An Overview of the Effectiveness of Forensic Science in the Australian Criminal Justice System Project." *Australian Journal of Forensic Sciences* 43, no. 4 (2011): 217–229.

Katz, Lawrence F., and Robert A. Margo. "Technical Change and the Relative Demand for Skilled Labor: The United States in Historical Perspective." In *Human Capital in History: The American Record*, pp. 15–57. University of Chicago Press (2014).

Klockars, Carl B., Sanja Kutnjak Ivkovic, and Maria R. Haberfeld. *The Contours of Police Integrity*. Sage (2003).

Knox, Dean, Will Lowe, and Jonathan Mummolo. "Administrative Records Mask Racially Biased Policing." *American Political Science Review* 114, no. 3 (2020): 619–637.

Koper, Christopher S., Cynthia Lum, James J. Willis, Dan J. Woods, and Julie Hibdon. "Realizing the Potential of Technology in Policing: A Multi-site Study of the Social, Organizational, and Behavioral Aspects of Implementing Policing Technologies." In Report to the National Institute of Justice, US Department of Justice. Fairfax, VA: Center for Evidence-Based Crime Policy, George Mason University and Police Executive Research Forum. (2015).

Lawless, Christopher James. "Policing Markets: The Contested Shaping of Neo-liberal Forensic Science." *British Journal of Criminology* 51, no. 4 (2011): 671–689.

Lebron, Christopher J. *The Making of Black Lives Matter: A Brief History of an Idea.* Oxford University Press (2017).

Lee, Murray, and Alyce McGovern. "Force to Sell: Policing the Image and Manufacturing Public Confidence." *Policing and Society* 23, no. 2 (2013): 103–124.

Lefèvre, Thomas. "Big Data in Forensic Science and Medicine." (2018): 1–6.

Levesley, Tom, Amanda Martin, and G. Britain. *Police Attitudes to and Use of CCTV.* London: Home Office (2005).

Lindsay, Rachael, Thomas W. Jackson, and Louise Cooke. "Empirical Evaluation of a Technology Acceptance Model for Mobile Policing." *Police Practice and Research* 15, no. 5 (2014): 419–436.

Linke, Uli. "Fortress Europe: Globalization, Militarization and the Policing of Interior Borderlands." *TOPIA: Canadian Journal of Cultural Studies* 23 (2010): 100–120.

Loftus, Bethan. *Police Culture in a Changing World*. Oxford University Press (2009).

Lumsden, Karen, and Alex Black. "Austerity Policing, Emotional Labour and the Boundaries of Police Work: An Ethnography of a Police Force Control Room in England." *British Journal of Criminology* 58, no. 3 (2018): 606–623.

Lynch, Michael, Simon A. Cole, Ruth McNally, and Kathleen Jordan. *Truth Machine: The Contentious History of DNA Fingerprinting*. University of Chicago Press (2010).

Lyon, David. *Surveillance after September 11.* Vol. 11. Polity (2003).

Martin, Aaron K., Rosamunde E. Van Brakel, and Daniel J. Bernhard. "Understanding Resistance to Digital Surveillance: Towards a Multi-disciplinary, Multi-actor Framework." *Surveillance & Society* 6, no. 3 (2009): 213–232.

Mathieson, SA. "CCTV Cameras Have Led Police to Lose Their Focus." *The Guardian* (2011).

Mawby, Rob C. "Police Corporate Communications, Crime Reporting and the Shaping of Policing News." *Policing and Society* 20, no. 1 (2010): 124–139.

McDermott, Drew. "What Matters to a Machine." *Machine Ethics* (2011): 88–114.

McGrory, Kathleen and Neil Bedi. "Read the Pasco Sheriff's Office Response to Our Investigation." *Tampa Bay Times* (2020).

McGrory, Kathleen and Neil Bedi. "Targeted." *Tampa Bay Times* (2020).

McKinsey Global Institute. "Jobs Lost, Jobs Gained: Workforce Transitions in a Time of Automation" (2017).

Mennell, Julie, and Ian Shaw. "The Future of Forensic and Crime Scene Science: Part I. A UK Forensic Science User and Provider Perspective." *Forensic Science International* 157 (2006): S7-S12.

Millie, Andrew. "What Are the Police for? Re-thinking Policing Post-austerity." In *The Future of Policing*, pp. 82–93. Routledge (2013).

Mokyr, Joel. *The Lever of Riches: Technological Creativity and Economic Progress*. Oxford University Press (1992).

Nadler, Anthony, Matthew Crain, and Joan Donovan. "Weaponizing the Digital Influence Machine." *Data & Society* (2018).

National Academy of Sciences. *Strengthening Forensic Science in the United States: A Path Forward*, Washington, DC: National Academies Press (2009).

Office for National Statistics. "Crime in England and Wales: Year Ending June 2018" (2018).

Office for National Statistics. "Crime in England and Wales: Year Ending March 2020" (2020).

Oliveira, Arlindo L. "Biotechnology, Big Data and Artificial Intelligence." *Biotechnology Journal* 14, no. 8 (2019): 1800613.

O'Neil, Cathy. *Weapons of Math Destruction: How Big Data Increases Inequality and Threatens Democracy*. Crown (2016).

Organisation for Economic Co-operation and Development. "How Technology and Globalisation Are Transforming the Labour Market." In *OECD Employment Outlook 2017*. Paris: OECD Publishing (2017).

Orwell, G., *Nineteen Eighty-Four*. London: Secker and Warburg (1949).

Papachristos, Andrew V., and Christopher Wildeman. "Network Exposure and Homicide Victimization in an African American Community." *American Journal of Public Health* 104, no. 1 (2014): 143–150.

Pepper, Ian, Colin Rogers, and Helen Martin. "Evidence Based Policing: A View on Its Development within the Police Service." *Journal of Work-Applied Management* (2020).

Perez, Caroline C., and Lauren Klein. "Is Bad Data Killing Women?." *The Conversation* [Podcast], BBC (2020).

Perry, Walt L. *Predictive Policing: The Role of Crime Forecasting in Law Enforcement Operations*. Rand Corporation (2013).

Phillips, Scott W. "Eyes Are Not Cameras: The Importance of Integrating Perceptual Distortions, Misinformation, and False Memories into the Police Body Camera Debate." *Policing: A Journal of Policy and Practice* 12, no. 1 (2018): 91–99.

Piquero, Alex R. "Disproportionate Minority Contact." The Future of Children (2008): 59–79.

Pontier, Matthijs, and Johan Hoorn. "Toward Machines That Behave Ethically Better Than Humans Do." In *Proceedings of the Annual Meeting of the Cognitive Science Society*, vol. 34, no. 34 (2012).

Porter, Glenn, Roberta Julian, and Sally F. Kelty. "Forensic Science as 'Risky Business': Identifying Key Risk Factors in the Forensic Process from Crime Scene to Court." *Journal of Criminological Research, Policy and Practice* (2015).

Punch, Maurice. *Police Corruption: Deviance, Accountability and Reform in Policing*. Routledge (2009).

Reiner, Robert. "Power to the People? A Social Democratic Critique of the Coalition Government's Police Reforms." *Accountability of Policing* (2016): 132–149.

Reiner, Robert. "The Dialectics of Dixon: The Changing Image of the TV Cop." In *Police Force, Police Service*, pp. 11–32. London: Palgrave (1994).

Reiner, Robert. *The Politics of the Police.* Oxford University Press (2010).

Reiss, Albert J. Jr. "Police Organization in the Twentieth Century." *Crime and Justice* 15 (1992): 51–97.

Ren, Ling, Liqun Cao, Nicholas Lovrich, and Michael Gaffney. "Linking Confidence in the Police with the Performance of the Police: Community Policing Can Make a Difference." *Journal of Criminal Justice* 33, no. 1 (2005): 55–66.

Robinson, William I. "Accumulation Crisis and Global Police State." *Critical Sociology* 45, no. 6 (2019): 845–858.

Robinson, William I. "The Next Economic Crisis: Digital Capitalism and Global Police State." *Race & Class* 60, no. 1 (2018): 77–92.

Rosenfeld, Richard, Robert Fornango, and Eric Baumer. "Did Ceasefire, Compstat, and Exile Reduce Homicide?." *Criminology & Public Policy* 4, no. 3 (2005): 419–449.

Ross, Karen. *Gendered Media: Women, Men, and Identity Politics*. Rowman & Littlefield (2009).

Saks, Michael J., and Jonathan J. Koehler. "The Coming Paradigm Shift in Forensic Identification Science." *Science* 309, no. 5736 (2005): 892–895.

Salter, Michael. "Toys for the boys? Drones, Pleasure and Popular Culture in the Militarisation of Policing." *Critical Criminology* 22, no. 2 (2014): 163–177.

Schulweis, Harold M. *Conscience: The Duty to Obey and the Duty to Disobey*. Jewish Lights Publishing (2010).

Sharkey, Noel. "The Ethical Frontiers of Robotics." *Science* 322, no. 5909 (2008): 1800–1801.

Shearing, Clifford, and Les Johnston. "Nodal Wars and Network Fallacies: A Genealogical Analysis of Global Insecurities." *Theoretical Criminology* 14, no. 4 (2010): 495–514.

Skogan, Wesley G. "Concern about Crime and Confidence in the Police: Reassurance or Accountability?." *Police Quarterly* 12, no. 3 (2009): 301–318.

Skogan, Wesley G. "The Police and Public Opinion in Britain." *American Behavioral Scientist* 39, no. 4 (1996): 421–432.

Skolnick, Jerome H., and James J. Fyfe. *Above the Law: Police and the Excessive Use of Force*. New York: Free Press (1993).

Solenov, Dmitry, Jay Brieler, and Jeffrey F. Scherrer. "The Potential of Quantum Computing and Machine Learning to Advance Clinical Research and Change the Practice of Medicine." *Missouri Medicine* 115, no. 5 (2018): 463.

Sousa, William H., Terance D. Miethe, and Mari Sakiyama. "Inconsistencies in Public Opinion of Body-Worn Cameras on Police: Transparency, Trust, and Improved Police–Citizen Relationships." *Policing: A Journal of Policy and Practice* 12, no. 1 (2018): 100–108.

Spratt, Brian G. "Multilocus Sequence Typing: Molecular Typing of Bacterial Pathogens in an Era of Rapid DNA Sequencing and the Internet." *Current Opinion in Microbiology* 2, no. 3 (1999): 312–316.

Squires, Peter. "Cops and Customers: Consumerism and the Demand for Police Services. Is the Customer Always Right?." *Policing and Society: An International Journal* 8, no. 2 (1998): 169–188.

Srnicek, Nick, and Alex Williams. *Inventing the Future: Postcapitalism and a World Without Work*. Verso Books (2015).

Stearns, Peter N. *American Fear: The Causes and Consequences of High Anxiety*. Routledge (2012).

Strom, Kevin. "Research on the Impact of Technology on Policing Strategy in the 21st Century, Final Report." Report, Department of Justice, September (2017).

Sulleyman, Aatif. "Durham Police to Use AI to Predict Future Crimes of Suspects, Despite Racial Bias Concerns." *The Independent* (2017).

Svensson, Lennart G. "New Professionalism, Trust and Competence: Some Conceptual Remarks and Empirical Data." *Current Sociology* 54, no. 4 (2006): 579–593.

Taylor, J. A., and Howard Williams. "Police Management, Office Automation and Organizational Change." *New Technology, Work and Employment*, 7/1 (1992): 44–53.

Thompson, William C. "Forensic DNA Evidence: The Myth of Infallibility." Essay. In *Genetic Explanations: Sense and Nonsense*, edited by Sheldon Krimsky and Jeremy Gruber. Cambridge, MA: Harvard University Press (2013).

Tilley, Nick, and Michael Townsley. "Forensic Science in UK Policing: Strategies, Tactics and Effectiveness." *Handbook of Forensic Science* (2009): 359–379.

Topak, Ozgun. "The Making of a Totalitarian Surveillance Machine: Surveillance in Turkey under AKP Rule." *Surveillance & Society* 15, no. 3/4 (2017): 535–542.

Turner, Jacob. *Robot Rules: Regulating Artificial Intelligence*. Springer (2018).

Valentine, Tim, and Josh P. Davis. *Forensic Facial Identification: Theory and Practice of Identification from Eyewitnesses, Composites and CCTV*. John Wiley & Sons (2015).

Walklate, Sandra. *Gender, Crime and Criminal Justice*. Routledge (2013).

Wall, David S. "Catching Cybercriminals: Policing the Internet." *International Review of Law, Computers & Technology* 12, no. 2 (1998): 201–218.

Williams, Hubert. "Core Factors of Police Corruption across the World." In *Forum on Crime and Society*, vol. 2, no. 1, pp. 85–99 (2002).

Wolf, Martin. "Enslave the Robots and Free the Poor." *Financial Times* 11 (2014): 7.

Wood, Dominic A. "Embedding Learning and Assessment within Police Practice: The Opportunities and Challenges Arising from the Introduction of the PEQF in England and Wales." *Policing: A Journal of Policy and Practice* 14, no. 2 (2020): 374–382.

Zedner, Lucia. "Pre-crime and Pre-punishment: A Health Warning: Lucia Zedner Calls for Restraint." *Criminal Justice Matters* 81, no. 1 (2010): 24–25.
Zou, James, and Londa Schiebinger. "Design AI so That It's Fair." *Nature* 559, no. 7714 (2018): 324–326.

NOTES

1. See Beck, Ulrich, Scott Lash, and Brian Wynne. *Risk Society: Towards a New Modernity.* Vol. 17. Sage (1992); Beck, Ulrich, Anthony Giddens, and Scott Lash. *Reflexive Modernization: Politics, Tradition and Aesthetics in the Modern Social Order.* Stanford University Press (1994).

2. Hudson, Barbara. *Justice in the Risk Society: Challenging and Re-affirming "Justice" in Late Modernity.* Sage (2003).

3. Fyfe, Nicholas R., J. B. Terpstra, and Pieter Tops. "Centralizing Forces? Comparative Perspectives on Contemporary Police Reform in Northern and Western Europe." (2013).

4. See Holdaway, Simon. "The Re-professionalization of the Police in England and Wales." *Criminology & Criminal Justice* 17, no. 5 (2017): 588–604; den Boer, Monica. "9 Intelligence-Led Policing in Europe." *The Future of Intelligence: Challenges in the 21st Century* (2014): 113

5. Hoogenboom, Bob. "The Governance of Policing and Security." In *The Governance of Policing and Security*, pp. 73–81. London: Palgrave Macmillan (2010).

6. See Cook, James, and Hannah Boland. "'Cummings' Plan to Create a UK Trillionaire Tech Giant Is Admirable—But Is It Realistic?" *The Telegraph* (2020); Featherstone, Mike, and Roger Burrows, eds. *Cyberspace/Cyberbodies/Cyberpunk: Cultures of Technological Embodiment*. Sage (1996).

7. Shearing, Clifford, and Les Johnston. "Nodal Wars and Network Fallacies: A Genealogical Analysis of Global Insecurities." *Theoretical Criminology* 14, no. 4 (2010): 495–514.

8. See Autor, David H., and David Dorn. "The Growth of Low-Skill Service Jobs and the Polarization of the US Labor Market." *American Economic Review* 103, no. 5 (2013): 1553–97; Acemoglu, Daron, and David Autor. "Skills, Tasks and Technologies: Implications for Employment and Earnings." In *Handbook of Labor Economics*, vol. 4 (2011): 1043–1171

9. Katz, Lawrence F., and Robert A. Margo. "Technical Change and the Relative Demand for Skilled Labor: The United States in Historical Perspective." In *Human Capital in History: The American Record*, pp. 15–57. University of Chicago Press (2014).

10. Spratt, Brian G. "Multilocus Sequence Typing: Molecular Typing of Bacterial Pathogens in an Era of Rapid DNA Sequencing and the Internet." *Current Opinion in Microbiology* 2, no. 3 (1999): 312–316; Mennell, Julie, and Ian Shaw. "The Future of Forensic and Crime Scene Science: Part I. A UK Forensic Science User and Provider Perspective." *Forensic Science International* 157 (2006): S7–S12.

11. See Home Office. "Market exploration: future policing." Defence and Security Accelerator, Defence Science and Technology Laboratory, and Home Office (2020); Feldstein, Steven. *The Global Expansion of AI Surveillance*. Vol. 17. Washington, DC: Carnegie Endowment for International Peace (2019); Lawless, Christopher James. "Policing Markets: The Contested Shaping of Neo-liberal Forensic Science." *The British Journal of Criminology* 51, no. 4 (2011): 671–689.

12. Clarke, John. "Citizen-Consumers and Public Service Reform: At the Limits of Neoliberalism?." *Policy Futures in Education* 5, no. 2 (2007): 239–248.

13. Mawby, Rob C. "Police Corporate Communications, Crime Reporting and the Shaping of Policing News." *Policing and Society* 20, no. 1 (2010): 124–139.

14. Evetts, Julia. "Introduction: Trust and Professionalism: Challenges and Occupational Changes." (2006): 515–531.

15. Svensson, Lennart G. "New Professionalism, Trust and Competence: Some Conceptual Remarks and Empirical Data." *Current Sociology* 54, no. 4 (2006): 579–593.

16. Giddens, Anthony. *The Consequences of Modernity*. Cambridge, UK: Polity. (1990).

17. Evetts, Julia. "The Construction of Professionalism in New and Existing Occupational Contexts: Promoting and Facilitating Occupational Change." *International Journal of Sociology and Social Policy* (2003).

18. Jackson, Jonathan, and Ben Bradford. "Crime, Policing and Social Order: On the Expressive Nature of Public Confidence in Policing." *British Journal of Sociology* 60, no. 3 (2009): 493–521.

19. Ren, Ling, Liqun Cao, Nicholas Lovrich, and Michael Gaffney. "Linking Confidence in the Police with the Performance of the Police: Community Policing Can Make a Difference." *Journal of Criminal Justice* 33, no. 1 (2005): 55–66.

20. Hough, Mike. "Researching Trust in the Police and Trust in Justice: A UK Perspective." *Policing and Society* 22, no. 3 (2012): 332–345.

21. IPSOS Mori. Two in Three Britons Say They Generally Trust the Police to Tell the Truth (2014).

22. Independent Police Complaints Commission. Public Confidence in the Police Complaints System (2014).

23. Home Affairs Committee. The Macpherson Report: Twenty-Two Years On (2021).

24. BMG Research Ltd. *Public Perceptions of Policing in England and Wales 2018*. Birmingham: BMG (2019).

25. Lynch, Michael, Simon A. Cole, Ruth McNally, and Kathleen Jordan. *Truth Machine: The Contentious History of DNA Fingerprinting*. University of Chicago Press (2010).

26. Home Office. "New Technology to Detect Knives in Public Places." (2019).

27. Ariel, Barak. "Police Body Cameras in Large Police Departments." *Journal of Criminal Law and Criminology* (2016): 729–768.

28. Pontier, Matthijs, and Johan Hoorn. "Toward Machines that Behave Ethically Better Than Humans Do." In Proceedings of the Annual Meeting of the Cognitive Science Society, vol. 34, no. 34 (2012).

29. Phillips, Scott W. "Eyes are Not Cameras: The Importance of Integrating Perceptual Distortions, Misinformation, and False Memories into the Police Body Camera Debate." *Policing: A Journal of Policy and Practice* 12, no. 1 (2018): 91–99.

30. Galloway, Robert A. "Quality Management in Police Services." *TQM Magazine* (1994).

31. Squires, Peter. "Cops and Customers: Consumerism and the Demand for Police Services. Is the Customer Always Right?." *Policing and Society: An International Journal* 8, no. 2 (1998): 169–188.

32. Lee, Murray, and Alyce McGovern. "Force to Sell: Policing the Image and Manufacturing Public Confidence." *Policing and Society* 23, no. 2 (2013): 103–124.

33. Hummer, Don, and James Byrne. "Technology, Innovation and Twenty-First-Century Policing." In *The Routledge Handbook of Technology, Crime and Justice*, pp. 375–389. Taylor and Francis 2017.

34. Sousa, William H., Terance D. Miethe, and Mari Sakiyama. "Inconsistencies in Public Opinion of Body-Worn Cameras on Police: Transparency, Trust, and Improved Police–Citizen Relationships." *Policing: A Journal of Policy and Practice* 12, no. 1 (2018): 100–108.

35. Bromberg, Daniel E., Étienne Charbonneau, and Andrew Smith. "Public Support for Facial Recognition via Police Body-Worn Cameras: Findings from a List Experiment." *Government Information Quarterly* 37, no. 1 (2020): 101415.

36. Skogan, Wesley G. "The Police and Public Opinion in Britain." *American Behavioral Scientist* 39, no. 4 (1996): 421–432.

37. Daugherty, Paul R., and H. James Wilson. *Human+ Machine: Reimagining Work in the Age of AI*. Harvard Business Press (2018).

38. Mokyr, Joel. *The Lever of Riches: Technological Creativity and Economic Progress*. Oxford University Press (1992).

39. Taylor, J. A., and Howard Williams. "Police Management, Office Automation and Organizational Change." *New Technology, Work and Employment*, 7/1 (1992): 44–53.

40. Ericson, Richard V., and Clifford D. Shearing. "The Scientification of Police Work." In *The Knowledge Society*, pp. 129–159. Dordrecht: Springer (1986).

41. Tilley, Nick, and Michael Townsley. "Forensic Science in UK Policing: Strategies, Tactics and Effectiveness." *Handbook of Forensic Science* (2009): 359–379.

42. Barry, Andrew. *Political Machines: Governing a Technological Society*. A&C Black (2001).

43. Johnson, Derek, Erin Faulkner, Georgia Meredith, and Tim J. Wilson. "Police Functional Adaptation to the Digital or Post Digital Age: Discussions with Cybercrime Experts." *Journal of Criminal Law* 84, no. 5 (2020): 427–450.

44. Wall, David S. "Catching Cybercriminals: Policing the Internet." *International Review of Law, Computers & Technology* 12, no. 2 (1998): 201–218.

45. Loftus, Bethan. Police culture in a changing world. Oxford University Press, USA, (2009).

46. Goold, Benjamin J. CCTV and Policing: Public Area Surveillance and Police Practices in Britain. Oxford University Press on Demand (2004).

47. Grace, Katja, John Salvatier, Allan Dafoe, Baobao Zhang, and Owain Evans. "When Will AI Exceed Human Performance? Evidence from AI Experts." *Journal of Artificial Intelligence Research* 62 (2018): 729–754.

48. Levesley, Tom, Amanda Martin, and G. Britain. Police Attitudes to and Use of CCTV. London: Home Office (2005).

49. Davis, Josh P., Charlotte Forrest, Felicia Treml, and Ashok Jansari. "Identification from CCTV: Assessing Police Super□Recognizer Ability to Spot Faces in a Crowd and Susceptibility to Change Blindness." *Applied Cognitive Psychology* 32, no. 3 (2018): 337–353.

50. Turner, Jacob. *Robot Rules: Regulating Artificial Intelligence*. Springer (2018).

51. See, Jawad, Rana. "Coronavirus: Tunisia Deploys Police Robot on Lockdown Patrol." *BBC News* 3 (2020); British Broadcasting Corporation "Robot Police Officer Goes on Duty in Dubai" (2017).

52. Coglianese, Cary, and David Lehr. "Regulating by Robot: Administrative Decision Making in the Machine-Learning Era." *Georgetown Law Journal* 105 (2016): 1147.

53. See Findley, Keith A. "Innocents at Risk: Adversary Imbalance, Forensic Science, and the Search for Truth." *Seton Hall Law Review 38 (2008): 893, Gardner, Ross M., and Donna Krouskup. Practical Crime Scene Processing and Investigation.* CRC Press (2018).

54. Christensen, Angi M., Christian M. Crowder, Stephen D. Ousley, and Max M. Houck. "Error and Its Meaning in Forensic Science." *Journal of Forensic Sciences* 59, no. 1 (2014): 123–126.

55. Dutelle, Aric W. "Fingerprint Evidence." An Introduction to Crime Scene Investigation. Burlington, VT: Jones and Bartlett Learning (2014): 169–202.

56. Julian, Roberta D., Sally F. Kelty, Claude Roux, Peter Woodman, James Robertson, Anna Davey, Robert Hayes et al. "What Is the Value of Forensic Science? An Overview of the Effectiveness of Forensic Science in the Australian Criminal Justice System Project." *Australian Journal of Forensic Sciences* 43, no. 4 (2011): 217–229.

57. Porter, Glenn, Roberta Julian, and Sally F. Kelty. "Forensic Science as 'Risky Business': Identifying Key Risk Factors in the Forensic Process from Crime Scene to Court." *Journal of Criminological Research, Policy and Practice* (2015).

58. National Academy of Sciences. Strengthening Forensic Science in the United States: A Path Forward, Washington, DC: National Academies Press (2009).

59. See, Skogan, Wesley G. "Concern about Crime and Confidence in the Police: Reassurance or Accountability?" *Police Quarterly* 12, no. 3 (2009): 301–318; Jang, Hyunseok, Hee-Jong Joo, and Jihong Solomon Zhao. "Determinants of Public Confidence in Police: An International Perspective." *Journal of Criminal Justice* 38, no. 1 (2010): 57–68.

60. Lefèvre, Thomas. "Big Data in Forensic Science and Medicine." (2018): 1–6.

61. Saks, Michael J., and Jonathan J. Koehler. "The Coming Paradigm Shift in Forensic Identification Science." *Science* 309, no. 5736 (2005): 892–895.

62. Braithwaite, John. "Restorative Justice: Assessing Optimistic and Pessimistic Accounts." *Crime and Justice* 25 (1999): 1–127.

63. Lebron, Christopher J. *The Making of Black Lives Matter: A Brief History of an Idea*. Oxford University Press (2017).

64. Carney, Nikita. "All Lives Matter, but so Does Race: Black Lives Matter and the Evolving Role of Social Media." *Humanity & Society* 40, no. 2 (2016): 180–199.

65. Klockars, Carl B., Sanja Kutnjak Ivkovic, and Maria R. Haberfeld. *The Contours of Police Integrity*. Sage (2003).

66. Johnson, Roberta Ann. "Whistleblowing and the Police." *Rutgers JL & Urb. Pol'y* 3 (2006): 74.

67. Skolnick, Jerome H., and James J. Fyfe. *Above the Law: Police and the Excessive Use of Force*. New York: Free Press (1993).

68. Bowling, Ben, and Coretta Phillips. "Disproportionate and Discriminatory: Reviewing the Evidence on Police Stop and Search." *Modern Law Review* 70, no. 6 (2007): 936–961.

69. Williams, Hubert. "Core Factors of Police Corruption across the World." In *Forum on Crime and Society*, vol. 2, no. 1, pp. 85–99 (2002).

70. Carter, David L. "Drug-Related Corruption of Police Officers: A Contemporary Typology." *Journal of Criminal Justice* 18, no. 2 (1990): 85–98.

71. Punch, Maurice. *Police Corruption: Deviance, Accountability and Reform in Policing.* Routledge (2009).

72. Eubanks, Virginia. *Automating Inequality: How High-Tech Tools Profile, Police, and Punish the Poor*. St. Martin's Press (2018).

73. See, Robinson, William I. "The Next Economic Crisis: Digital Capitalism and Global Police State." *Race & Class* 60, no. 1 (2018): 77–92; Robinson, William I. "Accumulation Crisis and Global Police State." *Critical Sociology* 45, no. 6 (2019): 845–858.

74. Frey, Carl Benedikt, and Michael A. Osborne. "The Future of Employment: How Susceptible are Jobs to Computerisation?." *Technological Forecasting and Social Change* 114 (2017): 254–280.

75. McKinsey Global Institute. *Jobs Lost, Jobs Gained: Workforce Transitions in A Time of Automation* (2017).

76. Organisation for Economic Co-operation and Development. "How Technology and Globalisation Are Transforming the Labour Market." In *OECD Employment Outlook 2017*. Paris: OECD Publishing (2017).

77. Wolf, Martin. "Enslave the robots and free the poor." *Financial Times* 11 (2014): 7.

78. Holzer, Harry J., and Robert I. Lerman. The Future of Middle-Skill Jobs. Vol. 41. Brookings, Center on Children and Families (2009).

79. Valentine, Tim, and Josh P. Davis. *Forensic Facial Identification: Theory and Practice of Identification from Eyewitnesses, Composites and CCTV*. John Wiley & Sons (2015).

80. Sharkey, Noel. "The Ethical Frontiers of Robotics." *Science* 322, no. 5909 (2008): 1800–1801.

81. Mathieson, S. A. "CCTV Cameras Have Led Police to Lose Their Focus." *Guardian* (2011).

82. Levesley, Tom, Amanda Martin, and G. Britain. Police Attitudes to and Use of CCTV.London: Home Office (2005).

83. Srnicek, Nick, and Alex Williams. *Inventing the Future: Postcapitalism and a World without Work.* Verso Books (2015).

84. Reiner, Robert. "Power to the People? A Social Democratic Critique of the Coalition Government's Police Reforms." *Accountability of Policing* (2016): 132–149.

85. Millie, Andrew. "What Are the Police For? Re-thinking Policing Post-austerity." In *The Future of Policing*, pp. 82–93. Routledge (2013).

86. Her Majesty's Inspectorate of Constabulary. Policing in Austerity: Meeting the Challenge. London: Her Majesty's Inspectorate of Constabulary and Fire and Rescue Services (2014).

87. Home Office. "Home Office Announces First wave of 20,000 Police Officer Uplift" (2019).

88. See, Office of National Statistics. "Crime in England and Wales: Year Ending June 2018" (2018); Office of National Statistics. "Crime in England and Wales: Year Ending March 2020" (2020).

89. Lumsden, Karen, and Alex Black. "Austerity Policing, Emotional Labour and the Boundaries of Police Work: An Ethnography of a Police Force Control Room in England." *British Journal of Criminology* 58, no. 3 (2018): 606–623.

90. Holdaway, Simon. "The Re-professionalization of the Police in England and Wales." *Criminology & Criminal Justice* 17, no. 5 (2017): 588–604.

91. Wood, Dominic A. "Embedding Learning and Assessment within Police Practice: the Opportunities and Challenges Arising from the Introduction of the PEQF in England and Wales." *Policing: A Journal of Policy and Practice* 14, no. 2 (2020): 374–382.

92. Pepper, Ian, Colin Rogers, and Helen Martin. "Evidence Based Policing: A View on Its Development within the Police Service." *Journal of Work-Applied Management* (2020).

93. Hoggett, James, and Cli□ord Stott. "Post G20: The Challenge of Change, Implementing Evidence-Based Public Order Policing." *Crowds in the 21st Century* (2015): 64–74.

94. See Hough, Mike, B. Stanko, W. Agnew-Pauley, J. Belur, J. Brown, David Gamblin, Gillian Hunter et al. "Developing an Evidence Based Police Degree-Holder Entry Programme." (2018); Stearns, Peter N. *American Fear: The Causes and Consequences of High Anxiety*. Routledge (2012).

95. Chan, Janet. "Changing Police Culture." *British Journal of Criminology* 36, no. 1 (1996): 109–134.

96. Reiner, Robert. *The Politics of the Police*. Oxford University Press (2010).

97. Reiss Jr, Albert J. "Police Organization in the Twentieth Century." *Crime and Justice* 15 (1992): 51–97.

98. Chan, Janet B. L. *Changing Police Culture: Policing in a Multicultural Society*. Cambridge University Press (1997).

99. Eubanks, Virginia. *Automating Inequality: How High-Tech Tools Profile, Police, and Punish the Poor.* St. Martin's Press (2018).

100. Cascriani, Dominic. "Covid: Police Watchdog Says Officers Confused by Unclear Pandemic Laws." *BBC* (2021).

101. British Broadcasting Corporation. "Met Police Technology 'Ineffective and Outdated," Report Claims' (2013).

102. Chan, Janet B. L. "The Technological Game: How Information Technology Is Transforming Police Practice." *Criminal Justice* 1, no. 2 (2001): 139–159.

103. Cockcroft, Tom. *Police Culture: Themes and Concepts*. Routledge (2012).

104. Koper, Christopher S., Cynthia Lum, James J. Willis, Dan J. Woods, and Julie Hibdon. "Realizing the Potential of Technology in Policing: A Multi-site Study of The Social, Organizational, and Behavioral Aspects of Implementing Policing Technologies." In Report to the National Institute of Justice, US Department of Justice. Fairfax, VA: Center for Evidence-Based Crime Policy, George Mason University and Police Executive Research Forum. (2015).

105. See Lindsay, Rachael, Thomas W. Jackson, and Louize Cooke. "Empirical evaluation of a technology acceptance model for mobile policing." *Police Practice and Research* 15, no. 5 (2014): 419–436; Chan, Janet, David Brereton, Margot Legosz, and Sally Doran. "E-policing: The Impact of Information Technology on Police Practices." Brisbane: Criminal Justice Commission (2001).

106. Strom, Kevin. "Research on the Impact of Technology on Policing Strategy in the 21st Century, Final Report." Report, Department of Justice, September (2017).

107. Lynch et al. (2010), 30; Thompson, William C. "Forensic DNA Evidence: The Myth of Infallibility." Essay. In *Genetic Explanations: Sense and Nonsense*, edited by Sheldon Krimsky and Jeremy Gruber. Cambridge, MA: Harvard University Press (2013).

108. Helbing, Dirk, Bruno S. Frey, Gerd Gigerenzer, Ernst Hafen, Michael Hagner, Yvonne Hofstetter, Jeroen Van Den Hoven, Roberto V. Zicari, and Andrej Zwitter. "Will Democracy Survive Big Data and Artificial Intelligence?." In *Towards Digital Enlightenment*, pp. 73–98. Springer, Cham (2019).

109. Oliveira, Arlindo L. "Biotechnology, Big Data and Artificial Intelligence." *Biotechnology Journal* 14, no. 8 (2019): 1800613.

110. O'Neil, Cathy. *Weapons of Math Destruction: How Big Data Increases Inequality and Threatens Democracy*. Crown (2016).

111. Berk, Richard A. "Artificial Intelligence, Predictive Policing, and Risk Assessment for Law Enforcement." *Annual Review of Criminology* 4 (2020).

112. Coleman, Roy, and Michael McCahill. *Surveillance and Crime*. Sage (2010).

113. Rosenfeld, Richard, Robert Fornango, and Eric Baumer. "Did Ceasefire, Compstat, and Exile Reduce Homicide?." *Criminology & Public Policy* 4, no. 3 (2005): 419–449.

114. Papachristos, Andrew V., and Christopher Wildeman. "Network Exposure and Homicide Victimization in an African American Community." *American Journal of Public Health* 104, no. 1 (2014): 143–150.

115. Ferguson, Andrew G. "The Exclusionary Rule in the Age of Blue Data." *Vanderbilt Law Review 72 (2019): 561.*

116. Brayne, Sarah. "Big Data Surveillance: The Case of Policing." *American Sociological Review* 82, no. 5 (2017): 977–1008.

117. Reiner, Robert. "The Dialectics of Dixon: The Changing Image of the TV Cop." In *Police Force, Police Service*, pp. 11–32. London: Palgrave (1994).

118. Clancy, Anna, Mike Hough, Rebbecca Aust, and Chris Kershaw. *Crime, Policing and Justice: The Experience of Ethnic Minorities*. London, England: Home Office Research Development and Statistics Directorate (2001); Piquero, Alex R. "Disproportionate Minority Contact." The Future of Children (2008): 59–79.

119. Knox, Dean, Will Lowe, and Jonathan Mummolo. "Administrative records Mask Racially Biased Policing." *American Political Science Review* 114, no. 3 (2020): 619–637.

120. Zou, James, and Londa Schiebinger. "Design AI So That It's Fair." *Nature* 559, no. 7714 (2018): 324–326.

121. Ross, Karen. *Gendered Media: Women, Men, and Identity Politics*. Rowman & Littlefield (2009); Walklate, Sandra. *Gender, Crime and Criminal Justice*. Routledge (2013).

122. Perez, Caroline C., and Lauren Klein. "Is Bad Data Killing Women?" *The Conversation* [Podcast], BBC (2020).

123. Dick, Philip K. *The Philip K. Dick Reader*. Citadel Press (1997).

124. Zedner, Lucia. "Pre-crime and Pre-punishment: A Health Warning: Lucia Zedner Calls for Restraint." *Criminal Justice Matters* 81, no. 1 (2010): 24–25.

125. McGrory, Kathleen and Neil Bedi. "Targeted." *Tampa Bay Times* (2020).

126. McGrory, Kathleen and Neil Bedi. "Read the Pasco Sheriff's Office Response to our Investigation." *Tampa Bay Times* (2020).

127. Dearden, Lizzie. "Police Testing Technology to 'Assess the Risk of Someone Committing a Crime' in UK." *Independent* (2019).

128. Sulleyman, Aatif. "Durham Police to Use AI to Predict Future Crimes of Suspects, Despite Racial Bias Concerns." *Independent* (2017).

129. Giroux, Henry A. "Totalitarian Paranoia in the Post-Orwellian Surveillance State." *Cultural Studies* 29, no. 2 (2015): 108–140.

130. Salter, Michael. "Toys for the Boys? Drones, Pleasure and Popular Culture in the Militarisation of Policing." *Critical Criminology* 22, no. 2 (2014): 163–177.

131. Linke, Uli. "Fortress Europe: Globalization, Militarization and the Policing of Interior Borderlands." *TOPIA: Canadian Journal of Cultural Studies* 23 (2010): 100–120.

132. Haggerty, Kevin D., and Richard V. Ericson. "The Surveillant Assemblage." *British Journal of Sociology* 51, no. 4 (2000): 605–622; Lyon, David. *Surveillance after September 11*. Vol. 11. Polity (2003).

133. Nadler, Anthony, Matthew Crain, and Joan Donovan. "Weaponizing the Digital Influence Machine." *Data & Society* (2018).

134. Feldman, Leonard. "Neoliberalism and Police Reform." In *Rethinking Neoliberalism: Resisting the Disciplinary Regime*, edited by Marianna Pavlovskaya and Sanford Schram. New York: Routledge (2018).

135. Schulweis, Harold M. *Conscience: The Duty to Obey and the Duty to Disobey*. Jewish Lights Publishing (2010); McDermott, Drew. "What Matters to a Machine." *Machine Ethics* (2011): 88–114.

136. Topak, Ozgun. "The Making of a Totalitarian Surveillance Machine: Surveillance in Turkey under AKP rule." *Surveillance & Society* 15, no. 3/4 (2017): 535–542.

137. Giroux (2015), 146.

138. Orwell, G., *Nineteen Eighty-Four*. London: Secker and Warburg (1949).

139. Freeman, Daniel, Felicity Waite, Laina Rosebrock, Ariane Petit, Chiara Causier, Anna East, Lucy Jenner et al. "Coronavirus Conspiracy Beliefs, Mistrust, and Compliance with Government Guidelines in England." *Psychological Medicine* (2020): 1–13; Martin, Aaron K., Rosamunde E. Van Brakel, and Daniel J. Bernhard. "Understanding Resistance to Digital Surveillance: Towards a Multi-disciplinary, Multi-actor Framework." *Surveillance & Society* 6, no. 3 (2009): 213–232.

140. Heilbroner, Robert L. "Do Machines Make History?." *Technology and Culture* 8, no. 3 (1967): 335–345; Fischer, Claude S. *America Calling: A Social History of the Telephone to 1940*. University of California Press (1992).

141. Solenov, Dmitry, Jay Brieler, and Jeffrey F. Scherrer. "The Potential of Quantum Computing and Machine Learning to Advance Clinical Research and Change the Practice of Medicine." *Missouri Medicine* 115, no. 5 (2018): 463.

142. Asaro, Peter M. "AI Ethics in Predictive Policing: From Models of Threat to an Ethics of Care." *IEEE Technology and Society Magazine* 38, no. 2 (2019): 40–53.

143. Perry, Walt L. *Predictive Policing: The Role of Crime Forecasting in Law Enforcement Operations*. Rand Corporation (2013).

Chapter 6

Artificial Intelligence and the Use of Algorithms in the Criminal Judicial System: Chimera or Panacea?

Raquel Borges Blázquez

ARTIFICIAL INTELLIGENCE AND 21ST-CENTURY SOCIETY: FROM UTOPIA TO DYSTOPIA

Artificial Intelligence (AI) is a field of work that includes professionals from diverse disciplines: mathemathicians, engineers, philosophers, jurists, etc. Among all these fields we are mainly interested in Artificial Intelligence and criminal justice. The use of AI in Criminal justice will have to maintain the principles and fundaments of criminal law intervention within the limits set by constitutions and respecting fundamental rights.[1] Criminal procedural legislation will be called upon to set the conditions for its use in the courts.[2] This task will be shared with administrative science when talking about police actions outside the investigation of a crime. It is precisely this holistic nature that makes the analysis and determination of the best conditions for its use to be at risk of staying in no man's land.[3]

What Is Artificial Intelligence and Why Does It Matter?

We use the term "AI" to refer to those systems that show us an "intelligent" behavior. These systems are capable of analyzing their environment and making decisions with a certain degree of autonomy to achieve specific objectives. These systems can be simple software (voice assistants, image analysis programs, search engines, and recognition systems among others), or AI that can be incorporated into hardware devices (drones, autonomous cars, the internet of things).[4]

Nowadays AI is a part of our lives. We use it on a daily basis without even realizing it. We live in a society based, designed and structured from and with technology. In our society social media, the cloud, IoT, big data, machine learning, deep learning, etc. drive us to an intelligent world. A world with a movable and mundial internet that changes our way of living, working, and interacting with each other.[5] We use AI the moment our e-mail account blocks an e-mail that it considers spam, when we translate a text, when whe use GPS apps to decide the best route to our destination. Lots of these technologies require huge amounts of data to improve their performance. For example, a GPS system that predicts a traffic jam in real time. In theory, AI can offer us more concrete predictions than a human decision-making process as AI will ignore subjective elements. However, we forget about the fact that humans are the ones that programmed the machine and humans can include biased data in it. A German artist managed to trick Google Maps and made it believe that there was a traffic jam in secondary streets of Berlin when there were actually only a few cars parked. He did this with a simple trick: riding around in a wheelbarrow carrying 99 mobile phones. Upon receiving this information, the algorithm modified the route of the rest of the cars, sending them to different routes in order to avoid passing through those streets. Google Maps makes virtual changes on the real city as the German artist explained on his Twitter account.[6]

Artificial Intelligence: Reality vs. Fiction

When we think of AI we imagine a robot that ignores its programming to rebel itself against humanity and cause harm to people. Science fiction has contributed to this. The moment an AI acquires its own intelligence is the moment in which it decides in its cold calculations that the best thing that can happen to the Earth is humanity disappearing. This is precisely the argument of the 1984 film *Terminator*. Talking about AI makes us think about robotics even though it is a different discipline with different origins that converge in the present and probably in the future.[7]

The term "AI" is a mixture of euphemism and desideratum. Firstly, it is a euphemism because the correct definition would really be a system for the automatic processing and analysis of information. Secondly, it is a desideratum because behind those systems there is a will to make them intelligent and to make them capable of having or imitating the cognitive processes of human beings.[8] Even though some scholars defend that in the near future it will be possible to elaborate artificial systems that are capable of assimilating all human mental processes or creating different ones, the reality is that they are simply mathematical models and the only similarity with human intelligence is their capacity for calculation. The machines are not capable of interpreting complex concepts and/or introducing new variables. They make decisions based on a basic logical premise that was previously introduced or considered by a human being. Today, the idea of consciousness through which systems will be able to learn autonomously from the environment and adapt to it is a utopian reality.[9]

Virtual Space as a Mirror of Physical Space

Today we live immersed in cyberspace. We buy from Amazon through our computer, tablet, or mobile phone. We communicate with our loved ones using instant messaging platforms like WhatsApp. Owing to COVID-19, we have been confined to our homes, and our way to keep in touch with our friends and family has been via video calls. The applications providing us with that opportunity have multiplied themselves: Skype, FaceTime, Zoom, Hangouts, Microsoft Teams, Jitsi Meet. Nowadays, everything moves with data. For centuries, the currency of exchange was money, but nowadays data is the instrument that moves society.[10]

We dissociate the internet as the virtual space and the physical world as the tangible and real space, but we forget that the virtual world is increasingly present in our lives. This has led to the emergence of new crimes associated with the technological field (such as sexting) or to others acquiring more force and vileness (such as cyberbullying).[11] Virtual space is only a reflection of physical space. Discriminated groups aregoing to more harshly suffer the consequences of digitalization. In recent years, we have witnessed women committing suicide because their ex-partners viralized sex tapes without their consent.[12] We have heard the testimonies of minors who wish they were dead because bullying continues when they leave school.[13] Cyberspace magnifies the offenses and makes them last forever. Here, words are not carried off by the wind but rather stay feeding the Big Data.[14] The analysis of the massive data we use is not neutral. The Big Data is the reality of the 21st century. Through the use of Big Data, the world that is offered is a world of prediction including the predictability of many vital components. Data is the eye that sees all the world and that causes the world to move.[15] Microsoft had to disconnect a robot because it turned out to be sexist, racist, misogynist, and it even began to defend Adolf Hitler.[16] This situation makes us rethink about AI and its goodness or badness. However, AI is neither good nor bad in itself. AI is not even intelligent, if we understand intelligence from a hominid perspective. AI feeds on the data we offer it and its actions reflect ours: our way of thinking, feeling, and acting.

Advances in the ICTs (information and communication technologies) not only have improved crime prevention and investigation in traditional or "physical" crime, but also have generated new opportunities to commit crimes in cyberspace. Security agencies are thus responding to the needs for prediction and prevention of cybercrime. Although traditionally the focus was on detecting vulnerabilities in digital infrastructures that could lead to intrusions and threats, in recent decades police AI has become increasingly sophisticated, flexible, adaptable, and robust. It is capable of detecting and preventing a wide variety of threats and making intelligent decisions in real time. In contrast to the previous interest in predicting and preventing more technical cybercrime there is now a growing interest in the human factor of cybercrime and cybersecurity. International cross-border police concern about the role of social networks in radicalization processes brings with it the need to develop tools capable of automated analysis of large amounts of data from digital platforms that are useful in the investigation, prediction, and prevention of these forms of crime.[17]

The fourth industrial revolution has not only enabled the positive progress of criminal justice but it has also incorporated harmful consequences that are arising from the use of AI. Delimitation of territorial spaces has been broken up and therefore crime transcends borders. States have shown their lack of capacity to fight these crimes because the prosecution of these types of infractions requires them to adapt to a virtual reality. As a reaction to these infractions, we have witnessed the evolution of machines at the service of criminal investigation that involves the use of AI in unthinkable realities. It is argued that facial recognition technology will give us more security even though it is ignoring the fact that it brings us closer to the Orwellian scenario of a society under the control of a not very well known "who or what."[18] A society where you do not know how often you can be watched in order to achieve a common interest: security.[19]

Bias In, Bias Out

Algorithms reproduce our prejudices. We cannot assume that numbers are impartial. Numbers have been fed with biased data due to our way of seeing reality through centuries of history. If we want to use AI in the criminal system we have to be aware that no risk management tool will be able to reverse and change centuries of racial injustice and gender inequality. AI is a desideratum and it is not intelligent. AI only makes calculations and forecasts with the data we offer it. In the criminal system this data is going to involve gender, race, and class bias.[20]

How Do Algorithms Work in Practice?

Algorithms are a series of mathematical equations that are interwoven to provide us with a result. Their purpose is not to certify the veracity of a hypothesis but to look for determinist correlations between some specific data and other data. The algorithm uses a large database arranged in an understandable way (smart data). A mathematical model will use these data later in a random way to establish patterns of correlation between different data that will allow us to make accurate assessments. There are more advanced algorithms: learning algorithms. These algorithms are more effective in anticipating behavior but they bring with them a problem that is difficult to solve: their operations at a certain point of inclusion of data and variables are incomprehensible to the human mind. We are unable to recognize the patterns the machine has made to reach a conclusion.[21] If we were able to recognize them it would take months, weeks, or even years to explain some of its decisions. This makes it difficult to legitimize the decisions that are made.[22]

This is precisely where dystopia begins. If the human loses control over the machine how are we going to get an explanation of why the machine has produced a certain result? These algorithms predict but do not explain. They are capable of reorganizing their own variables and they can find relationships between the final result to be measured (the veracity of the statement of a witness or a defendant) and data such as age, gender, nationality, religious beliefs, ideological, etc. They can even use data without it being requested, and this is what is called the bias of algorithms.[23]

A Practical Example: *State of Wisconsin v. Eric L. Loomis*

Predictive algorithms assist the judge in making judicial decisions. These mechanisms do not lack controversy. Their use can affect and even violate several fundamental rights such as the right to a fair trial, the prohibition of discrimination, privacy, freedom of expression, and the right to an effective remedy.[24] We can place the turning point on July 13, 2016, with the appeal decided by the Wisconsin State Supreme Court of Appeals.[25] The *Loomis* case and the use of the COMPAS system (Correctional Offender Management Profiling for Alternative Sanctions) is the best known and paradigmatic example of the use of AI in the judicial system. COMPAS is an AI system created by the Northpoint Company, which works using a non-public algorithm that is protected by intellectual property law and therefore hidden from public scrutiny. COMPAS combines data of different kinds in its analysis to assess the risk that a person has to commit an offence in various scenarios: 1) when the defendant is being tried and the judge/court has to decide whether to issue a pretrial detention or provisional freedom and 2) the moment the court has to determine which one is going to be the specific punishment to a convicted person (prison, protection measures, release on bail).[26] Regarding this, its creators were against the system being used in the courts but in practice more American judges are using it.[27]

If we want to make use of algorithms in the criminal justice system, we must ask ourselves the level of transparency that the result of the algorithm has, how it has handled the data and what value it has given to each variable. COMPAS is a software that assesses the risk of recidivism of a defendant and then advises judges on the type of penalty and the years to be imposed. This mathematical program was developed by a private company and it is totally opaque.[28] This application owes its fame to the *Wisconsin Supreme Court State v. Loomis*.[29]

Eric Loomis was charged with five felonies for his alleged involvement in a drive-by shooting. In total, he was charged with two counts of firearms possesion, one count of attempted escape in front of a traffic officer, endangering public safety, and driving a vehicle belonging to another person without authorization. Loomis denied participating in the shooting but admitted to driving someone else's vehicle without authorization and reached an agreement with the prosecution to accept the latter two charges. The judge accepted the agreement and considered the subject's risk assessment with the COMPAS tool to determine the sentence. COMPAS indicated that Eric Loomis presented a high risk of recidivism. Loomis was sentenced to six years in prison and five years of postconviction supervision. The possibility of suspending the sentence was excluded because of the seriousness of the crime, Loomis' record of judicial supervision, and because the risk-assessment tools applied to his case resulted in him being classified in the group with extremely high risk of recidivism.[30]

Loomis asked the court to review the sentence arguing among other reasons that the COMPAS result violated his right to a fair trial. The court did not change the sentence and explained that the COMPAS risk-assessment system only served to corroborate the conclusions that they had previously reached. The penalty would therefore have been the same regardless of whether or not the COMPAS system was used. Loomis appealed to the supreme court of Wisconsin claiming that the use of COMPAS for sentencing violated his right to a due process. He based his claim on three reasons: 1) He had not been convicted on the basis of reliable and accurate information. The commercial secrecy of the algorithm with which COMPAS works prevented him from knowing how the risk estimations were calculated. Without knowledge of them his right of defense was violated. 2) His right to obtain an individualized judgment was infringed. His judgment took into account data from past cases included in the algorithm. In summary, he claimed that the algorithm was studying the past in order to predict the future. 3) Finally, he claimed, his gender was improperly considered in order to determine his sentence.

None of these grounds for appeal were allowed. However, the importance of the case lies in the fact that the supreme court established some limitations on how and for what purpose risk assessment tools can be used in the sentencing phase.[31] The supreme court saw no violation of the right to information because it understood that company secrecy is essential to business. Loomis had access to both the results and the information used to calculate them. This information was objective data based upon the defendant's criminal history. The supreme court did not see a breach of the right to individualized sentencing because the sentence was not based solely on the results of COMPAS. It also considered that there was not a misuse of his gender. Both the prosecution and the defense accepted during the trial that all available scientific evidence indicated that men have higher rates of recidivism and violent crime than women.[32] Therefore, disregarding the gender factor would significantly diminish the accuracy of the estimations, which would increase the error rates for both men and women.[33] Moreover, there is no evidence that these recidivism rates are more detrimental to men than to women. Due to the fact that males have a higher risk of violent recidivism than females, the same raw score can be found in the low deciles of the male risk scale and conversely in the high deciles of the female risk scale.[34]

Despite this, the court imposed precautions that should be considered by American judges using risk assessment systems. Risk assessment tools cannot be used to decide the subject's imprisonment or to determine the severity of the sentence. Accordingly, they can only be used to (1) impose alternative measures to prison on low-risk offenders, (2) assess whether an offender can be effectively and safely supervised in the community, and (3) determine terms and conditions of a suspended sentence and probation as well as the consequences of their violation. Furthermore, they cannot be the determining element in deciding whether or not the subject evades a prison sentence.[35] The courts must also base themselves on other factors that they have considered and explain them in their sentence.

Following this case, the admissibility of the algorithms in the United States is consolidated. Several American courts have expressed a growing willingness to make use of AI tools to improve the functioning of justice. The use of AI in the criminal process expresses mixed feelings. Will AI help us to reinforce the criminal justice process or will it help us to liquidate it?[36] On the one hand, we have to accept that some of its applications can be very useful to cover multiple deficiencies that nowadays the judicial system has to face because of its lack of the appropriate tools. On the other hand, their use can imply violations of fundamental rights.[37]

After the Loomis case, ProPublica produced a report with the following title: "*Machine Bias. There's software used across the country to predict future criminals. And it's biased against blacks.*"[38] This report analyzed the reliability of the COMPAS predictions and questioned the fairness of a system that seemed to systematically discriminate against one group of the population.[39] This report contains several cases in which the algorithm gave a higher risk score for recidivism to black people than to white people. Therefore, Loomis' case is far from being an isolated case and rather seems to be a repeating pattern. The reason is probably that the data available to the machine shows a biased reality. It is impossible to predict the crime because there is a lack of data. We do not know all the crimes that had happened and therefore the data is biased. As computer scientists should say: bias in, bias out.[40]

With a score of 10 being very high risk and a score of 1 being nonexistent risk, we can see how the percentage of black defendants along the risk scale is distributed equally among the ten different groups. In contrast, the vast majority of white defendants are grouped in the very low risk with smaller groups in the higher risk groups. However, we have to avoid the pessimistic reading and learn from the past in order to be able to correct the algorithm. The facts of the past will be repeated in the future without intervention. Predictive analysis is a mirror of the past that is projected into the future. Predicting the future under the status quo conditions is simply projecting history forward. Due to the nature of prediction, a past with inequalities will project an unequal future. To be more specific, if we predict (based on

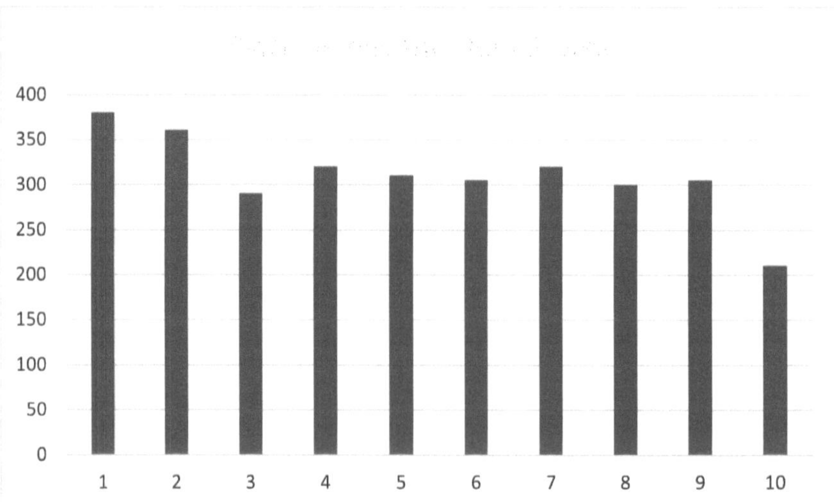

Figure 6.1. Black defendants risk score.

Source: Machine Bias. ProPublica (https://www.propublica.org/article/machine-bias-risk-assessments-in-criminal-sentencing).

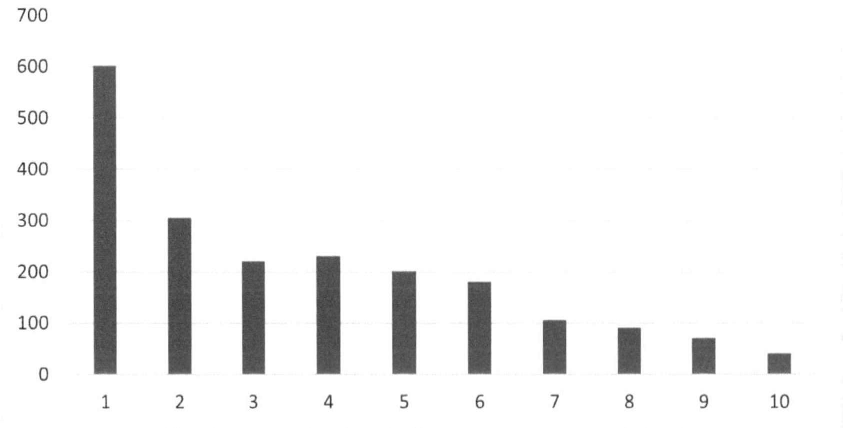

Figure 6.2. White defendants risk score.
Source: Machine Bias. ProPublica (https://www.propublica.org/article/machine-bias-risk-assessments-in-criminal-sentencing).

previous data) that arrest happens more often to black people than white people, the predictive analysis will always project that it will happen more often to black people than to white people in the future. The predicted event (the objective variable) is the key to the racial disparity in prediction.[41]

ALGORITHM SYSTEMS FOR RISK ASSESSMENT

Advances in empirical science mean that theories such as Lombroso's are gaining strength and that dystopian situations like the ones that we can read in *Minority Report* can be predicted with algorithms. The question we must ask ourselves is how far can we go in order to maintain the security in the streets without infringing fundamental rights contained with national constitutions and the European Convention of Human Rights.

Predictive systems such as sentencing guidelines are racist, class-biased, misogynist, and depersonalize the criminal justice system. Massive convictions and imprisonments are justified with promises of citizen security and maintaining public order.[42] Control and security are sold at a price.[43] This discourse is not exempt from risks because it compartmentalizes society into social groups and excludes those groups in which these risks exist.[44] The answer to the problem should be simple: we can only afford to use algorithmic systems if they do not infringe rights that we consider basic in our legal system. Every jurisdiction is different, but in Spain we cannot obtain statements under torture, nor can we accept a confession obtained through wiretapping without judicial authorization, neither can we base guilt solely on an algorithm.[45] It is better to have ten guilty people in the street than one innocent person in prison.[46]

The use of AI in the criminal justice system is already a reality that must be studied from a holistic perspective with the challenges posed by its use and the identification of limits and good practices.[47] At an academic and social level, the use of AI technologies in the criminal justice system raises a growing interest because of the enormous implications that their use can have toward the potential improvement of the justice system and because of the multiple risks that their use can pose to the rights and guarantees that we consider fundamental within the criminal process.[48]

The concept of dangerousness in a modern way was introduced into criminal political discourse and legislation with the positivist school of criminology of the late nineteenth and early twentieth centuries. Dangerousness was understood as a subjective characteristic or disposition that predisposed the subject to commit crimes in the future. Until the 1990s, the method for its determination was the clinical judgment of the expert (doctor, possibly psychiatrist or psychologist) in combination with the personal assessment of the judge.[49] Besides being a legal concept, dangerousness is also a concept in everyday language. Dangerousness has always been linked to violent crime and therefore has been an enigma that professionals in psychiatry, psychology, and forensic medicine have tried to solve. The belief that dangerousness is the cause of violent behavior has maintained a kind of chimera among professionals. According to it, if the identification of this attribute was done "right" it would mean that security and prevention of recidivism were guaranteed. In some cases, this has been what has happened, but in many others false negatives have been produced by rejecting dangerousness in individuals who have committed crimes again. On the other hand, some false positives have also been produced by identifying dangerousness in a subject who will not behave violently again in the future. The consequences of both errors are painful for society and for the individual. The intention of the aggressor, to cause harm, and the effects on the victim, the harm actually caused, is what actually identifies violent behavior.[50]

From the very moment the concept of "dangerousness" was born it was viewed with scepticism by criminal doctrine. A strong critical response to criminological positivism and trends oriented toward special prevention arose. In the 1970s and 1980s, this mistrust became widespread as a result of a very critical examination by medical and social scientists of the possibilities of "scientifically" detecting the dangerousness of a subject.[51] Dangerousness is not a fact but rather is a probability condition. Even if the person does not inflict any injury on anyone, this does not make him or her less dangerous to a certain extent. Traditionally, dangerousness was related to a condition of the aggressor, which was inherent to his way of being or his psychopathological state. Current risk management is based on understanding the reasons why the subject decided to act violently in the past, determining whether the risk/protection factors that influenced his choice are still present or will be in the future and promoting the factors that can lead to nonviolent decisions. This management refers to the application of available knowledge generated by the various risk assessment studies in order to reduce the behaviors and their effects.[52]

Until a few years ago, the basic strategy for predicting violent recidivism was clinical-forensic assessment and diagnosis of criminal dangerousness by the use of criminal profiles. The techniques for predicting future violence are currently based on the assessment of the risk of violence due to the fact that the dangerousness strategy is inadequate. This strategy was inadequate because of the low effectiveness of prediction and because of the lack of transparency in the basis of the diagnosis.[53] The idea of dangerousness has been replaced by violence risk assessment. Nowadays, it is not a question of assessing whether or not the individual possesses the quality of dangerousness but rather if he/she possesses personal and environmental factors that will be changing over time and will favor the commission of new crimes, thus allowing forecasts to be made about future recidivism in terms of probability. The change in the conceptualization from dangerousness to risk has also been accompanied by a change in the way risk is measured. The traditional clinical approach is considered unreliable, biased, and lacking an empirical basis.[54] It has gradually been replaced by structured methods of risk estimation. These estimations are sometimes obtained automatically by an algorithm.[55]

Risk assessment is a probability judgment that seeks to predict (re)offending.[56] Prevention is a key pillar in the fight against crime. Predictive techniques are the first step in combating violence at the level of an individual case to prevent it from becoming chronic. The assessment of the risk of violence will allow us to manage the adoption of safety measures toward the aggressor and protection measures for the victim.[57] The objective varies when replacing dangerousness with risk assessment. The objective now is not to find out whether the individual has the subjective quality of dangerousness but to assess a number of factors in both the individual and the environment that will lead to further crime and future delinquency.[58]

The use of algorithms is penetrating the sentence phase of criminal justice with suggestive denominations such as "evidence-based sentencing" or "smart sentencing." Risk assessments have been incorporated as one of the criteria to be considered when establishing the type and amount of penalty with the laudable aim of reducing recidivism. The incorporation of the assessments is based on three premises: First, the objective of avoiding recidivism as one of the legitimate aims pursued by the criminal law. Second, the fact that the judge's impression of the degree of danger posed by a subject is intuitive and, although motivated, will always be partly arbitrary, subjective, and biased. Third, that risk-management techniques provide rigorous and empirically based knowledge.[59]

We might think that instead of making decisions on subjective, arbitrary, and prejudicial estimates of danger, we do so on the basis of scientific estimates of the risk of recidivism. The reality is that scientific knowledge about risk is not as accurate and precise as it might seem and, furthermore, it is easy to misinterpret by those who are not experts in the field.[60] Two questions that will have to be answered arise: Is the use of violence risk assessment systems to determine the penalty compatible with the right to a due process?[61] Are we capable of understanding what mathematical operations the algorithm has gone through in order to place blind trust in it? If the answer to this second question is no, we do not need to ask any more questions. Behind the apparent simplicity of the results there is a convoluted web of numbers, formulas, and complicated calculations. The impression of transparency and objectivity only hide subjective and prejudicial assessments. These assessments are made invisible by the supposed impartiality of the numbers and formulas.[62] This can lead legal operators to exaggerated and unjustified confidence in the reliability of the risk estimates made by structured tools to the point of believing that they are better and more precise than human ones. Believing this discourse is very dangerous: excessive optimism about the performance of risk estimators leads to blind confidence in the virtues of the algorithms. This confidence facilitates decisions that limit the fundamental rights of the defendants due to the fact that courts think that they enjoy empirical support that they do not really have.[63] Therefore, it seems that by answering the second question we have also given an answer to the first one. In summary, if we want to apply mathematical formulas for sentencing we will have to understand them first.

THE USE OF ALGORITHMS IN THE CRIMINAL JUDICIAL SYSTEM: CHIMERA OR PANACEA?

AI has arrived to stay. It is only a matter of time before the Spanish judges end up including it in their daily lives like the Americans have already done. Law in general, and criminal justice in particular, are being reinterpreted from the Chicago School's economistic point of view. We seek effectiveness and efficiency and we use them as incentives for reforms, as budgets for financing institutions, and as criteria for adopting political decisions in justice matters. However, we cannot forget that both criteria must offer a "due" justice to citizens.[64] The use of AI to decide on the severity of the penalty to be imposed allows judges to corroborate their intuition with a risk-assessment algorithm and thus place the sentence with a clearer conscience.[65] We will have to be very specific in indicating the limits of what a machine can and cannot do. Today, we have the knowledge and the technology to create machines that assess the probability of recidivism of the convicted person and then opt for probation or prison. Whether we should let a machine decide on sensitive issues such as people's freedom is a different matter.[66]

We run the risk of becoming a *Minority Report* society. The risk of accepting a very dangerous discourse that works through the use of technology and its data allows us to foresee these possible future behaviors in order to justify a preventive guardianship and act ex ante.[67] This dilemma should be solved as things are solved in law: by pondering. The advantages that could be gained by incorporating risk assessments in sentencing should be disregarded in order to protect the fundamental rights of the accused if the risks to them are real and cannot be avoided by any other means.[68] This chapter asserts that there are certain red lines that we must not cross and that a machine should never be able to replace a judge's decision. The numbers, although clothed in (false) neutrality, are as biased as the reality in which we live. The information with which we have fed the algorithm is not neutral. It is the sum of different sentences in which different judges have resolved in one way or another.

Predicting the future by looking at the past involves the risk that the same gender, racial, and religious stereotypes that we are gradually overcoming as a society will continue to be repeated in the future. We must be cautious not only in the application phase of AI, but we should go one step further and ask ourselves who is behind the machine, how the algorithm was made, who does it benefit and who does it harm (consciously or unconsciously) because it can end up controlling global legal thinking.[69] AI can be very useful to us because it is capable of comparing in record time a quantity of sentences and data that a person could not compare during one year (or a lifetime), but its use has to be evaluated with caution and the functions that only concern the judge should not be deposited in the machine. Otherwise, we run the risk of going from utopia to dystopia without realizing it.

BIBLIOGRAPHY

Abidin, C., "La imagen del delincuente en la Escuela Clásica y en la Escuela Positiva" (2005), Cartapacio de Derecho: Revista Virtual de la Facultad de Derecho 8, 1–17.

Acosta, M. L.,"Violencia contra las mujeres: peligrosidad y valoración del riesgo" (2012), Revista Europea de Derechos Fundamentales.

Angwin, J., Larson, J., Mattu, Mattu, S., and Kirchner, L., "Machine Bias. There's Software Used across the Country to Predict Future Criminals. And It's Biased against Blacks" (2016), *ProPublica.*

Berk, R., Heidaric, H., Jabbaric, S., Kearnsc, M., and Roth, A., "Fairness in Criminal Justice Risk Assessments: The State of the Art" (2017), Berk, 1–42.

Bueno de Mata, F., "Macrodatos, Inteligencia Artificial y Proceso: Luces y Sombras" (2020) Revista General de Derecho Procesal 51, 1–31.

Buiten, M. C., "Towards Intelligent Regulation of Artificial Intelligence" (2019). *European Journal of Risk Regulation*, 10 1, 41–59.

Dick, P. K., *Minority Report* (2002). S.A. Ediciones B.

Echeburúa, E., and Andrés-Pueyo, A., "Valoración del riesgo de violencia: instrumentos disponibles e indicaciones de aplicación" (2010). *Psicothema* 22 3, 403–409.

Francesc, F., "¿Hacia una exención de responsabilidad por causas genéticas? A vueltas con Lombroso" (2016). *Gac. Int. Cienc. Forense* 19, 1–2.

Garay, L. M., "Peligrosidad, Algoritmos y Due Process: el Caso State v Loomis" (2018). *Revista de Derecho Penal y Criminología* 20, 485–502.

Garay, L. M., and Suay, F. M., "El uso de valoraciones del riesgo de violencia en Derecho Penal: algunas cautelas necesarias" (2018). *Indret* 2.

García, E. M., *La protección jurisdiccional contra la violencia de género en la Unión Europea (2019). Tirant Lo Blanch.*

González-Méndez, R. D., and Santana-Hernández, J., "Perceived risk and Safety-Related Behaviors after Leaving a Violent Relationship" (2014). *European Journal of Psychology Applied to Legal Context* 6.

Llinares, F. M., "Inteligencia artificial y justicia penal: más allá de los resultados lesivos causados por robots" (2018). *Revista de Derecho Penal y Criminología* 20, 87–130.

Mayson, S. G., "Bias In, Bias Out" (2019). *Yale Law Journal*, 2218–2300.

Moreno, J. V., "La biología humana y la conducta criminal" (2009). *QdC,* 35–42.

Orwell, G., *1984 (2020). Penguin Random House.*

Oswald, M., Grace, J., Urwin S., and Barnes, G. C., "Algorithmic Risk Assessment Policing Models: Lessons from the Durham HART Model and 'Experimental' Proportionality" (2018). *Information & Communications Technology Law* 27 2, 223–250.

Pérez Estrada, M. J., "Capítulo XI. El uso de algoritmos en el proceso penal y el derecho a un proceso con todas las garantías," in Silvia Barona Vilar (ed) *Claves de la Justicia Penal. Feminización, Inteligencia Artificial, Supranacionalidad y Seguridad* (2019). Tirant Lo Blanch, 235–253.

Pérez, G. V. "La concepción médico-biológica de la criminalidad (El caso de César Lombroso)" (2018). *Alegatos* 21 66, 377–388.

Rico, R. H. M., "El Delincuente Predeterminado: de la criminología positiva italiana a la neurocientificidad" (2017). *Criterio Jurídico* 5 2, 77–94.

Rodríguez, E. E., "Valoración de la peligrosidad criminal (riesgo-violencia) en psicología forense. Aproximación conceptual e histórica" (2003). *Psicopatología Clínica Legal y Forense* 3 2, 45–64.

Vilar, S. B., "Cuarta revolución industrial (4.0.) o ciberindustria en el proceso penal: revolución digital, inteligencia artificial y el camino hacia la robotización de la justicia" (2019). *Revista Jurídica Digital UANDES*, 1–17.
Vilar, S.B., "Inteligencia artificial o la algoritmización de la vida y de la justicia: ¿solución o problema?" (2019). *Rev. Boliv. de Derecho* 28, 18–49.

NOTES

1. Silvia Barona Vilar, "Cuarta revolución industrial (4.0.) o ciberindustria en el proceso penal: revolución digital, inteligencia artificial y el camino hacia la robotización de la justicia" (2019). *Revista Jurídica Digital UANDES*, 16.
2. Federico Bueno de Mata, "Macrodatos, Inteligencia Artificial y Proceso: Luces y Sombras" (2020). *Revista General de Derecho Procesal* 51, 29.
3. Fernando Miró Llinares, "Inteligencia artificial y justicia penal: más allá de los resultados lesivos causados por robots" (2018). *Revista de Derecho Penal y Criminología* 20, 90.
4. European Commission, Brussels, 25.4.2018 COM (2018) 237 final, *Communication from the Commission to the European Parliament, the European Council, the Council, the European Economic and Social Committee and the Committee of the Regions. Artificial Intelligence for Europe*, 1.
5. Barona (n 1), 2.
6. https://www.lavozdegalicia.es/noticia/sociedad/2020/02/04/99-moviles-carretilla-engano-artista-aleman-google-maps/00031580821490585336268.htm
7. Miró (n 3), 89.
8. "Machines 'think' differently to humans; 'When a computer learns and consequently builds its own representation of a classification decision, it does so without regard for human comprehension." Marion Oswald, Jamie Grace, Sheena Urwin, and Geoffrey C. Barnes, "Algorithmic Risk Assessment Policing Models: Lessons from the Durham HART Model and 'Experimental' Proportionality" (2018). *Information & Communications Technology Law* 27 2, 226.
9. Miró (n 3), 92.
10. Silvia Barona Vilar, "Inteligencia artificial o la algoritmización de la vida y de la justicia: ¿solución o problema?" (2019). *Rev. Boliv. de Derecho* 28, 22.
11. Miró (n 3), 88.
12. https://www.elmundo.es/madrid/2019/05/28/5ced493efdddffb0758b48fb.html; https://www.publico.es/internacional/joven-italiana-suicida-despues-exnovio.html
13. https://www.heraldo.es/noticias/salud/2016/03/15/espana-uno-los-paises-donde-mas-ciberacoso-sufren-los-menores-817032-2261131.html; https://www.elconfidencial.com/espana/2017-05-03/guardia-civil-evita-twitter-suicidio-victima-acoso-escolar_1374116/
14. "There are many definitions of Big Data, which differ depending on the specific discipline. Most of them focus on the growing technological ability to collect process and extract new and predictive knowledge from great volume, velocity, and variety of data. In terms of data protection, the main issues do not only concern the

volume, velocity, and variety of processed data, but also the analysis of the data using software to extract new and predictive knowledge for decision-making purposes regarding individuals and groups. For the purposes of these Guidelines, the definition of Big Data therefore encompasses both Big Data and Big Data analytics." Council of Europe, *Guidelines on the protection of individuals with regard to the processing of personal data in a world of big data,* 2017, 4.

15. Barona (n 10) 24.

16. Miriam C Buiten, "Towards Intelligent Regulation of Artificial Intelligence" (2019). *European Journal of Risk Regulation*, 10 1, 53.

17. Miró (n 3) 103–104.

18. Barona (n 1) 8.

19. George Orwell, *1984 (2020). Penguin Random House*, 10–11.

20. Richard Berk, Hoda Heidaric, Shahin Jabbaric, Michael Kearnsc, and Aaron Roth;,"Fairness in Criminal Justice Risk Assessments: The State of the Art" (2017). Berk 35.

21. "Even with these steps and the highest dedication to transparency, however, opacity seems difficult to avoid. The HART model contains over 4.2 million decision points, all of which are highly interdependent on the ones that precede them within the tree structure. These details could be made freely available to the public, but would require a huge amount of time and effort to fully understand. It is becoming increasingly difficult to explain to non-computer scientists and non-statisticians how a machine learning forecasting model arrives at its outcomes, and the potential for misunderstanding and even intentional misrepresentation is vast." Oswald, Grace, Urwin, and Barnes (n 8) 234.

22. Pérez Estrada, "Capítulo XI. El uso de algoritmos en el proceso penal y el derecho a un proceso con todas las garantías," in Silvia Barona Vilar (ed) *Claves de la Justicia Penal. Feminización, Inteligencia Artificial, Supranacionalidad y Seguridad (2019). Tirant Lo Blanch*, 238–239.

23. Pérez (n 20), 239.

24. FRA, *BigData: Discrimination in data-supported decision making*, 2018, 2.

25. Pérez (n 20), 236.

26. Miró (n 3), 108–109.

27. After Zilly was scored as a high risk for violent recidivism and sent to prison, a public defender appealed the sentence and called the score's creator, Brennan, as a witness. Brennan testified that he didn't design his software to be used in sentencing. "I wanted to stay away from the courts," Brennan said, explaining that his focus was on reducing crime rather than punishment. "But as time went on I started realizing that so many decisions are made, you know, in the courts. So I gradually softened on whether this could be used in the courts or not." Still, Brennan testified, "I don't like the idea myself of COMPAS being the sole evidence that a decision would be based upon." Julia Angwin, Jeff Larson, Mattu, Surya Mattu, and Lauren Kirchner, "Machine Bias. There's Software Used Across the Country to Predict Future Criminals. And It's Biased against Blacks" (2016), *ProPublica,* 12–13.

28. Pérez (n 20), 237.

29. Case No. 2015AP157-CR. *State of Wisconsin v. Eric L. Loomis*. July 13, 2016. Disponible en: https://www.wicourts.gov/sc/opinion/DisplayDocument.pdf?content=pdf&seqNo=171690
30. Lucía Martínez Garay, "Peligrosidad, Algoritmos y Due Process: el Caso State v Loomis" (2018). *Revista de Derecho Penal y Criminología* 20, 490.
31. Martínez (n 28), 491.
32. Martínez (n 28), 492.
33. Berk, Heidaric, Jabbaric, Kearnsc and Roth (n 18), 1–42.
34. Martínez (n 28), 502.
35. Also, in Europe: "Therefore, 'assessing the risk of future crime plays no role in sentencing decisions.' In contrast, risk assessment is a key instrument to implement the utilitarian approach, in which punishment is justified by the ability to decrease the probability of future crimes." European Parliament, *Understanding Algorithmic Decision-Making: Opportunities and Challenges*, 2019, 25.
36. Barona (n 10), 45.
37. Pérez (n 20), 250–251.
38. Angwin, Larson, Mattu, and Kirchner (n 25).
39. Miró (n 3), 109.
40. Sandra G. Mayson, "Bias In, Bias Out" (2019). *Yale Law Journal*, 2218–2300.
41. Mayson (n 38), 2224.
42. European Parliament, *Understanding Algorithmic Decision-Making: Opportunities and Challenges*, 2019, 25.
43. Barona (n 1), 11–12.
44. Barona (n 10), 43.
45. The Spanish constitution states in Article 117 that only judges and courts have jurisdictional function. Therefore, algorithms can help them on their decisions but not make the decision.
46. Martínez (n 28), 494.
47. Miró (n 3), 90.
48. Miró (n 3), 108.
49. Martínez (n 28), 492–498.
50. Miguel Lorente Acosta, "Violencia contra las mujeres: peligrosidad y valoración del riesgo" (2012). *Revista Europea de Derechos Fundamentales*, 19, 192–198.
51. Martínez (n 28), 486.
52. Lorente (n 47), 192.
53. Elena Martínez García, *La protección jurisdiccional contra la violencia de género en la Unión Europea* (2019). Tirant Lo Blanch, 97.
54. Martínez (n 28), 487.
55. Martínez (n 28), 487.
56. Enrique Echeburúa and Antonio Andrés-Pueyo, "Valoración del riesgo de violencia: instrumentos disponibles e indicaciones de aplicación" (2010). *Psicothema* 22 3, 403–409; Enrique Esbec Rodríguez, "Valoración de la peligrosidad criminal (riesgo-violencia) en psicología forense. Aproximación conceptual e histórica" (2003). *Psicopatología Clínica Legal y Forense* 3 2, 45–64.
57. Martínez García (n 50), 95.

58. Lucía Martínez Garay and Francisco Montes Suay, "El uso de valoraciones del riesgo de violencia en Derecho Penal: algunas cautelas necesarias" (2018). *Indret* 2, 5.
59. Martínez (n 28), 488.
60. Martínez and Montes (n 54), 7.
61. Martínez (n 28), 489.
62. Martínez and Montes (n 54), 36.
63. Martínez and Montes (n 54), 8.
64. Barona (n 1), 3–4.
65. Martínez (n 28), 496.
66. Barona (n 10), 46.
67. Barona (n 1), 13.
68. Martínez (n 28), 494.
69. Barona (n 1), 16.

Chapter 7

The Vulnerable Accused in Scotland

"A Fig for Those by Law Protected"?[1]

Eamon P. H. Keane

Like much else in human society in the tumultuous era of Covid 19, the manner in which criminal proceedings occur in Scotland has changed markedly in a remarkably short period of time.[2] As I write, jurors in the east and west of the country are assessing evidence and determining guilt, not from the austere and solemn confines of the jury box of the High Court of Justiciary, but rather from the relative comfort of the amply cushioned seats of various Scottish cinemas.[3] In Scotland's sheriff courts, there have also been convictions and acquittals in judge-only summary trials conducted entirely virtually, with parties participating in proceedings from various locations using information technology software.[4] There have been changes to the substantive Scots law of evidence itself, specifically the admissibility of hearsay as well.[5]

Amidst such far-reaching reform, there is a palpable sense of recognition in Scotland that notwithstanding whatever improvement to the public health situation widespread vaccination may bring, there will be no simple return to the status quo ante.[6] Indeed, the head of the judiciary in Scotland, the Lord Carloway, lord president, has remarked publicly that the pandemic has afforded the Scottish legal profession with "an opportunity as well as a challenge"[7] and that "the crisis has demonstrated that where change is a necessity, it can be made to happen."[8] It therefore seems an apt juncture, for me to write about an area of Scottish legal practice, namely the current legal framework governing the vulnerable accused in criminal proceedings who is not incapax, that requires urgent consideration and reform.[9] As I will show, the right of effective participation is the normative principle guiding measures of support for the vulnerable accused in Scots law. There is, however, no authoritative exposition of the principle of effective participation in Scots law in this context. As a result, such support that does exist is fragmented, and in places ill defined. This is a matter that now more than ever necessitates careful consideration from policy makers and practitioners, as the demographic in question, may be especially adversely impacted by increased digitalization and other changes made to criminal procedure deemed necessary due to the pandemic.[10]

DEFINITION OF THE VULNERABLE ACCUSED

It is necessary, prior to outlining and analysing the substantive legal framework protecting the vulnerable accused in Scotland, to first define what I mean by "the vulnerable accused," alongside noting a few other preliminary matters relating to questions of scope and definition. I acknowledge at the outset that the very definition of "vulnerability" in this context is multifaceted and often contested, in keeping with the use of the term generally in matters of socio-legal policy.[11] That being so, for the purposes of this chapter, I use the term "the vulnerable accused" to refer to any individual potentially facing criminal prosecution in Scotland, which I define as beginning at the stage of initial arrest and police interview,[12] t[13]hrough to the leading of evidence at trial, whose vulnerability is such that they engage a specific legal response, designed at assisting and enabling them to participate effectively in proceedings.[14] It should be noted that my definition of the vulnerable accused excludes from consideration the suite disposals commonly known as "diversionary measures" which, in general terms are alternatives to prosecution that may be offered by the procurator fiscal, but that is not to say that issues do not arise in this context for those who are vulnerable.[15] I also will not consider individuals whose alleged criminality is dealt with exclusively via the Scottish Children's Hearing System.[16] Vulnerability, too, in terms of my definition, is broad enough to cover a range of relevant personal factors in the accused that potentially engage a supporting measure.[17]

THE HISTORICAL FOUNDATIONS OF SUPPORT FOR THE VULNERABLE ACCUSED IN SCOTS LAW

I will now consider the historical foundations of the support for the vulnerable accused in Scots law. The obligation upon the court to take steps to ensure the effective participation of the vulnerable accused, can first be conclusively identified in a recognisable manner in the modern era in Scotland, in a reported case from the High Court of Justiciary in 1941, namely *HM*

Advocate v Olsson.[18] I use the phrase "the modern era" here to signify in very general terms the period which followed the move towards a mode of criminal trial which is broadly similar to that which is used today. Which for present purposes I define, as beginning in 1898 whereby the accused was given the right, previously denied under common law in Scotland, to give evidence at trial and at all stages of the case, in their own defense.[19] This change, and the resulting period, is important in the context of my analysis because it heralded an era whereby the Scottish courts, in theory at least, required to adapt to the prospect of the vulnerable accused giving evidence. As I will show, this led to several important changes in practice relating to the right of effective participation, that set the foundations for the contemporary legal position.

Returning to the case in hand, the accused, a Swedish sailor charged with a murder in Aberdeen, required the assistance of an interpreter in order to understand the evidence led at his trial. The case report notes that Lord Jamieson, who presided at first instance over the trial, ordered that such a step to be taken remarking that "the mere physical presence of the accused in this case will not satisfy the requirements of justice . . . ."[20] The judgment acknowledges too that a similar direction and practice had been adopted earlier by Lord MacKenzie in the High Court of Justiciary in an unreported case from 1913, with the hope that such a way of proceeding would be followed where appropriate.[21] While *Olsson* avoids the modern language of vulnerability and effective participation, the purpose of, and the principle behind, the judicial intervention may still be readily understood. Although the court is silent on why, exactly, the interpreter is required in the interests of justice, one can assume that the rationale behind such a step is to permit the accused in this case to understand the evidence led at trial, so that they may instruct their defense accordingly. Important here, as I have already mentioned, is the change in the late 19th century permitting the accused to give evidence in their own defense. Viewed in this context, the provision of the interpreter places the vulnerable accused on an equal footing such that they make an informed choice about whether to give evidence or not, in light of the Crown's case. Indeed, in the following year, the High Court of Justiciary determined that the failure to provide interpreters to three Polish accused at trial amounted to a miscarriage of justice and thus quashed their convictions.[22]

Importantly, the historical case law on the admission of extrajudicial confessions and statements made to the police from this era also features instances of evidence rendered inadmissible at trial on the grounds that its admission would be unfair, given the personal characteristics of the accused.[23] These cases, again while avoiding the language of vulnerability and effective participation, narrate instances where the youth, physical and mental condition, and the lack of English of the accused are all relevant in the assessment of fairness and thus admissibility. While these judgments are also directly concerned with myriad other political and legal factors, one can also clearly perceive a recognition that the vulnerability of certain individuals may require targeted support at early stages of the criminal investigation in order so that they can understand matters, thus facilitating their effective participation.[24] The limits to such "effective participation" do need to be acknowledged however in this context. Scots law's historical treatment of the legal definition of the suspect is complicated, and the law of evidence has varied throughout the modern era as to what is, and is not, permitted in terms of police practice.[25] The cases cited in this context arise from an era in which there was no legal power for police to detain a suspect for questioning, and where the only legal power was that of arrest, with police officers permitted to ask questions to clarify responses to caution and charge following arrest.[26] Nevertheless, the police often "invited" suspects to accompany them to police stations for questioning.[27] There was no right of access to legal advice for such individuals.[28] What is especially interesting therefore in this early body of case law, is the reference that is made in certain of the judgments to the importance of access to legal advice for those who are deemed vulnerable.[29] The rationale again here is not made explicit, and as alluded to above these decisions are multifaceted but within the court's analysis of fairness in the context of the inadmissibility of evidence, we can discern again a recognition that the personal circumstances of the vulnerable accused may require additional measures be taken (e.g., the provision of legal advice by a solicitor), such that they may understand proceedings and be placed on an even footing with others. In short, we can see again here via these early judgments, the recognition of the importance of additional steps being taken to facilitate the protection and understanding of the vulnerable accused throughout the criminal process.

What is interesting about these decisions, too, is that the early case law on the admissibility of statements and the vulnerable accused contains a relatively intelligible legal framework governing the requirements of and remedies for breach of the right of effective participation. This is attributable to the fact that, in this context, the right is subsumed within a broader legal process and analytical framework, namely, in this instance, the admissibility of extrajudicial confessions and statements. While this development is understandable in the sense that the right to effective participation encroaches on various and variable other areas of the substantive and adjectival Scots criminal law and procedure, this feature often obscures what the right to effective participation actually entails and makes generalizations about the requirement and consequences of breach of the right difficult to accurately predict.

Finally, the discussion of the historical position of the vulnerable accused in Scots law is illuminated by mentioning briefly the now abolished historical legal pleas governing capacity.[30] While the law in this respect predates what I define as the modern era, and detailed consideration of the area is beyond the scope of this chapter, one can nevertheless discern clearly general principles of crucial importance to our consideration of the topic at hand. Both the common law plea of insanity at the time of the criminal offense and as a plea in bar of trial were predicated on the understanding that the accused's mental condition was such that they had suffered an alienation of reason thus absolving them from criminal responsibility.[31] It is interesting, too, that Hume's discussion of the subject of insanity in the 19th century expressly acknowledges the existence of the vulnerable accused who is none the less *capax*, noting as he does that the law cannot and does not excuse criminal responsibility in a case of "mere weakness of intellect."[32]

Insanity as a plea in bar of trial also offers an insight into the matters which at the far end of the continuum of capacity, so to speak, render the accused unable to participate in the trial itself and are thus of use when delineating the development of the modern contours of the right of effective participation. Whether the accused was able to instruct their counsel in order to conduct their defense and whether they could intelligibly follow proceedings were key questions to be determined under the old common law governing the plea.[33] The core of the plea was therefore premised on a recognition that the accused was fundamentally unable to effectively participate in the trial, notwithstanding any remedial measures that could be enacted in their aid. Appreciating where the boundary of effective participation used to lie in this respect is beneficial when thinking about the modern law, as it enables one to identify the parameters within which the right to effective participation is situated.

In conclusion, an analysis of the historical legal protection of the vulnerable accused in Scotland illustrates clearly the lineage and existence of the right to effective participation in the modern era of criminal trials and reveals several characteristics of note. The right of effective participation can be shown to equate roughly to a right to understand legal proceedings so as to enable participation. I have outlined how historically the right has often necessitated a distinct legal response in order to facilitate its protection, but also how the exact requirements of the right and the consequences of its breach have varied.

THE MODERN LEGAL FRAMEWORK GOVERNING THE PROTECTION OF THE VULNERABLE ACCUSED IN SCOTS LAW: ARREST AND POLICE INTERVIEW

Having outlined the historical foundations for the support of the vulnerable accused, I will now turn my attention to a series of contemporary legal measures relevant in this context. My focus here is on two distinct stages of the criminal prosecution, namely arrest and interview and the leading of evidence at trial. The analysis undertaken in this section reveals that the normative principle that remains at the center of legal measures of support is the right to effective participation, and this again translates roughly to a right for the vulnerable accused to understand and participate in proceedings so that they may make decisions about the conduct of their defense. As important, I will reveal how in certain respects the right's requirements remain remarkably uncertain in Scots law.[34]

There is now a unitary statutory power of arrest without warrant in Scotland which may be utilized where there are reasonable grounds for suspecting that an individual has committed or is committing an offense.[35] Arrested individuals thereafter may be questioned under caution in relation to the alleged offense.[36] The statutory regime governing this process contains several provisions of note from the perspective of the vulnerable accused. The Criminal Procedure (Scotland) Act 2016 places an obligation upon the police when they consider an individual to be vulnerable who is in their custody, to communicate certain matters to what is known as an "appropriate adult" with a view to said individual providing support so that the person in custody can understand what is happening, and so that "effective communication" can be facilitated between the vulnerable accused and the police.[37] Vulnerability in this context is defined explicitly by the statute as any individual in police custody, over 16 years of age, who by reason of a mental disorder appears to the police to be unable to understand sufficiently what is happening or is unable to communicate effectively with the police.[38] "Mental disorder" is further defined in this context as per s.328 of the Mental Health (Care & Treatment) (Scotland) Act 2003 as any mental illness, personality disorder, or learning difficulty.[39] The definition of mental disorder utilized explicitly excludes from its ambit certain matters, in rather archaic fashion, related to, for example, sexual orientation.[40] It also states that no one shall be deemed to be mentally disordered solely by virtue of dependence on drink and drugs nor solely via the effect of certain types of behavior.[41] Oversight of the regime of appropriate adults is further regulated by specific provisions of the 2016 Act.[42] The act also contains several provisions which give those under the age of eighteen the right to have access to a parent or another individual, where a parent is not available, while they are in police custody.[43] The act permits the police to refuse or restrict access to such an individual in certain exceptional circumstances.[44]

Furthermore, the act strengthens the protection afforded to the vulnerable accused in respect of questioning by the police. In this respect, anyone who is deemed vulnerable by the police (using the aforementioned unable to understand and/or communicate effectively due to mental disorder criteria) may not consent to be interviewed by the police without a solicitor present.[45] A similar provision applies to those who are under the age of sixteen or are sixteen or seventeen and are subject to a compulsory supervision order, or an interim compulsory supervision order.[46] The act does permit sixteen or seventeen year olds to consent to interview without a solicitor present but only with the permission of a "relevant person."[47] The police are also permitted to proceed to interview without a solicitor being present in respect of any of the above classes of individual in exceptional circumstances, which are defined as being where it is necessary to interview the individual without delay in the interests of the investigation or the prevention of crime or the apprehension of offenders.[48] Only a constable at the rank of sergeant or above, who has not been involved in the investigation of the offense to which questioning pertains, may authorize this step.[49]

Several features of the contemporary regime of protection at arrest and interview for the vulnerable accused are worthy of comment. In the first instance, it requires to be noted that without contemporary empirical research on the topic, it is not possible to comment conclusively on the efficacy of police practice and protection in this area.[50] That being said, one can reasonably conclude that the legal infrastructure to protect the vulnerable accused at this stage of the criminal process appears prima facie adequate. The scheme of protection, as has been outlined, is centered around a clear definition of vulnerability. The clarity of definition provided here stands in stark contrast to the situation that pertains relating to the protection of the vulnerable accused at trial, as will be seen.

One can also readily identify in this context, without supposition, that the right of effective participation roughly equates to the right to understand proceedings (so as to make decisions relative to the conduct of one's defense), and this remains the normative basis for the legal interventions outlined. Scots law has in essence via the act, embedded protection for those whose vulnerability renders them liable to incriminate themselves at police interview. The statutory framework has myriad targeted interventions in this sense, which may all be roughly characterized as seeking to ensure that the vulnerable accused understands the processes that are occurring, and may react accordingly in order to participate and conduct their defense. This explains why children are entitled to access to a parent at an early stage of arrest and may only consent to interview without legal advice, with the approval of a third party. This conception of effective participation as the right to understand proceedings is also inherent in the suite of measures related to appropriate adults, whose very raison d'être is to aid understanding and facilitate communication. The act also centers legal representation and advice as a necessary component of the right to effective participation for the vulnerable accused in a manner which also has clear echoes from the historical era. Of course, the broader context here is, as has been noted, a general system of police interview for all suspects in Scotland that was badly out of kilter with practice both in England and Wales, most of Europe, and Article 6 when it came to access to legal advice.[51] Still, the act centers the solicitor as an important component for the protection for the vulnerable accused's effective participation rights by strengthening the right of access to legal advice for such individuals.

Admissibility of Extrajudicial Confessions by the Vulnerable Accused

While the 2016 Act entrenches support for the vulnerable accused at the stage of arrest and interview, it remains primarily the Scots common law of evidence, specifically the law relating to the admissibility of extrajudicial confessions, that regulates the breach of the statute, at least in terms of ongoing criminal proceedings.[52] The Scots law of evidence here continues to operate a general, and to a certain extent, nebulous, test of fairness, in this respect.[53] One can see here again how the regulation of the right to effective participation is thus subsumed within a broader legal framework.

The sea change to police practice at interview enacted by the 2016 Act means that whereas in the past challenges to the fairness of extrajudicial confessions made by the vulnerable accused at police interview were relatively commonplace, such challenges, at least in the reported Scottish case law, are now vanishingly rare.[54] It is important to acknowledge in this context that Scots law retains a right of silence at interview for those accused of criminal offending, which combined with the strengthened provisions described above relative to access to legal advice and an appropriate adult, might go some way to explaining the apparent falloff in reported judgments in the past few years.[55] This is not to suggest that there are no longer problems. As I have alluded to before, what is needed now in this context is a program of empirical research focused on the vulnerable accused following arrest so the efficacy of practice in the area can be properly assessed. One must remember that it remains primarily within the gift of the police officers to identify vulnerability in this context, and so much is contingent on their own training and behavior. What the pre-2016 Act law in this area tells us is that the personal characteristics of the accused may preclude the admission of an extrajudicial confession on the grounds of fairness, albeit the assessment of same is undertaken on a fact specific basis.[56] Much depends, in this context, on the stage at which suspicion has reached, albeit it should be remembered the 2016 Act now entitles any individual in police custody to receive legal advice regardless of whether they will be questioned under caution or not.[57]

Ultimately, whether a confession given by the vulnerable accused is deemed admissible or not will effectively be determined on a case by case basis. The exact nature of the fairness test is, in this context, as I have alluded to, relatively nebulous although Article 6 of the ECHR has made its mark. As mentioned previously, any reliance on an extrajudicial confession made by the vulnerable accused at police interview by the prosecuting authorities, given without access to legal advice, in contravention of the 2016 Act, is a violation of Article 6 and thus such evidence is clearly inadmissible.[58] One can posit, too, that any other substantive breach of the provisions of the 2016 Act relating to the vulnerable accused's right to effective participation, as outlined above, is certainly likely to render any concomitant extrajudicial confession inadmissible.[59] In this context, it should be noted that Scottish case law's trajectory over the past eighty or so years has been somewhat unpredictable.[60] Whereas, as noted previously, the original test referred explicitly to fairness to the accused alone as determining admissibility, the test was given a bipartite nature in later years whereby the public interest in the detection of crime became a relevant factor to be weighed in the court's consideration.[61] This position has subsequently fallen out of favor in recent years in the High Court of Justiciary, with the court noting that "it is not necessary to conduct empirical research into the fairness of the circumstances in every case, balancing the individual interest with that of the public. Indeed, that may be problematic in the modern era, where the emphasis is on the courts enforcing an individual's human rights as defined by the European Convention."[62] The specific nature of the test remains somewhat uncertain, although as mentioned, the protection of the 2016 Act and the lack of reported judgments concerning the vulnerable accused on the issue suggest that practice in this area has changed for the better.

THE TRIAL: THE VULNERABLE ACCUSED WHO GIVES EVIDENCE

I will now examine the measures available to the vulnerable accused at the stage of trial in Scots law.[63] There is a binary legal regime governing the vulnerable accused at this stage of the process, with different legal measures and protection applying contingent on whether the vulnerable accused is giving evidence or not. It is here, more than anywhere else, that the requirements of the right to effective participation in Scots law become obscure and ill-defined.

I will begin by considering the position of the vulnerable accused who gives evidence. The Criminal Procedure (Scotland) Act 1995[64] s. 271 represents years of successive statutory intervention aimed at accommodating and addressing the vulnerability of witnesses, in general, who elect to give evidence.[65] In general terms, the act operates to as to create two classes of vulnerable witness: those witnesses automatically entitled to special measures which may assist them to give evidence and those whose entitlement to such measures is discretionary.[66] Both categories may apply to the vulnerable accused.[67]

In respect of any measure of entitlement sought, an application requires to be drafted, intimated to the Crown, and lodged with the court.[68] Automatic entitlement to special measures applies to all of those under the age of eighteen at the commencement of the proceedings (referred to as "child witnesses" in the language of the act), and those who are deemed vulnerable witnesses, albeit the latter category of deemed vulnerable witness does not apply to the vulnerable accused, as such status applies only to other witnesses and is contingent on the nature of the offense allegedly committed against them.[69] Discretionary entitlement to special measures may apply to any individual, including the vulnerable accused, whose mental disorder or fear or distress in connection with giving evidence creates a significant risk that the quality of their evidence may be affected, or because there is considered to be a significant risk of harm to the person by reason only of the fact that the person is giving or is to give evidence in the proceedings.[70] The definition of mental disorder used in this context is the same as that outlined in respect of the 2016 Act above, and thus applies to any mental illness, personality disorder or learning disability.[71] In deciding whether a witness may be entitled to discretionary special measures, there are a wide range of circumstances that the court must take into account.[72] These factors, in the context of the vulnerable accused, include whether the accused is or could be legally represented, the nature and circumstances of the alleged offense, the accused's age and maturity, any physical disability or other physical impairment, and any behavior toward the accused by witnesses or co-accused, among others.[73] The court must have regard to the best interests and views of the witness in question (which applies to the vulnerable accused if he or she is the subject of the vulnerable witness application).[74] There is also an overarching obligation under the 1995 Act that requires the party seeking to lead evidence from a potentially vulnerable witness, including the vulnerable accused, to carry out an assessment to determine whether said individual may be vulnerable and thus if they require special measures in order to give evidence.[75] The party citing a vulnerable witness must also ascertain the vulnerable witnesses views and have regard to their interests prior to making an application for special measures.[76]

The 1995 Act contains a host of both standard and non-standard special measures which may be sought and implemented in respect of the vulnerable accused.[77] The distinction between the two classes of measure pertains to whether the grant of the measure is automatic or not, which is contingent on the designation of vulnerability, essentially in this context, whether the vulnerable accused is under eighteen or not at the commencement of proceedings.[78] The measures available under the 1995 Act include the presence of a supporter while giving evidence, giving evidence via video link, and giving evidence in chief in the form of a prior statement.[79] The first two of these measures are standard special measures under the act.[80] Certain measures in the statutory scheme are expressly excluded from use by the vulnerable accused, namely the use of screens blocking sight of other witnesses and the clearing of court of members of the public.[81] The provisions of the act, recently introduced, that apply to the giving of evidence on commission of child witnesses also do not apply to the vulnerable accused.[82]

The Crown or a co-accused may object to the application for special measures on behalf of the vulnerable accused.[83] Beyond the standard special measures, the court must be convinced that the measures sought are appropriate and that the individual in question is indeed vulnerable, and the act makes provision for the hearing of argument in this regard if the measures sought are contested, or the court itself ex proprio motu disagrees with the application.[84] The court retains the power to keep under review the grant of special measures and may on its own motion, or on motion of either party, revoke or amend any measures previously authorized.[85]

The statutory scheme, as summarized above, is unnecessarily complicated as far as it pertains to the vulnerable accused.[86] That being as it may, it still manages to center an identifiable scheme of assistance around a clear definition of vulnerability with a clear procedural framework. In the absence of comprehensive empirical research or data, it is impossible to comment authoritatively upon the efficacy and prevalence of the use of special measures for the vulnerable accused. One can still, however, make some observations relative to the normative basis for such measures, in the context of the wider analysis undertaken in this chapter, alongside commenting on the scope of the provisions themselves. In respect of the former matter, we can see here again clearly, that in a general sense, these measures are targeted at ensuring the effective participation of the vulnerable accused, albeit in this context it is the provision of the accused's evidence itself alone that attracts support. In isolation therefore, this area of the law is the first considered where prima facie the vulnerable accused's understanding of proceedings does not seem to be the matter primarily targeted by the legal intervention. This is interesting in itself. A broader conception of the right to effective participation, as inclusive of not only the right to understand proceedings, but also the right to give understandable evidence at trial, is implied by the 1995 Act. This goes further than the requirements of Article 6, as interpreted by the European Court of Human Rights.[87] What appears problematic in this context however is the practical measures provided to support such a right. For the vulnerable accused electing to give evidence, the measures available give no guarantee that their evidence will in fact be understood. Despite the lack of empirical research one can surmise that the use of video link and a supporter are of questionable assistance in this respect. The former merely changes the forum in which evidence is provided, and the latter's role is limited to merely being present beside the vulnerable accused while giving evidence.[88] In respect of the remaining special measure available, the use of a prior statement as evidence in chief, this section is arguably otiose in respect of the vulnerable accused, following the fact that legislative change brought about by the 2016 Act now means that any answer given to police at interview under caution is admissible as an exception to the hearsay rule.[89] This means in practice that if the vulnerable accused gives a position at interview under caution, then said position can be conveyed to the court as their evidence. The provision under the 1995 Act seems practically redundant in light of this change, given that if invoked it would still render the vulnerable accused liable to cross-examination, a choice unlikely to be made for obvious strategic reasons. So, while the right to effective participation in Scots law seems to encompass the right to give comprehensible evidence, one must question the efficacy of the measures that exist to further this aim. Tellingly, as will be seen in the following section considering the common law jurisdiction of the courts to address vulnerability, Scotland, unlike England, Wales, and Northern Ireland, has no statutory provision, or legal precedent, to allow third parties to act as intermediaries, providing active (and effective) assistance to the vulnerable accused in understanding and relying information during their evidence.[90] There is also no Scottish appellate case law without instances whereby the accused was incapax, on whether the inability of the accused to give comprehensible evidence in this respect constitutes a miscarriage of justice.

The Protection of the Vulnerable Accused Beyond the Giving of Evidence

Beyond the giving of evidence, it falls to the discretion at common law of the Scottish courts to regulate their own proceedings, to protect the vulnerable accused.[91] This power is well developed in one specific sense, namely the provision of an interpreter so that the accused may understand proceedings (and be understood in turn via the giving of evidence). We have seen earlier in the chapter how the importance of such a measure was recognized early in the modern era. The importance of the right has been underlined by both the text of Article 6 itself, which refers to the right "to free assistance of an interpreter if he cannot speak the language" and associated case law, which has held that this aspect of the provision is essential to the right of effective participation.[92] Scots law has continued to protect the right of the vulnerable accused to have evidence translated by an interpreter at trial, albeit the High Court of Justiciary has stressed that the right does not apply to all procedural diets and that the onus is on the defense to indicate any problems that arise.[93] The right has in recent years been characterized directly as an explicit part of the right to effective participation in terms of Article 6.[94] Unfortunately, the High Court of Justiciary's analysis in this respect has been somewhat perfunctory. In *Erkurt v. Higson* it was noted that in order for bill of advocation (which is a mechanism for challenging procedural irregularity prior to the determination of a case) to be sustained on the ground of a lack of effective translation, the appellant has to show that he was "prejudiced by his absence of understanding, in the sense of his being unable to participate effectively in the proceedings."[95] A similar principle applies in the context of postconviction appeals.[96] There has been little further detailed exposition however of the broader principles at play in the area, albeit guidance on the practicalities of interpretation at trial has been given.[97]

Beyond the context of the provision of the interpreter, and specific provisions related to the giving of evidence considered above, one is left mainly to speculate about the scope and extent of the right to effective participation for the vulnerable accused at trial, who is not incapax. Some assistance may be indirectly gained from the terms of the statutory defense of plea in bar of trial due to mental disorder.[98] The statute operates so as to avoid a criminal prosecution continuing when the accused is deemed unfit for trial, and this question is determined by reference as to whether, by reason of a mental or physical condition, they are incapable of effectively participating in proceedings.[99] In answering this question, the court is to have regard to the ability of the person to understand the nature of the charge and the requirement to tender a plea to the charge and the effect of same and any other factor the court considers relevant.[100] The court must also have regard to the ability of the person to understand the purpose of, and follow the course of the trial, to understand the evidence that may be given against the person and to instruct and otherwise communicate with their legal representative.[101] The plea must be established by the defense on the balance of probabilities.[102] These factors reflect Strasbourg jurisprudence.[103] While the statute helps one focus their mind on the relevant issues, this chapter is of course concerned with the position of the vulnerable accused who does not meet these criteria. In this specific sense, there remains no authoritative exposition of effective participation and no statutory guidance, and so one is left to guess as to what the right, in effect, means and how at trial if the right is impugned, that situation may be remedied. This is disappointing given that Strasbourg case law offers at least a template by which to approach and discuss the concept of effective participation in this context in the national setting.[104] What is illuminating too, for comparative purposes, is the relatively well-developed body of case law that exists on the concept of effective participation in the Children's Reporter System in Scotland.[105] There are of course different considerations applicable in the criminal context, and indeed often different articles of the European Convention on Human Rights at play, but the lack of meaningful analysis by the High Court of Justiciary results in uncertainty about what the right to effective participation actually guarantees in Scotland.[106]

This problem however is not merely doctrinal. It is difficult because of the unstructured and obscure nature of the courts' discretion to ascertain what is, and what is not, practically possible in the context of measures of support beyond those previously commented upon. The Equalities and Human Rights Commission and the Law Society of Scotland have both considered the issue in the past, albeit neither has conducted in-depth empirical research specifically in Scottish context, and as mentioned there is a dearth of case law on the subject.[107] One thing that we can be sure about though is that Scotland has no established system for the provision of intermediaries such as those that exist, in a limited fashion, in England, Wales, and Northern Ireland.[108] It is possible in Scotland, at common law, for the court to permit a supporter to be present beyond the giving of evidence of the vulnerable accused and for said individual to be tasked with ensuring that the vulnerable accused understands proceedings.[109] The grant of an active role to that individual however such that they may intervene to ensure that questions put to the vulnerable accused and their evidence given in reply are understood, while theoretically possible in Scotland under the common law, does not occur in practice.[110] This is a matter which requires urgent political attention. The overarching issue identified here relating to support, beyond the vulnerable accused who gives evidence, is that in the absence of any statutory regulation, and authoritative judicial guidance, the protection of the vulnerable accused at trial is left almost exclusively to individual discretion. Thus, such protection that does exist relies on the defense to raise the issue and on the individual judge to put in place the appropriate measure of support. Under a system configured in this way, in a criminal justice system under significant stress, one can safely assume there will be instances where practice varies greatly and the protection afforded to the vulnerable accused is inadequate to permit them to participate effectively.[111] It is telling to consider that over the course of many years the Scottish Parliament has (correctly) considered it necessary to legislate to protect the rights of vulnerable witnesses while giving evidence in Scottish courts.[112] What then to deduce from the fact that without instances whereby the vulnerable accused is to give evidence, they are still left wholly to rely on largely undirected judicial discretion alone for their protection at trial? While, of course, the court itself retains the overarching legal obligation to ensure that proceedings are compliant with Article 6, this disparity in treatment between the two classes of actor (vulnerable witness and the vulnerable accused) is, I suggest, none the less revealing.

CONCLUSION: A FIG FOR THOSE PROTECTED BY LAW?

In this chapter, I have analyzed the support available to the vulnerable accused in Scotland at distinct stages of the criminal process. I have shown how the level and structure of protection varies greatly depending upon the stage at which proceedings have reached. I have traced the historical development of the protection for the vulnerable accused in the contemporary era through to the present day, and have revealed how measures of support have consistently been centred around the right to effective participation, which loosely equates to a right to understand, and participate in, legal proceedings. This chapter reveals, however, that Scots law on this topic in respect of the vulnerable accused, who is not incapax, is fragmented and ill-defined. The scope of the right to effective participation is accordingly hard to identify and its meaning and requirements in places obscure. In some instances, the right has been subsumed into other aspects of the substantive and adjectival Scots criminal law. While in other respects, the protection of the right has been left entirely to the use of unstructured and unregulated discretion. Ultimately, I have suggested, channeling Burns, that those protected by law in Scotland often may be receiving little practical benefit from its auspices.

Scottish criminal justice is, as I remarked upon earlier in this chapter, currently amidst a period of almost unprecedented flux.[113] Changes to the manner of trial, such as the increased use of remote hearings, bring with them an increased risk to the ability of the vulnerable accused to effectively participate in proceedings.[114] The work undertaken in this chapter has revealed a distinct gap in knowledge about what is, and is not, occurring in the Scottish criminal justice system concerning the vulnerable accused. Now, more than ever, thorough empirical research is required, and politicians and practitioners need to carefully consider the current efficacy of the protection afforded by law for the vulnerable accused in Scotland. As Lord Carloway has said, the current era provides an opportunity as well as a challenge, it is hoped that in respect of the vulnerable accused, that opportunity is firmly seized.

BIBLIOGRAPHY

Barrie, D., "Coronavirus in Scotland: Jurors Take a Seat at Cinemas to Tackle Courts Backlog" *The Times* (London, 2 October 2020). https://www.thetimes.co.uk/article

/coronavirus-in-scotland-jurors-take-a-seat-at-cinemas-to-tackle-courts-backlog-s7h3j2wvg, accessed 7 December 2020.

Burns, R., *The Poetical Miscellany; Containing Posthumous Poems, Songs, Epitaphs and Epigrams* (Glasgow, 1800).

Carloway, "Annual Address on the Opening of the Legal Year" (Edinburgh, Judiciary of Scotland, 28 September 2020). https://www.judiciary.scot/home/media-information/media-hub-news/2020/09/28/opening-of-the-legal-year, accessed 7 December 2020.

Dewart, M., *The Scottish Legal System* (Bloomsbury 6th edition, 2019).

Duff, P., "Adversarial Ideology and Police Questioning after Charge" (2013) 1(1) *Juridical Review*, 1.

Duff, P., "Chalmers to Cadder: Full Circle on Police Interrogation" (2015) 19(2) *Edinburgh Law Review*, 186.

Equalities and Human Rights Commission, "Inclusive Justice: A System Designed for All" (EHRC April 2020).

Ford, J. D., *Law and Opinion in Scotland during the Seventeenth Century* (Hart Publishing, 2007).

Ho, H. L., "The Criminal Trial, the Rule of Law and the Exclusion of Unlawfully Obtained Evidence" (2016) 10(1) *Criminal Law and Philosophy*, 109.

Horne, M., "Lawyers Strike Over Legal Aid Crisis" *The Times* (London 1 December 2020). https://www.thetimes.co.uk/article/scottish-lawyers-strike-over-legal-aid-crisis-qqccfwtx2, accessed 7 January 2021.

Hume, D., *Commentaries on the Law of Scotland Respecting the Description and Punishment of Crimes* (2nd ed., Bell & Bradfute, 1819) Vol. I, 37.

Justice Scotland, "Legal Assistance in the Police Station" (Justice Scotland, June 2018).

Keane, E. & Davidson, F. (eds), *Raitt on Evidence: Principles, Policy and Practice* (3rd ed., W. Green, 2018).

Keane, E., "Alarm Bells Ring over Hearsay Proposals" *(Scottish Legal News*, 1 April 2020). https://www.scottishlegal.com/article/eamon-keane-alarm-bells-ring-over-hearsay-proposals, accessed 7 December 2020.

Macintosh, F., "Will the Risk of Covid-19 Lead to More Hearsay Evidence in Scottish Criminal Trials?" [2020] 166 *Criminal Law Bulletin*, 1.

"Next Stage of Vulnerable Accused Persons Project" (*Law Society News*, 28 August 2019). https://www.lawscot.org.uk/news-and-events/law-society-news/help-vulnerable-accused-persons-project/, accessed 14 December 2020.

Norrie, K., *Children's Hearings in Scotland* (W. Green, 3rd ed., 2013).

O'Sullivan, K., "Five Year Digital Strategy Aims Achieved in a Matter of Months, Says Scotland's Most Senior Judge" (*FutureScot*, 16 September 2020). https://futurescot.com/five-year-digital-strategy-aims-achieved-in-a-matter-of-months-says-scotlands-most-senior-judge/, accessed 7 December 2020.

Owusu-Bempah, A., "The Interpretation and Application of the Right to Effective Participation" (2018) 22(4) *International Journal of Evidence and Proof*, 321.

Owusu-Bempah, A., "Understanding the Barriers to Defendant Participation in Criminal Proceedings in England and Wales" (2020) 40 (4) *Legal Studies* (Society of Legal Scholars), 1.

Paterson, L., "Virtual Trials "Will Need to Be Used as Default Option" *The Times* (London, 4 July 2020). https://www.thetimes.co.uk/article/virtual-trials-will-need-to-be-used-as-default-option-n577bc6kd, accessed 7 December 2020.

Plotnikoff, J. & Woolfson, R., *Intermediaries in the Criminal Justice System: Improving Communication for Vulnerable Witnesses and Defendants* (Policy Press, 2015).

Price, T., Parkes, T., & Malloch, M., "'Discursive Struggles' between Criminal Justice Sanctions and Health Interventions for People Who Use Drugs: A Qualitative Exploration of Diversion Policy and Practice in Scotland" (2020). *Drugs: Education, Prevention and Policy.* https://www.tandfonline.com/doi/full/10.1080/09687637.2020.1775180.

Rahmatian, A., "The Role of Institutional Writers in Scots Law" (2018) 1 *Juridical Review* 42.

Ross, M. & Chalmers, J. (eds) *Walker & Walker: The Law of Evidence in Scotland* (Bloomsbury, 4th edition, 2015).

Scott, P. F., "Responding to Covid-19 in Scots Law" (2020) 24(3) *Edinburgh Law Review*, 421.

Sharp, L. & Ross, M. *The Vulnerable Witnesses (Scotland) Act 2004* (Dundee University Press, 2008).

The Law Society of England and Wales, "Law Under Lockdown: Covid 19 Measures on Access to Justice and Vulnerable People" (Law Society of England and Wales, September 2020).

The Scotland Institute, "Mental Health and Scotland's Prison Population" (The Scotland Institute, July 2015).

NOTES

1. My title borrows from Robert Burns' celebrated posthumous poem, "The Jolly Beggars." See Robert Burns, *The Poetical Miscellany; Containing Posthumous Poems, Songs, Epitaphs and Epigrams* (Glasgow 1800). I am grateful to Ryan Sloan and Tony Convery, who generously gave of their time to discuss matters that arose in my consideration of this area of practice. Any errors remain my own.

2. See Paul F. Scott, "Responding to Covid-19 in Scots Law" (2020) 24(3) *Edinburgh Law Review*, 421, for an overview of the various legal responses to the pandemic in Scotland.

3. Douglas Barrie, "Coronavirus in Scotland: Jurors Take a Seat at Cinemas to Tackle Courts Backlog" *The Times* (London, 2 October 2020), https://www.thetimes.co.uk/article/coronavirus-in-scotland-jurors-take-a-seat-at-cinemas-to-tackle-courts-backlog-s7h3j2wvg, accessed 7 December 2020.

4. Laura Paterson, "Virtual Trials "Will Need to be Used as Default Option"" *The Times* (London, 4 July 2020), https://www.thetimes.co.uk/article/virtual-trials-will-need-to-be-used-as-default-option-n577bc6kd, accessed 7 December 2020.

5. See s.259 (2A) of the Criminal Procedure (Scotland) Act 1995 as amended by Part 5 of the Coronavirus (Scotland) Act 2020. Analysis of the potential implications of the change are outlined at Eamon Keane, "Alarm Bells Ring over Hearsay Proposals" (*Scottish Legal News*, 1 April 2020), https://www.scottishlegal.com/article/eamon-keane-alarm-bells-ring-over-hearsay-proposals, accessed 7 December 2020. See also Fred Macintosh, "Will the Risk of Covid-19 Lead to More Hearsay Evidence in Scottish Criminal Trials?" (2020) 166 *Criminal Law Bulletin*, 1.

6. See Lord Carloway, "Annual Address on the Opening of the Legal Year" (Edinburgh, Judiciary of Scotland, 28 September 2020), https://www.judiciary.scot/home/media-information/media-hub-news/2020/09/28/opening-of-the-legal-year, accessed 7 December 2020.

7. Ibid.

8. See Lord Carloway's comments reported at Kevin O'Sullivan, "Five Year Digital Strategy Aims Achieved in a Matter of Months, Says Scotland's Most Senior Judge" (*FutureScot*, 16 September 2020), https://futurescot.com/five-year-digital-strategy-aims-achieved-in-a-matter-of-months-says-scotlands-most-senior-judge/, accessed 7 December 2020.

9. A different legal regime applies to the vulnerable accused who lacks legal capacity. From henceforth all references to "the vulnerable accused" should be read as referring to an accused who has legal capacity, unless otherwise stated.

10. See, e.g., the findings contained relating to remote hearings and vulnerable individuals in The Law Society of England and Wales, "Law Under Lockdown: Covid 19 Measures on Access to Justice and Vulnerable People" (September 2020, *Law Society of England and Wales*).

11. See Gillian Hunter, "Participation in Courts and Tribunals" in Jessica Jacobson and Penny Cooper (eds.) *Participation in Courts and Tribunals: Concepts, Realities and Aspirations* (BUP 2020) and Kate Brown, Kathryn Ecclestone, and Nick Emmel, "The Many Faces of Vulnerability" (2017) 16(3) *Social Policy and Society*, 497.

12. Given that my definition includes the police interview it would be more accurate to refer to the "vulnerable suspect" when referring to the individual at this stage of the process, but I have chosen the term "vulnerable accused" to cover the entirety of proceedings for the sake of simplicity.

13.

14. In Scotland, the police have a statutory power permitting them to arrest and ask questions of a suspect under caution without warrant as per the Criminal Justice (Scotland) Act 2016 s 1. A separate regime for questioning suspects also exists under the Terrorism Act 2000 s 41 and schedules 7 & 8 but consideration of same is excluded from this chapter.

15. For further information on the operation of such measures in the Scottish context see Tracey Price, Tessa Parkes, and Margaret Malloch, "'Discursive Struggles' between Criminal Justice Sanctions and Health Interventions for People Who Use Drugs: A Qualitative Exploration of Diversion Policy and Practice in Scotland"

(2020) *Drugs: Education, Prevention and Policy* https://www.tandfonline.com/doi/full/10.1080/09687637.2020.1775180, accessed 16 December 2020.

16. A civil forum, designed to safeguard the welfare of children, that may however consider the alleged commission of criminal offenses under its jurisdiction. See Kenneth Norrie, *Children's Hearings in Scotland* (W. Green, 3rd edition, 2013).

17. In using this term, I am not suggesting that any of the groups to which I apply the label are inherently vulnerable, rather that the specific institutional circumstances which they face render them such. There are also myriad other factors, beyond the scope of this chapter, that influence whether effective participation can be achieved or not.

18. *HM Advocate v Olsson,* 1941 JC 63.

19. See The Criminal Evidence Act 1898 s 1. A similar provision is now contained in The Criminal Procedure (Scotland) Act 1995. See Margaret Ross, James Chalmers, and Isla Callander (eds.) *Walker & Walker The Law of Evidence in Scotland* (Bloomsbury, 5th edition, 2020) 13.11.1.

20. *Olsson* (n 17) at 63.

21. Ibid.

22. *Liszewski v. Thomson*, 1942 JC 55.

23. E.g., *Olsson* (n 17), *HM Advocate v. Aitken,* 1926 JC 83; *HM Advocate v. M'Swiggan,* 1937 J.C. 50.

24. For further detailed analysis on the general factors that arise for consideration in this area of the law of evidence see Hock Lai Ho, "The Criminal Trial, the Rule of Law and the Exclusion of Unlawfully Obtained Evidence" (2016) 10(1) *Criminal Law and Philosophy*, 109.

25. For a full analysis see Peter Duff, "Adversarial Ideology and Police Questioning After Charge" (2013) 1(1) *Juridical Review*, 1; and Peter Duff, "Chalmers to Cadder: Full Circle on Police Interrogation" (2015) 19(2) *Edinburgh Law Review*, 186.

26. Ibid.

27. Lord Thomson described an individual's "theoretical" freedom to refuse such an invitation (and the likely consequences of same, i.e., formal arrest) in detail in *Swankie v. Milne,* 1973 JC 1 at 6.

28. See Duff, "Adversarial Ideology" (n 24) and Duff, "Chalmers to Cadder" (n 24). See also Justice Scotland, "Legal Assistance in the Police Station" (*Justice Scotland*, June 2018) 1.5.

29. See, e.g., *Olsson* (n 17) at 66 and *Aitken* (n 22) at 87.

30. For further information on the historical position in Scots law in respect of these matters see The Scottish Law Commission, *Report on Insanity and Diminished Responsibility* (*Scot Law Com*, No 92, 2004). These pleas were abolished by the Criminal Justice and Licensing (Scotland) Act s.171.

31. See the Scottish Law Commission (n 29) Part 2 and Part 4.

32. See David Hume, *Commentaries on the Law of Scotland Respecting the Description and Punishment of Crimes* (2nd ed., Bell & Bradfute, 1819) Vol. I, 37.

33. See, e.g., *HM Advocate v. Brown,* (1907) 5 Adam at 343 and *HM Advocate v. Wilson,* 1942 JC 75 at 79.

34. The European Court of Human Rights first recognized the implied right to effective participation as implicit in Article 6 in 1994 in *Stanford v. UK* (1994), Series A 282. The most comprehensive analysis of the right to date by the Strasbourg court occurred in 2005 in *SC v. UK* (2005) ECHR 263. See Abenaa Owusu-Bempah, "The Interpretation and Application of the Right to Effective Participation" (2018) 22(4), *International Journal of Evidence and Proof*, 321.

35. The Criminal Justice (Scotland) Act 2016 s. 1 (asp 1) hereafter "The 2016 Act." See also Eamon Keane and Fraser Davidson (eds), *Raitt on Evidence: Principles, Policy and Practice* (3rd ed., W. Green, 2018), 9.07–9.16 for a fuller consideration of the law and practice in this area.

36. The 2016 Act s.34. It is worth noting here that the statute uses the language of "a person not officially accused," given that said individual becomes officially accused only after formal charge by the police, I however have chosen to use the expression the vulnerable accused throughout in this chapter for reasons outlined at (n 12).

37. The 2016 Act s.42.

38. Ibid. s. 42(1)(a)-(c).

39. By virtue of The 2016 Act s. 33(6).

40. The Mental Health (Care & Treatment) (Scotland) Act 2003 (asp 13) ss. 328(2)(a).

41. Ibid. ss. 328(2)(e), (f) & (g). The types of behavior are behavior that causes or is likely to case harassment, alarm or distress to any other person and acting as no prudent person would.

42. The 2016 Act Part 6 Chapter 2.

43. Ibid. s. 40. See also s. 41 which allows social work to have access to the arrested individual in certain circumstances.

44. Ibid. s. 40(4).

45. Ibid. s 33(2)(c).

46. Ibid. s.33(3)-(5). These are orders made under the Children's Hearings (Scotland) Act 2011 (asp 1) that designate a local authority as responsible for the care of a child.

47. The 2016 Act s 33(3)-(5).

48. Ibid. s. 32(4).

49. Ibid. s. 32(5).

50. There is however concerning data available relative to the number of individuals who waive their right to legal advice at police interview generally in Scotland. The figure was thought to be as high as 75% in February 2017. See Justice Scotland (n 27) 2.7.

51. See Duff, "Chalmers to Cadder" (n 24) and *Cadder v. HM Advocate,* [2010] UKSC 43; 2011 SC (UKSC) 13.

52. A civil action for damages on the basis of a breach of convention rights following unlawful detention is competent in Scots law, see Human Rights Act 1998 s.8 & *McCaffer v. Lord Advocate, PF Glasgow and Chief Constable Police Scotland* 2015 SLT (Sh Ct) 44.

53. See *Gilroy v. HM Advocate* (2013) HCJAC 18, 2013 JC 163 at [56].

54. For examples of pre-2016 Act challenges involving vulnerability see *Codona v. HM Advocate*, 1996 SLT 1100, *Blagojevic v. HM Advocate,* 1995 SLT 1189 & *LB v. HM Advocate,* 2003 JC 94.

55. See *HM Advocate v Hawkins* (2017), HCJ 79; 2017 SLT 1328 for an instance whereby undue pressure was applied by police officers thus vitiating the admissibility of evidence obtained at a police interview.

56. See *Codona etc.* at (n 53).

57. See *Ambrose v. Harris* (2011), UKSC 43; 2012 SC (UKSC) 53. The 2016 Act s. 44(1).

58. *Cadder* (n 50).

59. Although pertaining to pre-2016 Act practice, see, e.g., *HM Advocate v. Mair,* 1982 SLT 471.

60. See Ross et al. (n 18) 9.12.1–9.12.4 for further details.

61. See, e.g., *Miln v. Cullen,* 1967 JC 21 at [30] and *Jamieson v. Annan*, 1988 JC 62.

62. *Gilroy* (n 52) at [56]. See also *B v. HM Advocate,* 1995 SLT 961.

63. Detailed consideration of these measures is outwith the scope of this chapter, albeit I will summarize their key features in the following section. For an examination of the subject in general, albeit one not including more recent changes, see Laura Sharp and Margaret Ross *The Vulnerable Witnesses (Scotland) Act 2004* (Dundee University Press 2008).

64. Hereafter "The 1995 Act."

65. See Keane & Davidson (n 34) 3.46 - 3.72.

66. The 1995 Act ss. 271(1)(a)(b)(c) & (d).

67. Ibid. s.271F.

68. Ibid. s.271C.

69. Ibid. s.271(1)(a) & (c).

70. Ibid. s.271(1)(b) & (d).

71. Ibid. s.271(1)(b)(i) which incorporates the definition given in The Mental Health (Care & Treatment)(Scotland) Act 2003 s. 328.

72. The 1995 Act S. 271(2) as read alongside s.271F.

73. Ibid.

74. Ibid. s.271(4A).

75. Ibid. s. 271BA.

76. Ibid. s.271E(1)(a).

77. Ibid. s.271H.

78. Ibid. s. 271A.

79. Ibid. s.271H.

80. Ibid. *s.* 271A.

81. Ibid. *s.* 271F(8).

82. Ibid. ss. 271BZA(1) & 271F(8).

83. Ibid. ss. 271A & 271C.

84. Ibid. s.271C.

85. Ibid. *s*.271D.

86. The 1995 Act utilizes a scheme of adjustment fairly described as "tortuous" in Ross et al. (n 18) 13.4.9.

87. See *SC* (n 33) & Owusu-Bempah (n 33).

88. The 1995 Act s 271L.

89. Ibid. s. 261ZA.

90. See Joyce Plotnikoff & Richard Woolfson, *Intermediaries in the Criminal Justice System: Improving Communication for Vulnerable Witnesses and Defendants* (Policy Press 2015).

91. *Hampson v. HM Advocate*, 2003 SLT 94. A power asserted by the High Court of Justiciary, albeit in the context of other vulnerable witnesses. See also the 1995 Act s. 271G.

92. *Stanford* (n 33) at [26].

93. See, e.g., *Mikhailitchenko v Normand*, 1993 SLT 1138 & *Erkurt v. Higson*, 2004 JC 23.

94. *Erkurt* (n 92) and *San Lee v. HM Advocate,* [2016] HCJAC 39; 2016 JC 133.

95. *Erkurt* (n 92) at [27].

96. *San Lee* (n 92).

97. Ibid.

98. s. 53F The 1995 Act.

99. Ibid. s.53F(1).

100. ibid s. 53F(2)(i) & (ii).

101. ibid s. 53F(2)(iii)–(v).

102. ibid s. 53F(1)

103. See *SC* (n 33).

104. ibid.

105. See, e.g., *ABC v Principal Reporter and Another* (2020) UKSC 26; 2020 SLT 679 & *Murtaza v Murtaza* (2011) CSOH 214.

106. Cases involving the Children's Reporter System in Scotland tend to invoke Article 8, but also often feature Article 6 in its civil context.

107. Although the Commission did undertake interviews with solicitors, judges, and accused in Scotland albeit the transcription of same is not available. It should be noted that there has been valuable work in Scotland on the topic of the vulnerable accused in recent years, see, e.g., the work of the Law Society of Scotland, "Next Stage of Vulnerable Accused Persons Project" (*Law Society News*, 28 August 2019), https://www.lawscot.org.uk/news-and-events/law-society-news/help-vulnerable-accused-persons-project/, accessed 14 December 2020 and the work of the Equality and Human Rights Commission, which specifically considered Scotland and digitalisation during its UK wide inquiry into the experiences of disabled defendants and accused persons, Equalities and Human Rights Commission, "Inclusive Justice: A System Designed for All" (EHRC April 2020).

108. See Plotnikoff and Richard Woolfson (n 89).

109. Data on file with author.

110. See the comments of the Equalities and Human Rights Commission (n 106), 28.

111. For information on the financial and other pressures on the Scottish criminal justice system at present, see, e.g., Marc Horne, "Lawyers Strike Over Legal Aid Crisis" *The Times* (London, 1 December 2020), https://www.thetimes.co.uk/article/scottish-lawyers-strike-over-legal-aid-crisis-qqccfwtx2, accessed 7 January 2021.

112. See, e.g., ss 274 & 275 of the 1995 Act.

113. If one ignores for present purposes Oliver's Cromwell's attempts to abolish Scots law in the 17th century. See John D. Ford, *Law and Opinion in Scotland during the Seventeenth Century* (Hart Publishing, 2007).

114. See, e.g., the comments of the English Law Society (n 10).

Chapter 8

The Group Decision-Making of the Jury

Challenges to a Fair Trial

Sarah Lloyd

Juries have been in place, in one form or another, for thousands of years. The modern jury has its roots in the 12th century with the idea of having a representative trial of one's equals. Today, the jury system is based on the fundamental principles of fairness and representativeness, however, questions have been raised with regard to this fairness in practice. This is particularly important to examine in terms of the group decision-making of the jury as very little is known about these collective decision-making processes.[1] These issues are important to examine in more detail, as lack of knowledge of how juries make their verdict decisions could result not only in miscarriages of justice, but also in a loss of faith in the jury system and criminal justice system (CJS) more widely. In this chapter, a brief history of the jury will be discussed, before looking at the role of the jury and how it is viewed by the public and criminal justice professionals. It will then look in more detail at the group decision-making processes of the jury and the implications this has on fairness. The chapter will end by briefly examining the impact of Covid-19 on the fairness of jury trials and new measures introduced to tackle this.

A BRIEF HISTORY OF THE JURY IN ENGLAND AND WALES

Before juries, conflicts tended to be resolved using trial by ordeal. As the church and state were closely connected, and it was the local priest's job to interpret God's will and resolve criminal and civil disputes. Trial by ordeal such as fire or water, were used to divine the truth. As time went on, trial by ordeal was replaced to trial by verdict. After the Norman conquest in 1066, local noblemen served as a type of jury who reported on the size and productivity of local estates for tax purposes. By 1166, in matters pertaining to land ownership, where ownership by the church or state was not clear, Henry II introduced a jury of twelve free and lawful men who heard these cases.[2] Henry II also experimented with juries to deal with criminal issues.[3] In 1166, he met with his barons and issued the Assize of Clarendon to draft local people to identify criminals.[4] This had become the grand jury, where a local sheriff or royal judge assembled a group of respected citizens who met periodically and were asked to write up a list of criminals in their area.

The Magna Carta of 1215 set out the idea of a representative jury of one's peers. The charter read, "To any man whom we have deprived or dispossessed of lands, castles, liberties, or rights without the lawful judgment of his equals, we will at once restore these."[5]

Although this mainly involved barons, it helped to codify the right to a jury trial in terms of judgment of peers, and guaranteed a trial, although not always by jury.[6]

The main development of the jury system was the Bushel case of 1670.[7] This case concerned the Quaker, William Penn, who defied a ban against public assembly and preaching in public. Bushel was a member of the jury in this case. The jury found Penn guilty of speaking of religion in a public place, but they refused to find this an unlawful assembly. As a result, the judge imprisoned the jury without food, heat or water for two nights. The jury remained defiant despite warnings from the lord mayor to provide the verdict the court would accept. Bushel petitioned the Court of Common Pleas for a writ of habeas corpus, used to bring a prisoner/detainee before the court to determine if their imprisonment was lawful. The subsequent proceedings confirmed the principle of juries as independent fact finders who have a right to give a verdict that reflects their conscience.[8] This means that a jury cannot be penalized for having a view that differs from the judge.[9] The right to a criminal trial by jury was noted as statute in 1688[10] and still exists today.

THE JURY TODAY IN ENGLAND AND WALES

There are a variety of legal systems around the world[11] and some operate an inquisitorial system where the judge decides the verdict, such as Italy or France, or an escabado or mixed system, e.g., Spain, where there may be a combination of professionals and laypeople who decide the verdict.[12] The legal system in England and Wales is an adversarial system. This means that the prosecution and defense represent two sides of the case (or evidence), and argue against each other, to persuade a jury of a defendant's guilt or innocence.[13]

In England and Wales, juries are made up of 12 people, aged between 18 and 75, who are randomly selected from the electoral roll. In order to be selected for jury service, you need to have lived in the UK, Channel Islands, or Isle of Man, for a period of at least 5 years since the age of 13. In addition, you must be on the electoral roll. Restrictions to jury service include those on bail, if you've been to prison or on a community order in the last 10 years, if you are regularly receiving treatment for a mental health condition or if you do not have the capacity to manage your own affairs or decisions.[14]

Around 400,000 people are called for jury service every year.[15] The summons is sent through the post by the Jury Central Summoning Bureau (JCSB). If the summons is ignored, it may constitute a breach of s.20 of The Juries Act, 1974 and result in a fine of £1000. People can though, apply for exemptions to jury service, for instance if you have a holiday booked, or if you are attending hospital for regular treatment.

All trials in England and Wales begin in the magistrates court. Jury trials take place in the crown court when a defendant pleads not guilty. This means that jury trials are reserved for the most serious of criminal cases, such as rape and murder. In reality, juries decide less than 1% of all criminal cases.[16] This may seem a small number, but it still represents thousands of cases. Furthermore, given the seriousness of these cases, they have the most profound consequences, not only for the defendant, but also for the victim, families and friends, and for society more widely.[17] It is therefore of the utmost importance that the way juries make their decisions is as fair and as informed as possible.

The Role of the Jury

Juries are supposed to be fair and representative.[18] The basic role of the jury is to be fact finders, i.e., to determine a defendant's guilt or innocence based solely on the evidence presented to them during the trial. This is complicated by the fact that the jury is a group that is unique in nature, and also as juries are governed by s.8 of the Contempt of Court Act, 1981, which will be discussed further on in this chapter.

Generally, juries are required to come to a unanimous decision and deliberate for at least 2 hours and 10 minutes.[19] If a unanimous decision cannot be reached, the judge will usually accept a majority decision of 10:2 or 11:1. Jury decision-making is dichotomous. The options open to them are guilt or innocence. They also make these dichotomous decisions at an individual and at a group level. At the individual level, research has primarily been concerned with psychosocial influences such as gender, age, confidence and attractiveness alongside basic psychological principles such as recall and biases.[20] Juries though, make their ultimate verdict decision as a group, but very little is known about these group decision-making processes. Additionally, there is limited understanding of how juries engage in meaningful deliberative decision-making processes, how they communicate, and how the group impacts these processes.[21] These factors are important to explore to increase our understanding of these processes and to ensure that they are fair to prevent wrongful conviction.

SECTION 8 OF THE CONTEMPT OF COURT ACT 1981

The Contempt of Court Act, 1981 restricts revealing information about researching jury deliberations, examining their decision-making processes and forbids jurors discussing details about the case and these processes outside of the jury room. Section 8 of this Act is the result of *Attorney General v. New Statesman & Nation Publishing Co Ltd* (1981), where one of the jurors in the trial that acquitted Jeremy Thorpe of conspiracy to murder released information about the trial to the *New Stateman* magazine in 1979.

The act states:

> It is a contempt of court to obtain, disclose, or solicit any particulars of statements made, opinions expressed, arguments advanced, or votes cast by members of a jury in the course of their deliberations in any legal proceedings.[22]

A breach of this act is punishable by fine or imprisonment for up to two years.

Many have argued that s.8 of the Contempt of Court Act, 1981 should be relaxed for academic interests to examine jury decision-making processes and their efficacy and fairness to ensure they are as fair and effective as possible and ensure informed decision-making.[23] In parts of Australia, e.g., NSW and Victoria, information the Attorney General can grant researchers to enter the jury room.[24] In England and Wales, though, this act forbids research on real deliberating juries and as a result jury decision-making is shrouded in secrecy.

THE UNIQUE NATURE OF THE JURY

Despite being a fundamental decision-making group, juries are also a unique decision-making group in our society. Firstly, is the fact that a jury is made up of 12 strangers, from all walks of life, who come together for the sole purpose of deciding whether someone is guilty or innocent of a serious crime.

Furthermore, members of the jury may not have any experience of the CJS, or knowledge of it, and no training is given.

They also bring with them their personal values, experiences, viewpoints, attitudes, etc. which may impact their decision-making. Once they have made their verdict decision, they go home and probably do not see one another again. So, for most jury members, jury service is a unique experience for which they have very little knowledge or experience and they have varying levels of education, different personal beliefs and value systems, who come together for a short time to make a profound, important decision about a stranger's life.

Secondly, jurors firstly listen to the evidence as individuals. At this pre-deliberation stage of proceedings, jurors also listen in silence, i.e., there is no discussion as they hear the evidence presented at trial. At this stage, they make a decision as individuals as to whether the defendant is guilty or not. The ultimate decision though, is made as a collective and is reached through discussion and argument, which means jurors must bring their individual decision to the group and try and persuade others to their way of thinking or be persuaded toward other's viewpoints. Given that this is a group of strangers where some members may be more dominant than others, this is no easy task.

HOW JURIES ARE MEANT TO MAKE DECISIONS VS. REALITY

Juries are expected to make their verdict decision based only on the evidence provided during the trial. Jury trials though, are extremely complex and consist of a variety of different players from a variety of different backgrounds, belief system, etc. all working toward a common goal in an environment that is alien to them. The legal system of England and Wales operates under the assumption that jurors can and do take in all of the trial information and process it rationally and objectively, discarding any irrelevant information, and then they retrieve this information in order to reach a verdict decision.[25]

During criminal trials, jurors are presented with various types of evidence, which is often complex and contradictory, that they need to evaluate, interpret, and use to reach a verdict.[26] Jurors are therefore expected to reach a decision about a suspect's guilt or innocence, objectively, rationally and without emotion. The reality of whether jurors can be truly impartial and objective has been questioned and this issue impacts the fairness of a jury trial,[27] particularly as we know very little about jury decision-making processes and other factors that could affect these decisions. In addition, a fundamental question underlying the use of juries is, to what extent do they base their decision on the evidence presented to them and what part do extra-legal factors play.

Extra-legal factors such as confidence, pre-trial publicity, ethnicity and gender have been examined in detail in research looking at individual jurors.[28] In fact, the majority of research on jury decision-making has examined this at an individual/juror level, and findings have then been extrapolated to the group/jury level.[29] Very few factors have been examined in looking at the jury however. Since the judicial system in England and Wales requires the jury to discuss, deliberate and reach a decision collectively, it is extremely important to understand more about these decision-making processes. Moreover, research has shown how group decisions differ from individual decisions in several ways, e.g., group decision-making can be more severe.[30]

Some issues that may influence the fairness of jury decision-making have come to light. One example is that of decision-making errors.[31]

Juries are made up of humans and human decision-making is fallible. Since we cannot directly study the deliberation/decision-making processes of real juries, due to s.8 of the Contempt of Court At 1981, it is not always clear where and when in the collective decision-making process these errors occur. Errors in decision-making can have disastrous consequences for victims, defendants, and families, such as wrongful convictions or acquitting someone who is guilty. These errors also can undermine public faith in the credibility of juries and in the CJS more widely and could affect public belief in the notion of a fair trial. Understanding these collective decision-making processes could lead to the development of strategies and legislation to reduce juror bias, make jury trials more informed and therefore facilitate fairer trials.[32]

Another factor undermining the fairness of jury trials is that juries have limited understanding of judicial instruction and of the evidence, particularly scientific/forensic evidence, presented to them.[33] A lack of understanding or overconfidence in understanding could impact the fairness of a jury trial by giving too much or too little weight to a piece of evidence for example. If juries can understand the evidence and instructions from the judge, for example beyond reasonable doubt, this will mean their decision-making processes will be more informed.[34]

There has been very little research examining how juries are able to adequately incorporate evidence and the information presented at trial into their decision-making processes.[35] This includes how they process and reason about scientific evidence.[36] This is important to consider as modern criminal trials are more and more dependent on scientific and forensic evidence and techniques.

There is then, limited understanding of how juries engage in meaningful deliberative and decision-making processes in reality, in spite of the importance of jury decision-making within the CJS.[37] There is also limited knowledge and understanding of the communicative aspects of these processes and the role the group plays. There have been a few questionable jury decision-making processes that have come to light in recent years and these examples illustrate the importance of understanding more about the differences between how the jury is expected to make decisions, and how they really do, to protect the right to a fair trial. One such case is the Ouija board case. This case illustrates the threat to fairness of a jury trial if those involved do not follow instruction or do not take their role seriously.

In 1994, Stephen Young was on trial for the murder of Harry and Nicola Fuller. The couple had been found shot dead in their home. The trial took 5 weeks to decide and the jury were housed in a hotel. It emerged that four of the jurors on the case got drunk and decided to consult a Ouija board and ask the spirit of Harry and Nicola Fuller who killed them. They claimed the Ouija board confirmed that Stephen Young had killed them. These jurors managed to persuade the other members of the jury that Stephen Young was guilty, and he was sentenced to two life terms. When the story emerged, Stephen Young received a retrial with a new jury. This jury found him guilty, without the use of an Ouija board, although Young maintains his innocence.[38]

THE PERCEPTIONS OF JURIES

Juries have been criticized on several levels, for example for being idealistic, costly and open to misconduct.[39] Despite criticisms, juries generally are viewed positively by the general public and many consider juries to be the cornerstone of the CJS.[40] In England and Wales, the jury play a central role in the CJS. A study by Roberts and Hough (2009) asked participants to rate six rights of a democratic society on a Likert scale 1–7 (1 = not important and 7 = very important). The right to a jury trial was included in this and 72% of participants rated this right as a 7 and 15/6% rated it a 6 on the Likert scale. This demonstrated that the right to a jury trial was the most important of the rights polled. Other rights included the right to protest against the government and the right to privacy.

WHAT WE KNOW ABOUT JUROR DECISION-MAKING

Much of what we know about jury decision-making has been from research conducted on individual jurors and on psychosocial factors such as gender, ethnicity, attractiveness and confidence[41] rather than the collective member's communicative processes.

Research on individual jurors has also focused on the outcome (verdict) rather than the processes by which the group reach this outcome. Additionally, factors such as sentencing have been studied in juries even though in England and Wales the jury has no say in sentencing.[42] This information has then been extrapolated to the group level (jury level). In addition, most of our knowledge has come from anecdotal evidence or retrospective interviews with legal professionals such as lawyers and judges who have a very different experience of criminal trials and the CJS than laypeople. This is important to note as legal professionals have not only been trained in legal matters and have a wealth of experience in criminal law, but also are not party to the decision-making processes of the jury and therefore do not know what factors influence these processes. Furthermore, most of the research on juror decision-making has been done in the US.[43] This is an issue as jury systems in the US are markedly different to those in England and Wales and therefore results are difficult to generalize to our legal system.

In addition to these issues with traditional research, there have also been several methodological issues. In a review of jury decision-making research, Devine (2014) found issues such as inadequate sampling, i.e., relying on small numbers, unrepresentative samples. Many studies rely on undergraduate samples of psychology students who are very young rather than a mix of jury eligible participants.[44] Also, the majority of studies have suffered from poor quality simulation/case material, such as a partial video of a fictional crime rather than a full trial which simulates a real trial.

Additionally, very few studies had any form of deliberative element and of those that did, the majority were facilitated by a researcher, were partial or timed.[45] My own research looking at the group decision-making processes has addressed these methodological issues by using a real case, tried in a mock courtroom using actors to play legal parts in front of a community of jury eligible mock jurors who then deliberate until they reach a unanimous decision. This aims to replicate the realities of jury decision-making as much as possible given the restrictions of s.8 of the Contempt of Court Act 1981. There is therefore a real need for more research in this area to ensure that everyone receives a fair trial and that juries understand their role and the instructions given.

RESPONSES TO COVID-19: THE REMOTE AND NIGHTINGALE COURTS

A recent factor to potentially impact the fairness of trial by jury is Covid-19. In March 2020, the lord chief justice decided to stop all jury trials. This was a response to protect public safety as it was difficult to implement social distancing in existing courtrooms.[46] Since then, several proposals have been implemented such as remote jury trials and Nightingale courts, however, there is a lack of evidence about how these might impact the fairness of a criminal trial. This is not the first time video link technology has been used in court, however, it is not used in court as a matter of course and some research has found the use of video may be detrimental to a fair trial.[46] Video link technology allows the court to use live streaming so that participants can take part and guidelines can be found from the MOJ (2020).[47] There are advantages to using remote trials, in that it is cost-effective, can livestream from anywhere and allow social distancing to be observed.[48]

A project piloted by JUSTICE[49] examined whether jury trials could be conducted remotely and ensure fairness. They used a fictional case and legal roles and jury members were played by volunteers and invited experts. Parts of the process were "extremely abbreviated" according to the project team. The remote trial took place on a single screen like a Zoom meeting. The jurors, clerk and judge had access to a private chat function where they could access relevant documents. The project team reported this was generally a positive experience, and once trained, participants seemed with the technology. However, there were also technological issues such as connectivity issues. This could mean that jurors miss important evidence, instructions, etc. They may fill in these gaps with what they thought happened during the trial and this could affect the fairness of their decision-making processes. Additionally, if jurors are watching the trial from their homes for example, it would be difficult to maintain confidentiality, and control over the sanctity of the jury room. It might also breach s.8 of the Contempt of Court Act 1981. Furthermore, training jurors and legal professionals takes time and resources and some do not have access to this technology.

Another implementation during Covid-19 is that of Nightingale courts. Nightingale courts are courts that take place in public buildings such as university halls, sports halls, conference centers, and were last used during World War II. There has been very little research examining the use of these courts and how they might impact fairness, however, the government has plans for 9 more of these by the end of January 2021. This will bring the total to 40. The idea behind these Nightingale courts was to clear backlog and keep criminal trials progressing through the pandemic according to Lord Chancellor Robert Buckland QC. These courts though, raise issues of whether these buildings have the gravitas and meaning of real criminal courts and how this affects the jury and their decision-making. In addition, they raise the question of where the jury deliberate and ultimately make their decision and how the right to a fair trial will be protected.

CONCLUSION

Juries in England and Wales are considered to be extremely important to ensure a fair and representative trial of one's peers. They are made up of laypeople with no training and usually very little experience of the CJS. They also come from a variety of backgrounds, attitudes, belief systems and biases. Research has been carried out at a mainly individual/juror level, despite juries in this country making their decision as a group through collective discussion and deliberation. In addition to these factors and our knowledge of extra-legal factors such as confidence and attractiveness that affect individual juror decision-making, very little is known about the group decision-making processes of juries and how these processes impact the fairness of a criminal trial. The jury as a collective is extremely important to examine as even though jury trials represent around 1% of all criminal cases in England and Wales,[50] these are the most serious with the most profound consequences. It is crucial that we learn more about the jury in order to ensure more informed decision-making and a fair, representative legal system for all.

BIBLIOGRAPHY

Bailey, S. H., Ching, J. P. L., and Taylor, N. W. (2007). *Smith, Bailey, and Gunn on the Modern English Legal System*. London: Sweet & Maxwell.

Bornstein, B. H., and Greene, E. (2011). "Jury Decision Making: Implications for and from Psychology." *Current Directions in Psychological Science, 20*(1), 63–67. doi: 10.1177/0963721410397282.

Carlson, K., and Russo, J. (2001). "Biased Interpretation of Evidence by Mock Jurors." *Journal of Experimental Psychology: Applied, 7*, 91–103.

Chesterton, M., Chan, J., and Hampton, S. (2001). "Managing Prejudicial Publicity." New South Wales and the Law and Justice Foundation's Justice Research Centre.

Daftary-Kapur, T., Dumas, R., and Penrod, S. D. (2010). Jury Decision-Making Biases and Methods to Counter Them. *Legal and Criminological Psychology, 15*(1), 133–154. doi: 10.1348/135532509X465624.

Darbyshire, P., Maughn, A., and Stewart, A. (2001). "What Can We Learn from Published Jury Research?: Findings for the Criminal Courts Review 2001." *Judicial Studies Institute Journal, 3*(1), 71–89.

de Keijser, J. W., and van Koppen, P. J. (2007). "Paradoxes of Proof and Punishment: Psychological Pitfalls in Judicial Decision Making." *Legal and Criminological Psychology, 12*(2), 189–205. doi: 10.1348/135532506x118721.

Devine, D. J. (2012). *Jury Decision-making: The State of the Science*. New York: New York University Press.

Devine, D. J., and Caughlin, D. E. (2014). "Do They Matter? A Meta-analytic Investigation of Individual Characteristics and Guilt Judgments." *Psychology, Public Policy, & Law, 20*, 109–134. Doi: 10.1037/law0000006.

Gastil, J. (2010). *The Group in Society.* London: Sage.

Gastil, J., Burkhalter, S., and Black, L. W. (2007). Do Juries Deliberate? A Study of Deliberation, Individual Difference, and Group Member Satisfaction at a Municipal Courthouse. *Small Group Research, 38*, 337–359. Doi: 10.1177/1046496407301967.

Gordon, S. (2015). All Together Now: Using Principles of Group Dynamics to Train Better Jurors. *Indiana Law Review, 48*, 415–455.

Hans, V. (2007). Judges, Juries, and Scientific Evidence. *Journal of Law and Policy, 16,* 19–46.

Holland, R. (2014). Magna Carta Muse & Mentor. Toronto, Canada: Thomson Reuters.

Johnston, E., and Smith, T. (2020). Criminal Procedure and Punishment. Saltford: Hall & Stott Publishing Ltd.

Kovera, M. B., and Borgida, E. (2010). "Social Psychology and Law." In S. T. Fiske, D. Gilbert, & G. Lindzey (eds.), *Handbook of Social Psychology* (5th ed., pp. 1353–1385). New York: Oxford University Press.

Lloyd, S. (2020). "Remote jury trials during COVID-19: What One Project Found about Fairness and Technology." *The Conversation 16/7/20.*

Lloyd-Bostock, S., and Thomas, C. (2003). "Decline of the 'Little Parliament': Juries and Jury Reform in England and Wales." *Law & Contemporary Problems*, 62(2), 7–40. Doi:10.2307/1192251.

McAuliff, B. D., Nemeth, R. J., Bornstein, B. H., and Penrod, S. D. (2003). Jury Decision-Making in the Twenty-First Century: Confronting Science and Technology in Court. In Carson, D., & Bull R. (Eds.), *Handbook of Psychology in Legal Contexts.* (pp. 303–327). Chichester, West Sussex: John Wiley & Sons Ltd.

McClure, D. (2007). *Focus Group on Scientific and Forensic Evidence in the Courtroom*. Washington, DC: National Institute of Justice.

Maeder, E. M., McManus, L. A., McLaughlin, K. J., Yamamoto, S., and Stewart, H. (2016). "Juror's Perceptions of Scientific Testimony: The Role of Gender and Testimony Complexity in Trials Involving DNA Evidence." *Cogent Psychology, 3*, 1–14. Doi: 10.1080/23311.908-2016.1264657.

Narutoshi, Y. (2015). The Case for Abolishing Jury Trials in the English Legal System. An Analysis of the Issues and Consequences. *PhD thesis Kings College.* http://kclpure.kcl.ac.uk/portal/-. Accessed 11.1.17.

Nunez, N., McCrae, S. M., and Culhane, S. E. (2011). Jury Decision Making Research. Are Researchers Focusing on the Mouse and Not the Elephant in the Room? *Behaviour, Science and Law, 29*, 439–451. doi: 10.1002/bsi.967.

Nusbaum, A. (2014). "The Jury Process: Racial Bias, Extraversion, Leadership and Sex." *College of Saint Benedict and St John's University Honors Thesis.* http://www.digitalcommons.csbsju.edu/honors_theses/47. Accessed 2.2.17.

Roberts, J. V., and Hough, M. (2009). *Public Opinion and the Jury: An International Literature Review.* Ministry of Justice Research Series 1/09.

Rossner, 2019. "Storytelling Rituals in Jury Deliberations." Oñati Sociolegal Series, ISSN 2079–5971.

Salerno, J., and Diamond, S. (2010). "The Promise of a Cognitive Perspective on Jury Deliberation." *Psychonomic Bulletin and Review, 17*, 174–179. Doi: 10.3758/PBR.17.2.174.

Shaw, J. I., and Skolnick, P. (2005). "Effects of Psycholegal Knowledge on Decision-making by Mock Juries." *Applied Psychology in Criminal Justice, 1*(2), 90–109.

Smith, L. L., Bull, R., and Holliday, R. (2011). "Understanding Juror Perceptions of Forensic Evidence: Investigating the Impact of Case Context on Perceptions of Forensic Evidence Strength." *Journal of Forensic Sciences, 56*(2), 1–7. doi: 10.1111/j.1556-4029.2010.01671x.

Thomas, C. (2007). *Diversity and Fairness in the Jury System.* Ministry of Justice Research Series 2/07. London: Ministry of Justice.

Thomas, C. (2010). *Are Juries Fair?* Ministry of Justice series 1/10. London: Ministry of Justice.

Tinsley, Y. (2001). *Juror Decision-making: A Look inside the Jury Room.* The British Criminology Conference: Selected Proceedings. Vol. 4. Leicester. 1–11.

Vidmar, N. (2003). Juror Discussions during Civil Trials: Studying an Arizona Innovation. *Arizona Law Review*, 45

Wilmott, D., Boduszek, D., Debowska, A., et al. (2018). "Validation of the Juror Decision Scale (JDS): An Empirical Investigation of the Story Model." *Journal of Criminal Justice, 57*, 26–34. Doi: 10.1016/j.jcrimjus.2018.03.004.

Zander, M. (2001). *A Response: Lord Justice Auld's Review of the Criminal Courts.* http://www.lse.ac.uk/collections/law/staff%20publications%20full%20text/zander/ault_response_web.pdf. Accessed 30.1.17.

NOTES

1. Rossner, M. (2019). "Storytelling Rituals in Jury Deliberations." Oñati Socio-Legal Series. Available https://onatifirstonline.wordpress.com/2005/05/24/rossner/; Salerno, J., & Diamond, S. S. (2010). "The Promise of a Cognitive Perspective on Jury Deliberation." *Psychonomic Bulletin & Review, 17(*2), 174–9. doi: 10.3758/PBR.17.2.174. Willmott, D., Boduszek, D., Debowska, A., & Hudspith, L. (2018). "Introduction and Validation of the Juror Decision Scale (JDS): An Empirical Investigation of the Story Model." *Journal of Criminal Justice, 57*, 26–34. https://doi.org/10.1016/j.jcrimjus.2018.03.004.

2. Holland, R. (2014). *Magna Carta Muse & Mentor*. Toronto, Canada: Thomson Reuters.

3. Ibid.

4. Ibid.

5. Gastil, J. (2008). "Political Communication and Deliberation." 10.4135/9781483329208.

6. See fn.2.

7. *Bushel* [1670] Vaughn 135, 124 Eng Rep 1006 CP 1670).

8. Bailey, S. H., Ching, J. P. L., and Taylor, N. W. (2003). *On the Modern English Legal System.* London: Sweet & Maxwell.

9. Lloyd-Bostock, S., and Thomas, C. (1999). "Decline of the 'Little Parliament': Juries and Jury Reform in England and Wales." *Law and Contemporary Problems*, 62(2), 7–40. https://doi.org/10.2307/1192251.

10. Bill of Rights 1688.

11. Chesterton, M., Chan, J., and Hampton, S. (2001). "Managing Prejudicial Publicity: An Empirical Study of Criminal Jury Trials in New South Wales." Justice Research Centre Law and Justice Foundation of NSW.

12. Hans, V. (2008). "Jury Systems around the World." https://scholarship.law .cornell.edu/facpub/305/, last accessed December 2021.

13. Johnston, E., and Smith, T. (2020). *Criminal Procedure and Punishment, 2nd edition*. Saltford: Hall & Stott Publishing Ltd.

14. For more, see the official guidance here: https://www.gov.uk/jury-service, Last accessed December 2021.

15. Narutoshi, Y. (2015). The case for abolishing jury trials in the English legal system. An analysis of the issues and consequences. *PhD thesis Kings College.* http: //kclpure.kcl.ac.uk/portal/-, last accessed December 2021.

16. Thomas, C. (2010). *Are Juries Fair?* Ministry of Justice series 1/10. London: Ministry of Justice.

17. Gordon, S. (2015). All Together Now: Using Principles of Group Dynamics to Train Better Jurors. *Indiana Law Review, 48*, 415–455.

18. Vidmar, N. (2003). "Juror Discussions During Civil Trials: Studying an Arizona Innovation." *Arizona Law Review*, 45.

19. The Juries Act, 1974.

20. Carlson, K., and Russo, J. (2001). "Biased Interpretation of Evidence by Mock Jurors." *Journal of Experimental Psychology: Applied,* 7, 91–103.

21. Gastil, J., Burkhalter, S., and Black, L. W. (2007). "Do Juries Deliberate? A Study of Deliberation, Individual Difference, and Group Member Satisfaction at a Municipal Courthouse." *Small Group Research, 38*, 337–359. Doi: 10.1177/1046496407301967.

22. *Attorney Gen v. New Statesman and Nation Publishing Co. Ltd.* (1980) ALLER644 (1981) QBI.

23. Zander, M. (2001). *A Response: Lord Justice Auld's Review of the Criminal Courts.* http://www.lse.ac.uk/collections/law/staff%20publications%20full%20text/zander/ault_response_web.pdf

24. See fn.15.

25. Daftary-Kapur, T., Dumas, R., and Penrod, S. D. (2010). "Jury Decision-Making Biases and Methods to Counter Them." *Legal and Criminological Psychology, 15*(1), 133–154. doi: 10.1348/135532509X465624.

26. Smith, L. L., Bull, R., and Holliday, R. (2011). "Understanding Juror Perceptions of Forensic Evidence: Investigating the Impact of Case Context on Perceptions of Forensic Evidence Strength." *Journal of Forensic Sciences, 56*(2), 1–7. doi: 10.1111/j.1556-4029.2010.01671x.

27. Nusbaum, A. (2014). "The Jury Process: Racial Bias, Extraversion, Leadership and Sex." *College of Saint Benedict and St Johns University Honors Thesis*. http://www.digitalcommons.csbsju.edu/honors_theses/47.

28. For a review see Devine, D. J., and Caughlin, D. E. (2014). Do they Matter? A Meta-Analytic Investigation of Individual Characteristics and Guilt Judgments." *Psychology, Public Policy, & Law, 20*, 109–134. Doi: 10.1037/law0000006.

29. Kovera, M. B., and Borgida, E. (2010). "Social Psychology and Law." In S. T. Fiske, D. Gilbert, & G. Lindzey (eds.), *Handbook of Social Psychology* (5th ed., pp 1353–1385). New York: Oxford University Press.

30. Salerno, J., Bottoms, B. L., and Peter-Hagene, L.C. (2017). "Individual versus Group Decision Making: Juror's Reliance on Central and Peripheral Information to Evaluate Expert Testimony." *Plos one*, 20(12;9). https://doi.org:10.1371/journal.pone.0183580.eCollection.

31. Darbyshire, P., Maughn, A., and Stewart, A. (2001). "What Can We Learn from Published Jury Research?: Findings for the Criminal Courts Review 2001." *Judicial Studies Institute Journal, 3*(1), 71–89.

32. Maeder, E. M., McManus, L. A., McLaughlin, K. J., Yamamoto, S., and Stewart, H. (2016). Juror's Perceptions of Scientific Testimony: The Role of Gender and Testimony Complexity in Trials Involving DNA Evidence." *Cogent Psychology, 3*, 1–14. Doi: 10.1080/23311.908-2016.1264657/.

33. See fn.26.

34. McClure, D. (2007). *Focus Group on Scientific and Forensic Evidence in the Courtroom*. Washington, DC: National Institute of Justice

35. Shaw, J. I., and Skolnick, P. (2005). "Effects of Psycholegal Knowledge on Decision-making by Mock Juries." *Applied Psychology in Criminal Justice, 1*(2), 90–109

36. McAuliff, B. D., Nemeth, R. J., Bornstein, B. H., and Penrod, S. D. (2003). "Jury Decision-making in the Twenty First Century: Confronting Science and Technology in Court." In Carson, D., and Bull R. (Eds.), *Handbook of Psychology in Legal Contexts*. (pp. 303–327). Chichester, West Sussex: John Wiley & Sons Ltd.

37. See fn. 21.

38. *R v. Young (Stephen)*, CACD 30 Dec. 1994.

39. See fn. 26.

40. Tinsley, Y. (2001). *Juror Decision-making: A Look inside the Jury Room*. The British Criminology Conference: Selected Proceedings. Vol. 4. Leicester. 1–11.

41. See fn. 28 for a comprehensive review.

42. de Keijser, J. W., and van Koppen, P. J. (2007). "Paradoxes of Proof and Punishment: Psychological Pitfalls in Judicial Decision Making." *Legal and Criminological Psychology, 12*(2), 189–205. doi: 10.1348/135532506x118721.

43. See 1 Willmott et al. (2018).

44. Nunez, N., McCrae, S. M., and Culhane, S. E. (2011). "Jury Decision Making Research. Are Researchers Focusing on the Mouse and Not the Elephant in the Room?" *Behaviour, Science and Law, 29*, 439–451. doi: 10.1002/bsi.967.

45. Devine, D. J. (2012). *Jury Decision-making: The State of the Science*. New York: New York University Press.

46. Lloyd, S. (2020). "Remote Jury Trials During COVID-19: What One Project Found about Fairness and Technology." *The Conversation 16/7/20.*

47. Ibid.

48. HM Courts and Tribunals Service, *The Use of Remote Hearings to Maintain Justice during the Coronavirus Outbreak*, available here: https://assets.publishing.service.gov.uk/government/uploads/system/uploads/attachment_data/file/901050/CVP_CFT_and_QA_-_Webinar_presentation_FINAL.PDF, last accessed December 2021.

49. JUSTICE covid-19 Response, available here: https://justice.org.uk/our-work/justice-covid-19-response/. See also the government response here: https://www.justice.gov.uk/downloads/publications/research-and-analysis/moj-research/virtual-courts.pdf.

50. See fn. 16.

Chapter 9

Victim Participation as a Right

From the International Criminal Court to the European Court of Human Rights

Freya Doughty

"WITNESSES ARE THE EYES AND EARS OF JUSTICE."[1]

Victim and witness participation across international courts and tribunals is still relatively novel in practice. The International Criminal Court (hereinafter "ICC") explicitly enshrined victim and witness participation in both the Rome Statute[2] and its corresponding Rules of Procedure and Evidence.[3] Two articles in particular were pivotal for the victim rights movement: 43(6)[4] established a duty for the registrar to create a dedicated Victims and Witnesses Unit (hereinafter "VWU"), and 68(3) permits victims to participate throughout proceedings. Despite greater victim-centric language potentially posing issues for the delicate balancing act between victims' rights, defendants' rights, and ensuring a fair trial,[5] the ICC's approach has largely been commended by the international legal community.[6]

While the ICC's prosecutorial powers focus on the niche of grand atrocities, its inclusive rules and regulations may be conducive to use in other international court systems that do not permit victim participation: namely the European Court of Human Rights (hereinafter "ECtHR"). Of the European Convention for the Protection of Human Rights and Fundamental Freedoms'[7] (hereinafter "ECHR") ratifying states, many have domestic provisions providing a right for victim standing. Civil law and Nordic jurisdictions provide opportunities for victim participation in criminal proceedings, otherwise known as "*partie civile*" or "*Adhasionsverfahren.*"[8] However, the same cannot be said about common law systems. Out of the 47 Council of Europe members, only the United Kingdom and the Republic of Ireland follow a common law system. Why does the ECtHR not follow the majority consensus? Is there a belief within the ECtHR that victim and witness participation does not provide a real and tangible benefit for its cases?

The central theme of this book is criminal justice, and this author believes providing the right to participation for impacted victim-witnesses is vital in achieving a just outcome for all parties involved. Should the ICC's system be viewed as the gold standard for the remaining exclusionary international court systems? Would the ECtHR benefit from a VWU of its own, and is this feasible? This chapter will respond to these queries through an exploration of international victim participation, alterations made as the International Court developed insight through cases, and by examining how the ECtHR could improve justiciability for victims by learning from the ICC's experience.

ATTEMPTING TO INCLUDE THE VICTIM-WITNESS

As was previously stated, the Rome Statute was the first *successful* attempt at giving victims and witnesses the right of participation in international cases, with Article 68(3)[9] providing "unprecedented access to the ICC and justice process for the victims of the world's most serious atrocities."[10] Some of the ICC's tribunal predecessors, including the International Criminal Tribunal for the former Yugoslavia and the International Criminal Tribunal for Rwanda, appeared to give a cursory glance toward victim and witness participation. Here, the permitted role of victims was "solely that of a witness"[11] and special attention was not paid to their "physical and psychosocial wellbeing."[12] Those involved in the Rwanda Tribunal even became "so frustrated [. . .] that they cut off all cooperation with the tribunal."[13] Consequently, these ad hoc tribunals have widely been deemed ineffective with regards to participation and forging a connection to the affected communities.[14] Nonetheless, international tribunals and special courts[15] helped lay the groundwork for what a more representative and powerful international body could enact for victims and witnesses on this scale.

The drafters of the Rome Statute were also influenced by the victim rights movement of the 1960s,[16] whose aim was to advocate for the "enhancement of the role and rights of victims during the criminal justice process."[17] The movement led to the United Nations' 40th General Assembly adopting the Declaration of Basic Principles of Justice for Victims of Crime and Abuse of Power[18] in 1985. These basic principles defined what it means to be a victim,[19] emphasized that treatment should be "with compassion and respect for their dignity,"[20] and urged states to allow "the views and concerns of victims to be presented and considered at appropriate stages of the proceedings"[21]—all marking a momentous step toward formalizing victim participation.[22] Three years later, a pivotal victim rights case was heard at the Inter-American Court of Human Rights (hereinafter "IACHR"): *Velásquez-Rodríguez*.[23] The first case to be heard at the IACHR, it permanently changed the "understanding of a State's duty to prosecute."[24] The IACHR in *Velásquez-Rodríguez* interpreted several fundamental principles within the American Convention on Human Rights[25] (hereinafter "ACHR") to ensure states "provide victims of right of life and personal integrity violations an effective remedy for [these] violations."[26] Paragraph 134 continues, cementing victims and their inclusion and protection within international human rights as indisputably fundamental in practice:

> The objective of international human rights law is not to punish those individuals who are guilty of violations, but rather to protect the victims and to provide for the reparation of damages resulting from the acts of the States responsible.[27]

Codifying Victim–Witness Participation at the ICC Level

The drafters of the Rome Statute purposefully constructed a broad framework so that narrow interpretation could occur once cases were deliberated.[28] Nonetheless, the plain language itself contains "ground breaking provisions,"[29] and recognizes the "unique voice [victims . . .] bring to proceedings."[30] Restorative justice themes underpin the major victim participation articles found within both the Rome Statute and the Rules of Procedure and Evidence (hereinafter "RoPE"), ensuring a central role for victims in an individually tailored process.[31] Moreover, the state assumes the role of the victim in the majority of domestic criminal trials, further alienating victims from an already traumatic time. The ILC were careful in ensuring said alienation did not find itself in provisions of the Rome Statute, giving victims and witnesses the chance to "regain a sense of control and empowerment over their own lives."[32]

The starting point for including victims is to define them. However, the drafters of the Rome Statute were unable to achieve consensus over a definition, so one was later drafted and placed within the rules.[33] Rule 85(a) of the RoPE states victims are "natural persons who have suffered harm as a result of the commission of any crime within the jurisdiction of the Court." Subsection (b) continues, remarking victims "may include organisations or institutions that have sustained direct harm to any of their property which is dedicated to religion, education, art or science or charitable purposes, and to their historic monuments, hospitals and other places and objects for humanitarian purposes." Provided the applicant is a natural or legal person, has suffered a harm that would fall within the court's jurisdiction *ratione materiae, loci, personae* and *temporis*, and a causal link exists between the crime and suffering, victim status should be met.[34]

The Rome Statute reminds readers of the grave reasons for its existence from the outset: "millions of children, women and men have been victims of unimaginable atrocities that deeply shock the conscience of humanity."[35] Article 15 continues, stating the prosecutor may conduct an investigation *proprio motu* provided there is sufficient "supporting material."[36] Where this evidence comes from is not defined; victims and witnesses may provide the supporting material themselves, thus playing a key role in the prosecutor's decision to investigate. Notably, this is the first example of vesting victims with rights before a case has even commenced. Further, Article 19 details an additional area in which victims hold power: when admissibility or jurisdiction of a case is challenged before the court. Once again, victims are invited to have a say through submitting their observations to the court.[37] When interpreted alone, both articles appear to be extraordinarily inclusive and supportive of victims' voices. Upon closer inspection and further assessment by the court, the case is far more complex.

Article 15(3) has its own limitations: participation and representations must be: (1) in accordance with the RoPE; (2) only where the victim's interests are "affected"[38] pursuant to Article 68(3); and (3) undertaken during the Pre-Trial Chamber process. Rule 50(1) of the RoPE requires the prosecutor to either inform the victims or the VWU of his or her decision to seek investigation authorization from the Pre-Trial Chamber.[39] However, as is often the case due to the scale of the crimes the ICC investigates, the prosecutor or the VWU may simply be unaware of many of the victims of the atrocity in question. This "innovative"[40] notification provides newly informed victims with the chance to make potentially significant representations to the prosecutor, which may "help the conduct of the investigation before it even begins."[41]

Points two and three became a focus of the *Situation in Uganda*,[42] a case deemed a "landmark decision of the ICC."[43] Here, an examination of previous decisions made by the court regarding applications for participation under Article 68(3) was undertaken—in particular, with reference to the victims wishing to participate in the pre-trial phase of the Uganda situation. Judge Mauro Politi was tasked with both "manag[ing] victims' issues"[44] and deciphering the relationship between Articles 15(3) and 68(3). He confirmed that the correct method in granting participatory rights was to pursue a broad approach.[45] Quoting the earlier *Situation in the Democratic Republic of the Congo*,[46] participation as a whole was consistent with the "object and purpose of the victims participation regime established by the drafters of the [Rome] Statute."[47]

Victims should have the right to engage without endless caveats, but some specificity is required concerning the "nature and scope of the proceedings in which victims may participate in the context of a situation."[48] A non-exhaustive list identifying when victims might expect to participate was published with this decision (in addition to those already posed within the Rome Statute).[49] In sum, it is a two-step process: identify if the person in question should be given victim status—this is set at a "relatively low threshold,"[50]—and secondly, ask if including the victim within an investigation phase would impair "fairness or efficiency."[51] The single judge added a stipulation to the latter point: if a victim is granted the right to participate, how their personal interests may be impacted must be indicated.[52] Essentially, Article 68(3) of the Rome Statute, pertaining to a victim's personal interests, is now a "further condition"[53] to Article 15(3): "the Court's discretion in determining the appropriateness of a victim's participation has to be exercized against the criterion of the existence of an impact on the personal interests of the applicant."[54]

Consistent and open communication with victims and their legal representatives from pre- to posttrial is another key component of effective victim participation. If a victim has already communicated with the court, several articles of the Rome Statute and its corresponding rules from the RoPE come in to play. Articles 15(3) and 19(3) together with Rule 59(1)(b) require the registrar to inform victims of any challenges to the jurisdiction or admissibility of the case; Article 53(2) together with Rule 92(2) compel the court to inform victims of the prosecutor's decision not continue an investigation or prosecute; and conversely Article 53(1) together with Rule 92(3) mandate the court to inform victims of a decision to hold a hearing to confirm charges. Possessing rights of notification before having formally participated in proceedings is a remarkable choice made by the ICC, demonstrating their dedication to victim inclusion throughout every step of the process.

VICTIM PARTICIPATION *DURING* PROCEEDINGS: ARTICLE 68

Article 68 details the ways in which the court must protect "victims and witnesses and their participation in the proceedings." Sub-paragraph three is arguably the most important section of Article 68, and is the subject of such vast discussion that its every facet is beyond the remit of this chapter. It reads:

> Where the personal interests of the victims are affected, the Court shall permit their views and concerns to be presented and considered at stages of the proceedings determined to be appropriate by the Court and in a manner which is not prejudicial to or consistent with the rights of the accused and a fair and impartial trial. Such views and concerns may be presented by the legal representatives of the victims where the Court considers it appropriate, in accordance with the Rules of Procedure and Evidence.[55]

One party believes 68(3) to be "frustratingly vague,"[56] another commends it for being revolutionary in its granting victims "expansive powers to argue."[57] This author falls on the side of the former, primarily because it is definitionally lacking and as such, has left vast room for interpretation beyond that of the intentions of the drafters. Specifically, the terms "views and concerns," "proceedings," and once again, "personal interests" have all presented their own definitional issues. The *Situation in the Democratic Republic of the Congo*[58] (hereinafter "Situation in the DRC") plainly exemplifies this through the contrasting opinions of the prosecutor and defense, and the victims' legal representation. The prosecutor actively opposed victims' applications to take part in proceedings, but their legal representatives insisted upon broad interpretation of Article 68(3) by the chambers[59]—both takes had the potential to be realized given this sub-paragraph's wide scope. Nevertheless, thus far the chambers has tended to support "extensive participation"[60] for victims.

We shall start with defining "proceedings," and how the different ICC sub-bodies construed this term. As part of the wider *Situation in the DRC*, six applicants requested participation in proceedings on June 14, 2005, "be it at the investigation, trial or sentencing stage and to invoke all provisions of the Statute, RoPE[61] and Regulations of the court concerning the rights of victims who have applied to participate in proceedings."[62] One month later, the VWU submitted their observations on the protection of witnesses.[63] Emmanuel Daoud, their legal representative, assumed it would be as simple as the Pre-Trial Chamber I setting out the modalities for their participation. However, two questions were posed in response: do these applicants constitute victims under Rule 85 of the RoPE? And if so, is victim participation permitted at this early investigative stage of proceedings?[64]

The Office of the Prosecutor rejected the applications on the basis of this second question—it was argued investigation is a distinct phase from proceedings itself,[65] reinforced by Article 68(3)'s placement in the Rome Statute: Part 6, "The Trial." Further, they believed participation at this stage was inappropriate. Pre-Trial Chamber I disagreed, highlighting historic decisions from the ECtHR and IACHR.[66] Article 6(1) of the ECHR—right to a fair trial—has applied to victims in the early investigation phase, and the Inter-American Court held Article 8 of the ACHR to mean victims subject to human rights abuses may take steps "from the investigation stage and prior to the confirmation of the charges."[67] What is more, when interpreting victim participation within the Rome Statute from a teleological perspective, it is consistent with the object and purpose established by the original drafters. Pre-Trial Chamber II in the *Uganda Situation* aided in concretizing this interpretation, by determining that Kony's victims may participate in proceedings, *including* the investigation period, and perhaps as early as "prior to the consideration of the merits of their application."[68]

"Views and concerns" has also been the subject of a variety of submissions before the chambers. The victims' legal representation in the *Situation in the DRC* asserted that to effectively participate in proceedings, victims must be able to obtain reparations, express views and concerns, verify facts, and protect their dignity throughout.[69] Participation on the victims' side is consistently construed liberally, and in the views and concerns context the Pre-Trial and Trial Chambers have concurred. The stage of proceedings in which views and concerns are to be expressed seemingly is "whenever necessary [. . .] through statements, examination of witnesses or by filing written submissions."[70] Whenever necessary is literal in its meaning: victims have the right to introduce, tender, and examine evidence if it will assist in "the determination of the truth."[71] Ostensibly, victims may express concerns and possess the same rights as the defence and prosecution regarding evidence introduction, provided submissions are relevant.[72]

The ICC prosecutor at the time, Luis Moreno-Ocampo, staunchly disagreed with this broad liberal approach. The prosecution insisted victim participation "should remain within the boundaries established by the Statute and the existing jurisprudence";[73] interpretation should not unnecessarily expand upon the already carefully crafted consensus. Judge Pikis in his Separate Opinion stated that "[a]n opportune stage at which the views and concerns of participating victims may be presented is at the outset of the proceedings,"[74] rather than this right being expressed through involving oneself in evidence examination, or even witness questioning. Victims and their participation are a fundamental part of the international criminal justice process, but Pikis argued they should not concern themselves with duties belonging to the prosecution. He continued, citing the equality of arms principle: "the defendant cannot be required to confront more than one accuser."[75]

While this level of participation does pose a complication for the defendant(s)' right to a fair trial, Pikis,' and the prosecutor's take remains a dissent. The Appeals Chamber explained their stance: if "victims were generally and under all circumstances precluded from tendering evidence relating to the guilt or innocence of the accused [. . .] their right to participate in the trial would potentially become ineffectual."[76] In the balance between victims' and defendants' rights, ensuring the relevant views and concerns of victims are expressed throughout proceedings triumphs.

The "personal interests" element of Article 68(3) has also been subject to scrutiny. The primary criterion for participation to be allowed is having one's personal interests be impacted. Unsurprisingly, this, too, has been interpreted broadly by the chambers. Pre-Trial Chamber I deemed the personal interests of the victim to be affected "in general at the investigation stage, since the participation of victims at this stage can serve to clarify the facts, to punish the perpetrators of crimes and to request reparations for the harm suffered."[77] Pre-Trial Chamber II similarly argued the personal interest requirement is met when a victim "applies for participation in proceedings following the issuance of a warrant or arrest or of a summons to appear for one or more individuals."[78] These conclusions appear overwhelmingly redundant additions to Article 68(3), adding no real clarity. A meager attempt was made by the Trial Chamber in January 2008: a "general interest in the outcome of the case or in the issues or evidence the Chamber will be considering at that stage is likely to be insufficient."[79]

The Appeals Chamber has taken an archetypal approach, suggesting determining if personal interests are affected should be made on a case by case basis.[80] The chamber must actively decide participation is appropriate, rather than it being an automatic right. As with debate surrounding "views and concerns," questioning appropriateness is a matter of securing balanced rights for the accused—personal interests pertain to the accused, too. Judge Song in his Separate Opinion reminds us of Article 82(1)(b) of the Rome Statute, which deems the appropriate stage for victims to present "after the submission of the document in support of the appeal, once the arguments of the appellant have been fully expressed."[81] He noted this because the *Situation in the DRC* had been severely delayed, and additional victim participation to express views and concerns would unnecessarily extend proceedings.[82] Regardless, Judge Song argued in his dissent that this particular appeal in the Lubanga case affected the victims' personal interests, but appropriate timing must be questioned. While he differed from Judges Kourula, Kirsh, Pillay, and Pikis, a consensus of sorts was reached: participation on the basis of personal interests *is* limited.

The continuity throughout the key words of Article 68(3) indicates the court's primary intention: to give victims the chance to share their stories. Achieving justice for victims by liberally interpreting 68(3) and its relevant RoPE attachments has been a means for the court to recognize one of the major reasons for its creation. Giving victims a voice by allowing participation throughout proceedings—with partial stipulations dotted throughout decisions of the chambers—has been instrumental for the victim rights movement, but occasionally suggests the rights of the victim trump that of the accused. Balancing the two is an incredible feat, and something that will never be achieved perfectly. However, critics have suggested the court has an impartiality blind spot when it comes to victim participation. If this is so, should victim participation continue in this manner, if at all?

A Review of Arguments for and against Victim Participation

Perhaps the most commonly presented argument for participation is to give victims a voice. In the context of the ICC (and occasionally the ECtHR), crimes committed will have impacted thousands of members of a community who "[a]bove all [. . .] feel a need to understand why the social group which they belong to was the target of these crimes."[83] Providing victims with a platform to question the court and present their stories should help prevent secondary victimization.[84] Being given the chance to be listened to, and respected by the International Criminal Court after having been the victim of a widespread atrocity is the minimum catharsis deserved. This process may even contribute to rehabilitation[85]—testifying itself can have a "profoundly healing effect."[86] Participation beyond the sharing of experiences, for example by playing a role in the prosecution, can assist in restoring dignity by providing additional agency. Fair treatment of victims, leading to at least partial recovery, is an indisputable benefit of participation.

Secondly, participation may be sought for more than having views and concerns expressed—reparations. While retribution is often assumed to be the primary reason for victim participation, "restitution or compensation, plus the opportunity to make a fresh start, to recover and to be protected from further victimization"[87] has been found to supersede in importance. Strang identified the needs of victims in criminal proceedings, and two of the five primary needs were to obtain material and emotional restoration, and an apology.[88] It is not the victims' duty to secure a prosecution, but aiding the prosecutor by providing information may lead to a more just outcome. Participating in a way that secures their own fair fate not only helps victimized individuals, but other communities impacted by the human rights atrocity in question.[89]

Finally, participation may even result in "more successful prosecutions."[90] This point intertwines with the earlier mentioned facets of the Rome Statute—having the chance to share information from victims' perspectives provides the court with context and potentially crucial evidence. In the *Situation in Uganda*, the legal representative for victims highlighted how they can "assist the Court to fight impunity,"[91] perhaps enhancing the chance of a successful prosecution.[92]

Contrariwise, critics have suggested participation in criminal proceedings may *cause* secondary victimization as a result of the "arbitrary, cynical and non-emphatic treatment"[93] typical of a criminal case. An experience cannot be shared without recalling and reliving the likely distressing details, doubling the trauma suffered. Without a system in place to deal with the psychological harm caused from participation, not only would participation prove ineffective but would likely be a deterrent for those needing to come forward in the future. However, if time and resources are given to participating victims to the detriment of the accused, this may "impede the accused in exercising his/her right to defence."[94]

A sizeable asterisk must be added to all the above plaudits and critiques: as with many aspects of international law, reasons for or against a domestic issue become significantly more complex when exclusively applied on an international level. Given the ECtHR finds itself in the position of an international court, but often with very few applicants per case, the European Court may benefit from acknowledging victim participation plights domestically. However, were the ECtHR to examine reasons given for or against adding a victim participation strategy, the international critique should be the European Court's primary focus.

Secondary victimization often stems from factors commonly found in domestic criminal courts, not in a body with a Victims and Witnesses Unit specifically designed to address said issues. Causes of secondary victimization include an inability to find "necessary counselling or medical treatment"[95] and "intrusive or inappropriate conduct by police or other criminal justice personnel."[96] Article 68 in particular details the duty of the court to "protect the safety, physical and psychological well-being, dignity and privacy of victims and witnesses." Of course, this is not ensured just by being present in the Rome Statute, but is an example of an ambitious protectionary article that the European Court may benefit from including.

This duty does not cease after leaving the safety of the court; the VWU's assistance continues with outreach programs. UC Berkeley interviewed 109 witnesses who had testified at The Hague: when asked how they would respond were they to be called to the court again, 75% of women said yes to returning and 15% said they did not know, while 85% of men said yes with 13% not knowing.[97] Being identified and harassed after trials is another common fear and critique of domestic criminal courts. The ICC has been meticulous in ensuring retaliation does not occur. Again, of the 109 surveyed, 82% of women used facial distortion, an equal number used pseudonyms, and 78% used voice distortion, while 61% of men used at least one of the available protective methods.[98]

Achieving reparations and some form of rehabilitation again must be viewed through the comparative international lens. Domestic criminal trials usually only have one victim, unlike trials for crimes against humanity where dozens as a minimum are involved. This many people may make it "impossible for an individual victim to participate in a meaningful way,"[99] especially when most power is deferred to the assigned common legal representative. What is more, thousands of individuals may be seeking reparations from just the one applicant. The chamber cannot seize assets before an admission of guilt, so perpetrators have the opportunity to hide assets. Even if this is not done, "virtually no defendant will have the personal resources to pay meaningful compensation to [all] victims,"[100] preventing victims' needs from being met. If unable to participate meaningfully, nor receive compensation, the tangible benefits of victim participation quickly dwindle. Lastly, some scholars argue the idea that participation could positively assist the prosecution is dubious at best,[101] given the prosecutor's tendency to push back against victims' requests to participate.

In summary, opinions, beliefs, and statistics concerning victim participation on an international level, specifically through an ICC lens, do not fall squarely to the pro or con side. The specificities of the role and an analysis of the effectiveness of the VWU, additional accompanying rules found within the Rome Statute and the RoPE, and the limited resources of the court to adequately attend to every victim are all further elements of the ICC that would have to be considered to fully assess the practicability of the ECtHR having a similar system. Unfortunately, those are beyond the remit of this chapter. Regardless, on the basis of that included within this chapter, what would the European Court look like if they chose to include greater victim participation by taking on the assessments discussed above? What benefits or detriments would they be absorbing by doing so?

WHAT CAN THE ECTHR LEARN FROM THE ICC?

The ECHR is often considered to be "the most successful of all regional human rights tools."[102] If we are to deem the opportunity for victims to participate as a mandatory successful pillar of a human rights instrument, then the ECHR has vast room for improvement. Article 13 at least provides for a right to an effective remedy, and in addition to financial compensation "where appropriate, a thorough and effective investigation capable of leading to the identification and punishment of those responsible, [. . .] including effective access for the complainant to the investigatory procedure,"[103] may be permitted. The European Court used to exclusively apply Article 13 to cases involving civil or administrative remedies, or those involving due process rights.[104] Slowly the ECtHR began to prosecute violations of the right to life and allegations of inhumane treatment with Article 13 in mind.[105] In finding a separate Article 13 violation the ECtHR *also* finds that a "states' failure to prosecute right to life and human treatment violates an individual victim's right to an effective remedy."[106]

Rather than having specific articles and rules dedicated to victim participation, the European Court has interpreted Articles 2, right to life, and 13 to afford victims' rights in the course of proceedings. An application may be made to the ECtHR provided the applicant is "directly and personally the victim of the alleged violation,"[107] after all domestic remedies have been exhausted. However, predominantly in cases against Turkey, the European Court has allowed some exceptions. If the victim has passed or consented to being represented, their next of kin may participate on their behalf. Parents,[108] spouses,[109] siblings[110] and other familial relationships provided it is one close in fact,[111] may allege a violation "arising from procedural errors or lack of victim access to the criminal process"[112] too. Whomever participates must not only be provided a remedy under Article 13, but be ensured the entire remedy system be *effective*.[113]

The European Court in cases against the United Kingdom regarding a potential Article 13 violation differed from its Turkey conclusions.[114] Procedural errors violating the state's duty to conduct an effective criminal investigation were found under Article 2, but no breaches under Article 13 were found. A distinction was made between southeast Turkey and the United Kingdom because pursuing damages from the state is a civil matter, separate from the criminal outcome. The right to an effective remedy as per Article 13 can still be met, solely through civil recourse.[115] Being able to secure a remedy deemed effective is part and parcel of victim participation, but only scrapes the surface of what the ICC offers as rights of participation.

Interestingly, despite the European Court following the British common law system of an absence of participation, it has been critical of several aspects of its criminal justice system in relation to victims. There is no requirement for the prosecutor to justify a decision not to prosecute, undermining "public confidence in the administration of justice";[116] when a state agent is implicated, victims should have the right to know why proceedings have ceased. Further, the frequent use of public interest immunity, preventing the revelation of material facts and thus an effective investigation, has been condemned by the court.[117] It is natural that if the only real article in the ECHR tangentially concerning victim participation is centered around the right to an effective remedy that the ECtHR will offer its opinions and critique of states within the remit of Article 13.

While this appears limited in application, the European Court in 2012 expanded upon Article 13's meaning of effective access to the court: "a victim must be involved in the procedure to the extent necessary to safeguard his or her legitimate interests."[118] It is not entirely clear yet if Article 13 could be relied upon to provide the broad range of participatory rights eluded to in *Kolpak*, but Article 47 of the EU Charter of Fundamental Rights[119] (hereinafter "the Charter") offers some insight. The Charter links the right to an effective remedy with fair trial rights, going beyond the restriction of the ECHR.[120] Seemingly the right to a fair trial extends to victim participants. Other secondary EU legislation, including the Victims' Rights Directive,[121] textually follows the decisions of the ICC: victims "should be protected from secondary and repeat victimisation, from intimidation and retaliation, should receive appropriate support to facilitate their recovery and should be provided with sufficient access to justice."[122] The European Court could benefit from incorporating aspects of these texts into its own rules and legislation, especially as Brexit means not every party to the ECHR may rely upon the text of the Charter[123] or Directive.

A human-rights and dignity-based approach must be the way forward for the European Court, otherwise any edits or additions would prove detrimental to the victim rights movement and ambitions of the Directive. Balancing this with the right to a fair trial for the state or accused party is of course a necessity, especially when renegotiating the already tight finances of the European Court: "criminal justice cannot be about the rights of the individual victim *alone*."[124] Resources have not been extraordinarily designated to victims at the ICC level. The most recent program budget for the ICC had €3.22 million designated to the Secretariat of the Trust Fund for Victims,[125] representing only 2% of the total programming budget. Presumably the accused's rights have not been impeded by this, so perhaps the ECtHR could follow suit.

Formally defining a victim and recognizing victims as having rights that have been violated should be the first steps of the European Court. One cannot participate in a court proceeding if their rights under the ECHR have not been infringed upon. The fear of secondary victimization as the result of an inconsiderate and ineffectual court is a matter the ECtHR should also pay heed to. Without a designated Victims and Witnesses Unit of their own and a specialized team to assist victims throughout an incredibly traumatic process, adding victim participation rights would ultimately prove futile. Provided everything enacted to allow victim participation is in line with a rights-based victim concept, the ECtHR will be following the original intent of the Rome Statute's drafters and their "major innovation."[126]

A constant source of debate surrounding the ICC is meaningful participation—if the ECtHR were to provide a platform to participate and have an attached supportive team, the next step would be to ensure participation is more than a way of placating victims. Having hundreds if not thousands of victims all wanting to participate in a meaningful manner is nigh on impossible. However, the European Court rarely has this issue—of the most recently published judgments (available in English), two Russian nationals,[127] one Spanish national,[128] and one national of Tajikistan[129] were the applicants. While often representing an issue far greater than themselves, the victim(s) in these particular judgments are small in number and thus more able to contribute meaningfully than were they at the ICC. Another quandary surrounding the term "meaningful" is compensation. The accused in the ECtHR context is a state, so financial compensation, unless a wildly exorbitant ask, should be able to be fulfilled. A concrete finding of the violation itself may be retribution enough when the damage is non-pecuniary. So long as a violation is found, "just satisfaction" under Article 41[130] will be awarded to the applicants. Meaningful compensation in light of the particular circumstances of the European Court should not be as difficult to achieve as it is at the ICC level.

The European Court also has the benefit of secondary EU legislation detailing the importance of victim participation and how to make this successful. By following many aspects of the Victims' Rights Directive and incorporating those into ECtHR judgments, the European Court could become the second international court to make rights for victims a priority. Lastly, given the court's criticism of the United Kingdom's attitudes toward victims domestically, and the repercussions of Brexit preventing the being held to account under the Charter or persuaded by the Directive, formalizing the Directive's text into something affecting all parties to the ECHR should be of great import for the European Court in coming years.

CONCLUSION

The International Criminal Court's victim participation strategy should not be simply replicated in its entirety by the European Court of Human Rights. The latter body can however learn from its international court companion, as the ICC did from its tribunal predecessors. Concretely defining key elements of victim participation including proceedings, views and concerns, and personal interests should prevent limited ECtHR time and resources from being wasted on definitional "sub-judgments." The Victims' Rights Directive already defines what it means to be a victim,[131] the role of victims in the criminal justice system,[132] and the minimum communication expected,[133] so a solid framework for the introduction of victim participation exists. Given the relative novelty of the ICC and the work it has already achieved for the victim rights movement, the European Court has significant work ahead of it if it wishes to remain "the most successful of all regional human rights tools."[134]

The right to participate in international proceedings is not exclusively positive, as we have seen. Participation may result in greater stress than the rights violation itself, and compensation may be insufficient. Regardless, participation should be a *choice*. If the primary objective of human rights law really is to protect and provide for victims, being able to have a voice in your own case should be customary. The remaining member states of the

EU overwhelmingly believe in the right for victims to participate in domestic criminal proceedings. Despite the divisions and challenges facing the EU, this broadly unifying element should swiftly become a policy mirrored by its highest human rights court.

BIBLIOGRAPHY

Aldana-Pindell, Raquel. "An Emerging Universality of Justiciable Victims' Rights in the Criminal Process to Curtail Impunity for State-Sponsored Crimes" (2004) Vol. 26, No. 3 *Hum. Rights Quarterly* 605.

Aldana-Pindell, Raquel. "In Vindication of Justiciable Victims' Rights to Truth and Justice for State-Sponsored Crimes" (2002) 35 *Vand. J. Transnat'l L.* 1399.

Amnesty International. "International Justice" (Amnesty International) https://www.amnesty.org/en/what-we-do/international-justice/, accessed 20 October 2020.

Bassiouni, M. Cherif (ed.). "The Statute of the International Criminal Court: A Documentary History" (Transnational Pub. Inc., 1999).

Bassiouni, M. Cherif. "International Recognition of Victims' Rights" (2006) *Hum. Rts. L. Rev.* 203.

Baumgartner, Elisabeth. "Aspects of Victim Participation in the Proceedings of the International Criminal Court" (2008) 90 *Int'l Rev Red Cross* 409.

Bentham, Jeremey A. *Treatise on Judicial Evidence Extracted from the Manuscripts of Jeremy Bentham, Esq.* (1st ed., Baldwin, 1825).

Brienen, Marion E. & Hoegen, Ernestine H. "Victims of Crime" in 22 *European Criminal Justice Systems* (WLP, 2000).

Chung, Christine H. "'Victims' Participation at the International Criminal Court: Are the Concessions of the Court Clouding the Promise?" (2008) 6 NW. *U. J. Int'l Hum. Rts.* 459

Cohen, Miriam "Victim's Participation Rights within the International Criminal Court: A Critical Overview" (2009) 37 *Denv. J. Int'l L. & Pol'y* 351.

European Union Agency for Fundamental Rights. "'Victims' Rights as Standards of Criminal Justice; Justice for Victims of Violent Crime, Part 1" (Publications Office of the European Union, 2019).

Garkawe, Sam "Victims and the International Criminal Court: Three Major Issues" (2003) 3 *Int'l Crim L. Rev.* 345, 347.

Glasius, Marlies "The International Criminal Court: A Global Civil Society Achievement" (Routledge, 2006).

Human Rights Center, UC Berkeley School of Law, Bearing Witness at the International Criminal Court: An Interview Survey of 109 Witnesses (University of California, Berkeley, School of Law, 2014).

International Bar Association. "Witnesses before the International Criminal Court" (IBAHRI Trust, 2013).

Irish Human Rights Commission, European Convention on Human Rights Guide for the Civil & Public Service (Irish Human Rights Commission, 2012).

Jouet, Mugambi. "Reconciling the Conflicting Rights of Victims and Defendants at the International Criminal Court," (2007) 26 *St. Louis U. Pub. L. Rev.* 249.

Kelly, Siobhan. "The Role of Victims in the International Criminal Court: Challenges and Opportunities" (2012) 18 *New Eng. J. Int'l & Comp L.* 243.

Lee, Roy, S. "Introduction: The Rome Conference and Its Contributions to International Law" in Roy S. Lee (ed.) The International Criminal Court: The Making of the Rome Statute: Issues, Negotiations, Results (Kluwer Law International, 1999).

McAsey, Bridie. "Victim Participation at the International Criminal Court and Its Impact on Procedural Fairness" (2011) 18 *Austl. Int'l L. J.* 105.

Rauschenbach, Mina and Scalia, Damien. "Victims and International Criminal Justice: A Vexed Question?" (2008) 90 *Int'l Rev Red Cross* 441.

Stickels, John W. "Victims Impact Evidence: The Victims' Right That Influences Criminal Trials" (2001) 32 *Tex. Tech L. Rev* 231.

Strang, Heather. *Repair or Revenge: Victims and Restorative Justice* (Clarendon Studies in Criminology) (Oxford University Press, 2004).

Trumbull IV, Charles P. "The Victims of Victim Participation in International Criminal Proceedings" (2008) 29 *Mich J Int'l L* 777.

United Nations Office for Drug Control and Crime Prevention. Handbook on Justice for Victims—On the Use and Application of the Declaration of Basic Principles of Justice for Victims of Crime and Abuse of Power (Centre for International Crime Prevention, 1999).

Victims' Rights Working Group. "Gender Focus" (Victims' Rights Working Group, 2007) http://www.vrwg.org/victims-rights/gender-focus, accessed 22 October 2020.

von Hebel, Herman. "An International Criminal Court—A Historical Perspective" in Herman A. M. von Hebel, Johan G. Lammers, and Jolien Schukking (eds), Reflections on the International Criminal Court: Essays in Honour of Adriaan Bos. (T.M.C. Asser Press, 1999).

War Crimes Research Office, Obtaining Victim Status for Purpose of Participating in Proceedings at the International Criminal Court (American University Washington College of Law, 2013).

Wemmers, Jo-Anne. "Victims' Experiences in the Criminal Justice System and Their Recovery from Crime" (2013) 19(3) *Int'l Rev Victimology*.

NOTES

1. Jeremy Bentham, *A Treatise on Judicial Evidence Extracted from the Manuscripts of Jeremy Bentham, Esq* (1st ed., Baldwin, 1825) 226.

2. Rome Statute of the International Criminal Court, 1998 U.N. Doc. A/CONF. 183/9 (hereinafter "Rome Statute").

3. International Criminal Court, *Rules of Procedure and Evidence,* 2013 ICC-ASP/1/3, R. 48.

4. Rome Statute, Article 43(6).

5. Siobhan Kelly, "The Role of Victims in the International Criminal Court: Challenges and Opportunities" (2012) 18 *New Eng. J. Int'l & Comp L.* 243.

6. Two NGOs were central in the fight for this right: Human Rights Watch and Amnesty International have long called for "effective access to justice for victims," on an international platform; Amnesty International, "International Justice" (*Amnesty International*) https://www.amnesty.org/en/what-we-do/international-justice/, accessed 20 October 2020. See more at Amnesty International, The International Criminal Court: Ensuring an effective role for victims, AI Index: IOR 40/10/1999, July 1, 1999, available at https://www.amnesty.org/en/documents/IOR40/006/1999/en/.

7. European Convention on Human Rights and Fundamental Freedoms 1950.

8. Marion E. Brienen & Ernestine H. Hoegen, *Victims of Crime in 22 European Criminal Justice Systems* (WLP, 2000) 3.

9. Rome Statute, Article 68(3).

10. *supra* 5 at 243.

11. Miriam Cohen, "Victim's Participation Rights within the International Criminal Court: A Critical Overview" (2009) 37 Denv. *J. Int'l L. & Pol'y* 351, 356.

12. Victims' Rights Working Group, "Gender Focus" (Victims' Rights Working Group, 2007) http://www.vrwg.org/victims-rights/gender-focus, accessed 22 October 2020.

13. Charles P. Trumbull IV, "The Victims of Victim Participation in International Criminal Proceedings" (2008) 29 *Mich J Int'l L* 777, 787.

14. *supra* 5 at 244.

15. The Special Court for Sierra Leone, for example.

16. *supra* 13 at 780.

17. Sam Garkawe, "Victims and the International Criminal Court: Three Major Issues." (2003) 3 *Int'l Crim L. Rev.* 345, 347.

18. Declaration of Basic Principles of Justice for Victims of Crime and Abuse of Power, UNGA A/RES/40/34 (29 Nov. 1985).

19.*supra* 18 at para 1.

20. *supra* 18 at para 4.

21. *supra* 18 at para 6(b).

22. *supra* 13 at 783.

23. *Velásquez-Rodríguez v Honduras* (1988) *Inter-Am. Ct. H. R.* (Ser. C) No. 4.

24. *supra* 13 at 785.

25. American Convention on Human Rights 1969: Articles 1(1) obligation to respect rights; 8(1) right to a fair trial; 25 right to judicial protection.

26. Raquel Aldana-Pindell, "In Vindication of Justiciable Victims' Rights to Truth and Justice for State-Sponsored Crimes" (2002) 35 *Vand. J. Transnat'l L.* 1399, 1417.

27. Velásquez-Rodríguez, para 134.

28. For example: *Prosecutor v. Lubanga*, Case No. ICC-01/04–01/06 OA 10, Judgment on the Appeals of the Prosecutor and the Defence against Trial Chamber I'2 Decision on Victims' Participation of 18 January 2008, P 96 (July 11, 2008).

29. *supra* 5 at 243.

30. *supra* 5 at 245.

31. *supra* 5 at 243.
32. *supra 5* at 246.
33. Elisabeth Baumgartner, "Aspects of Victim Participation in the Proceedings of the International Criminal Court" (2008) 90 *Int'l Rev Red Cross* 409, 417.
34. *supra* 33 at 418.
35. Rome Statute, preamble para 2.
36. Rome Statute, Article 15(3).
37. Rome Statute, Article 19(3).
38. Rome Statute, Article 68(3).
39. Article 50(1) reads: "When the Prosecutor intends to seek authorization from the Pre-Trial Chamber to initiate an investigation pursuant to article 15, paragraph 3, the Prosecutor shall inform victims, known to him or her or to the Victims and Witnesses Unit, or their legal representatives, unless the Prosecutor decides that doing so would pose a danger to the integrity of the investigation or the life or well-being of victims and witnesses."
40. *supra* 11 at 360.
41. Id.
42. Situation in Uganda (*Prosecutor v. Kony et al.*), Decision on victims' applications for participation a/0010/06, a/0064/06 to a/0070/06, a/0081/06 to a/0104/06 to a/0127/06, ICC-02/04–101 (Aug. 10, 2007).
43. *supra* 11 at 359.
44. Christine H. Chung, "Victims' Participation at the International Criminal Court: Are the Concessions of the Court Clouding the Promise?" (2008) 6 NW. *U. J. Int'l Hum. Rts.* 459, 471.
45. *supra* 42 at para 83.
46. Situation in the Democratic Republic of the Congo, Situation No. ICC-01/04–101-tEN-Corr, Decision on the Applications for Participation in the Proceedings of VPRS 1, VPRS 2, VPRS 3, VPRS 4, VPRS 5, and VPRS 6, Public Redacted Version (Jan 17, 2006).
47. Id. para 50.
48. *supra* 42 at para 88.
49. *supra* 42 at paras 90–95.
50. *supra* 46 at para 97.
51. *supra* 44 at 72.
52. *supra* 42 at para 89.
53. *supra* 11 at 359.
54. *supra* 42 at para 89.
55. Rome Statute, Article 68(3).
56. Trumbull, 793 *supra* 13 at 793.
57. Mugambi Jouet, "Reconciling the Conflicting Rights of Victims and Defendants at the International Criminal Court," [2007] 26 *St. Louis U. Pub. L. Rev.* 249, 269.
58. Situation in the Democratic Republic of the Congo (*Prosecutor v. Lubanga Dyilo*), Case No. ICC-01/04–01/06–119, Decision on Victims' Participation (Jan. 18 2008).
59. *supra* 46 at paras 50–51.

60. *supra* 13 at 794.
61. Acronym by author.
62. *supra* 46 at para 19.
63. *supra 46* at para 12.
64. *supra* 46 at para 22.
65. *supra 46* at para 35.
66. Inter-American Court of Human Rights, *Blake v. Guatemala*, "Judgment," 24 January 1998, Series C No 36.
67. *supra* 46 at para 53.
68. *supra* 42 at para 99.
69. *supra* 58 at para 39.
70. *supra* 58 at para 98.
71. *supra* 58 at para 108.
72. Rome Statute, Article 69(3).
73. Situation in the Democratic Republic of the Congo (*Prosecutor v. Lubanga Dyilo*), Case No. ICC-01/04–01/06–1136, Application for leave to Appeal Trial Chamber I's January 18 Decision on Victims' Participation (Jan. 28, 2008) p. 3.
74. Situation in the Democratic Republic of the Congo (*Prosecutor v. Lubanga Dyilo*), Case No. ICC-01–04–01/06 OA8, Decision of the Appeals Chamber on the Joint Application of Victims a/0001/06 to a/0003/06 and a/0105/06 concerning the "Directions and Decision of the Appeals Chamber" of 2 February 2007 (Jun. 13, 2007) para 20.
75. *supra* 74 at para 19.
76. Situation in the Democratic Republic of the Congo (*Prosecutor v. Lubanga Dyilo*), Case No. ICC-01/04–01/06 OA 9 OA 10, Judgment on the appeals of The Prosecutor and The Defence against Trial Chamber I's Decision on Victims' Participation of 18 January 2008 (Jul. 11, 2008) para 97.
77. *supra* 46 at para 63.
78. *supra* 42 at para 9.
79. *supra* 58 at para 96.
80. *supra* 74 at para 21.
81. Joint Application, Separate Opinion of Judge Sang-Hyun Song, para 21.
82. *supra* 81 at para 21.
83. Mina Rauschenbach and Damien Scalia, "Victims and International Criminal Justice: A Vexed Question?" (2008) 90 *Int'l Rev Red Cross* 441, 453.
84. Jo-Anne Wemmers, "Victims' Experiences in the Criminal Justice System and Their Recovery from Crime" (2013) 19(3) *Int'l Rev Victimology*.
85. *supra* 13 at 802.
86. *supra* 83 at 443.
87. *supra* 83 at 444.
88. Heather Strang, *Repair or Revenge: Victims and Restorative Justice (Clarendon Studies in Criminology)* (Oxford University Press, 2004).
89. *supra* 13 at 803.
90. Id.

91. Situation in Uganda, Case No. ICC-02/04–106, Response of Legal Representative of Victims a/0119/06 to the Prosecutor's Application for Leave to Appeal the Decision on Victims' Applications for Participation a/0010/06, a/0064/06 to a/0070/06, a/0081/06 to a/0111/06 to a/0127/06 (Aug. 31, 2007) para 23.

92. M. Cherif Bassiouni, "International Recognition of Victims' Rights" (2006) *Hum. Rts. L. Rev.* 203, 205–206.

93. *supra* 83 at 445.

94. *supra* 83 at 449–450.

95. *supra* 13 at 805.

96. United Nations Office for Drug Control and Crime Prevention, *Handbook on Justice for Victims—On the use and application of the Declaration of Basic Principles of Justice for Victims of Crime and Abuse of Power* (Centre for International Crime Prevention, 1999) 9.

97. Human Rights Center, UC Berkeley School of law, *Bearing Witness at the International Criminal Court: An Interview Survey of 109 Witnesses),* (University of California, Berkeley, School of Law, 2014) 40.

98. Id. 39.

99. *supra* 13 at 806.

100. *supra* 57 at 302.

101. *supra* 13 at 807.

102. Irish Human Rights Commission, *European Convention on Human Rights Guide for the Civil & Public Service* (Irish Human Rights Commission, 2012) 22.

103. *Aksoy v. Turkey* 100/1995/606/694 (ECHR, 18 December 1996) para. 98.

104. See, e.g., *James and Others v. The United Kingdom* [1986] ECHR App. No. 8793/79, paras 83–87; *Leander v Sweden* [1987] ECHR App. No. 9248/81 paras 76–84.

105. See, e.g., *McCann and Others v. The United Kingdom* [1996] App. No. 18984/91, 21. Eur. H.R. Rep. 97 para 161; *Assenov and Others v Bulgaria* [1998] App. No. 24760/94, 28 Eur. H. R. Rep. 652, para 102.

106. Raquel Aldana-Pindell, "An Emerging Universality of Justiciable Victims' Rights in the Criminal Process to Curtail Impunity for State-Sponsored Crimes" (2004) Vol. 26, No. 3 *Hum. Rights Quarterly* 605, 635.

107. *supra* 102 at 25.

108. See, e.g., *Gül v. Turkey* [2000] 34 Eur. H.R. Rep. 28.

109. See, e.g., *Salman v. Turkey* [2000] 34 Eur. H.R. Rep. 17.

110. See, e.g., *Ilhan v. Turkey* [2000] 34 Eur. H.R. Rep. 36.

111. In *Ilhan v. Turkey*, his brother submitted on his behalf. The closeness of their relationship as demonstrated evidentially and the special circumstances of the case led the court to dismiss preliminary objections to the brother's intervention. Id, paras 53–55.

112. *supra* 26 at 1417.

113. *supra* 26 at 1421. See also *Ergi v. Turkey* [2001] App. No. 23818/94, Eur. H.R. Rep. 18.

114. See, e.g., *Jordan v. The United Kingdom* [2001] ECHR 300; *Kelly v. The United Kingdom* [2001] ECHR 240.

115. Id.
116. *supra* 26 at 1435.
117. *McKerr v. The United Kingdom* [2001] ECHR App. No. 28883/95.
118. *Kolpak v. Russia* [2012] ECHR App. No. 41408/04, para 62.
119. Charter of Fundamental Rights of the European Union [2000], Article 47.
120. European Union Agency for Fundamental Rights, "'*Victims' Rights as Standards of Criminal Justice; Justice for Victims of Violent Crime Part I*" (Publications Office of the European Union, 2019) 21.
121. Directive 2012/29/EU of the European Parliament and of the Council [2012] establishing minimum standards on the rights, support and protection of victims of crime, replacing Council Framework Decision 2001/220/JHA.
122. *supra* 121 at 9.
123. European Union (Withdrawal) Act 2018 S.5(4).
124. European Union Agency for Fundamental Rights, 22.
125. Resolution ICC-ASP/18/Res.1, Resolution of the Assembly of States Parties on the proposed programme budget for 2020, the Working Capital for 2020, the scale of assessment for the apportionment of expenses of the International Criminal Court, financing operations for 2020 and the Contingency Fund (Dec. 6 2019).
126. *supra* 5 at 261.
127. *Plokhovy v. Russia* [2020] ECHR, App. No. 45024/07.
128. *J.A. v. Switzerland* [2020] ECHR, App. No. 6325/15.
129. *Usmanov v. Russia* [2020] ECHR, App. No. 43936/18.
130. ECHR, Article 41.
131. *supra* 121 at Article 19.
132. *supra* 121 at Article 20.
133. *supra* 121 at Article 21.
134. *supra* 102 at 22.

Chapter 10

Out-of-Court Disposals in the Dutch Criminal Process

An Affront to a Fair Trial?

Anna Pivaty

The proliferation of out-of-court disposals in criminal cases attracts growing international attention.[1] An influential report from Fair Trials states that since 1990 there has been a three-fold increase in the number of trial waiver models introduced across the globe.[2] In many Western European legal systems, the main form of avoiding a criminal trial is an out-of-court disposal, which involves pre-trial case termination decisions administered by law enforcement authorities—police or prosecution—without direct involvement from a judge.[3] A well-known legal comparativist Máximo Langer has termed this global development as the "administrativization of criminal convictions."[4] Administrative out-of-court disposals are increasingly viewed as an appropriate way of dealing with low-level criminal offenses.[5] In contrast to the 1970s models driven largely by re-socialization ideals, the goals of efficiency and cost-saving have become the main driving force behind the use of out of-court disposals at the turn of the 21st century.[6] Consequently, in criminal law literature, the proliferation of out-of-court disposals is often viewed negatively. Criminal law attaches great importance to the right of access to court and other procedural rights, which may be compromised when cases do not undergo a full trial.[7] Empirical research from England and Wales points at overly punitive, inconsistent and otherwise inappropriate use of out-of-court disposals.[8] The most critical accounts, notably from the US, view administrative case disposals in low-level criminal cases as an instrument of surveillance and social control.[9]

At the same time, relatively little is known about how out-of-court case disposal mechanisms operate in non-common law and non-English speaking jurisdictions.[10] This contribution seeks to address this gap by examining the developments of administrative out-of-court disposals in the Dutch criminal legal system. This chapter analyzes the most recent developments in the use of out-of-court disposals in the Netherlands—the introduction of the prosecutorial penal order and the so-called ZSM program, aiming to implement penal orders in practice.[11] These developments are frequently criticized in Dutch literature. The criticisms revolve around the possible threats to the right to a fair trial, legal certainty and transparency; the increased punitiveness of the new system; as well as its orientation toward efficiency and managerialist goals. In this contribution, I reflect further on these criticisms. I argue that while the policy discourse around the new form of out-of-court settlements is indicative of a more punitive and efficiency-driven approach, more empirical research is needed to establish whether it operates in this way in practice. I furthermore question whether the traditional fair trial framework, namely that of Article 6 of the European Convention of Human Rights (hereinafter—ECHR), is suited to assess procedural fairness of out-of-court disposals. I argue that instead the process by which out-of-court disposals are reached should be assessed from the viewpoint of procedural justice.

This chapter reads as follows. Section 2 describes the system of out-of-court disposals in Dutch criminal proceedings that had existed before the introduction of the prosecutorial penal order in 2008. Section 3 describes the changes that have taken place after 2008. Section 4 describes the criticisms voiced against the "new" system of out-of-court disposals. In Section 5, I offer further reflections on some of these criticisms.

THE DUTCH SYSTEM OF OUT-OF-COURT DISPOSALS BEFORE 2008

The widespread use of out-of-court disposals has been a feature of the Dutch criminal legal system since many decades. This possibility was implied in the principle of opportunity of prosecution, codified in the 1926 Code of Criminal Procedure.[12] In the Netherlands, out-of-court disposals are mostly issued by the prosecutor, in contrast for instance to England and Wales, where they are used predominantly by the police.[13] The proportion of (prosecutorial) out-of-court disposals has always been relatively high: around half or more of all criminal cases brought before the prosecutor. The trends in the numbers of out-of-court disposals have generally followed the trends in the numbers of new cases brought for prosecution. A peak in the use of out-of-court disposals—notably, as a means of diversion from prosecution[14]—was observed in 1983, when 166,000 of 270,000 new cases were dealt with out of court.[15] However, since 1983 the relative proportion of out-of-court disposals had slightly decreased due to the hardening of the criminal policy (as discussed further). In 1990–1999 both the total number of cases brought for prosecution and the number of out-of-court disposals had been decreasing,[16] then increasing again in 2000–2009 (and decreasing in 2010–2018).[17] The proportion of out-of-court disposals has remained relatively stable at slightly more than half of new criminal cases.

Cases can be dismissed for "technical" or "policy" reasons.[18] "Technical" reasons include the situations where no grounds for prosecution exist, including where there is not sufficient evidence to prosecute.[19] Dismissals for "policy" reasons are applied where there is in principle sufficient evidence for prosecution, but it is deemed inopportune, for instance due to the lack of public interest or reconciliation between the suspect and the victim.[20] When deciding to dismiss the case, the prosecutor can do so unconditionally (take no further action), usually when dismissing the case for "technical" reasons. Before the mid-1980s, decisions to take no further action were often used for "policy" reasons in trivial crimes, usually involving a reprimand or a warning.[21] However, since the mid-1980s, policy dismissals with no punitive consequences had been discouraged as being in conflict with the government's policy of stricter reaction to street and petty crime.[22] As a result, the numbers of such dismissals had decreased two-fold between 2000 and 2009.[23]

Out-of-court dismissals may also be issued conditionally, although the proportion of conditional dismissals is relatively low.[24] The kinds of conditions or the situations in which they may be applied are not regulated by law.[25] These measures should primarily have a rehabilitative, but not punitive, goal.[26] The conditions may include compensation of the damage caused by the offense, or a prohibition to attend certain places or areas, an obligation to undertake a course or a treatment, including in a closed institution.[27] Although a confession is not required for a conditional case dismissal, in practice if a case has been dismissed conditionally, it is implied that the suspect is guilty. For instance, in the Public Prosecutor's Office guidelines a conditional case dismissal counts toward "recidivism."[28] Moreover, it is possible that a conditional case dismissal would not be offered again for a similar offense.[29] Conditional case dismissals do not result in a criminal record, meaning they are not registered in the register of criminal offenses established by the law on judicial and criminal-law related information (except for transaction, see below).[30] However, the fact that the person was offered a conditional case dismissal is registered in the police and judicial records, and it may have an effect on the future criminal proceedings against that person, for instance as additional proof, if they are suspected of a similar offense, or in the eventual choice of the sanction.

A specific type of a conditional dismissal is the so-called transaction: a decision based on Article 74 of the Dutch Criminal Code. In the rhetoric of the law, transaction has a voluntary character (it is "offered" to the suspect).[31] In practice, it is hardly a free choice because the consequence of non-accepting a transaction is criminal prosecution.[32] A transaction may only be applied in cases punishable by no more than six years of imprisonment, and the list of conditions attached to it are defined by law, for instance, a fine, community works, or damage compensation. Transactions are not registered in the register of criminal offenses as "conviction," but they are mentioned there "for information." This has the consequence that, for instance, a certificate of good behavior (*verklaring omtrent het gedrag*), necessary to exercize certain professions, may not be issued for the person concerned. Although transaction is considered a specific type of conditional case dismissal,[33] there are certain differences between them. Transaction, unlike the conditional case dismissal, has an explicit legal basis, the measures attached to it have a more punitive character, and it is likely to be perceived by suspects as less voluntary in nature than a conditional case dismissal.[34] Thus, transaction is viewed as a more punitive measure than a dismissal with conditions.

Since the mid-1980s, the system of out-of-court disposals as described above was criticized as inappropriately "mild." At that time, the Dutch criminal justice policy has acquired a new element—a strong orientation toward the "law and order" agenda—which has radically changed its nature.[35] The historic emphasis on due process and humane sentencing policies was replaced by the politics of crime control, emerging in response to a concern about the growing crime rates and the inability of the justice system to adequately combat crime.[36] This transformation became explicit in the 1985 government plan entitled "The Society and Criminality," which has called for, inter alia, more streamlined, efficient and coordinated administration of the criminal process.[37] The criticisms of the then-existing system of out-of-court disposals seemed to revolve around two main points. First, suspects had been required to take additional action to accept the disposal or to meet the conditions of a conditional disposal or a transaction. Where suspects failed to do so, the Public Prosecutor's Office had to bring the case before the judge, which was viewed as a waste of public resources.[38] Another point of criticism was the absence of an explicit and official recognition that the suspect was guilty of the impugned crime(s), where the latter has accepted a conditional dismissal or a transaction.[39]

DEVELOPMENTS SINCE 2008: PENAL ORDERS AND THE ZSM PROGRAM

These criticisms led to reforming the system of out-of-court disposals by introducing a new instrument, the so-called penal order, by the Law on Case-Ending Decisions by a Public Prosecutor (*Wet OM-afdoening*), which entered into force in 2008.[40] The penal order was supposed to gradually replace the transaction, although it has not yet been fully achieved.[41] The goal was to introduce a form of pre-trial case disposal expressly construed as criminal punishment imposed by prosecutor[42] or police,[43] unlike a transaction which had (possibly, only in theory) a consensual element in it.[44] A penal order may be applied in cases which carry a maximum sanction of 6 years of imprisonment. The prosecutor or police may choose among a limited list of sanctions: work penalty, fine, temporary prohibition to drive a vehicle, etc.[45] They may not however impose a prison punishment. The decision to issue a penal order is taken unilaterally and no consent of the suspect is required. If a suspect disagrees with the decision, or with the imposed sanction, he may challenge it in court, which possibly forms an obstacle toward contesting penal orders.[46] Unlike a transaction, a penal order constitutes an official pronouncement that the suspect is guilty of the impugned offense(s), which implies that it may only be issued if there is sufficient evidence of suspect's guilt. In certain situations a suspect must be heard before a penal order is issued.[47] However, an admission of the offense by the suspect is not formally necessary. The issuance of the penal order results in a criminal record, similarly to a court sentence.

Currently about half of all cases referred to the Public Prosecutor's Office are sent to a judge, and another half is dealt with out of court.[48] Penal orders represent only about one-third of out-of-court disposals, although over time, penal orders have largely replaced transactions, particularly as regards low-level criminality. If in 2008 the Prosecutor's Office issued 66,000 transactions and 4,600 penal orders, in 2019 the proportion was reversed to 3,700 and 32,000, respectively.[49] Currently, transactions seem to be reserved mostly for economic crime and often involve high settlement amounts, which leads to specific criticisms of this disposal modality (for instance, those linked to "class justice").[50]

In March 2011, the so-called ZSM program was launched by the Dutch Public Prosecutor's Office. ZSM stands for "as soon, smart, selective, simple, together and society-oriented as possible."[51] The program aims at accelerated disposal, before the end of police detention if possible,[52] or within 7 days from the suspect's arrest or interrogation,[53] of "frequently occurring criminal cases" considered evidentially "simple."[54] This should be achieved by bringing together the public prosecutor and other "stakeholders"—police, social services, etc. (lawyers not included)—in one location, to enable speedy exchange of information on cases potentially eligible for ZSM. In 2019, about 70 percent (129,300 cases) of all new criminal prosecutions (188,600 cases) were referred to the ZSM procedure.[55] This does not, however, mean that an out-of-court disposal was reached in all cases referred to the ZSM procedure. The proportion of out-of-out disposals in relation to court prosecutions in 2019 was about 52 percent,[56] thus a certain number of ZSM cases was referred to a court.

Criticisms of the New System of Out-of-Court Disposals

Some of the long-standing criticisms of the "old" transaction-dominated system are also applicable to the "new" penal-order focused system. These revolve around the lack of transparency and judicial control of out-of-court disposals (impacting on their legitimacy), as well as the lack of consistency in their application.[57] The argument of potential "net-widening" has also been advanced. It was suggested that a more punitive measure (e.g., a transaction instead of no further action) might be used in cases, where there is not sufficient evidence to prosecute.[58] Several commissioned studies sought to examine legality and consistency in the use of penal orders.[59] Early research found that prosecutorial records of penal orders did not always include sufficient evidence of guilt, or sufficient legal justification of responsibility for the impugned offense(s).[60] Follow up studies, however, have shown improvements, as well as evidence of "great efforts" made by the Public Prosecutor's Office to improve justification and recording of legal grounds for issuing penal orders.[61] Despite this, the percentage of acquittals following appeals of penal orders remains rather high: about one-fifth of such appeals.[62]

Prosecutorial penal orders and the ZSM program were also subjected to other, more specific, criticisms. These concerned, firstly, the lack of procedural and fair trial guarantees in the design of the "new" system. Penal orders administered by law enforcement authorities, whilst leading to a full-fledged criminal conviction, do not provide the same procedural guarantees as judge-led trials. The new modality of out-of-court disposal grant excessive powers to (already powerful) prosecutors within an essentially inquisitorial setting, and without any supervision or counterbalancing guarantees.[63] It was also suggested that the "new" system would shorten the distance between the public prosecutor and law enforcement, thus preventing prosecutors from exercising an impartial "magisterial" role and turning them into zealous "crime fighters."[64] The "new" system of out-ot-court disposals is furthermore in tension with a number of fair trial rights, including the right of access to a court, the rights of defense (the rights to information and access to evidence, to adequate time and facilities for the preparation of the defense, to call and question witnesses), the right to equality of arms, and the right to silence, among others.[65] It was also noted that out-of-court disposals may operate in a coercive manner for the accused, given their emphasis on the speed and the lack of information given to suspects about the consequences of a penal order.[66]

A frequently voiced criticism of the ZSM program in particular was that it did not guarantee sufficient access to legal assistance to suspects referred to it. When the ZSM approach was being rolled out, no consideration had been given to the need to accommodate legal assistance.[67] In contrast to the summary proceedings before the court,[68] within the ZSM model, defense lawyers had had no opportunity to comment on the accusation, evidence and the envisaged sanction, or to discuss them with their client.[69] If the case was handled through the ZSM procedure, the lawyer's involvement would usually end after the first lawyer-client consultation, or approximately at the moment when a decision to send the case down the ZSM path was just being taken by the authorities.[70] It should, however, be noted that the position of legal assistance in the ZSM program has improved since its inception. Presently, every suspect accused of an offense, potentially to be processed by ZSM (except for minor offenses) would have a mandatory preliminary meeting with a lawyer.[71] Another consultation would take place if the prosecutor plans to terminate the case directly at the police station.[72] Furthermore, the target ZSM "throughput times" were increased to accommodate the need for the provision of legal assistance.[73]

Another argument against the "new" system of out-of-court disposals was that it was more punitive than the "old" system. This argument was substantiated on the one hand, with reference to the underlying goals of the "new" disposal modality—to impose criminal punishment—and the punitive discourse that accompanied it.[74] It was also noted that the immediacy of punishment was unlikely to play a preventative role in respect of the kind of crimes targeted by the ZSM program, which are usually emotional and unpremeditated.[75] Another frequently raised argument of a similar nature was that prosecutors, when issuing penal orders, supposedly tend to issue higher penalties than judges in respect of similar offenses. This argument was supported by the finding that judges issued lower sentences in a large number of cases, where penal orders were appealed (currently, about 10 percent of penal orders are being appealed).[76] As transpired from interviews, judges were inclined to lower the sanction for various reasons, for instance due to lengthy court processing times, due to suspect's personal circumstances, but also because they found prosecutorial sanctioning guidelines too strict or disproportionate. In response to this criticism, the Public Prosecutors' Office has pledged to align its sanctioning practice with that of the judiciary. The current internal regulation on penal order requires that the sanction imposed by the prosecutor should generally be lower than the expected judicial sentence.[77] The latest internal report from the Public Prosecutor's Office suggests that the discrepancies in the sentences issued by prosecutors and courts might be decreasing.[78]

Yet another criticism raised against the ZSM program was that it might be perceived as procedurally unjust by its participants (suspect and victims).[79] The theory of procedural justice was developed in late 1970s and early 1980s by American social psychologists, and it is commonly associated with the name of Tom Tyler.[80] It argues that people's perception of justice is based not only on the instrumental factors (desired outcomes), but also on the normative factors (procedural fairness).[81] In the other words, people value procedural fairness because it makes them feel more dignified, respected and empowered. Four elements of procedural justice were distinguished: the opportunities for participation in the proceedings (voice); the neutrality of the decision-maker (impartiality and objectivity of the authorities); the trustworthiness of the decision-maker (genuine concern for the parties' interests and opinions, shown, e.g., by careful consideration and explanation of the parties' arguments); and the treatment with dignity and respect in the course of the proceedings.[82] In the context of the Dutch ZSM program, Jacobs and van Kampen argued that the goal of achieving speedy resolution and the role given to the prosecutor might impact negatively the perceptions of procedural fairness of its participants. Thus, the position of the prosecutor as both an actor (closely) supervising police investigations and deciding on the suspect's guilt and sanction might affect the perception of neutrality of the decision-maker in the ZSM procedure. Participation of the suspect (and victim) might also be problematic in view of the challenges with providing access to legal assistance described above, and the potential challenges with adequately informing and involving suspects (as well as victims) in the decision-making process. This is particularly due to the need to ensure speedy decisions and the oral exchange of information between police and prosecutors, which makes it difficult to easily share it with other actors. The principles of respect and trust might also be under threat within the ZSM program, for instance because participants believe that their procedural rights are not sufficiently respected.

Finally, an important criticism of the ZSM program was that due to its emphasis on achieving a speedy resolution, it results in decision-making that is, firstly, insufficiently thorough, and secondly, insufficiently individualized or tailor-made (contrary to the proclaimed goal of achieving a "meaningful" resolution).[83] This argument is supported, on the one hand, by the research, which found that penal order decisions were not always sufficiently substantiated. On the other hand, two recent qualitative studies supply important evidence of the potential lack of thoroughness and/or individualization in the ZSM process.[84] The first study was based mainly on (focus group) interviews with professionals involved in implementing the "ZSM programme" carried out in late 2015/early 2016.[85] The interviewed police and social workers reported tensions with the prosecutor's goal to finalize cases speedily, evoke parallels with the "conveyor belt" approach.[86] In their view, contextual information about the suspect was not always sufficiently brought to light. Reportedly, thoroughness of decision-making was especially at risk when the ZSM unit was confronted with a large number of cases, and when the cases were complex. Another reported concern was the quality of the investigation files supplied by the police, especially given significant time pressures. At the same time, prosecutors reportedly did not always critically assess the evidence supplied by the police. This was attributed by authors to time pressures, relative lack of experience of "assistant prosecutors" (lower-grade employees of the Public Prosecutor's Office) charged with the decision-making, but also to the lack of necessary distancing of prosecutors from the interests of law enforcement (the lack of a "magisterial" role mentioned above). Finally, some respondents in the study noted that insufficient attention was paid with the ZSM program to possibilities for diversion, or resolving cases outside of the domain of criminal law. Instead, the process was aimed at obtaining a quick and standardized outcome, which implies one of the "standard" criminal law interventions: usually, a penal order or a conditional case dismissal.

The lack of time and space within the ZSM program to apply individualized solutions was emphasized in another qualitative study carried out in 2014–2015, which involved observations and interviews with 160 ZSM officers (as well as 17 lawyers) at 13 local police stations.[87] This study concluded that while the ZSM program resulted in greater attention being paid to petty crime, doubts remained concerning whether the ZSM decision-making process was sufficiently thorough, and whether it led to "meaningful" resolution. These findings were largely in line with the conclusions of the research described above. In addition, the authors argued that several factors interfered with the ability of the ZSM program to achieve non-standard and individualized outcomes, such as the emphasis on speed, as well as the fact that police were often not incentivized to provide contextual information about the suspect and the victim to ZSM prosecutors.[88] Other Dutch authors pointed at the relatively marginal use of mediation and alternatives to prosecution by the Public Prosecutor's Office, despite the existence of such possibilities in the law and in practice.[89]

Reflections on the Criticisms

Is the New System of Out-of-Court Disposal More Punitive?

Firstly, it is clear that an important policy goal behind the penal order and the ZSM program, in addition to increasing efficiency, is to strengthen the use of criminal sanctions.[90] The Explanatory Memorandum to the Law on Case-Ending Decisions by a Public Prosecutor states, for instance, that the rationale for the new law lies in increasing public safety.[91] The "new" system of out-of-court disposals does not anymore create an impression that criminal offenses remain unpunished, as the penal order creates the possibility for the prosecutor to formally prosecute and sanction crime. The ZSM program, designed as the means of (speedy) implementation of public orders (although so far this objective has not been achieved, as only a minority of ZSM cases result in penal orders)[92] thus also aims to contribute to the goal of strengthening the use of criminal sanctions.

It is, however, not entirely clear whether the punitive discourse around penal orders has resulted in greater punitiveness of the out-of-court disposal system viewed as the whole. Interestingly, the proportion of (conditional) dismissals issued by the Public Prosecutor's Office as compared to other forms of out-of-court disposals has been increasing in parallel with the increasing use of penal orders. For instance, from 2007 to 2016 the number of conditional and unconditional dismissals has increased from 32.975 to 49.180.[93] An internal report from the Public Prosecutor's Office suggests that one reason is the increasing number of "technical" dismissals due to insufficient evidence to prosecute (suggesting that prosecutors now assess cases more critically).[94] The other suggested reason is the increased attention to searching for alternative solutions, resulting from the change in the internal policy of the Public Prosecutor's Office.[95] The change was reflected in the internal policy document "Vision for 2015," which envisions a greater emphasis on "meaningful" resolution within the "ZSM approach."[96] Thus, it might be that certain less serious matters, which would previously have been dealt with by means of transaction are now settled with a (conditional) case dismissal, whilst a penal order, being more punitive in nature, is reserved for more "serious" offenses. This explanation appears plausible, and consistent with research findings, suggesting that certain elements of the ZSM program reflect the goals of criminal de-escalation, offender rehabilitation and "restorative justice": for instance, the involvement of probation services and the victim.[97]

It is also unclear whether and to what extent the "new" system of out-of-court disposals is more punitive than the "old" system (or is experienced as such by suspects) in practice. Although a transaction is considered "voluntary" in the rhetoric of the law, it also contains important punitive elements, as described in Section 2 above. The practice of penal orders, in its turn, as demonstrated by empirical research, seems to contain consensual elements, contrary to the meaning of the respective law. For instance, prosecutors tend to secure consent of the suspect and the lawyer to the penal order, as a (informal) guarantee that the order will not be appealed.[98] Finally, the argument that judges would impose, on average, lower sentences than prosecutors for similar crimes remains rather theoretical. Despite the intention for penal orders to replace (a part of) judicial sentences, the proportion of cases settled by prosecutors did not greatly increase following the introduction of penal orders.[99] Thus, it may be hypothesized that penal orders have rather replaced the "old" transactions, which could very well be as "severe" as penal orders.

RESPECT OF FAIR TRIAL RIGHTS

Concerning the arguments that the design or the practice of penal orders creates tension with fair trial rights—which appear justified—two further remarks should be made. Firstly, the application of the "traditional" fair trial rights' framework arguably results in an incomplete picture of procedural fairness of out-of-court disposals. That is not to say that, for instance, the right of access to a court or the adversarial rights of the defense are irrelevant, but that other aspects of procedural fairness—for example, those related to the thoroughness or neutrality of decision-making—might be even more relevant in the context of administrative out-of-court disposals.

As noted by Vriend, human rights law does not protect the right to a fair out-of-court settlement, but only the right to a fair trial.[100] In the other words, out-of-court disposals are viewed as a corollary to the trial process, but not as a self-standing procedure leading to case resolution. The procedural safeguards applied to out-of-court disposals are thus derived "by analogy" from those applied to waivers of the right to the court,[101] to abbreviated trial proceedings,[102] or from those used in pre-trial proceedings.[103] None of these models however accurately describes prosecutorial out-of-court disposals, which have arguably developed into a self-standing procedural mechanism of resolving criminal cases. Acknowledging this fact, Vriend attempted to develop a self-standing fairness framework for out-of-court settlements, which is, however, still derived from Article 6 ECHR. His framework is based on the participatory, or adversarial model of proof, which in Vriend's view leads to most accurate fact-finding. He therefore distinguishes four elements of procedural fairness also applicable to out-of-court settlements: non-compulsion, informed involvement, the right to challenge evidence, and the right to a reasoned decision. Although this framework is a valuable addition to understanding procedural fairness of out-of-court settlements, its underlying assumptions may be questioned. Thus, the model is based on the "adversarial" presentation of proof representing an "ideal" model of procedural fairness (understood only as outcome-based fairness, namely, fact-finding accuracy).[104] An adversarial model, however, presupposes the existence of an independent and impartial authority, taking a decision after hearing evidence presented by two parties, having equal opportunities to present their case. Thus, the procedural safeguards embedded in the adversarial model are those related to the parties' control and participation in the proceedings.[105] It would, however, seem unrealistic to apply an "adversarial" model in a procedural setting of an out-of-court disposal, where the role of investigation and decision-making is granted to the same authority. In this respect a criminal out-of-court disposal in the Netherlands resembles more of an administrative procedural setting. In such settings, however, procedural fairness is construed mostly around the quality and integrity of decision-making of the respective authority, rather than the principle of adversarialism.[106]

Another potential issue with the application of the traditional fair trial rights framework to out-of-court disposal proceedings—or any other legal proceeding—is that it does not automatically equal to procedural justice.[107] The procedural justice perspective, described above in Section 3, transcends the perspective of formal law in determining whether a certain legal procedure is "fair." Although some of the guarantees embedded in the framework of fair trial correspond to certain elements of procedural justice (particularly in the procedural setting involving an impartial arbiter), they do not match entirely. The elements embedded in the procedural justice perspective are more subtle than those incorporated in the formal legal guarantees: for instance, providing a consultation with the lawyer to every suspect "processed" via a ZSM program might meet the requirements of "fair trial," but the procedure may still be experienced by the suspect as unfair, because the lawyer, having little information about the suspect's background and the case, can only provide superficial advice. Thus, formal compliance with fair trial guarantees does not as such guarantee procedural justice.

Procedural Justice Concerns

Given the important limitations of formal legal frameworks of fairness as described above, it seems appropriate to assess the fairness of the "new" Dutch system of out-of-court disposals primarily from the standpoint of procedural justice. However, no such empirical study has been undertaken so far.

Research findings described in Section 3 suggest that several elements of the "new" Dutch system of out-of-court disposals might enter into conflict with the procedural justice perspective. Thus, the elements of participation (voice) and quality of decision-making seem to be of importance in any type of (criminal) legal procedure. The research findings summarized above suggest that both aspects might be under threat within the current procedural design and practice of out-of-court disposals in the Netherlands. Voice, for instance, depends on the amount and quality of information provided to the participants, and on the availability and quality of legal assistance. Both aspects, as suggested by numerous studies, are potentially problematic within the ZSM procedure. The quality of decision-making includes in particular such elements as thoroughness of fact-finding, neutrality (absence of bias), and the quality of reasoning and justification. All these aspects of decision-making are potentially under threat within out-of-court disposal procedures and even more so, at it seems, within the ZSM program, where managerial pressures are especially high.[108]

However, more empirical research is needed to examine how the various elements of procedural justice are reflected the actual practice of out-of-court disposals. This practice might be more uneven and complex than the theoretical arguments suggesting a link between certain elements of ZSM procedural design and negative perceptions of procedural justice. Besides, the practices of out-of-court disposals and of the ZSM program in the Netherlands are still evolving. The design and implementation of prosecutorial penal orders is an area of increased political concern, and they are therefore subject to frequent adjustments and reforms.

The developments concerning access to legal assistance in the ZSM program is one illustration of such adjustments. For instance, in my fieldwork research into legal assistance at police stations (which ended in 2015), I found that at that time the practices of accommodating lawyers within the various regional ZSM programs were uneven.[109] However, already by 2015, the participation of lawyers had improved as compared to the moment of inception of the ZSM project. In reaction to criticisms mounted by defense lawyers[110] and reflected in evaluation reports,[111] the Public Prosecutor's Office sought to enhance the position of legal assistance within the ZSM program. This has led, inter alia, to the so-called "legal assistance pilots," which ran from the end of 2014 to early 2015 in four different locations.[112] In the pilots, lawyers had an opportunity to consult the case file before the second consultation.[113] My research demonstrated that lawyers involved in the pilots had some, although limited, possibilities to influence decisions taken within the ZSM proceedings (more so than in the other regions).[114] At the same time, lawyers participating in the "pilots" still reported challenges with accessing ZSM procedures. For instance, they were rarely provided access to written documents or other information on the authorities' own initiative.[115] These findings were confirmed by other research described in Section 3, suggesting that the exchange of information with lawyers was deficient (at that time). It would be interesting to follow up on these and other relevant developments, and assess their potential impact on participants' perceptions of procedural justice in the practice of penal orders and of the ZSM program.

CONCLUSION

In view of the growing scholarly attention to the (global) increase of criminal trial waivers and out-of-court settlements, and the scarcity of information about the respective phenomena from non-English jurisdictions, this chapter sought to critically examine the design and practice of out-of-court settlements in Dutch criminal proceedings. It was observed, firstly, that although in the international literature the proliferation of trial waivers is viewed as a relatively recent development, the Dutch criminal legal system has relied on widespread use of out-of-court disposals since several decades.

The recent developments in the Netherlands involved not so much an increase in the use of out-of-court settlements, but a change in the nature of the legal instruments used. The adoption of the new instrument of out-of-court disposal, the so-called penal order, and the implementation of this instrument via the so-called ZSM program of the Public Prosecutor's Office has attracted much attention in the Dutch literature. The prevailing opinion seems to be that this has resulted in a more punitive out-of-court disposal system. However, it is somewhat unclear whether and to what extent the Dutch system of out-of-court disposals has become more punitive in practice following the introduction of the penal order. To assess this, the system of (out-of-court) criminal sanctions should arguably be viewed in its entirety.

This chapter has furthermore critically assessed the various arguments against the "new" Dutch system of out-of-court disposals. The potential tensions of the system with fair trial rights, such as the right of access to a court or the rights of the defense are often mentioned in the Dutch legal literature. However, I argued that the fair trial rights framework is insufficient to assess procedural fairness of out-of-court disposals in criminal proceedings. Instead, this chapter suggested that fairness of out-of-court disposal mechanisms should be assessed primarily from the standpoint of procedural justice. Although the existing research findings related to the design and operation of prosecutorial penal orders and the ZSM program suggest potential areas of tension, no empirical study into procedural justice of out-of-court disposals has yet been undertaken in the Netherlands. Such research appears necessary to shed further light on the controversial question of whether administrative out-of-court disposals in criminal proceedings are or can be procedurally fair.

BIBLIOGRAPHY

Abels, D., and others. *Evaluatie Wet OM-afdoening* (Universiteit van Amsterdam, 2018).

van den Biggelaar G. J. M. *De buitengerechtelijke afdoening van strafbare feiten door het Openbaar Ministerie (diss. Maastricht)* (Gouda Quint, 1994).

Bijlsma, J. *Het voorwaardelijk sepot. Normering, praktijk, evaluatie* (Boom Juridisch, 2019).

Boek, J. "Sepot en transactie; afdoeninb van strafzaken buiten geding" in WODC (ed), *Justitiele herkenningen Honderd jaar strafrecht*, vol. 25 (Gouda Quint, 1999).

Boone, M. and P. Langbroek. "Problem-Solving Initiatives in Administrative and Criminal Law in the Netherlands" (2019) 14 *Utrecht Law Review*, 64.

Brants, C. "Prosecutorial Sanctions in the Netherlands" in U. Sieber and others (eds), *Alternative Systems of Crime Control* (Duncker & Humblot, 2018).

Brants, C. H., and B. Stapert. "Buitengerechtelijke afdoening: discretie en macht " in M. Boone and others (eds), *Discretie in het strafrecht* (Boom Juridische Uitgevers, 2004).

Brouwer, D. V. A. "ZSM en de verdediging" (2015) 26 *Delikt en Delinkwent*, 265.

Brûle, I. van den. "Gezocht: rol voor de advocatuur bij ZSM" (2014) *Proces*, 89.

Buruma, Y. "Het Openbaar Ministerie in zwaar weer" (2013) 2300 *Nederlandse Juristenblad*, 2727.

Corstens, G. J. M. "Consensualiteit en strafsancties" (1997) *Ars Acqui* 139.

Crijns, J. H. "Het wetsvoorstel OM-afdoening: een wolf in schaapskledij" (2004) 4 *Sancties*, 225.

Crijns, J. H. "Rationaliteiten achter de Wet OM-afdoening" in C.P.M. Cleiren and others (eds), *Op zoek naar samenhang Het Algemeen kader herziening strafvordering nader beschouwd* (Kluwer, 2006), 56.

Crijns, J. H. *De strafrechtelijke overeenkomst. De rechtsbetrekking met het Openbaar Ministerie op het grensvlak van publiek-en privaatrecht (diss. Leiden)* (Kluwer, 2010).

Crijns, J. H. and R. S. B. Kool. "Afscheid van de klassieke strafrechtelijke procedure?," *Handelingen Nederlandse Juristen-Vereniging; Afscheid van de klassieke procedure? /preadviezen* (Wolters Kluwer, 2017), 285.

van Daele, D. *De openbaar ministerie en de afhandeling van strafzaken in de Nederland* (Universitaire Pers Leuven, 2003).

Damaška, M. R. *The Faces of Justice and State Authority: A Comparative Approach to the Legal Process* (Yale University Press, 1986).

Downes, D., and R. van Swaaningen. "The Road to Dystopia? Changes in the Penal Climate of the Netherlands" (2007) 35 *Crime and Justice*, 31.

Evans, R., and C. Wilkinson. "Variations in Police Cautioning Policy and Practice in England and Wales" (1990) 29 *Howard Journal of Criminal Justice*, 155.

Fair Trials. *The Disappearing Trial* (2017).

Farrington, D. P. and T. Bennett. "Police Cautioning of Juveniles in London" (1981) 21 *British Journal of Criminology*, 123.

Franken, A. A. "Het geduldige papier en de weerbarstige praktijk" (2013) 16 *Delikt en Delinkwent*, 157.

Galligan, D. *Due Process and Fair Procedures: A Study of Administrative Procedures* (Oxford University Press, 1997).

Gelsthorpe, L. and V. Kemp. "Youth Justice Discretion in Pre-Court Decision-Making" in L. Gelsthorpe and N. Padfield (eds.), *Exercising Discretion* (Willan, 2003).

Groenhuijsen, M. C., and A. M. van Kalmthout. "Transactie en voorwaardelijk sepot: lood OM oud ijzer?" (1983) 6 *Delikt en Delikwent* 16, 474–478.

Grotelaar HAM, *Interacting with Procedural Justice in Courts (diss. Utrecht)* (2018).

Hartmann, A. R. "Buitengerechtelijke afdoening II" in M. S. Groenhuijsen and G. Knigge (eds.), *Dwangmiddelen en rechtsmiddelen Derde interim-rapport onderzoeksproject strafvordering 2001* (Kluwer, 2001).

Jacobs, P. and P. van Kampen. "Dutch 'ZSM Settlements' in the Face of Procedural Justice: The Sooner the Better?" (2014) 10 *Utrecht Law Review*, 73.

Kessler, M., and B. F. Keulen. *De strafbeschikking* (Kluwer, 2008).

Knigge, G., and M. Peters. *Beschikt en Gewogen. Over de naleving van de wet door het openbaar ministerie bij het uitvaardigen van strafbeschikkingen* (2014).

Knigge, G., and M. Peters. *Beproefd verzet. Over de naleving van de wet door het openbaar ministerie bij de afhandeling van het verzet tegen een OM-strafbeschikking* (2017).

Knigge, G., and M. Peters. *Wordt vervolgt: beproefd verzet* (2019).

Kohler-Hausmann, I. *Misdemeanorland: Criminal Courts and Social Control in an Age of Broken Windows Policing* (Princeton University Press, 2018).

Kwakman, N. "Snelrecht en de ZSM-aanpak" (2012) 3 *Delikt en Delinkwent*, 188.

Landau, S. F., and G. Nathan. "Selecting Delinquents for Cautioning in London Metropolitan Area" (1983) 23 *British Journal of Criminology*, 128.

Langer, M. "Plea Bargaining, Conviction without Trial, and the Global Administratization of Criminal Convictions" (2021) 4 *Annual Review of Criminology*, 377.

Leliveld, J. "ZZM afhandeling van strafzaken" (2012) *Nederlands Juristenblad*, 1952.

Leliveld, J. and P. van Kampen. "Rechtsbijstand in de voorfase van het strafproces" (2014) *Nederlandse Juristenblad*, 2604.

Lent, L. van., M. A. Simon Thomas, and P. van Kampen. "De ZSM-werkwijze in praktijk—Op zoek naar balans" (2016) 37 *Nederlands Juristenblad*, 2753.

Lind, E. and T. Tyler. *The Social Psychology of Procedural Justice* (Springer Science & Business Media, 1988).

Meij, P. van der. "De andere kant van de ZSM-medaille: Het gebrek aan controle op beleid en beslissingen van het Openbaar Ministerie" (2014) 25 *Nederlandse Juristenblad*, 1666.

Meij, P. van der and L. Hartjes. "Twijfels bij de toekomstigheid van ZSM. Een toets van het ZSM-beleid aan huidige en voorzienbare ontwikkelingen" in N. Achterberg and others (eds.), *Vrouwe Justitia zucht en steunt Hoe houden we de rechtsstaat toekomstbestendig?* (Stichting NJCM-Boekerij, 2015).

Ministerie van Justitie, *Samenleving en criminaliteit. Een beleidsplan voor de komende jaren* (1985).

Openbaar Ministerie, *Landelijke bevindingen 2-meting OM-strafbeschikking en 1-meting verzet* (2020).

Packer, H. L. *The Limits of Criminal Sanction* (Stanford University Press, 1969)

Pakes, F. "The Ebb and Flow of Criminal Justice in the Netherlands" (1996) 34 *International Journal of the Sociology of Law*, 141.

Pivaty, A. *Criminal Defence at Police Stations: A Comparative and Empirical Study* (Routledge, 2019).

Ridder, J. D. *Sepots. Trends en ontwikkelingen* (2018).

Salet, R. and J. Terpstra. *VVC onder de aandacht: Een onderzoek naar ZSM en de gevolgen voor het politiewerk* (Politie en wetenschap, 2017).

Salet, R., and J. Terpstra. "Criminal Justice as a Production Line: ASAP and the Managerialization of Criminal Justice in the Netherlands" (2020) 17 *European Journal of Criminology*, 826.

Sikkema, E., and F. Kristen. "Strafbeschikking en ZSM: verschuivingen binnen de strafrechtshandhaving" in F. de Jong and R. S. B. Kool (eds.) *Relaties van gezag en verantwoordelijkheid: strafrechtelijke ontwikkelingen* (Boom/Lemma, 2012).

Solum, L. B. *Procedural Justice* (2004).

Spronken, T. "Het strafrecht als vergiet en het ZSM-model als snelkookpan" (2012) 4 *Nieuwsbrief Strafrecht*, 373.

Spronken, T. "De wasstraat" (2015) 5 *Nederlands Juristenblad*, 295.

Tak, P. J. "Methods of Diversion Used by the Prosecution Services in the Netherlands and other Western European countries" (2008).

Thaman, S. C. "The Penal Order: Prosecutorial Sentencing as a Model for Criminal Justice Reform?" in E. Luna and M. Wade (eds.) *The Prosecutor in Transnational Perspective* (Oxford University Press, 2012).

Thibaut, J., and L. Walker. *Procedural Justice: A Psychological Analysis* (L. Erlbaum Associates, 1975).

Thomas, M. S., and others. *Snel, Betekenisvol en Zorgvuldig. Een tussenevaluatie van de ZSM-werkwijze*, 2016).

Tyler, T. "Social Justice: Outcome and Procedure" (2000) 35 *International Journal of Psychology*, 117.

Tyler, T. "Enhancing Police Legitimacy" (2004) *Annals of the American Academy of Political and Social Science*, 84.

Vriend, K. *Avoiding a Full Criminal Trial: Fair Trial Rights, Diversions and Shortcuts in Dutch and International Criminal Proceedings* (Springer, 2016).

Wetenschappelijk Onderzoek en Documentatie-Centrum (WODC), *Criminaliteit en rechtshandhaving 2001. Ontwikkelingen en samenhangen* (Boom Juridisch Uitgevers, 1999).

Wetenschappelijk Onderzoek en Documentatie-Centrum (WODC), *Criminaliteit en rechtshandhaving 2010. Ontwikkelingen en samenhangen* (Boom Juridisch Uitgevers, 2009).

Wetenschappelijk Onderzoek en Documentatie-Centrum (WODC), *Criminaliteit en rechtshandhaving 2019. Ontwikkelingen en samenhangen* (Boom Juridisch Uitgevers, 2020).

de Zanger, W. S., and E. Sikkema. "Schikken of beschikken?: Buitengerechtelijke afdoening van (grote en bijzondere) strafzaken in een gemoderniseerd Wetboek van Strafvordering" (2019) 2 *Platform Modernisering Strafvordering.*

NOTES

1. Máximo Langer. "Plea Bargaining, Conviction without Trial, and the Global Administratization of Criminal Convictions" (2021) 4 *Annual Review of Criminology*, 377; Fair Trials, *The Disappearing Trial* (2017).

2. Fair Trials. *The Disappearing Trial*, p. 23.

3. See Stephen C. Thaman. "The Penal Order: Prosecutorial Sentencing as a Model for Criminal Justice Reform?" in Erik Luna and Marianne Wade (eds.), *The Prosecutor in Transnational Perspective* (Oxford University Press, 2012) for Germany; Chrisje Brants. "Prosecutorial Sanctions in the Netherlands" in Ulrich Sieber and others (eds) *Alternative Systems of Crime Control* (Duncker & Humblot, 2018) for the Netherlands.

4. Langer. "Plea Bargaining, Conviction without Trial, and the Global Administratization of Criminal Convictions."

5. Issa Kohler-Hausmann, *Misdemeanorland: Criminal Courts and Social Control in an Age of Broken Windows Policing* (Princeton University Press, 2018).

6. Peter J. P. Tak. "Methods of diversion used by the prosecution services in the Netherlands and other Western European countries" (2008), p. 1.

7. See Fair Trials, *The Disappearing Trial*; K. Vriend, *Avoiding a Full Criminal Trial: Fair Trial Rights, Diversions and Shortcuts in Dutch and International Criminal Proceedings* (Springer, 2016).

8. Roger Evans and Christine Wilkinson. "Variations in Police Cautioning Policy and Practice in England and Wales" (1990) 29 *Howard Journal of Criminal Justice*, 155; David P. Farrington and Trevor Bennett. "Police Cautioning of Juveniles in London" (1981) 21 *British Journal of Criminology*, 123; L. Gelsthorpe and V. Kemp. "Youth Justice Discretion in Pre-Court Decision-Making" in L. Gelsthorpe and N. Padfield (eds.) *Exercising Discretion* (Willan: 2003); Simha F. Landau and Gad Nathan. "Selecting Delinquents for Cautioning in London Metropolitan Area" (1983) 23 *British Journal of Criminology*, 128.

9. Kohler-Hausmann, *Misdemeanorland: Criminal Courts and Social Control in an Age of Broken Windows Policing.*

10. Langer. "Plea Bargaining, Conviction Without Trial, and the Global Administratization of Criminal Convictions," p. 389.

11. See section 3.

12. Art. 167 para. 2 Dutch Criminal Procedure Code (hereinafter, CCP).

13. Police can only issue penal orders in very minor cases. Art. 257b CCP.

14. See below.

15. Wetenschappelijk Onderzoek en Documentatie-Centrum (WODC), *Criminaliteit en rechtshandhaving 2001. Ontwikkelingen en samenhangen.* (Boom Juridisch Uitgevers, 2001), p. 116.

16. Ibid., p.111.

17. Wetenschappelijk Onderzoek en Documentatie-Centrum (WODC), *Criminaliteit en rechtshandhaving 2019. Ontwikkelingen en samenhangen* (Boom Juridisch Uitgevers 2020), p. 59–60.

18. J. Boek. "Sepot en transactie; afdoeninb van strafzaken buiten geding" in WODC (ed), *Justitiele herkenningen Honderd jaar strafrecht*, vol. 25 (Gouda Quint, 1999).

19. Aanwijzing sepot en gebruik sepotgronden (2020A013), Staatscourant 2020, 62570.

20. Ibid.

21. Dirk van Daele, *De openbaar ministerie en de afhandeling van strafzaken in de Nederland* (Universitaire Pers Leuven, 2003), p. 416–418.

22. Ministerie van Justitie, *Samenleving en criminaliteit. Een beleidsplan voor de komende jaren* (1985); D. van Daele, *De openbaar ministerie en de afhandeling van strafzaken in de Nederland* (Universitaire Pers Leuven, 2003), p. 417.

23. From approximately 25% to about 12% of all decisions not to prosecute. See Wetenschappelijk Onderzoek en Documentatie Centrum (WODC), *Criminaliteit en rechtshandhaving 2009* (2010), p. 109.

24. In 2019: 53,000 unconditional dismissals and 8,400 conditional dismissals. (WODC), *Criminaliteit en rechtshandhaving 2019. Ontwikkelingen en samenhangen*, p. 61.

25. Exception for specific types of conditional case dismissals, namely the HALT-project or a transaction (see below). HALT or the "alternative" (*Het alternatief*) is a special kind of a conditional case dismissal applied to juvenile offenders, with legal basis in Art. 77e of the Dutch Criminal Code. it is not further discussed here.

26. J. Bijlsma, *Het voorwaardelijk sepot. Normering, praktijk, evaluatie* (Boom Juridisch, 2019), p. 47.

27. Ibid., p. 50–51.

28. Aanwijzing kader voor strafvordering meerderjarigen (2019A003), Stcrt. 2019, 14890.

29. Ibid.

30. Wet van 7 november 2002 tot wijziging van de regels betreffende de verwerking van justitiële gegevens en het stellen van regels met betrekking tot de verwerking van persoonsgegevens in persoonsdossiers.

31. On the legal nature of transaction, see J. H. Crijns, *De strafrechtelijke overeenkomst. De rechtsbetrekking met het Openbaar Ministerie op het grensvlak van publiek-en privaatrecht (diss. Leiden)* (Kluwer, 2010).

32. Ibid., p. 527–532.

33. G. J. M. van den Biggelaar, *De buitengerechtelijke afdoening van strafbare feiten door het Openbaar Ministerie (diss. Maastricht)* (Gouda Quint, 1994), p. 59.

34. M. C. Groenhuijsen, A. M. van Kalmthout. “Transactie en voorwaardelijk sepot: lood OM oud ijzer?” (1983) 13(6) *Delikt en Delikwent*, 474; Crijns, *De strafrechtelijke overeenkomst. De rechtsbetrekking met het Openbaar Ministerie op het grensvlak van publiek-en privaatrecht (diss. Leiden)*, p. 179–813.

35. D. Downes and R. van Swaaningen. “The Road to Dystopia? Changes in the Penal Climate of the Netherlands” (2007) 35 *Crime and Justice*, 31, 32.

36. F. Pakes. “The Ebb and Flow of Criminal Justice in the Netherlands” (1996) 34 International Journal of the Sociology of Law 141; Downes and van Swaaningen. “The Road to Dystopia? Changes in the Penal Climate of the Netherlands.”

37. Ministerie van Justitie, Samenleving en criminaliteit. Een beleidsplan voor de komende jaren.

38. J. H. Crijns and R. S. B. Kool. “Afscheid van de klassieke strafrechtelijke procedure?,” *Handelingen Nederlandse Juristen-Vereniging; Afscheid van de klassieke procedure? / preadviezen* (Wolters Kluwer, 2017), p. 285.

39. A. R. Hartmann. “Buitengerechtelijke afdoening II” in M. S. Groenhuijsen and G. Knigge (eds.) *Dwangmiddelen en rechtsmiddelen Derde interim-rapport onderzoeksproject strafvordering 2001* (Kluwer, 2001), p. 101–102.

40. Wet van 7 juli 2006, Stb. 330.

41. W. S. de Zanger and E. Sikkema. “Schikken of beschikken?: Buitengerechtelijke afdoening van (grote en bijzondere) strafzaken in een gemoderniseerd Wetboek van Strafvordering” (2019) 2 Platform Modernisering Strafvordering, p. 8.

42. Art. 257a CCP.

43. Art. 257b CCP.

44. Memorie van Toelichting, Wet OM-afdoening, Tweede Kamer, vergaderjaar 2004–2005, 29 849, nr. 3. p.1.

45. Art. 257a para. 2 CCP.

46. Art. 257e CCP.

47. M. Kessler and B. F. Keulen, *De strafbeschikking* (Kluwer, 2008), p. 31.

48. In 2019, 192,000 decisions were taken by the Public Prosecutor’s Office, among which 93,000 cases were referred to court and 99,000 cases were finalized with an out-of-court disposal. (WODC), *Criminaliteit en rechtshandhaving 2019. Ontwikkelingen en samenhangen*, p. 58.

49. de Zanger and Sikkema. “Schikken of beschikken?: Buitengerechtelijke afdoening van (grote en bijzondere) strafzaken in een gemoderniseerd Wetboek van Strafvordering,” p. 2.

50. Crijns and Kool. “Afscheid van de klassieke strafrechtelijke procedure?” p. 286–287; for an overview of criticisms, see de Zanger and Sikkema. “Schikken of beschikken?: Buitengerechtelijke afdoening van (grote en bijzondere) strafzaken in een gemoderniseerd Wetboek van Strafvordering,” p. 5–6.

51. Marc Simon Thomas and others, *Snel, Betekenisvol en Zorgvuldig Een tussenevaluatie van de ZSM-werkwijze* (Universiteit Utrecht, 2016), p. 7.

52. The maximum duration of police detention in the Netherlands is 3 days and 18 hours. Article 59a CCP.

53. M.S. Thomas and others, *Snel, Betekenisvol en Zorgvuldig. Een tussenevaluatie van de ZSM-werkwijze*, 2016), p. 20–24.

54. There is no clear definition of "frequently occurring cases," or set eligibility criteria for cases to be referred to ZSM. Ibid, 22–3.

55. Jaarbericht 2019 Openbaar Ministerie (2020), p. 35.

56. *Criminaliteit en rechtshandhaving 2019. Ontwikkelingen en samenhangen*, p. 58.

57. For an overview, see Vriend *Avoiding a Full Criminal Trial: Fair Trial Rights, Diversions and Shortcuts in Dutch and International Criminal Proceedings*, p. 195–197; G. J. M. Corstens. "Consensualiteit en strafsancties" (1997) *Ars Acqui*, 139.

58. Vriend, *Avoiding a Full Criminal Trial: Fair Trial Rights, Diversions and Shortcuts in Dutch and International Criminal Proceedings*, p. 196.

59. Procureur-Generaal bij de Hoge Raad der Nederlanden, *Beschikt en Gewogen*, 2014); G. Knigge and M. Peters, *Beproefd verzet. Over de naleving van de wet door het openbaar ministerie bij de afhandeling van het verzet tegen een OM-strafbeschikking* (2017).

60. Nederlanden, *Beschikt en Gewogen*, p. 59–62.

61. Knigge and Peters, *Beproefd verzet. Over de naleving van de wet door het openbaar ministerie bij de afhandeling van het verzet tegen een OM-strafbeschikking*; G. Knigge and M. Peters, *Wordt vervolgt: beproefd verzet* (2019). See also an internal report of the Public Prosecutor's Office: Openbaar Ministerie, *Landelijke bevindingen 2-meting OM-strafbeschikking en 1-meting verzet* (2020).

62. Ministerie, *Landelijke bevindingen 2-meting OM-strafbeschikking en 1-meting verzet*, p. 32.

63. Eelke Sikkema and François Kristen. "Strafbeschikking en ZSM: verschuivingen binnen de strafrechtshandhaving" in F. de Jong and R. S. B. Kool (eds.), *Relaties van gezag en verantwoordelijkheid: strafrechtelijke ontwikkelingen* (Boom/Lemma 2012); C. H. Brants and B. Stapert. "Buitengerechtelijke afdoening: discretie en macht" in M. Boone and others (eds), *Discretie in het strafrecht* (Boom Juridische Uitgevers 2004); J. J. Crijns. "Het wetsvoorstel OM-afdoening: een wolf in schaapskledij" (2004) 4 Sancties 225, p. 232.

64. Sikkema and Kristen. "Strafbeschikking en ZSM: verschuivingen binnen de strafrechtshandhaving," p. 193–197.

65. Vriend, *Avoiding a Full Criminal Trial: Fair Trial Rights, Diversions and Shortcuts in Dutch and International Criminal Proceedings;* Ybo Buruma. "Het Openbaar Ministerie in zwaar weer" (2013) 2300 *Nederlandse Juristenblad*, 2727; N. Kwakman. "Snelrecht en de ZSM-aanpak" (2012) 42 *Delikt en Delinkwent*, 188; P. Jacobs and P. van Kampen. "Dutch 'ZSM Settlements' in the Face of Procedural Justice: The Sooner the Better? " (2014) 10 *Utrecht Law Review*, 73; Sikkema and Kristen. "Strafbeschikking en ZSM: verschuivingen binnen de strafrechtshandhaving."

66. T. Spronken. "Het strafrecht als vergiet en het ZSM-model als snelkookpan" (2012) *Nieuwsbrief Strafrecht*, 373.

67. The ZSM approach was implemented nationwide in 2012 and 2013. See information brief on the website of the Public Prosecutor's Office. "Landelijke invoering van de ZSM werkwijze," available from: www.om.nl/vaste-onderdelen/zoeken/@24445/factsheet-zsm/, last accessed on 10 April 2021.

68. Kwakman. "Snelrecht en de ZSM-aanpak."

69. T. Spronken. “Het strafrecht als vergiet en het ZSM-model als snelkookpan” (2012) 4 Nieuwsbrief Strafrecht, 373; I. van den BrÛle. “Gezocht: rol voor de advocatuur bij ZSM” (2014) Proces 89; A. A. Franken. “Het geduldige papier en de weerbarstige praktijk” (2013) 16 Delikt en Delinkwent, 157.

70. P. van der Meij. “De andere kant van de ZSM-medaille: Het gebrek aan controle op beleid en beslissingen van het Openbaar Ministerie” (2014) 25 Nederlandse Juristenblad, 1666, 1667. According to the 2011 statistics, a great majority of suspects “processed” through ZSM waived their right to a lawyer. P. Jacobs and P. van Kampen. “Dutch ‘ZSM Settlements’ in the Face of Procedural Justice: The Sooner the Better?” (2014) 10 Utrecht Law Review, 73, p. 79.

71. Letter of the Minister of Security and Justice to the Parliament “Rechtsbijstand in de eerste fase van het opsporingsonderzoek” of 22 August 2016, Kamerstukken II, 2015/16, 31 753, nr. 109, p. 3.

72. Ibid., p. 3.

73. Also, the proportion of cases, initially selected for ZSM, but then referred to courts, appeared to have been increasing; thus, by 2016 about one-third of cases initially processed by the ZSM were being referred to courts. Thomas and others, Snel, Betekenisvol en Zorgvuldig. Een tussenevaluatie van de ZSM-werkwijze, p. 106–108.

74. Brants and Stapert. “Buitengerechtelijke afdoening: discretie en macht.”

75. N. Kwakman. “Snelrecht en de ZSM-aanpak” (2012) 3 Delikt en Delinkwent 188, p. 196.

76. Knigge and Peters, *Beproefd verzet. Over de naleving van de wet door het openbaar ministerie bij de afhandeling van het verzet tegen een OM-strafbeschikking*, p. 120–121; Denis Abels and others, *Evaluatie Wet OM-afdoening* (Universiteit van Amsterdam 2018), p. 103–104.

77. Aanwijzing om-strafbeschikking (2020A014), Staatscourant 2020, 62572.

78. Ministerie, Landelijke bevindingen 2-meting OM-strafbeschikking en 1-meting verzet, p. 19–21.

79. Jacobs and van Kampen. “Dutch ‘ZSM Settlements’ in the Face of Procedural Justice: The Sooner the Better?”

80. See the seminal work of T. Tyler “Why People Obey the Law” and his other works. The foundations of the procedural justice theory were developed by J. Thibaut and L. Walker. J. Thibaut and L. Walker, Procedural Justice: A Psychological Analysis (L. Erlbaum Associates, 1975).

81. E. Lind and T. Tyler, The Social Psychology of Procedural Justice (Springer Science & Business Media, 1988), p. 237.

82. See, e.g., T. Tyler. “Enhancing Police Legitimacy” (2004) The Annals of the American Academy of Political and Social Science, 84, p. 94–5; T. Tyler. “Social Justice: Outcome and Procedure” (2000) 35 International Journal of Psychology, 117, p. 121–2.

83. L. van Lent, M.A. Simon Thomas, and P. van Kampen. “De ZSM-werkwijze in praktijk—Op zoek naar balans” (2016) 37 Nederlands Juristenblad, 2753; T. Spronken. “De wasstraat” (2015) 5 Nederlands Juristenblad, 295; D.V.A. Brouwer. “ZSM en de verdediging” (2015) 26 Delikt en Delinkwent, 265.

84. Thomas and others, *Snel, Betekenisvol en Zorgvuldig Een tussenevaluatie van de ZSM-werkwijze*; Renze Salet and Jan Terpstra, *VVC onder de aandacht: Een onderzoek naar ZSM en de gevolgen voor het politiewerk* (Politie en wetenschap, 2017); also reported in: R. Salet and J. Terpstra. “Criminal Justice as a Production Line: ASAP and the Managerialization of Criminal Justice in the Netherlands” (2020) 17 *European Journal of Criminology*, 826.

85. Thomas and others, Snel, Betekenisvol en Zorgvuldig Een tussenevaluatie van de ZSM-werkwijze.

86. Packer argued that the efficiency-oriented “crime control” model of criminal justice encourages uniform and routine procedures to guarantee speed, which operate similarly to a conveyor belt. H. Packer, *The Limits of the Criminal Sanction* (Stanford University Press, 1969), p. 159.

87. Salet and Terpstra, *VVC onder de aandacht: Een onderzoek naar ZSM en de gevolgen voor het politiewerk.*

88. Ibid., p. 839–840.

89. Art. 51h CCP. See, e.g., M. Boone and P. Langbroek. “Problem-Solving Initiatives in Administrative and Criminal Law in the Netherlands” (2019) 14 Utrecht Law Review, 64, p. 75–76.

90. See also Jan Crijns. “Rationaliteiten achter de Wet OM-afdoening” in C. P. M. Cleiren and others (eds), *Op zoek naar samenhang Het Algemeen kader herziening strafvordering nader beschouwd* (Kluwer, 2006), p. 56–58.

91. Memorie van Toelichting, Wet OM-afdoening, Tweede Kamer, vergaderjaar 2004–2005, 29 849, nr. 3, p.1.

92. See the statistics in the end of Section 2.

93. J. de Ridder, *Sepots. Trends en ontwikkelingen* (2018), p. 7.

94. Ibid., p. 24–26.

95. Ibid., 21–24.

96. Ibid.; Bijlsma, *Het voorwaardelijk sepot. Normering, praktijk, evaluatie*, p. 13–14.

97. Thomas and others, *Snel, Betekenisvol en Zorgvuldig Een tussenevaluatie van de ZSM-werkwijze*. The use of conditional case dismissal to achieve resocialization of suspects with multiple (social) issues including mental health problems was criticized; see Bijlsma, *Het voorwaardelijk sepot. Normering, praktijk, evaluatie*, p. 159–162.

98. Thomas and others, *Snel, Betekenisvol en Zorgvuldig Een tussenevaluatie van de ZSM-werkwijze*, Abels and others, *Evaluatie Wet OM-afdoening*, p. 261, 267.

99. See the statistics in Section 2.

100. Vriend, *Avoiding a Full Criminal Trial: Fair Trial Rights, Diversions and Shortcuts in Dutch and International Criminal Proceedings*, p. 255–256.

101. Jacobs and van Kampen. “Dutch ‘ZSM Settlements’ in the Face of Procedural Justice: The Sooner the Better?; Anna Pivaty, *Criminal Defence at Police Stations: A Comparative and Empirical Study* (Routledge, 2019), pp. 30–31.

102. Vriend. *Avoiding a Full Criminal Trial: Fair Trial Rights, Diversions and Shortcuts in Dutch and International Criminal Proceedings.*

103. Sikkema and Kristen, “Strafbeschikking en ZSM: verschuivingen binnen de strafrechtshandhaving.”

104. Lawrence B. Solum, *Procedural Justice* (2004), p. 42 onward.

105. While in inquisitorial settings, procedural safeguards are built *inter alia* around powers of higher-level authorities to review decisions of lower-level authorities. See Mirjan R. Damaška, *The Faces of Justice and State Authority: A Comparative Approach to the Legal Process* (Yale University Press, 1986), p. 181.

106. See in particular Denis Galligan, *Due Process and Fair Procedures: A Study of Administrative Procedures* (Oxford University Press, 1997), p. 241–247 arguing that participation should not be considered the (only) normative basis for administrative justice procedures.

107. On the relationship between legal standards of fair trial and procedural justice, see H. A. M. Grotelaar, *Interacting with Procedural Justice in Courts (diss. Utrecht)* (2018), p. 9–11.

108. See Salet and Terpstra, “Criminal Justice as a Production Line: ASAP and the Managerialization of Criminal Justice in the Netherlands”

109. Published in: Pivaty, *Criminal Defence At Police Stations: A Comparative And Empirical Study.*

110. See J. Leliveld, “ZZM afhandeling van strafzaken” (2012) *Nederlands Juristenblad,* 1952J. Leliveld and P. van Kampen. “Rechtsbijstand in de voorfase van het strafproces” (2014) *Nederlandse Juristenblad,* 2604; Meij. “De andere kant van de ZSM-medaille: Het gebrek aan controle op beleid en beslissingen van het Openbaar Ministerie.”

111. Procureur-Generaal bij de Hoge Raad van Nederlanden, *Beschikt en Gewogen*; Thomas and others, *Snel, Betekenisvol en Zorgvuldig. Een tussenevaluatie van de ZSM-werkwijze*.”

112. See Public Prosecutor’s Office. “Start pilot “ZSM en rechtsbijstand,” available from: www.om.nl/@86989/start-pilot-zsm, last accessed on 10 April 2021.

113. P. van der Meij and L. Hartjes. “Twijfels bij de toekomstigheid van ZSM. Een toets van het ZSM-beleid aan huidige en voorzienbare ontwikkelingen” in N. Achterberg and others (eds.), *Vrouwe Justitia zucht en steunt Hoe houden we de rechtsstaat toekomstbestendig?* (Stichting NJCM-Boekerij, 2015), p. 39.

114. Thomas and others, *Snel, Betekenisvol en Zorgvuldig. Een tussenevaluatie van de ZSM-werkwijze*, p. 104.

115. Ibid.

Chapter 11

The Over-Representation of Aboriginals in Canadian Correctional Facilities

An Issue before Canada

Eric Myles

This chapter will discuss a distinctive feature of contemporary Canadian law and society—the interaction of Canada's Aboriginals with the criminal justice system.[1] Often, Aboriginal offenders serving sentences in federal correctional facilities have committed offenses different from those perpetrated by their non-Aboriginal counterparts.[2] Moreover, as crime rates fall in Canada overall, as in other western States,[3] Aboriginals are strongly over-represented in corrections. If Aboriginals formed approximately five percent of the aggregate Canadian population in 2016–2017, they represented 23.1% of the offender population; and 41.4% of all women in federal correctional facilities in 2019 were Aboriginal.[4]

The preceding observations about Canadian Aboriginals' interaction with the criminal justice system evoke two issues. Of these, the first is what circumstances cause Aboriginals to be over-represented in corrections. This issue prompts several narrower questions. Is the over-representation ascribable primarily to the historical, social and economic circumstances impelling Aboriginals to commit offenses of particular kinds and at high rates? Or does the over-representation result chiefly from the operation of the criminal justice system itself? Furthermore, what underlies the current increase in the extent of the over-representation?[5] The second issue is what remedial measures Canada should adopt to lessen Aboriginal over-representation in corrections—an issue also raising more restricted questions. Which circumstances contributing to the over-representation warrant priority when remedial measures undergo contemplation? How might Canada's constitution circumscribe the measures taken?[6] Are changes in societal attitudes toward Canada's Aboriginal peoples required to reduce the over-representation?

The purpose of this chapter is to analyse afresh the two above-stated issues, hoping that the resulting analysis will stimulate new reflection and research.

ABORIGINAL CRIME AND OVER-REPRESENTATION IN CANADIAN CORRECTIONAL FACILITIES: PRIOR EXAMINATION

Aboriginal over-representation in Canadian correctional facilities is attested since World War II.[7] By the late-mid 1960s, Aboriginal crime rates and representation in corrections animated the Canadian Corrections Association to make submissions to the then Minister of Indian Affairs and Northern Development.[8] Assorted examinations of Aboriginals' interaction with Canada's criminal justice system followed these submissions between the late 1960s and the early 1990s.[9]

In 1996, the Royal Commission on Aboriginal Peoples released the most authoritative examination thus far of the subject. According to the Commission, high levels of crime among Aboriginal peoples and discrimination they suffer within the criminal justice system combine to explain their over-representation in it.[10] The Commission traced high levels of Aboriginal crime to the historical and contemporary legacy of Aboriginals' colonial relationship to Euro-Canadian society: in the Commission's view, the relationship has "systematically undermined the social, cultural and economic foundations of Aboriginal peoples, including their distinctive forms of justice."[11] Moreover, the Commission held that Aboriginals encounter discrimination at multiple points as they navigate the criminal justice system.[12]

Striking were the remedial measures that the Commission proposed to lessen Aboriginal over-representation in the criminal justice system and particularly, correctional facilities. Positing that Canada's Aboriginal peoples possess an inherent right to self-government under section 35 of the *Constitution Act, 1982*,[13] the Commission deduced that they have a right to establish and administer their own justice systems.[14] Additionally, the Commission suggested that Aboriginal courts—governed by Aboriginal understandings of substantive justice and the proper procedures for achieving it and presided over by Aboriginal judges—would offer more productive fora for assessing Aboriginals' conduct.[15] When sentencing offenders, Aboriginal courts could utilise the holistic methods characteristic of Aboriginal justice systems in addressing wrongdoing rather than the retributive approaches to sentencing typical of Euro-Canadian criminal justice.[16] Such methods would presumptively diminish Aboriginal representation in corrections.

To advocate Aboriginal courts was, the Commission acknowledged, to query their interplay with the Canadian constitutional and legal order. The Commission anticipated that the *Charter* would remain Canada's paramount law, with which the legislation and acts of Aboriginal governments—presumably embracing their criminal codes—would necessarily comply.[17] Furthermore, the Commission envisaged appellate bodies organised within individual Aboriginal peoples or through the cooperation of several peoples and urged consideration of a pan–Aboriginal appellate body; final appeal would lie to the Supreme Court of Canada.[18]

No later enquiry into Aboriginal crime and over-representation in Canada's criminal justice system can discount the Commission's analysis and proposed remedies. A quarter-century after the Commission released its findings and recommendations, though, they require reexamination in light of subsequent research and changes to Canadian law.

HYPOTHESIS

A propos the two above-stated issues, one hypothesis of this chapter is that the Commission could justifiably impute high levels of crime by Aboriginals to their colonial relationship to Euro-Canadian society and ascribe their over-representation in the criminal justice system and especially, corrections to systemic discrimination. Nevertheless, legislative changes subsequent to the Commission's analysis can be correlated with Aboriginals' increasing over-representation in Canada's correctional facilities. A second hypothesis is that the Commission's proposals for remedying the over-representation by instituting Aboriginal courts as an incident of Aboriginal self-government have not been adopted wholesale. Rather incremental remedial measures, expanding the role of Aboriginal culture and understandings of justice in processing Aboriginal accused without subjecting the Canadian criminal justice system to massive surgery, have gained traction. This preference, buttressed by the successes of such measures in reducing Aboriginal crime and recidivism, informs the remedial measures advanced presently.

Aboriginal Crime Rates and the Over-Representation in Canadian Correctional Facilities

Five circumstances are treated as potentially or actually related to Aboriginals' high crime rates and their over-representation in Canadian correctional facilities.

Demographics

Demographics is a foundational circumstance contributing to Aboriginal over-representation in Canadian correctional facilities. Statistics confirm that Aboriginals constitute a rapidly mounting share of Canada's population: between the censuses of 2006 and 2016, the Aboriginal population rose by 42.5%—a figure more than four times the corresponding growth rate of the non-Aboriginal population; and in 2016, Aboriginals formed 4.9% of the total population, up from 3.8% in 2006 and 2.8% in 1996.[19] If the speedy growth in the Aboriginal population is concurrent with Aboriginals' increasing over-representation in corrections, however, demographics alone do not explain it.[20]

Colonialism, Marginalization and Canada's Aboriginal Peoples

Colonialism and Its Aftermath

A second circumstance fuelling Aboriginals' crime rates and over-representation in Canada's correctional facilities is their colonial relationship to Euro-Canadian society.[21] This relationship stems from continuity between the mindset of pre-Confederation Canada's European colonial masters—France and the United Kingdom—and the attitudes of Canada's leaders after Confederation in 1867 respecting Aboriginals. If the colonial masters displaced Aboriginals from their traditional lands to prepare same for European settlers and facilitate natural resource extraction,[22] Canada regulated Aboriginals intensively after 1867 through the *Indian Act.*[23] More strikingly again, Canada's leaders, confident that Euro-Canadian culture was intrinsically superior to that of Aboriginals, compelled Aboriginal children to attend residential schools that attempted to expunge their culture.[24]

Marginalization

A corollary to Aboriginals' colonial relationship to Euro-Canadian society is their marginalization from it.[25] Marginalization has assumed four forms exceptionally germane to examining high Aboriginal crime rates and over-representation in corrections.

Aboriginals' Attendance at Indian Residential schools

Aboriginals' attendance at Indian residential schools has played a uniquely baneful part in disposing them to criminal conduct. Whichever school Aboriginal children attended, they suffered verbal abuse disparaging of their aboriginality; they were forbidden to speak their own language; and they routinely underwent corporal punishment.[26] Frequently, they faced graver abuse still, embracing severe physical abuse, sexual abuse, and other wrongful acts with serious consequences.[27] On leaving residential school, a sizeable share of them used alcohol and drugs to gain relief from their school memories; today alcohol and drug abuse characterizes a majority of Aboriginal offenders.[28] Another considerable share subjected their children to the violence and abuse they had sustained at residential school;[29] children who learned to construe this conduct as appropriate became likely candidates to interact with the Canadian criminal justice system,[30] ensuring that the reverberations of residential school attendance would be intergenerational.

The "Sixties Scoop"

From the early 1950s, after Indian residential school enrolment peaked, into the early 1990s, child welfare authorities in multiple parts of Canada arranged placement in foster homes or adoption for respective Aboriginal children.[31] Implicit in the arrangements, labeled the "Sixties Scoop,"[32] was the same goal pursued in residential schools of eradicating the children's Aboriginal identity and culture: white Christian Euro-Canadian families almost invariably provided the foster homes; and adoptive parents usually belonged to the same collective.[33] Aboriginals who underwent the "Sixties Scoop" as children have demonstrated high crime rates.[34]

Socioeconomic Marginalization

Aboriginals' low levels of education, limited employment opportunities and widespread poverty reveal a third form of marginalization that has augmented their crime rates. A significant number of Aboriginal schoolchildren reportedly find their schooling, frequently led by white Euro-Canadian teachers, unappetising;[35] moreover, the disciplinary measures that many Aboriginal schoolchildren undergo dampen their inclination to remain in school.[36] Unsurprisingly, studies show that Aboriginal offenders in correctional facilities usually possess, at most, modest education.[37] Aboriginal youths who fail to complete their schooling have few marketable skills, in another gap that displays significant correlation with Aboriginals' representation in corrections.[38] Besides, the reflections of a young Aboriginal show how Aboriginals can view correctional facilities as an escape from poverty and remain nonchalant on interacting with the Canadian criminal justice system. He related: "[J]ail is better than the over-crowded houses, where there is no running water and there are few jobs and recreational opportunities. I [do not] feel anything any more when I go to court."[39]

The Marginalization of Aboriginal Women

Finally, Aboriginal women evince a distinctive form of marginalization that renders them especially prone to committing crimes. While Aboriginal women are marginalized relative to Euro-Canadian society,[40] their marginalization is heightened in their own communities, where they often experience domestic violence, sexual abuse, and egregious impoverishment.[41] Even perhaps more than Aboriginal men, Aboriginal women who forsake their communities to improve their lot encounter formidable obstacles to extricating themselves from penury—and the incentives to perpetrate crimes it furnishes.[42] Certainly, Aboriginal women are more strongly over-represented than Aboriginal men in Canadian correctional facilities.[43]

Concluding Observations

That Aboriginals' colonial relationship to Euro-Canadian society and their consequent marginalization have nurtured high crime rates is well-documented, supporting the finding of the Royal Commission on Aboriginal Peoples. A driving role for the relationship and its incidents in stimulating Aboriginals' over-representation in corrections is less apparent.[44] An appraisal of its role necessitates comparison with the part of other putatively contributing circumstances in triggering the over-representation.

Racism

Racial animosities between Euro-Canadian society and Aboriginals, while promoting Aboriginal crime rates,[45] form a third circumstance contributing to their over-representation in correctional facilities. A celebrated instance stems from the report of the Nova Scotia Royal Commission on the Donald Marshall Jr. Prosecution: in the Commission's view, Marshall, a Mi'kmaq of the Membertou First Nation, was wrongfully convicted of murder and sentenced to life imprisonment at least partly because he was Aboriginal.[46] Latterly, the Supreme Court of Canada has admitted that racial discrimination remains a hazard of the criminal justice system, emphasizing that sentencing judges offer a bulwark against it.[47]

The Supreme Court of Canada on the Sentencing of Aboriginal Offenders

A fourth circumstance deserving mention in respect of Aboriginals' over-representation in corrections is the Supreme Court of Canada's judgment in *R. v. Gladue*.[48] Key to the judgment was the Supreme Court's interpretation of section 718.2(e) of the *Criminal Code*,[49] added in 1995—amidst Parliament's first major review of sentencing[50]—to counter the over-representation. Section 718.2(e) stipulates:

> 718.2 A court that imposes a sentence shall also take into consideration the following principle:
>
> . . . .
>
> (e) all available sentences other than imprisonment that are reasonable in the circumstances shall be considered for all offenders, with particular attention to the circumstances of Aboriginal offenders.

According to the Supreme Court, section 718.2(e) assigned judges sentencing Aboriginal offenders a positive duty to elicit information on all elements of the offense's context, including the offender, the victims, the community and "the unique circumstances of the offender as an Aboriginal person."[51] In practice, Aboriginal offenders have found ineffective the sentencing approach that the Supreme Court deduced from section 718.2(e).[52] Most importantly, the approach outlined in *Gladue* has not reduced Aboriginal over-representation in correctional facilities.[53]

A partial exception to this conclusion arises from the so-called "Gladue courts" instituted in Toronto and various other Canadian centers to provide culturally appropriate sentences for Aboriginal accused.[54] An Aboriginal who pleads guilty to a charge may be diverted to a community-based sentencing process guided by a plan of care: under the plan, the accused is connected with culturally relevant services, including sweat lodges, counselling for substance abuse, and employment assistance.[55] Aboriginal's sentenced via "Gladue courts" have exhibited a lower rate of recidivism than their Aboriginal counterparts tried and sentenced through the standard courts—and are less likely to enter corrections.[56]

Mandatory Minimum Sentences for Offenses

Finally, a circumstance that almost certainly contributes to Aboriginal over-representation in correctional facilities is the substantial increase in the criminal offenses for which a mandatory minimum sentence fixed by statute follows conviction. If in 1987, when the Supreme Court of Canada first addressed the constitutional propriety of mandatory minimum sentences,[57] nine offenses attracted mandatory minimum sentences, today the matching figure is approximately 100.[58] Whether the mandatory minimum sentences added more recently pass constitutional muster is a matter for ongoing determination.[59] Whether they help to deter crime is equally a subject for debate.[60] Still, of the circumstances contributing to Aboriginal over-representation in correctional facilities, they can probably be correlated most clearly with its current growth.[61]

Remedies for Aboriginal Over-Representation in Correctional Facilities

The Proposed Remedy of the Royal Commission on Aboriginal Peoples

Since the "Gladue courts" and assorted other fora have demonstrated that holistic healing in culturally appropriate settings can lessen Aboriginals' rates of incarcerations and recidivism,[62] the proposal of the Royal Commission on Aboriginal Peoples for Aboriginal courts appears well-suited to combating Aboriginal over-representation in corrections. Yet, formidable obstacles oppose the proposal's implementation.

Probably the foremost obstacle is the government of Canada's apparent reluctance to relinquish control of the criminal justice system. To date, the government has instigated no generalized grant of self-government to Aboriginal groups enabling them to institute their own criminal codes and court systems; rather the government has proceeded piecemeal, enacting agreements with specific Aboriginal groups for self-government.[63] These agreements allow the resulting Aboriginal governments little latitude to modify the processes for handling the accused that the existing criminal justice system specifies. The Nisga'a Final Agreement, signed in April/May 1999 by representatives of the Nisga'a First Nation, the Canadian government and the British Columbia government as Canada's first self-government agreement, is paradigmatic: Article 61 of Chapter 11 denies the forthcoming Nisga'a government any authority in respect of criminal law.[64]

Another significant obstacle to implementing the commission's proposal is the task of integrating the protections that the charter accords the accused with Aboriginal groups' preferences for responding to malfeasance.[65] Take, for example, section 10(b) of the charter: stipulating that everyone has the right on arrest or detention to retain and instruct counsel, it furnishes a platform for the accused to exercise further rights.[66] Yet the sentencing circles widely used by Canadian courts since the early 1990s—even before *Gladue*—when fixing sentences for Aboriginal offenders present a context where the traditional roles of defence counsel may prove unproductive.[67] Attempts by the defense counsel to undermine the credibility of participants in the sentencing circle or zealously to advocate a sentence that other participants oppose probably contravene the goals of healing and harmony that a sentencing circle promotes.[68]

Elimination of Mandatory Minimum Sentences for Offenses

An alternative approach to reducing Aboriginal over-representation in correctional facilities is to limit the range of offenses with a mandatory minimum sentence. In 2017, the Standing Senate Committee on Legal and Constitutional Affairs concluded that the elimination of mandatory minimum sentences would allow various criminal matters to be resolved at an early stage, lowering the volume of cases before the courts and decreasing the delays in managing the remaining cases.[69] Therefore, the Committee recommended a thorough review of the existing mandatory minimum sentences, to be informed by two goals: to ensure that "a reasonable evidence-based approach" determines when mandatory minimums are appropriate; and to establish whether offenders with mental health issues might be candidates for alternative sentencing options or treatment.[70] In 2020, Bill S-207—An act to amend the criminal code (independence of the judiciary)—was submitted to the senate of Canada, where it is presently undergoing second reading.[71] Sections 1 and 2 of the bill anticipate widened scope for judges to exercise discretion when sentencing offenders, notwithstanding statutory mandatory minimum sentences. However, the extent to which either the committee's recommendation or Bill S-207 will bear fruit remains questionable.

Miscellaneous Approaches to Reducing Aboriginal Over-Representation in Correctional Facilities

Although the present chapter cannot canvass exhaustively the possible approaches to countering Aboriginal over-representation in correctional facilities, four miscellaneous approaches deserve particular deliberation. Among these approaches, further education of all participants in the over-representation is fundamental. Education presumably begins within Aboriginal communities themselves. Certainly, Aboriginal men and women alike would benefit from education and training that would enhance their marketable skills, helping them to overcome the poverty closely linked with crime. By contrast, the goal of expurgating the racist attitudes that the Royal Commission on the Donald Marshall Jr. Prosecution and the Supreme Court of Canada have discerned within the criminal justice system would inform the education of police investigators, prosecutors,[72] judges, and corrections officials. Although progress in educating these actors on Aboriginal perspectives has been evident more recently,[73] the task is incomplete.

A second approach is to ensure that Aboriginals accused of a criminal offense have all chances that Canadian law affords to mount a cogent defense. Surely, the foremost goal of this approach is to make certain that Aboriginal accused have competent legal representation. Because very many Aboriginals are impoverished, Aboriginal accused must often seek representation through legal aid. However, its availability can be variable, and it is lacking altogether in assorted small communities.[74] Therefore, the Canadian government, in collaboration with the provincial and territorial governments, might commit funds to improve Aboriginals' access to legal assistance.[75]

A third approach is to expand the possibilities that Canada's criminal justice system offers for holistic healing of Aboriginal offenders instead of incarceration in correctional facilities. The "Gladue courts" are the most familiar fora that stress healing but are accompanied by other courts with the same emphasis.[76] Given the successes of holistic healing methods in handling Aboriginal offenders and preventing recidivism, the Canadian, provincial, and territorial governments might consider expanding the number of such courts.

Finally, a fourth approach is to make certain that Aboriginal offenders sentenced to correctional facilities undergo rehabilitation assisting their reintegration into civil society and rendering them unlikely to reoffend.[77] This approach passes beyond education and training to improve offenders' employment prospects upon release. For assorted Aboriginal inmates, a correctional facility affords them their first opportunity to regain their Aboriginal identity and culture, after attempts at eradication.[78] The role of Aboriginal elders in rendering them cognizant of their identity and culture and lessening the disorientation that can leave them vulnerable to crime is vital and should be reinforced.[79]

ISSUES FOR RESEARCH

Systematic research of the following issues will most likely yield deeper insights into Aboriginal over-representation in Canadian correctional facilities:

- the consequences of the markedly higher growth rate of Aboriginal populations off-reserve than on-reserve, which evoke the ways whereby Aboriginals experience marginalization;[80]
- the extent to which the loss of self-esteem various Aboriginals suffered through abuse in Indian residential schools or elsewhere has enabled them psychologically to commit crimes;[81]
- the experiences of Aboriginals in sentencing fora arising subsequent to *Gladue;*[82]
- the impact of mandatory minimum sentences on racial groups in Canada;[83]
- Aboriginal inmates' reactions to their sojourn in correctional facilities;[84] and
- the particularities of the interactions of Métis and Inuit accused with the criminal justice system.[85]

CONCLUSIONS

Three interrelated conclusions convey the foremost results of this chapter's enquiry. Of these conclusions, the first asserts that the over-representation of Aboriginals in Canadian correctional facilities is a complex phenomenon to which multiple circumstances contribute, with roles variable over time. Apropos the first above-stated hypothesis, subsequent analysis and research have, with respect, confirmed the finding of the Royal Commission on Aboriginal Peoples that the over-representation is presently rooted in Aboriginals' colonial relationship to Euro-Canadian society and the discrimination they encounter in Canada's criminal justice system. However, the colonial relationship antedated any significant over-representation of Aboriginals in Canadian corrections; and the increase in the over-representation apparent during the past quarter-century is most evidently correlated with the conspicuous increase in the offenses eliciting a statutorily prescribed mandatory minimum sentence.

Another conclusion, consistent with the second above-stated hypothesis, is that the wide-ranging remedial measures necessary to counter the over-representation will require a sustained commitment by the federal, provincial and territorial governments, working with Aboriginal leaders and groups, to effect their implementation. These measures include: programs to assist Aboriginals in combatting substance abuse; education of Aboriginals, men and women alike, to improve their employment prospects, as a step in overcoming socioeconomic marginalization; education of all elements of the criminal justice system to counter racist attitudes towards Aboriginals; expanded recourse to holistic healing methods consonant with Aboriginal understandings of justice when Aboriginal accused need to be processed; and measures to extend programs within correctional facilities to make incarceration more truly rehabilitative for Aboriginal inmates. Since Canada, having ratified the *United Nations Declaration on the Rights of Indigenous Peoples* ("UNDRIP"),[86] has incorporated its provisions into domestic law (Footnote 87), these measures will become more pressing still.

A third conclusion is that Canadian societal attitudes toward the Aboriginal population must evolve to underpin abiding governmental commitment to remedying Aboriginals' over-representation in corrections. Earlier questions relating to Aboriginals have been "background noise" amidst ongoing debates over Canada's political, social, and economic issues.[87] As Aboriginals participate increasingly in Canadian life, societal attitudes toward them appear to evolve.[88] Nevertheless, non-Aboriginals' appreciation of Aboriginals' historical and contemporary circumstances will require refinement if the over-representation is to diminish. Whether a deepened appreciation will arise is an issue before Canada.

BIBLIOGRAPHY

Blackstock, C. & N. Trocmé. "Community-Based Child Welfare for Aboriginal Children: Supporting Resilience through Structural Change" (2005) 24 *Soc Pol'y J NZ*, 12.

Canada, *Indian Treaties and Surrenders from 1680–1902*, 3 vols. (Ottawa: Queen's Printer, 1891–1912).

Canadian Broadcasting Corporation, "Canada Officially Adopts UN Declaration on Rights of Indigenous Peoples," online: Canadian Broadcasting Corporation, http://www.cbc.ca/news/indigenous/canada-adopting-implementing-un-rights-declaration-1.3575272.

Canadian Corrections Association, *Indians and the Law: A Survey Prepared for the Honourable Arthur Laing, Department of Indian Affairs and Northern Development* (Ottawa: Canadian Corrections Association, 1967).

Canadian Parliamentary Documents

Cardoso, T. Security Risk: Maximum; Reintegration Potential: Low" *[Toronto] Globe and Mail* (24 October 2020) A11.

Chalifoux, T. "A Need for Change: Cross-cultural Sensitization of Lawyers" (1994) 32 *Alta LRev*, 762.

Chartrand, L. "The Appropriateness of a Lawyer as Advocate in Contemporary Aboriginal Justice Initiatives" (1995) 33 *Alta LRev*, 874.

Clamp, K. *Restorative Justice in Transition* (Abingdon, Oxon.: Routledge, 2014).

Corrado, R. R., & I. M. Cohen. "Needs Profile of Serious and/or Violent Aboriginal Youth in Prison" (2002) 14:3 *Forum Corrections Res*, 20.

Crosby, A., & J. Monaghan. "Settler Governmentality in Canada and the Algonquins of Barriere Lake" (2012) 43:5 *Security Dialogue*, 421.

Crown-Indigenous Relations and Northern Affairs Canada. "Indian Residential Schools," online: Crown-Indigenous Relations and Northern Affairs Canada, https://www.rcaanc-cirnac.gc.ca/eng 1100100015576/1571581687074#sect4.

Crown-Indigenous Relations and Northern Affairs Canada. "Self-government," online: Crown-Indigenous Relations and Northern Affairs Canada, https://www.rcaanc-cirnac.gc.ca/eng/1100100032275/1529354547314.

Crown-Indigenous Relations and Northern Development Canada. "The Government of Canada's Approach to Implementation of the Inherent Right and the Negotiation of Aboriginal Self-government," online: Crown-Indigenous Relations and Northern Affairs Canada, https://www.rcaanc-cirnac.gc.ca/eng/1100100031843/1539869205136.

Department of Justice Canada. "Mandatory Sentences of Imprisonment in Common Law Jurisdictions: Some Representative Models," online: Department of Justice Canada, https://www.justice.gc.ca/eng/rp-pr/csj-sjc/ccs-ajc/rr05_10/toc-tdm.html.

DeWall, C. N., ed. *The Oxford Handbook of Social Exclusion* (New York: Oxford University Press, 2013).

Friedland, H. "Different Stories: Aboriginal People, Order, and the Failure of the Criminal Justice System" (2009) 72 *Sask LRev*, 105.

Gauthier, M. "The Impact of the Residential School, Child Welfare System and Intergenerational Trauma upon the Incarceration of Aboriginals" (MEd thesis, Queen's University, 2010).

General Assembly Resolution 61/95, *United Nations Declaration on the Rights of Indigenous Peoples*, A/Res/61/95 (13 September 2007).

Gevikoglu, J. "Ipeelee/Ladue and the Conundrum of Indigenous Identity in Sentencing" (2013) 63 *SC LRev*, 205.

Gover, K., "Equality and non-discrimination in the UNDRIP: Articles 2, 6, and 7(1)," in J. Hohmann & M. Weller, eds., *The UN Declaration on the Rights of Indigenous Peoples: A Commentary* (Oxford: Oxford University Press, 2018) 179.

Green, Justice M., "The Challenge of Gladue Courts" (2012) 89 CR (6th) 362.

Hamilton, A. C. & C. M. Sinclair. *Report of the Aboriginal Justice Inquiry of Manitoba*, 2 vols (Winnipeg: Queen's Printer, 1991), Vol. 1, *The Justice System and Aboriginal People*.

House of Commons Standing Committee on Public Safety and National Security. *Indigenous People in the Federal Correctional System* (Ottawa: House of Commons, 2018).

House of Commons Standing Committee on the Status of Women. *A Call to Action: Reconciliation with Indigenous Women in the Federal Justice and Correctional Systems* (Ottawa: House of Commons Canada, 2018).

Indigenous and Northern Affairs Canada "First Nations People in Canada," online: Indigenous and Northern Affairs Canada, https://www.aadnc-aandc.gc.ca/eng/1303134042666/1303134337388.

Jackson, M. *Locking up Natives in Canada: Report of the Canadian Bar Association Committee on Imprisonment and Release* (Vancouver: Canadian Bar Association, 1988), repr. (1989) 23 *UBC LRev*, 220.

La Prairie, C. *Examining Aboriginal Corrections in Canada* (Ottawa: Aboriginal Corrections, Ministry of the Solicitor General, 1996).

LaForme, Justice H. S. "The Justice System in Canada: Does It Work for Aboriginal People?" (2004) 4 *Indig LJ*, 1.

Law Society of British Columbia. "Law Society Adopts Indigenous Intercultural Competency Training," online: Law Society of British Columbia, https://www.lawsociety.bc.ca/about-us/news-and-publications/news/2019/law-society-adopts-indigenous-intercultural-compet /.

Leslie, J. & R. Maguire, eds. *The Historical Development of the Indian Act*, 2nd ed. (Ottawa: Indian and Northern Affairs Canada, 1978).

Manikis, M. "The Recognition of Prosecutorial Obligations in an Era of Mandatory Minimum Sentences of Imprisonment and Over-representation of Aboriginal People in Prisons" (2015) 71 *SC LRev*, 277.

McKenzie, H. A. et al. "Disrupting the Continuities among Residential Schools, the Sixties Scoop, and Child Welfare: An Analysis of Colonial and Neocolonial Discourses" (2016) 7:2 *Intl Indig Pol'y*, J 1.

McMillan, L. J. *Truth and Conviction: Donald Marshall Jr. and the Mi'kmaw Quest for Justice* (Vancouver: University of British Columbia Press, 2018).

Milloy, J. *A National Crime: The Canadian Government and the Residential School System* (Winnipeg: University of Manitoba Press, 1999).

Milward, D. L. "Raven Grows New Feathers: Realizing Contemporary Indigenous Visions of Justice in Canada through the Culturally Sensitive Interpretations of Legal Rights" (Ph.D. dissertation, University of British Columbia, 2009).

Monchalin, L. *The Colonial Problem: An Indigenous Perspective on Crime and Injustice in Canada* (Toronto: University of Toronto Press, 2016).

Monture-Angus, P. A. "Women and Risk: Aboriginal Women, Colonialism, and Correctional Practice" (1999) 19:1/2 *Can Womens Stud*, 24.

Mulgrew, I., "Canada's Growing Indigenous Prison Population 'A National Travesty'" *Vancouver Sun* (30 January 2020), online: *Vancouver Sun*, https://vancouversun .com/opinion/ columnists/ian-mulgrew-canadas-growing-indigenous-prison-population-a-national-trave sty/.

NationTalk, "New Survey Reveals How Mainstream Society Views Aboriginal Peoples in Canada," online: https://nationtalk.ca/story/new-survey-reveals-how -mainstream-socuety-views-aboriginal-peoples-in-Canada.

Native People and Justice: Report on the National Conference and the Federal/ Provincial Conference on Native People and the Criminal Justice System (Ottawa: Solicitor General of Canada, 1975).

Nisga'a Lisims Government, "Nisga'a Final Agreement," online: http://www.nnkn.ca /files/u28/nis-eng.pdf.

Office of the Correctional Investigator, "2017–2018 Annual Report," online: www.oci -bec.gc.ca/cnt/rpt/pdf/annrpt/annrpt20172018-eng.pdf.

Office of the Correctional Investigator, "2018–2019 Annual Report," online: https:// www.oci-bec.gc.ca/cnt/rpt/pdf/annrpt/annrpt20182019-eng.pdf.

Parliament of Canada, "Bill C-15," online: Parliament of Canada, https://parl.ca/ DocumentViewer/en/43-2/bill/C-15/first-reading.

Parliament of Canada, "Bill S-207," online: Parliament of Canada, https://parl.ca/ DocumentViewer/en/43-2/bill/S-207/first-reading.

Perreault, S. "The Incarceration of Aboriginal People in Adult Correctional Services" (2009) 29:3 *Juristat* 5.

Rehavi, M. M. & S. B. Starr. "Mandatory Sentencing and Racial Disparity: Assessing the Role of Prosecutors and the Effects of *Booker*" (2013) 123:1 *Yale LJ*, 39.

Research and Statistics Division, Department of Justice Canada, *Spotlight on Gladue: Challenges, Experiences, and Possibilities in Canada's Justice System* (Ottawa: Research and Statistics Division: Department of Justice Canada, 2017).

Richardson, C., & B. Nelson. "A Change of Residence: Government Schools and Foster Homes as Sites of Forced Aboriginal Assimilation: A Paper Designed to Provoke Thought and Systemic Change" (2007) 3:2 *First Peoples Child & Fam Rev*, 75.

Roach, K., "One Step Forward, Two Steps Back: *Gladue* at Ten and in the Courts of Appeal" (2009) 64 *Crim LQ*, 470.

Ross, R., *Returning to the Teachings: Exploring Aboriginal Justice* (Toronto: Penguin Books Canada, 1996).

Royal Canadian Mounted Police, *Departmental Results Report 2017–18* (Ottawa: Minister of Public Safety and Emergency Preparedness, 2018).

Royal Commission on Aboriginal Peoples, *Bridging the Cultural Divide: A Report on Aboriginal People and Criminal Justice in Canada* (Ottawa: The Commission, 1996).

Royal Commission on Aboriginal Peoples, *Report of the Royal Commission on Aboriginal Peoples,* 5 vols. (Ottawa: The Commission, 1996).

Royal Commission on the Donald Marshall Jr. Prosecution, *Commissioners' Report: Findings and Recommendations* (Halifax: The Commission, 1989).

Rudin, J., "Aboriginal Over-representation and *R. v. Gladue*: Where We Were, Where We Are and Where We Might Be Going" (2008) 40 *SC LRev* (2d), 687.

Rudin, J., "Looking Backward, Looking Forward: The Supreme Court of Canada's Decision in *R. v. Ipeelee*" (2012) 57 *SC LRev*, 375.

Ryan, N. *et al.*, "Prison Life and Prior Social Experiences: Understanding Their Importance for Indigenous Peoples' Re-entry Outcomes" (2019) 59:1 *Br J Crim*, 188.

Rymhs, D., *From the Iron House: Imprisonment in First Nations Writing* (Waterloo: Wilfrid Laurier University Press, 2008).

Senate of Canada, https://sencanada.ca/en/content/sen/chamber/432/journals/040jr_2021-05-25-e.

Standing Senate Committee on Legal and Constitutional Affairs, *Delaying Justice Is Denying Justice: An Urgent Need to Address Lengthy Court Delays in Canada (Final Report)*(Ottawa: Senate of Canada, 2017).

Statistics Canada, "Aboriginal Peoples in Canada: Key Results from the 2016 Census," online: Statistics Canada, https://www150.statcan.gc.ca/n1/daily-quotidien/171025/dq171025a-eng.htm?indid=14430-1&indgeo=0.

Stirrett, N., "Re-visiting the Sixties Scoop: Relationality, Kinship and Honouring Indigenous Stories" (MA thesis: Queen's University, 2015).

Stonefish, B., *Moving Beyond: Understanding the Impacts of the Residential School* (Owen Sound: Ningwakwe Learning Press, 2007).

Stuart, Justice B., "Circle Sentencing in Canada: A Partnership of the Community and the Criminal Justice System" (1996) 20:2 *Intl J Comp App Crim Justice*, 291.

Sugar, F. & Fox, L., *Survey of Federally Sentenced Aboriginal Women in the Community* (Ottawa: Native Women's Association of Canada, 1990).

Supreme Court of Canada, "Applications for Leave," online: Supreme Court of Canada, https://decisions.scc-csc.ca/scc-csc/scc-|-csc-a/en/item/18646/index.do?q=Sharma.

Task Force on Aboriginal Peoples in Federal Corrections, *Final Report* (Ottawa: Solicitor General of Canada, 1988).

Tonry, M., "Why Crime Rates Are Falling throughout the Western World" (2014) 43:1 *Crime Justice*, 1.

Truth and Reconciliation Commission of Canada, *Canada's Residential Schools: The Final Report of the Truth and Reconciliation Commission of Canada*, 6 vols (Montreal: McGill-Queen's University Press, 2015).

Waldram, J., "The Aboriginal Peoples of Canada: Colonialism and Mental Health," in I. Al-Issa & M. Tousignant, eds, *Ethnicity, Immigration and Psychopathology* (New York: Plenum Press, 1997), 169.

Wesley, M., *Marginalized: The Aboriginal Women's Experience in Federal Corrections* (Ottawa: Public Safety Canada, 2012).

Wesley-Esquimaux, C., & Smolewski, M., *Historic Trauma and Aboriginal Healing* (Ottawa: Aboriginal Healing Foundation, 2004).

Whonnock, K., "Aboriginal Courts in Canada," online: The Scow Institute, http://scow-archive.libraries.coop/library/documents/Aboriginal_Courts_Fact_Sheet.pdf.

Yang, C. S., "Free at Last? Judicial Discretion and Racial Disparities in Federal Sentencing" (2015) 44:1 *J Legal Stud*, 75.

NOTES

1.In Canada, the term "Aboriginals" comprehends the First Nations, formerly styled "Indians," alongside the Inuit of the Arctic and the Métis. Indigenous and Northern Affairs Canada, "First Nations People in Canada," online: Indigenous and Northern Affairs Canada https://www.aadnc-aandc.gc.ca/eng/1303134042666/1303134337388.

2. The five leading offenses for Aboriginal offenders are: assault causing injury; robbery; second-degree murder; manslaughter; and sexual assault. By contrast, the five foremost offenses for non-Aboriginal offenders are: robbery; assault causing injury; trafficking; second-degree murder; and firearms offenses. C. La Prairie, *Examining Aboriginal Corrections in Canada* (Ottawa: Aboriginal Corrections, Ministry of the Solicitor General, 1996), at 39–40.

3. M. Tonry, "Why Crime Rates Are Falling throughout the Western World" (2014) 43:1 *Crime Justice*, 1.

4. Office of the Correctional Investigator, "2018–2019 Annual Report," online: Office of the Correctional Investigator, https://www.oci-bec.gc.ca/cnt/rpt/pdf/annrpt/annrpt20182019-eng.pdf at 64. Together subsections 91(28) and 92(6) of the *Constitution Act, 1867* (UK), 30 & 31 Vict., c. 3, as am. ("the *Constitution Act, 1867*"), assign both the Canadian and the provincial governments a part in maintaining correctional facilities: federal facilities house offenders sentenced to at least two years, while the offenders accommodated in provincial facilities have received sentences under two years. Aboriginal over-representation in provincial facilities, variable across Canada, is strongest on the Prairies: in 2017–2018, Aboriginal adults reportedly formed 75% and 74% of admissions to custody in Manitoba and Saskatchewan respectively. I. Mulgrew, "Canada's growing indigenous prison population 'a national travesty'" *Vancouver Sun* (30

January 2020), online: *Vancouver Sun*, https://vancouversun.com/opinion/ columnists/ ian-mulgrew-canadas-growing-indigenous-prison-population-a-national-travesty/.

5. Between March 2009 and March 2018, the number of Aboriginal offenders incarcerated in Canada's federal correctional facilities grew by 42.8%; whereas the overall population of the facilities rose by less than 1% during the same period. Office of the Correctional Investigator, "2017–2018 Annual Report," online www.oci-bec.gc .ca/cnt/rpt/pdf/annrpt/annrpt20172018-eng.pdf.

6. Remedial measures must respect the allocation of powers between the Canadian and the provincial governments that the *Constitution Act, 1867* prescribes and reckon with the provisions of the *Canadian Charter of Rights and Freedoms* ("the *Charter*"), Part 1 of the *Constitution Act, 1982*, being Schedule B to the *Canada Act 1982* (UK), 1982, c. 11 ("the *Constitution Act, 1982*") on how offenders are to be processed.

7. Before 1945, Aboriginals were not over-represented in Canadian corrections. J. Rudin, "Aboriginal over-representation and *R. v. Gladue*: where we were, where we are and where we might be going" (2008) *40 SC LRev* (2d) 687, at 687.

8. Canadian Corrections Association, *Indians and the Law: A Survey Prepared for the Honourable Arthur Laing, Department of Indian Affairs and Northern Development* (Ottawa: Canadian Corrections Association, 1967).

9. *Native People and Justice: Report on the National Conference and the Federal/ Provincial Conference on Native People and the Criminal Justice System* (Ottawa: Solicitor General of Canada, 1975); M. Jackson, *Locking up Natives in Canada: Report of the Canadian Bar Association Committee on Imprisonment and Release* (Vancouver: Canadian Bar Association, 1988), repr. (1989) 23 UBC LRev 220; A. C. Hamilton & C. M. Sinclair, *Report of the Aboriginal Justice Inquiry of Manitoba*, 2 vols (Winnipeg: Queen's Printer, 1991), vol. 1, *The Justice System and Aboriginal People*.

10. Royal Commission on Aboriginal Peoples, *Bridging the Cultural Divide: A Report on Aboriginal People and Criminal Justice in Canada* (Ottawa: The Commission, 1996), at 309.

11.Ibid.

12. Bail provisions offer an important example: the Commission established that systemic discrimination triggered higher rates of pretrial detention for Aboriginal than for non-Aboriginal accused. *Ibid.*, at 239.

13. Subsection 35(1) stipulates: "The existing aboriginal and treaty rights of the aboriginal peoples of Canada are hereby recognmarginalization and affirmed." Since 1995, the Government of Canada has accepted that Aboriginals have an inherent right to self-government under section 35, exercisable within the Canadian State's structures. The Government's approach is expounded in Crown-Indigenous Relations and Northern Development Canada, "The Government of Canada's approach to implementation of the inherent right and the negotiation of Aboriginal self-government," online: Crown-Indigenous Relations and Northern Affairs Canada, https://www.rcaanc-cirnac.gc.ca/eng/1100100031843/1539869205136. Nevertheless, the Supreme Court of Canada has been chary of inferring an Aboriginal right to self-government from section 35.

14. Royal Commission on Aboriginal Peoples, *supra* note 10, at 310.

15. Ibid.

16. *Ibid.* at 3–5, 19, 78, 137. Aboriginal justice systems reveal affinities with restorative justice, to which its aficionados assign the following attributes: abuses qualify as acts against individuals rather than offenses against the State; those most immediately affected have an opportunity to participate actively; the emphasis is on repairing harm; and a balanced approach to the needs and responsibilities of all stakeholders prevails. K. Clamp, *Restorative Justice in Transition* (Abingdon, Oxon.: Routledge, 2014) at 4. While the Supreme Court of Canada has encouraged judges to espouse restorative approaches when sentencing Aboriginal offenders *(R. v. Ipeelee*, [2012] 1 SCR 433 ("*Ipeelee*") at para 59), Gevikoglu has cautioned against conflating Aboriginal justice systems too readily with ideas of restorative justice. J. Gevikoglu, "Ipeelee/Ladue and the conundrum of indigenous identity in sentencing" (2013) 63 *SC LRev* 205, at 221–222.

17. Royal Commission on Aboriginal Peoples, *supra* note 10, at 311. Nonetheless, the Commission remarked that section 25 of the *Charter*, which provides that guarantee of rights and freedoms made elsewhere in the Charter "shall not be construed so as to abrogate or derogate from any aboriginal, treaty or other rights or freedoms that pertain to the aboriginal peoples of Canada," would affect the *Charter*'s impact on Aboriginal justice systems. At the same time, the Commission proposed that Aboriginal charters of rights enacted by Aboriginal peoples would help to ensure that Canada's *Charter* was interpreted flexibly. *Ibid.*

18. *Ibid.*, at 313.

19.Statistics Canada, "Aboriginal Peoples in Canada: Key Results from the 2016 Census," online: Statistics Canada, https://www150.statcan.gc.ca/n1/daily-quotidien/171025/dq171025a-eng.htm?indid=14430-1&indgeo=0. Statistics Canada imputes the increase in the Aboriginal population recorded in 2016 to natural growth, including high fertility rates, and the choice of multiple census respondents for the first time to identify as Aboriginals. *Ibid.*

20. S. Perreault, "The Incarceration of Aboriginal People in Adult Correctional Services" (2009) 29:3 *Juristat* 5 at 12. The Ontario Court of Justice accepted this conclusion in *R. v. T.M.B.*, [2011] OJ No. 4836, 2011 *ONCJ*, at para 119.

21. Royal Commission on Aboriginal Peoples, *supra* note 10, at 47–49; A. Crosby & J. Monaghan, "Settler Governmentality in Canada and the Algonquins of Barriere Lake" (2012) 43:5 *Security Dialogue* 421; H. Friedland, "Different Stories: Aboriginal People, Order, and the Failure of the Criminal Justice System" (2009) 72 *Sask LRev* 105, at 120–126; L. Monchalin, *The Colonial Problem: An Indigenous Perspective on Crime and Injustice in Canada* (Toronto: University of Toronto Press, 2016).

22. The land surrenders Aboriginals made to the Crown through the early twentieth century are found in Canada, *Indian Treaties and Surrenders from 1680–1902*, 3 vols. (Ottawa: Queen's Printer, 1891–1912).

23. RSC 1985, c. I-5, as amended ("the *Indian Act*"). When first passed in 1876, the *Indian Act* was a consolidation of pre-1867 statutes relating to Aboriginals. J. Leslie & R. Maguire, eds, *The Historical Development of the Indian Act*, 2nd ed. (Ottawa: Indian and Northern Affairs Canada, 1978), at 52–70.

24. The foremost exploration of Canada's Indian residential schools is the Truth and Reconciliation Commission of Canada, *Canada's Residential Schools: The Final Report of the Truth and Reconciliation Commission of Canada*, 6 vols. (Montreal: McGill-Queen's University Press, 2015).

25. On social marginalization, see C. N. DeWall, ed., *The Oxford Handbook of Social Exclusion* (New York: Oxford University Press, 2013).

26. Truth and Reconciliation Commission of Canada, *supra* note 24, Pt 1, at 175, 186, 188, 191–192, 194, Pt. 2, at 538–539.

27. The Independent Assessment Process, part of the Settlement Agreement concluded in May 2006 to resolve the class action—Canada's largest to date—gathering Aboriginals' claims for abuse in Indian residential schools, unequivocally acknowledged these kinds of abuse. The Independent Assessment Process is accessible through Crown–Indigenous Relations and Northern Affairs Canada, "Indian Residential Schools," online: Crown–Indigenous Relations and Northern Affairs Canada, https://www.rcaanc-cirnac.gc.ca/eng 1100100015576/1571581687074#sect4.

28. J. Milloy, *A National Crime: The Canadian Government and the Residential School System* (Winnipeg: University of Manitoba Press, 1999); J. Waldram, "The Aboriginal Peoples of Canada: Colonialism and Mental Health," in I. Al-Issa & M. Tousignant, eds, *Ethnicity, Immigration and Psychopathology* (New York: Plenum Press, 1997), 169.

29. B. Stonefish, *Moving Beyond: Understanding the Impacts of the Residential School* (Owen Sound: Ningwakwe Learning Press, 2007), at 16.

30. Justice H.S. LaForme, "The Justice System in Canada: Does It Work for Aboriginal People?" (2004) 4 *Indig LJ* 1, at 17; C. Wesley-Esquimaux & M. Smolewski, *Historic Trauma and Aboriginal Healing* (Ottawa: Aboriginal Healing Foundation, 2004), at 2–3.

31. The circumstances animating these arrangements are treated in C. Blackstock & N. Trocmé, "Community-Based Child Welfare for Aboriginal Children: Supporting Resilience through Structural Change" (2005) 24 *Soc Pol'y J NZ* 12, at 15–16.

32. On the "Sixties Scoop," see H. A. McKenzie *et al.*, "Disrupting the Continuities among Residential Schools, the Sixties Scoop, and Child Welfare: An Analysis of Colonial and Neocolonial Discourses" (2016) 7:2 *Intl Indig Pol'y J* 1; N. Stirrett, "Re-visiting the Sixties Scoop: Relationality, Kinship and Honouring Indigenous Stories" (MA thesis: Queen's University, 2015).

33. C. Richardson & B. Nelson, "A Change of Residence: Government Schools and Foster Homes as Sites of Forced Aboriginal Assimilation—A Paper Designed to Provoke Thought and Systemic Change" (2007) 3:2 *First Peoples Child & Fam Rev* 75, at 77, 79–80. The Ontario Superior Court of Justice, rendering judgment in *Brown v. Canada (Attorney General)* (2017), 136 OR (3d) 497 at 501, portrayed vividly the effects of loss of Aboriginal identity, including psychiatric disorders, suicide, and so forth. The judgment was the first where a Canadian superior court held that Canada had a common law duty of care to safeguard Aboriginal children's identity and failed to discharge it.

34. On visiting Prince Albert, Saskatchewan, the Royal Commission on Aboriginal Peoples learned that 95 percent of the Aboriginal inmates of the local correctional

facility had been in foster care or group homes. Royal Commission on Aboriginal Peoples, *Report of the Royal Commission on Aboriginal Peoples,* 5 vols (Ottawa: The Commission, 1996), III, at 17–18.

35. R. R. Corrado & I. M. Cohen, "Needs Profile of Serious and/or Violent Aboriginal Youth in Prison" (2002) 14:3 *Forum Corrections Res* 20 at 21.

36. A probe of serious and violent Aboriginal offenders in British Columbia showed that of 100 Aboriginal youths, 96% of the males and 85% of the females had undergone school discipline for misconduct serious enough to warrant suspension or expulsion. *Ibid.*

37. Thus, a study of 84 Aboriginal and 793 non-Aboriginal inmates of federal correctional facilities who became eligible for release in 1983–1984 showed that under 20 percent of the Aboriginal offenders had received a grade 10 education or less, whereas more than 30 percent of non-Aboriginal offenders had achieved that level of education. Task Force on Aboriginal Peoples in Federal Corrections, *Final Report* (Ottawa: Solicitor General of Canada, 1988), at 26.

38. The aforementioned study of 84 Aboriginal and 793 non-Aboriginal inmates of federal correctional facilities revealed that only 22.5 percent of the Aboriginal inmates had vocational training and that approximately two-thirds had no previous skilled employment. *Ibid.*

39. Quoted in M. Gauthier, "The Impact of the Residential School, Child Welfare System and Intergenerational Trauma upon the Incarceration of Aboriginals" (MEd thesis, Queen's University, 2010), at 7.

40.The report of the Royal Commission on Aboriginal Peoples, *supra* note 10, embodies the marginalization of Aboriginal women: it remains silent on the issue how Aboriginal women might benefit additionally from their time in corrections. P. A. Monture-Angus, "Women and Risk: Aboriginal Women, Colonialism, and Correctional Practice" (1999) 19:1/2 *Can Womens Stud* 24, at 24.

41. M. Wesley, *Marginalmarginalization: The Aboriginal Women's Experience in Federal Corrections* (Ottawa: Public Safety Canada, 2012) at 4. Sometimes the domestic violence, sexual abuse, and extreme impoverishment Aboriginal women frequently suffer in their communities lead them to commit crimes precisely to enter a correctional facility, which they perceive as a safer environment. Cp. House of Commons Standing Committee on the Status of Women, *A Call to Action: Reconciliation with Indigenous Women in the Federal Justice and Correctional Systems* (Ottawa: House of Commons Canada, 2018), at 44.

42. Aboriginal women leaving their communities for cities are not seldom hampered, among others, by minimal education, few marketable skills and sentiments of dislocation and isolation, compounded by whatever racial discrimination they experience. Wesley, *supra* note 41, at 5.

43. Office of the Correctional Investigator, *supra* note 4, at 64.

44. Significantly, the relationship antedated any noteworthy over-representation of Aboriginals in corrections. Thus in 1950, the Supreme Court of Canada spoke of "the accepted view" of Aboriginals as "in effect, wards of the State." *St. Ann's Island Shooting and Fishing Club v. The King*, [1950] SCR 211, at 219.

45. An Aboriginal woman undergoing incarceration described as follows the effects of racism on Aboriginal women: "Racism lies at the root of our life experiences. The effect is violence, violence against us, and in turn our own violence." F. Sugar & L. Fox, *Survey of Federally Sentenced Aboriginal Women in the Community* (Ottawa: Native Women's Association of Canada, 1990), at 18.

46. Royal Commission on the Donald Marshall Jr. Prosecution, *Commissioners' Report: Findings and Recommendations* (Halifax: The Commission, 1989) at 17. Particularly the Commission found that racist attitudes shaped the police investigation of the murder with which Marshall was charged and prejudiced the representation he received from defense counsel at trial. *Ibid.* at 41, 77. Marshall's wrongful conviction is explored in L. J. McMillan, *Truth and Conviction: Donald Marshall Jr. and the Mi'kmaw Quest for Justice* (Vancouver: University of British Columbia Press, 2018), especially chapters 1–4.

47. *Ipeelee*, *supra* note 16, at paras 66–67; *R. v. Ewert*, [2018] 2 SCR 165 at para 57. A contemporary study suggests that racist attitudes still influence the risk assessments made by corrections officers in establishing how readily inmates of correctional facilities can be reintegrated into civil society and by extension, whether they are fit candidates for parole: Aboriginal men are 30% more likely than their white counterparts to obtain the lowest possible reintegration potential score. T. Cardoso, Security risk: maximum; reintegration potential: low" *Toronto Globe and Mail* (24 October 2020), A11.

48. [1999] 1 SCR 688 ("*Gladue*"). While *Gladue* is the Supreme Court's foremost judgment of the past quarter-century on the sentencing of Aboriginal offenders, *Ipeelee* passes beyond reiterating strongly the principles it articulated: in *Ipeelee*, the Court clarified that Aboriginal over-representation in corrections is the responsibility of all elements of the criminal justice system. J. Rudin, "Looking Backward, Looking Forward: The Supreme Court of Canada's Decision in *R. v. Ipeelee*" (2012) 57 *SC LRev* 375, at 381.

49. RSC 1985, c. C-46, as am.

50. *An Act to Amend the Criminal Code (sentencing) and Other Acts in Consequence Thereof*, SC 1995, c. 22.

51. *Gladue*, *supra* note 48, at para 81. Consistent with the sentencing approach enjoined in *Gladue*, section 23 of *An Act to Amend the Corrections and Conditional Release Act and Another Act*, SC 2019, c. 27, obliges the Correctional Service of Canada to apply the following considerations when taking decisions under the *Corrections and Conditional Release Act*, SC 1992, c. 20, as am., that affect Aboriginal offenders: systemic and background factors involving Canada's Aboriginal peoples; systemic and background factors contributing to Aboriginal over-representation in the criminal justice system; and the offender's Aboriginal culture and identity. These considerations may not be considered in evaluating the risk an Aboriginal offender poses, unless they diminish the risk level.

52. Research and Statistics Division, Department of Justice Canada, *Spotlight on Gladue: Challenges, Experiences, and Possibilities in Canada's Justice System* (Ottawa: Research and Statistics Division: Department of Justice Canada, 2017), at 20.

53. K. Roach, "One Step Forward, Two Steps Back: *Gladue* at Ten and in the Courts of Appeal" (2009) 64 *Crim LQ* 470, at 471.

54. "Gladue Courts" are not trial courts. Research and Statistics Division, Department of Justice Canada, *supra* note 52, at 41.

55. *Ibid.* Section 81 of the *Corrections and Conditional Release Act*, SC 1992, allows the Minister of Public Safety and Emergency Preparedness to enter agreements with Aboriginal governing bodies or organizations to provide correctional services for Aboriginal offenders; section 84 of the same Act contemplates the release of Aboriginal offenders into Aboriginal communities.

56. Research and Statistics Division, Department of Justice Canada, *supra* note 52, at 42. On "Gladue courts," see alternatively Justice M. Green, "The Challenge of Gladue Courts" (2012) 89 CR (6th) 362.

57. In *R.* v. *Smith*, [1987] 1 SCR 1045, the Supreme Court ruled unconstitutional the minimum seven-year prison sentence for importing or exporting narcotics, specified by subsection 5(2) of the *Narcotic Control Act*, RSC 1970, c. N-1: the minimum sentence infringed the protection against "cruel and unusual treatment or punishment" that section 12 of the *Charter* afforded; and the infringement was not saved by section 1.

58. M. Manikis, "The Recognition of prosecutorial obligations in an era of mandatory minimum sentences of imprisonment and over-representation of Aboriginal people in prisons" (2015) 71 *SC LRev* 277 at 277. The offenses eliciting a mandatory minimum prison sentence are classified in Department of Justice Canada, "Mandatory sentences of imprisonment in common law jurisdictions: some representative models," online: Department of Justice Canada, https://www.justice.gc.ca/eng/rp-pr/csj-sjc/ccs-ajc/rr05_10/toc-tdm.html.

59. A majority of the Supreme Court of Canada held in *R. v. Nur*, [2015] 1 SCR 774 that the mandatory minimum sentences that subparagraphs 95(2)(a)(i) and(ii) of the *Criminal Code* stipulated for the possession of loaded prohibited firearms violated section 12 of the *Charter* and were not saved by section 1. The Ontario Court of Appeal's judgment in *R. v. Sharma*, 2020 ONCA 478, reveals other grounds for invalidating mandatory minimum sentences. Ms. Sharma, an Ojibway of the Saugeen First Nation, challenged the constitutional propriety of sections 742.1(c) and 741.1(e)(ii) of the *Criminal Code*, inserted by the *Safe Streets and Communities Act*, SC 2012, c. 1. Under these sections, conditional sentences servable in the community under strict conditions were unavailable to offenders convicted of certain categories of offenses; instead, such offenders were liable to incarceration. The Court of Appeal held that the sections denied the benefits of a conditional sentence in a manner "reinforcing, perpetuating or exacerbating" the historical disadvantages of Aboriginal offenders and therefore infringed the equality guarantees of section 15 of the *Charter*. Moreover, the Court ruled that the incarceration Ms. Sharma suffered pursuant to the sections infringed the requirements of fundamental justice, contrary to section 7. Since section 1 saved neither infringement, the sections were constitutionally improper. The Supreme Court of Canada granted leave to appeal on 14 January 2021. Supreme Court of Canada, "Applications for Leave," online: Supreme Court

of Canada, https://decisions.scc-csc.ca/scc-csc/scc-|-csc-a/en/item/18646/index.do?q =Sharma, last accessed December 2021.

60. A widespread public perception that excessively lenient sentences failed to deter would-be offenders furnished impetus for mandatory minimum sentences. Nevertheless, Lamoureux J. expressed unusually forthrightly in *R. v. Vandyke*, 2013 ABPC 347 the doubts accompanying mandatory minimums, writing at para 24: "Mandatory minimum penalties do not advance proper sentencing principles set forth in s. 718 of the *Criminal Code*, they do not advance any realistic goal of deterrence, they do not target dangerous offenders but rather catch in their net a very broad spectrum of citizens. Mandatory minimum penalties have an egregious impact on the groups who are already over represented in the Canadian penal system."

61. Mandatory minimum sentences for the greatest share of the offenses listed in Department of Justice Canada, *supra* note 58, are dated the mid-1990s, and mandatory minimum sentences were added to other offenses after 2000. This chronology buttresses the statistical correlation between mandatory minimum sentences and the increase in Aboriginal over-representation in corrections.

62. The Hollow Water Healing Circle Program has proved successful in resolving pervasive sexual abuse in a Manitoba Aboriginal community: of 48 identified offenders in Hollow Water, only five were incarcerated, mainly because they joined inadequately in the healing program; and only two of the remaining 43 repeated their offenses. R. Ross, *Returning to the Teachings: Exploring Aboriginal Justice* (Toronto: Penguin Books Canada, 1996), at 36.

63. Twenty-five self-government agreements are currently attested, engaging 43 Aboriginal communities across Canada. Crown-Indigenous Relations and Northern Affairs Canada, "Self-government," online: Crown-Indigenous Relations and Northern Affairs Canada, https://www.rcaanc-cirnac.gc.ca/eng/1100100032275 /1529354547314.

64. The text of the Nisga'a Final Agreement is accessible through Nisga'a Lisims Government, "Nisga'a Final Agreement," online: Nisga'a Lisims Government, http: //www.nnkn.ca/files/u28/nis-eng.pdf.

65. The barriers to integration are expounded in D. L. Milward, "Raven Grows New Feathers: Realizing Contemporary Indigenous Visions of Justice in Canada through the Culturally Sensitive Interpretations of Legal Rights" (Ph.D. dissertation, University of British Columbia, 2009), *passim*.

66. *R. v. Sinclair*, [2010] 2 SCR 310, at para 26.

67. Sentencing circles were pioneered by Mr. Justice Barry Stuart in *R. v. Moses* (1992), 11 CR (4th) 357 (YT TerrCt). He assembled a cross-section of community representatives, including Crown and defense counsel, police, a probations officer, and members of the defendant's Aboriginal group, striving to ensure that all pertinent perspectives on sentencing were canvassed and that the sentence he established was broadly acceptable. Sentencing circles are probed at greater length in Justice B. Stuart, "Circle Sentencing in Canada: A Partnership of the Community and the Criminal Justice System" (1996) 20:2 *Intl J Comp App Crim Justice*, 291.

68. T. Chalifoux, "A Need for Change: Cross-Cultural Sensitization of Lawyers" (1994) 32 *Alta LRev* 762, at 776–779; L. Chartrand, "The Appropriateness of a

Lawyer as Advocate in Contemporary Aboriginal Justice Initiatives" (1995) 33 *Alta LRev* 874, at 875–880.

69. Standing Senate Committee on Legal and Constitutional Affairs, *Delaying Justice Is Denying Justice: An Urgent Need to Address Lengthy Court Delays in Canada (Final Report)* (Ottawa: Senate of Canada, 2017), at 55.

70. *Ibid.* at 56. The second goal is exceptionally topical for Aboriginal offenders: Correctional Services Canada, probing a sampling of female inmates in corrections, verified that almost all of the Aboriginal women had a diagnosis of mental health disorders over their lifetime. Office of the Correctional Investigator, *supra* note 4, at 106.

71. The text of Bill S-207 is accessible through Parliament of Canada, "Bill S-207," online: Parliament of Canada, https://parl.ca/DocumentViewer/en/43-2/bill/S-207/first-reading.

72. The education of prosecutors is especially important insofar as they play a key role in shaping the over-representation of Aboriginals in corrections: they have discretion over whether an alleged instance of criminal conduct by an Aboriginal is charged before the trial court as an offense attracting a mandatory minimum sentence or otherwise; and their exercise of discretion is challengeable only for abuse. A majority of the Supreme Court of Canada characterized this bar in *Nur*, *supra* note 59, at para 94 as "extremely high."

73. In 2018, the Royal Canadian Mounted Police reported that it had provided all employees with training in reconciliation and Aboriginal perceptions (Royal Canadian Mounted Police, *Departmental Results Report 2017–18* (Ottawa: Minister of Public Safety and Emergency Preparedness, 2018),at 3. In 2019, the Law Society of British Columbia determined that from 2021 onward, all practicing counsel in that province will be required to take a course on Aboriginal intercultural competence (Law Society of British Columbia, "Law Society adopts Indigenous intercultural competency training," online: Law Society of British Columbia, https://www.lawsociety.bc.ca/about-us/news-and-publications/news/2019/law-society-adopts-indigenous-intercultural-compet/). Since 9.5 percent of Correctional Services Canada Staff is currently Aboriginal, though, the need for education is partially reduced. House of Commons Standing Committee on Public Safety and National Security, *Indigenous People in the Federal Correctional System* (Ottawa: House of Commons, 2018), at 21.

74. House of Commons Standing Committee on the Status of Women, *supra* note 41, at 58–59.

75. Cp. *ibid.*, at 59.

76. On the courts established in British Columbia, Alberta and Saskatchewan that emphasize holistic healing of Aboriginal offenders, see K. Whonnock, "Aboriginal Courts in Canada," online: The Scow Institute, http://scow-archive.libraries.coop/library/documents/Aboriginal_Courts_Fact_Sheet.pdf.

77. By comparison, Aboriginal Australians have a significantly higher risk of reincarceration than their non-Aboriginal counterparts. N. Ryan *et al.*, "Prison Life and Prior Social Experiences: Understanding Their Importance for Indigenous Peoples' Re-entry Outcomes" (2019) 59:1 *Br J Crim*, 188.

78. House of Commons Standing Committee on the Status of Women, *supra* note 41, at 100.

79. The role of Aboriginal elders in assisting Aboriginal inmates is expounded in Office of the Correctional Investigator, *supra* note 4, at 73–75.

80. The 2016 census showed that of 744,866 First Nations people with registered or treaty Indian status, 44.2% lived on-reserve, while the remaining 55.8% lived off-reserve. Since the 2006 census, the on-reserve and off-reserve First Nations populations had grown by 12.8% and 49.1%, respectively. Statistics Canada, *supra* note 19.

81. Cp. Gauthier, *supra* note 39, at 46–47.

82. Research and Statistics Division, Department of Justice Canada, *supra* note 52, at 48.

83. American research has demonstrated that mandatory minimum sentences affect racial minorities in the United States more strongly than the population at large: M. M. Rehavi & S. B. Starr, "Mandatory Sentencing and Racial Disparity: Assessing the Role of Prosecutors and the Effects of *Booker*" (2013) 123:1 *Yale LJ*, 39; C. S. Yang, "Free at Last? Judicial Discretion and Racial Disparities in Federal Sentencing" (2015) 44:1 *J Legal Stud*, 75. The corresponding Canadian research is less developed.

84. Noteworthy, though, is D. Rymhs, *From the Iron House: Imprisonment in First Nations Writing* (Waterloo: Wilfrid Laurier University Press, 2008).

85. Cp. House of Commons Standing Committee on the Status of Women, *supra* note 41, at 28.

86. General Assembly Resolution 61/95, *United Nations Declaration on the Rights of Indigenous Peoples*, A/Res/61/95 (13 September 2007). Canada abandoned its objections to the UNDRIP only on 9–10 May 2016 (Canadian Broadcasting Corporation, "Canada officially adopts UN declaration on rights of indigenous peoples," online: Canadian Broadcasting Corporation, http://www.cbc.ca/news/indigenous/canada-adopting-implementing-un-rights-declaration-1.3575272. Since racist attitudes within the Canadian criminal justice system contribute to Aboriginal over-representation in corrections, Article 2 of the UNDRIP, asserting that Indigenous peoples and individuals "have the right to be free from any kind of discrimination" in exercising their rights, is topical. On Article 2, see K. Gover, "Equality and Non-discrimination in the UNDRIP: Articles 2, 6, and 7(1)," in J. Hohmann & M. Weller, eds, *The UN Declaration on the Rights of Indigenous Peoples: A Commentary* (Oxford: Oxford University Press, 2018), 179.

87. *United Nations Declaration on the Rights of Indigenous Peoples Act*, SC 2021, c. 14

88. According to a national survey reported on 8 June 2016, an increasing majority of non-Aboriginal Canadians recognize the long-standing marginalization of Aboriginals and their contemporary challenges. Particularly an increasing majority of non-Aboriginals acknowledge that Aboriginal peoples encounter daily discrimination at least comparable to if not more severe than that suffered by other marginalized communities; and many believe that they experience discrimination in the educational and criminal justice systems. Nation Talk, "New Survey Reveals How Mainstream Society Views Aboriginal Peoples in Canada," online: Nation Talk, https://nationaltalk.ca/story/new-survey-reveals-how-mainstream-society-views-aboriginal-peoples-in-Canada, last accessed December 2021.

Chapter 12

Contemporary Issues in the Penitentiary System of the Republic of Macedonia

Fundamentals of Criminal Justice Reform and Penitentiary Reform

Gordana Lažetić and Elena Mujoska-Trpevska

The criminal code (hereinafter: CC) was adopted on 29 July 1996, and 38 modifications and amendments were made since then. 99% of the criminal code's initial version was modified. Such frequent changes seriously complicated the CC's application in practice and the inconsistency in criminal punishment.

Table 12.1: Criminal Code Statistics

Criminal Code	
First Publication	29.07.1996
Number of Modifications and Amendments	38
Last Consolidation	31.12.2018
Total Articles	540
Modified Articles	376
Total Modifications	903
Added Articles	114
Deleted Articles	48
Modification of Articles	99%
Additional Provisions	54
References to Articles	409

Source: Assembly of the Republic of Northern Macedonia

The frequent modifications to the CC[1] that transform its innovation into continuous reform are followed by reforms in other areas of the criminal law (procedural law, execution of sanctions), the new system of justice for children and misdemeanor law. From the laws directly related to the criminal law, the Law on Criminal Procedure (hereinafter: LCP) of 2010[2], the adoption of the new Law on Execution of Sanctions of 2019[3] and the new Law on Misdemeanors of 2019[4], and especially the adoption of the Law on Justice for Children in 2013[5] are of particular importance.

The new model of criminal procedure, inspired by the Anglo-American concept of fair trial, leaving the judicial paternalism, procedural instruments well known in the accusatory procedure (sentence bargaining), was introduced with the adoption of the new LCP in 2010. However, the changes were not well-accepted by the practitioners, especially public prosecutors, so the implementation and interpretation have caused numerous inconsistencies and weaknesses as well as uneven judicial practice. Thus, the pending process for improving the legislative text and overcome the inconsistencies is quite significant.

The new Law on Justice for Children, which came into force as of 1 December 2013, regulates children exposed at risk and children in conflict with the law for committed criminal offenses. The new legislative model indicated the need to promote its legal frame and its application mechanisms to further comply with the international principles and standards.[6]

The complementary part of the criminal justice reform is the misdemeanor reform. The Law on Misdemeanors of 17 May 2019 follows the modern tendencies in the sphere of misdemeanors and the apparent problems from the past are resolved with the new law.

PENITENTIARY LEGISLATIVE FRAMEWORK AND STRATEGIC DOCUMENTS

The new law on the execution of sanctions (hereinafter: LES) was enacted in the Republic of North Macedonia on 29 May 2019, implementing and adjusting the Mandela rules regarding the prisoners' treatment and strengthening their rights (health care, education, vocational training, etc.).

Why was the adoption of new LES necessary? Because the system for the execution of sanctions is a complex and sensitive matter that regulates an adult and juvenile offender's rights. There was a need for upgrade, improvement, and compliance with the international standards and best practices for effective execution of sanctions. In the past few years, great efforts were made in the area covering the penitentiary system to improve the overall situation with the execution of sanctions. That implies improving the conditions for serving a prison sentence and reviving the alternative measures into practice. During this process, all international standards regulating this area were considered as guidelines, including the European Committee's recommendations for the Prevention of Torture and Inhumane or Degrading Treatment or Punishment (CPT).[7] In fact, the new law was adopted as a response to the established weaknesses and inconsistencies in the prison system's functioning.

The new law is based on rules that apply impartially with a strict ban on discrimination based on race, skin color, origin, nationality or ethnicity, sex, gender, sexual orientation, gender identity, belonging to marginalized group, language, citizenship, social origin, education, religion or confession, political orientation, other belief, disability, age, family or marital status, property status, health status, personal characteristic or social status, or any other basis toward the sanctioned person (Article 4 paragraph 1 and 2 of LES). In a multiethnic society such as Macedonia, the upgrade of the rights of prisoners was necessary by promoting and respecting religious feelings, personal belief, and moral norms of the sanctioned persons (Article 4 paragraph 3 of the LES).

On the other hand, the resocialization of prisoners is the penal and correctional institutions' primary function. The new penitentiary law's main feature is the protection of the convicted person's psychophysical and moral integrity and the respect of his/her personality and dignity. All of the aforementioned is in line with the European Prison Rules and the United Nations Standard Minimum Rules for the Treatment of Prisoners (the Mandela Rules),[8] including essential rules accepted as good principles and practices in prisoners' treatment by the prison management. The same context is the commitment specified in the European Parliament Resolution of 5 October 2017 on Prison Systems and Conditions.[9]

The question about the arrangement of the prison system is quite complicated. Therefore, there is a continuous need for development and improvement. The Macedonian penitentiary system took a step closer to the modern and contemporary prison systems with the National Strategy for Penitentiary System Development (2015–2019).[10] This crucial strategic document's primary mission was to ensure an efficient and professional approach in the organization and supervision of the functioning of the penal and correctional institutions and establishing the probation system in the country. The strategy encompasses prisoners serving a prison sentence, persons in detention, and juveniles imposed with the corrective measure to "transfer to a correctional-educational facility."

The drafting of the new National Strategy for Penitentiary System Development (2021–2025) started after the previous strategy expiry.[11] The new strategy will continue to promote and upgrade the penitentiary system in line with the latest standards, by establishing a modern penitentiary system for acting with persons deprived of liberty in a safe environment, dignity and respect, proper education and professional training, support of their personal development, constructive use of their free time, and support for their reintegration in the society after serving their term of imprisonment.

The main strategic goals of the contemporary penitentiary policy in RNM are as follows:

- Improvement of material conditions in penal institutions;
- Strengthening of leadership capacities and penitentiary system supervision;
- Strengthening the professional relations of the prison institutions via structural and advanced training;
- Ensuring a safe environment for the prisoners and the staff in prison and correctional institutions;
- Strengthening the re-socialization and reintegration process of prisoners, including care after prison;
- Improvement of the treatment and care for persons imposed with the measure—referral in a correctional institution;
- Improvement of corporate integrity, strengthening the mechanisms for handling cases of improper action and corruption;
- Strengthening the provisioning of health care of prisoners, including the mental health of those persons;
- Strengthening the educational structures for training based on individual needs;
- Addressing radicalization leading to forced extremism in prisons;
- Probation; and
- Introduction of efficient internal and external structures for communication aimed at resocialization support.

THE ORGANIZATIONAL STRUCTURE OF PENAL AND CORRECTIONAL INSTITUTIONS

In RNM, there is a network of 11 penal institutions (five penitentiary institutions and six prisons) and one correctional-educational facility (hereinafter: CEF). The penitentiaries are located in different parts of the country, such as Idrizovo Penitentiary in Skopje with an open unit in Veles, Shtip Penitentiary with an open unit in Kriva Palanka, Kumanovo Penitentiary, and Prilep Penitentiary (institutions of closed type), and Struga Penitentiary (open type). There are six semi-open type institutions (prisons) on a national level: Bitola Prison, Gevgelija Prison, Skopje Prison, Strumica Prison, and Tetovo Prison, as well as Ohrid Prison, which functions as a special institution for juvenile imprisonment. The detention units are within the prisons where accused men and women await their trials.

The institutions' internal organization, departments and units are organized in each of them handling issues from re-socialization, security, and the executive, administrative and financial area. Also, a special reception unit functions in every institution for observing the newly arrived prisoners, where they stay for 30 days. An expert team performs a social-medical and psychological-pedagogic examination of the convicted's personality by applying scientific methods. As of that moment, the convicted is introduced with the institution's prison rules for prisoners serving a sentence in a penal institution (hereinafter: prison rules),[12] the rights and responsibilities during the serving of the penalty, and the manner of their realization (Article 152 LES).

One of the main problems the prison system faced was introducing a mechanism for efficient management where the directors of prisons and correctional institutions correctly report their activities to the director of the directorate for execution of sanctions (hereinafter: DES). The new LES strengthened the director of the DES's position via established clear penitentiary system hierarchy. LES also strengthened the supervisory function of the DES on the functioning of the penal and correctional institutions. The DES's supervision includes supervision of the conditions and the status of prisoners and persons in detention and children in correctional institutions and preventing torture and inhumane or degrading treatment in the penal and correctional institutions.

Accommodation Capacity and Overcrowding of Prisons

The prison system's total capacity is 2,256, which should be enough for a small country like ours.[13] But inadequate prison conditions and overcrowding are still challenging questions that we need to overcome. In the past, the frequent imposition of imprisonment, followed by overcrowded prison facilities, has led to exceptional demands such as the adoption of amnesty laws. In 2018, after adopting the Law on Amnesty,[14] the number of sentenced persons in certain prisons had significantly decreased. The trend of reduced prison capacity continued in 2019 and 2020. In general, the prison system's overall picture began to improve intensively with the change of the government in 2017 and the transformation of authorities in the DES.

These activities are followed by the adoption of a new law on probation[15] and the establishment of special probation service in the country following the example of several European countries, which gives good results in reducing the prison population, improving the re-socialization of convicts, and reducing recidivism.

Although we managed the overcrowding problem, we still face serious accusations in terms of accommodation, nutrition, general and personal hygiene, insufficient and inadequate healthcare, poor sanitation, and frequent conflicts between the prisoners. In its annual reports, the ombudsman is reporting and elaborating the grounds of appeals regarding cases of noncompliance with the domestic and international standards for the accommodation of persons deprived of liberty[16].

Health Care in Penal and Correctional Institutions

The problems of health care of prisoners and offenders in detention and the lack of medical staff the prison system were solved by applying and complying with the recommendations of European prison rules. The rules indicate that prisons' health policy should be an integral part of the national health policy. The right to health care is guaranteed to prisoners and the right to necessary medical assistance and treatment according to the regulations of health care and health insurance (Article 182). With the new LES for the first time, the prisoners have the right to secondary and tertiary health care levels. The costs for their health care in penal institutions are borne by the state.

Education of Prisoners

The educational process of prisoners is a serious problem that persists for many years. This significant segment may improve the resocialization and social adaptation process of prisoners after serving their term of imprisonment. According to the current legal regulation, the primary education of prisoners must be organized in all penal and correctional institutions as part of the general education system in the state. Even though the law and the Strategy for Penitentiary System (2015–2019) specify that the Ministry of Education and Science shall be the responsible authority for organizing and funding the primary education of prisoners upon a proposal of the DES, this is not the case. There is an inability of the penitentiary system to realize the educational process since the Ministry of Education and Science does not provide the necessary staff and funds. In practice, the penitentiary system is facing a situation where the educational process is supported only by several international organizations in the country. On the other hand, when it comes to professional education (vocational trainings), even though formally conducted in every penitentiary, there is no wide range of professions that can be offered to the convicted adults and juveniles. There is also a lack of formal verification for the prisoners about their acquired profession and skills by relevant institutions that can be used after leaving the facility for their effective inclusion in the labor market.

By the end of December 2020, only one institution, Shtip Penitentiary, provided basic education for 60 prisoners.[17] Idrizovo Penitentiary has the largest number of prisoners, totaling 1,024, but there is no current education program.

Work Treatment for Prisoners

There are two options for performing work while serving a sentence. The employment of prisoners is organized and done within the institution as a rule; however, prisoners with treatment in an open unit can work outside the institution. The majority of prisoners who perform working activities are classified within the open and semi-open treatment. In contrast, prisoners in closed units are rarely engaged in any working activities, which may negatively affect their resocialization process. In general, penal and correctional institutions do offer a wide range of professions for which the prisoners could be engaged to perform, but rarely have the conditions to implement it. Since January 2020, there is a new rulebook for establishing unified criteria for proper compensation and payment method for the prisoners that are engaged in working activities.[18] The rulebook determines that prisoners engaged in working activities are paid in advance for the work performed on monthly basis. The amount is based on the complexity and responsibility of the performed job.

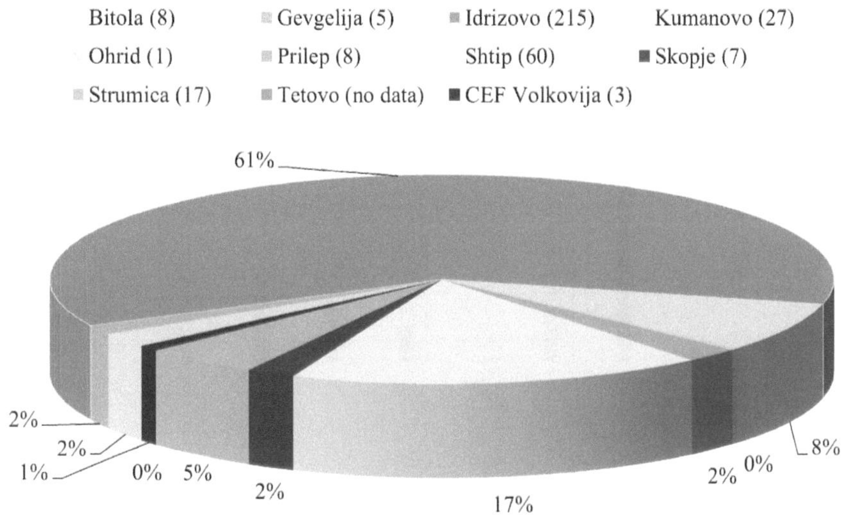

Figure 12.1. Education in prisons. Note: The Idrizovo total prisoners' number of 1,024 is not displayed on this chart, for better visualization.

Source: Data was compiled from a questionnaire that was prepared for and filled by an official in the directorate for the execution of sanctions (DES) in December 2020.

From the gathered data from the penal institution,[19] the experts and specialists put the main emphasis on work as a treatment measure because it is proven to be the most useful for all prisoners. Whether the convicted person will be engaged in or out of the institution additionally depends on knowledge, interests, abilities, and consent for engagement. Consent for engagement outside the institution is given by DES. According to the Article 164 and 165 of LES and Article 27 of the prison rules, prisoners can perform activities in the fields of fruit growing, poultry raising, farming, agriculture, construction work (repairs and maintenance), woodworking, mechanical work, horticulture, hygiene maintenance, laundry work, courier activity, baking, emergency services,, etc. The type of work mostly depends on the geographical location of the prisons.

In the previous period, the work outside of prisons was limited by the order for action in all prisons in the country due to COVID-19 prevention. On 18 November 2020, the director of the DES issued this order to limit the convicts' contacts with the outside world including work engagement outside the institution. The duration of the measures imposed with this order was 30 days (18 November 2020 to 18 December 2020). However, there is still limitation for engagements outside the prisons.

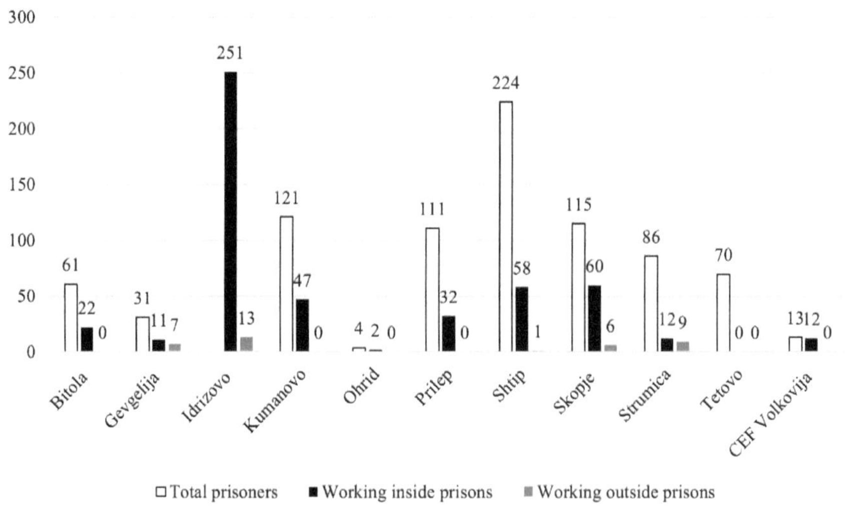

Figure 12.2. Work in prisons, Note: The Idrizovo total prisoners' number of 1,024 is not displayed on this chart, for better visualization.

Source: Data was compiled from a questionnaire that was prepared for and filled by an official in the directorate for the execution of sanctions (DES) in December 2020.

Juvenile Prison

Ohrid Prison is a special institution for juveniles sentenced to prison. According to the Articles 40–41 of the instructions, special attention shall be paid to education and vocational training, health prevention and health education, creating work habits, developing a sense of responsibility toward oneself, other personalities and social requirements, organizing free time in the form of sports and creative activities, contacts with family or legal guardians, positive social contacts with the outside world, and preparation for the post-penal period. Special care during treatment activities with children shall be paid to children that have suffered physical, sexual, or psychological violence. The treatment of children is determined by the specific needs and developmental characteristics of the person in childhood and youth and enables socialization of the child and elimination of repression.

The reality is quite different. Until the end of 2020, four children were sentenced to prison for children. Unfortunately, the committed criminal offenses included violence, as they are serving a prison sentence for murder and robbery. Although the juveniles do not have mental illnesses, they are provided with permanent health care and mental support as well as conversations with a psychiatrist once a week or more. Education remains to be the biggest issue. Some programs were provided by international organizations in the past. However, some classes given by the teachers from the local schools proved to be incomplete and insubstantial. If an underaged inmate is without education and is still illiterate after leaving the facility, it will undoubtedly make his post-penal social adaptation and future life more difficult. The children are allowed to work in the prison's cafeteria, laundry, and kitchen, which are in poor condition. They can also spend their time in recreation and sports as far as the inadequate and poor conditionsallow.

Correctional-Educational Facility

Until November 2020, the juvenile prisoners were located in the same prison with the juvenile offenders who serve correctional-educational measures. Now, the new CEF in Volkovija, Tetovo[20] offers much better conditions for implementing the correctional-educational process for juvenile offenders than the previous facility in Ohrid Prison. Today, there are possibilities for respecting and promoting children's rights while they are involved in different social and sports activities.[21] Currently, there are 13 juvenile offenders of which six have committed violent criminal offenses. Although there are no drug-addicted juveniles, two have mental disorders. One has a court order for a referral to a psychiatric clinic. One is undergoing therapy for mental disorders under medical supervision. In the CEF, the work engagement is in the primary working treatment for creating work habits. So, two children are learning to be caterers, three are learning mechanical skills, four are becoming plumbers, and three are involved in economics. Unfortunately, three are illiterate and do not have basic education.

Statistical Overview

According to the State Statistical Office data,[22] the total number of reported offenders for all offenses in the period 2008–2014 marks a relatively stable trend with an average number of 9,500 prisoners per year. The number increased significantly in 2014 and 2015 to a total record number of 21,995 prisoners. Compared to 2014 and 2015, there was a drastic decrease in 2016 of the reported crime, which results in lower numbers of prisoners. Afterward, the trend remains relatively constant—with an insignificant decrease in the years that follow.

As mentioned above, the authors asked the DES to provide them with the updated information on the situation in the penal and educational institutions. The data refers to adult men and women, children, drug-addicted prisoners, violent prisoners, and prisoners with mental illness, but also to their education, social activities, work, and postpenal treatment.[23]

Since May 2020, new instructions determine the types and methods of treatment of prisoners[24] (hereinafter: instructions). According to these instructions, there are specific programs based on the identified needs in the individual treatment program, in addition to the general treatment measures for prisoners. Specific treatment measures can be implemented for certain categories of convicts, as follows:

- treatment of prisoners who abuse drugs and other psychotropic substances
- treatment of prisoners who abuse alcohol
- treatment of convicted perpetrators of sexual offenses
- treatment of violent convicts in prison
- treatment of prisoners for crimes with elements of violence
- treatment of younger adult convicts
- treatment of children
- treatment of convicted women
- treatment of convicts with long sentences and life imprisonment
- treatment of radicalized convicts
- treatment of convicts with high and very high security risk
- medical psychological treatment of prisoners (for a certain period of time or for the entire period of the execution of the sentence) (Article 30)

Table 12.2. Prisoners total, 2007–2019.

Prisoners According to the Different Groups													
	2007	2008	2009	2010	2011	2012	2013	2014	2015	2016	2017	2018	2019
Total	9636	9503	9801	9169	9810	9042	9539	11683	10312	8172	6273	5857	4712

Source: MAKstat Database, State Statistical Office

As of December 2020, 1,847 prisoners were serving their sentences. Additionally, 23 prisoners had certain termination of the sentence and 267 prisoners have been in detention. Idrizovo Penitentiary has the only woman's department for female prisoners. Currently, 55 women are serving their sentences. There is no underaged female serving time in prison.

Violent Prisoners

Article 31 of the Instructions stipulates that the treatment of violent convicts in prison is determined by the specific needs and characteristics of prisoners with violent behavior and allows acceptance of responsibility for violent behavior in prison. There are three possibilities depending on whether the prisoners are under open, semi-open, or closed-type treatment. The prisoners are learning social and self-control skills that would reduce the potential risk of further violent behavior in prison.

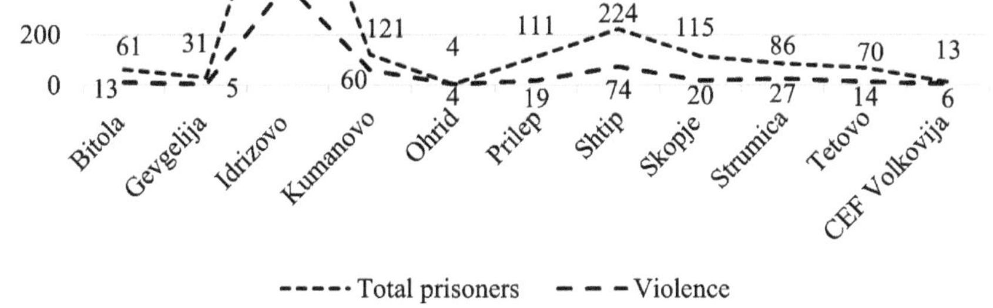

Figure 12.3. Violent crimes and behavior.
Source: MAKstat Database, State Statistical Office

Drug-Addicted Prisoners

The high rate of drug addiction among the prison population has grown rapidly in recent years and is of particular concern. This problem is faced by many prison systems and undoubtedly contributes toward increasing the reoffending rate. The treatment of convicts who abuse drugs and other psychotropic substances is determined by their specific needs and characteristics and enables the establishment of a stable psychophysical condition and reduction of risky behavior. Additionally, the treatment of convicts who abuse alcohol is determined by the specific needs and characteristics of convicts who abuse alcohol and allows for the establishment of a stable psychophysical condition and reduction of risky behavior.

Prisoners with Mental Illness

If the prisoner becomes mentally ill or shows severe mental disorder while serving a sentence, he must be transferred to an appropriate health facility for treatment and care. A psychiatrist determines that condition. The prisoner may request a special medical examination at his/her own expense if the doctor of the institution does not specify such an examination. The institution's director decides on the request of the convicted person after obtaining an opinion from the doctor in the institution (Article 186–187 LES). This practice is widespread and applied by all institutions. For example, in Shtip

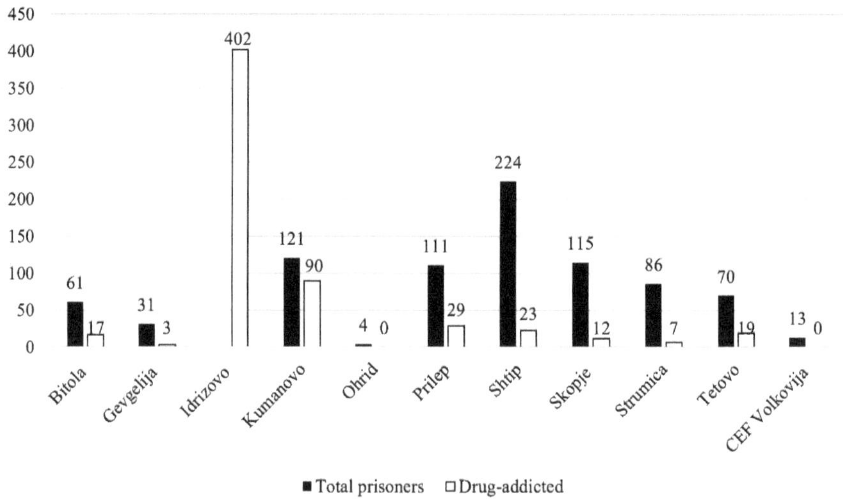

Figure 12.4. Drug-addicted prisoners, Note: The Idrizovo total prisoners' number of 1,024 is not displayed on this chart, for better visualization.

Source: Data was compiled from a questionnaire that was prepared for and filled by an official in the directorate for the execution of sanctions (DES) in December 2020.

Penitentiary, 53 inmates have mental health problems and need pill therapy prescribed by a psychiatrist. If the mental condition worsens, they are taken to hospital for treatment at the Negorci Mental Hospital, where there are currently two prisoners. Similarly, in Bitola Prison there are two registered prisoners with mental health problems and are currently under treatment from PHI Clinical Hospital Bitola. The five prisoners in Prison Tetovo and 12 prisoners in Prison Skopje, are treated within the prisons.

In the other penal institutions, there are no registered prisoners with mental illness but the practice remains the same. Hence, in Prison Prilep, the prisoners who have mental problems are taken to the PHI Hospital Prilep in the neuropsychiatric ward and the prisoners in Strumica are taken to the neurological department at Strumica Hospital or PI Negorski banji Gevgelija.

Resocialization and Free Activities

The process of resocialization of prisoners is an essential function of every penal and correctional facility. Within the institutions, there are organizational units for resocialization activities. Any prison in accordance with the limits linked with the conditions, space and prison staff are organizing different activities. Due to COVID-19 restrictions, every activity is conducted within prisons. For example, Skopje Prison applies so-called occupational treatment by organizing sports tournaments in football, chess, oksan, ping-pong, basketball, etc.; visiting the prison library; and organizing a small music concert within the institution. These games and tournaments are practiced in other institutions as well. Once the restrictions are over, the prisoners can visit theater performances and cinema and sports competitions in the city (as reported by Bitola Prison, Tetovo Prison, and Shtip Penitentiary).

ECtHR Judgments against RNM Regarding Article 3 of ECHR

Article 3 of the European Convention on Human Rights (ECHR) belongs to the ECHR group of nonderogable articles. It does not allow exemptions and derogations even in an emergency or situations when there is a health threat.[25] The significance of Article 3 of the ECHR arises from the fact that it guarantees one of the fundamental values of democratic societies, the prohibition of acts involving torture, inhumane and degrading treatment, proceedings, and punishments—even in the most complex circumstances, such as the fight against terrorism and organized crime.[26]

While the traditional protection of human rights is primarily provided by the so-called "negative" obligations, which imply that states refrain from violating human rights, the interpretation of the effects of individual articles of the ECHR necessarily have created "positive" obligations according to which states are obliged to take active steps. Namely, the positive obligations have a "growing importance" in the jurisdiction of the ECtHR.[27]

In this context, Articles 1 and 3 of the ECHR impose numerous positive obligations toward the states aimed at preventing and compensation for torture and other forms of inhuman and degrading treatment.[28] The investigation into serious allegations of ill treatment must be thorough, which means that the authorities must always make a serious attempt to establish the facts, hold accountable those at fault, and provide appropriate redress to the victim.[29] A positive procedural obligation of the state under Article 3 of the ECHR implies conducting of an effective investigation regarding all alegations and the investigation shall be assessed as effective if the following conditions are to be met: the persons responsible for the investigation and those conducting the investigative actions have to be independent of those involved in the events as alleged perpetrators (this condition is not met if there is a hierarchical position, affiliation to the same police or military unit, if the investigation was conducted by prison authorities who did not include an external person or external body, etc.); the investigation shall be urgent, fast, and thorough and shall lead to the identification and punishment of persons involved into the inhuman or degrading treatment; there shall be established effective external, public oversight of the investigation. The authorities should not rely on hasty or ill-founded conclusions to close their investigation or as the basis of their decisions and shall be aware of the ECtHR attitude that any deficiency in the investigation that undermines its ability to establish the cause of injuries or the identity of the persons responsible will risk falling foul of the standard within the scope of the Article 3.[30]

Starting from January 1, 1998, when the RNM has recognized the jurisdiction of the EctHR, there are 12 judgments against the RNM regarding violations of different aspects of the Article 3. The judgments were rendered in the period 2007–2020. In half of the judgments, there were violations of the procedural aspect of Article 3. In five judgments, there was a violation of both material and procedural aspects, and in one case there was a violation of both Articles 2 and 3 of the ECHR, cumulatively in material and procedural aspects. In most of the judgments, the applicants stated that they had been victims of inhumane treatment by the police, but that the domestic authorities did not conduct an effective investigation.[31] In several cases, the ECtHR found that the police reacted beyond their competences and have exceeded the use of physical means.[32]

There is one case regarding the violation of Article 3 in Macedonian prison, where the ECtHR holds that there has been a violation of Article 3 of the ECHR on account of the failure of the authorities to conduct an effective investigation into the applicant's allegations.[33] Namely, the applicant was sentenced to six months' imprisonment for causing serious injury to a third person and on the prison farm, he was attacked by a bull, which was not castrated, as a result of which he sustained numerous bodily injuries. Before the incident, the applicant warned the prison guard several times that the bull had become aggressive, but there was no reaction from the prison administration. The ECtHR found that prior to the incident the authorities generally knew that the bull was a risk to the applicant's physical integrity and that the state had not complied with its obligation to take measures to protect the inmate and to prevent possible incidents. After the incident, he was transferred by prison vehicle to the hospital, where he underwent surgery. The state covered the medical expenses. On the same day, when the applicant was released from the hospital, the prison governor ordered him to be released early from prison due to a good behavior. The applicant reiterated his arguments that the prison authorities had been alerted before the incident to the aggressiveness of the bull and that despite that fact they had failed, contrary to section 12 of the Execution of Sanctions Act, to take any measure to protect his physical integrity.

The court reiterates that when an individual makes an arguable claim that he has suffered treatment infringing Article 3 at the hands of agents of the state, it is the duty of the national authorities to carry out "an effective official investigation" capable of establishing the facts and identifying and punishing those responsible.[34]

The most famous case is *El-Masri v. FYR Macedonia*, where the ECtHR found a violation of Article 3 of the ECHR due to two reasons: first one regarding ill-treatment of the applicant, who was a foreign national, and was subjected to torture, inhumane, and degrading treatment during detention, and the second reason due to the transfer to a third country, where there was a real risk that the applicant could be exposed to the treatments prohibited by Article 3 of the ECHR. In the same case, the ECtHR found that there had been a violation of Article 3 of the ECHR in the procedural aspect due to the failure of the Macedonian investigative authorities to conduct an effective investigation for identification and punishment of the offenders of the ill-treatment and torture.[35]

The last case against RNM in 2020 where the ECtHR found a violation of Article 3, is a case where the applicant is an eight-year-old child with mental disorder, so on his behalf the application was submitted by a nongovernmental organization. There was violation of the rights of a child with a disability who had been placed within a state institution for child care since he was three months old. During the ombudsman's visit, they found him tied to his bed and received the reply that "it is for his own safety." Accoding to the ECtHR, the Macedonian authorities were responsible for placing the child in an institution that could not meet his needs, found a lack of necessary care and inhumane and degrading treatment. There is also conclusion that in this case the procedural aspect of Article 3 was also violated because the national authorities did not adequately investigate the case and punish the offenders.[36]

External Oversight Mechanism

Reasons for Establishing the Mechanism

Some research regarding the best practices emphasized that prison oversight mechanism shall be established in a way that will encourage prisoners to file complaints and to be sure that there is a system to keep information confidential and protect complainant-inmates from retaliation. There should be a prisons ombudsman who accepts and arbitrates complaints about prisons, but also a multifaceted system should be developed with the purpose of strengthening prison oversight with active participation of the civil society organizations. Best practice prioritizes meaningful independence, clarity of mandate, functions, and powers, and the holistic practice of oversight that includes, at the very least, inspection, monitoring, investigative, and reporting powers. Meaningful independence requires that the oversight body enjoy financial, legal, operational, and institutional independence, as well as security of tenure for its staff.[37]

According to the assessment of the European Commission (EC) in the report on RNM for 2016, the Sector for Internal Control and Professional Standards within the Ministry of the Interior is not efficient enough—especially when it comes to brutality and inhuman treatment by police officers. Even when sentences are imposed toward police officers, they are not dissuasive enough. So, there was a proposal for establishing an independent and effective external oversight mechanism over the police.[38] During 2015, the Ombudsman office received 21 complaints regarding inhuman and degrading treatment by the police. Although the unit for internal control and professional standards in the Ministry of the Interior received 62 complaints on the same grounds, the results are disappointing because in only three cases did the unit decide that there was an unjustified physical force by the police officers, and only one police officer was charged for inhumane and degrading treatment.[39]

The European Commission pointed out that the prison system violates international human rights standards, as pointed out by the Committee for the Prevention of Torture (CPT) in relation to the Republic of North Macedonia.[40] Such mechanism can provide guarantees that reports of police brutality are being investigated seriously and thoroughly.

The Council of Europe has supported the national authorities in the RNM regarding the process of developing the concept and legislative framework for establishing an external oversight mechanism over police officers and prison police.[41]

THE CONCEPT OF "PROSECUTOR PLUS"

The concept of "prosecutor plus" was established as a specialized unit for investigation and prosecution of criminal offenses committed by police officers and members of the prison police, by the law on amendments to the Law on Public Prosecutor's Office in 2018 (hereinafter: LPPO 2018).[42] However, there are changes introduced by the new LPPO, which began implementation on June 30, 2020 (hereinafter: LPPO 2020).[43] The specialized unit has been effective since December 1, 2018, and its establishment was positively assessed by the GRECO.[44]

A specialized unit for investigation and prosecution of criminal offenses committed by police officers and members of the prison police was established within the Basic Public Prosecutor's Office for prosecution of organized crime and corruption.

The public prosecutors from the specialized unit shall manage the preliminary procedure and undertake the actions independently or through the public prosecutor's investigators regarding the:

- criminal offenses committed by persons with police powers[45] and members of the prison police while performing the official duties and powers,
- offenses committed outside the service with the use of a serious threat, force, or means of coercion resulting in death, severe bodily injury, bodily injury, unlawful deprivation of liberty, torture, and other cruel, inhumane or degrading treatment, or punishment for offenses ex-officio prosecuted by the public prosecutor as a competent authority. Aside from the above-mentioned criminal offenses, the specialized unit shall, by ex officio decision, initiate a procedure for:
- assessing the merits of using firearms, as well as the use of force or means of coercion resulting in death or severe bodily injury by the persons with police powers and members of the prison police.

The competences of the specialized unit have the reflection toward the the organizational unit in the Ministry of Interior responsible for internal control and professional standards. This unit in the MOI shall take actions for initiating a disciplinary procedure in relation to the acts that fall within the competetnce of the specialized unit, only upon approval of the competent public prosecutor from the specialized unit.

For successful and effective functioning of the specialized unit, the legislative solution related to the investigation center is important. LPPO 2018 had a provision that the specialized unit shall undertake actions independently or through investigators assigned to this unit. However, the LPPO 2020 does not contain an explicit provision that there are investigators assigned to a specialized unitwho might be assessed as a solution that contribute toward reducing the effectiveness of this unit.

There is increased hierarchical control regarding deployment of public prosecutors and the head of the specialized unit. Previously, LPPO 2018, the deployment was the competence of the head of the Basic Public Prosecutor's Office for prosecuting organized crime and corruption, and according to the LPPO 2020, there is additional condition—prior consent of the public prosecutor of the RNM. Bearing in mind that the public prosecutor of the RNM is elected by the parliament upon proposal of the government, this legislative solution increases the risk of possible political influence regarding the personal structure of the specialized unit.

In the context of transparency, the changes in LPPO 2020 no longer contain the obligation for the specialized unit to prepare an annual report that shall be submitted to the head of the Basic Public Prosecutor's Office for prosecution of organized crime and corruption, the council of the public prosecutors, the public prosecutor of the RNM, and to the parliament. Given that such a solution was in line with the recommendations of GRECO in the context of a higher level of transparency,[46] there is a possibility for our country to receive a new recommendation in this regard in the following evaluation rounds.

THE OVERSIGHT MECHANISM OVER PRISON POLICE

The oversight mechanism over the prison police was introduced by amendments to the LES 2018. Penal institutions and educational correctional facilities as well as the directorate for the execution of sanctions shall not delay any report to the specialized unit in the PPO in the case where there is existence of grounds for suspicion that a prison police officer committed a criminal offense, which prosecution is within the competence of the public prosecution.

The subject of the report are criminal offenses committed during undertaking official actions, but also criminal offenses committed outside the service, where the important way of acting (modus operandi) is: the use of a serious threat, force, or means of coercion.

The consequences of the criminal offense shall be: death, severe bodily injuty, infliction of bodily harm, unlawful deprivation of liberty, torture, and other cruel, inhumane, or degrading treatment or punishment. Additionally, the provisions of the new LES 2019 stipulate that professional supervision of penal and educational correctional institutions by the directorate for execution of sanctions, includes direct supervision of work. One of the goals of this supervision is the prevention of torture and inhumane and degrading treatment in these institutions. Whenever the directorate for execution of sanctions considers that such proceedings have taken place, its obligation is to report the case to the specialized unit.

The rights of the convicts are strengthened with the LES 2019, by the possibility the convict person to submit a request to the CPT and the UN High Commissioner for Human Rights, when the convict considers that some basic human rights have been violated while serving his sentence within the penal institution. When there is a request from the CPT or the UN High Commissioner, the director of the directorate for execution of sanctions is obliged to examine all allegations and through the Ministry of Justice to inform the competent authority what was determined. Whenever there is a request from the convicted person, the director of the directorate for execution of sanctions is obliged to provide the international representatives direct contact with the convicted person, insight, and meetings with the officials in the institution, in order to establish the facts related to the specific case.

Civil Control Mechanism: "Ombudsman Plus"

The ombudsman mechanism is set up in the Ombudsman Office as the ombudsman. It is taking actions together with representatives of three civil society organizations, elected through a public announcement in the parliament, as follows:

- Association for Criminal Law and Criminology of Macedonia,[47]
- Macedonian Association of Young Lawyers[48] and
- Helsinki Committee for Human Rights.[49]

The ombudsman takes actions and measures to provide support and protection of victims, their rights and the representation of their interests in all cases before the public administration bodies, as well as before the prosecution and the courts. The competence (ratione materiae) mechanism of civil control coincides with the competence of the specialized unit in the PPO.

The ombudsman shall initiate proceedings upon request of the victims or members of his family, upon the initiative of a civil society organization's representative, as well as at its own initiative after receives notification about possible violations of the right to life and prohibition of torture in the context of ECHR.

In order to successfully perform the competences, the Ombudsman is competent for the following actions and measures:

- monitoring of actions to all involved bodies, organizations, and institutions,

- reviewing records of police investigations and other investigations conducted by a competent authority,
- to inspect the cases, access all relevant documents (medical documentation, statements of the victim, witness, and perpetrator),
- meetings with the victims, witnesses, and offenders,
- visiting the involved bodies, organizations, and institutions and proposing a renewing of a certain procedure before the competent body and public prosecution,
- legal support for victims and their family members,
- early warning of persons with police powers and members of the prison police,
- monitoring the implementation of regulations, identifying gaps, and submitting initiatives on amendments to laws and other bylaws and their harmonization with international agreements ratified in accordance with the constitution of the RNM and
- taking other measures provided by law.

Because of the transparency of work, the ombudsman is obliged to submit a report, which is an integral part of the ombudsman's annual report regarding the respect, promotion, and protection of constitutional and legislative rights of citizens, that is submitting to the parliament and shall be available to the public. However, taking into account the nature of the competences, in certain cases, the ombudsman may prepare and publish special reports. This obligation and possibility is a mechanism for civil control in accordance with the requirements of GRECO. Namely, as in relation to the public prosecutor's office, GRECO recommends that the available mechanisms for external oversight of police forces, including the ombudsman, be subject to adequate transparency regarding the cases and providing appropriate statistics. Technical support for the activities of the ombudsman—external mechanism of civil control—is provided through the separate unit within the administrative service of the ombudsman's office.

CONCLUSION

Establishing the rule of law, constitutionality and legality, responsibility of public function holders, nonselective, fast, and effective criminal justice remain the key challenge of Republic of North Macedonia on its way to the EU. Its central areas are prevention and repression of crime, as a strategy for efficient fight against crime, which inspires the law makers and as practical activity of the courts and other bodies in the fight for repression of crime.

The results from numerous conferences and published materials, which present the opinions supported with arguments about the situation of the Macedonian judiciary, indicate the addressed critics and suggestions on how to continue in the future. It is an encouraging indicator that there is a capacity to direct the reforms in the right way toward the European integration of RNM.

The new law is an expression of the efforts for the continuous upgrade and improvement of the national penitentiary system, modernization, and humanization thereof, in order to reach the goals for punishing prisoners and reducing the tendency of the prisoners to reoffend. LES can be assessed as a comprehensive systematic law that fully regulates the execution of sanctions, pronouncing sanctions based on the person's age, offense, types of sanctions, status, rights, and obligations of the prison police. The increase of accommodating capacities, efficient utilization of the existing capacities in penitentiaries, as well as establishing a special probation unit as an alternative for imprisonment are feasible solutions and may contribute to a reduction of the numbers of people in prison, as well as the overcrowding in the prison system.

The ambitiously prepared reform in the penitentiary sphere will not give the wanted results, unless the risks from application thereof are analyzed especially from the aspect of preparedness of the judiciary, public prosecution, and other institutions of criminal justice for coherent implementation of its provisions.

BIBLIOGRAPHY

Andonovski v. the former Yugoslav Republic of Macedonia, no. 24312/10 (ECtHR, 23 July 2015).

Annual Reports on the Work of the Ombudsman (ombudsman.mk, 2021), http://ombudsman.mk/%D0%9F%D0%BE%D1%87%D0%B5%D1%82%D0%BD%D0%B0/%D0%93%D0%BE%D0%B4%D0%B8%D1%88%D0%BD%D0%B8_%D0%B8%D0%B7%D0%B2%D0%B5%D1%88%D1%82%D0%B0%D0%B8.aspx, accessed 28 November 2021.

Arnaudovski, Lj., and A. Gruevska Drakulevsk. *Law on Execution of Sanctions: Integral Text with Preface, Brief Explanations and Register of Terms with Attachments* (1st ed., Studiorum Center for Regional Research and Cooperation, 2011).

Asenov v. Bulgaria, no. 42026/98 (ECtHR, 15 July 2005).

Asllani v. the former Yugoslav Republic of Macedonia, no. 24058/13 (ECtHR, 10 December 2015).

Boicenco v. Moldova, no. 41088/05 (ECtHR, 11 July 2006).

Breuer, M., and William A. Schabas. "The European Convention on Human Rights: A Commentary Referent." *Archiv des Völkerrechts* 54, no. 2, pp. 228–232.

Chahal v. the United Kingdom (ECtHR, 15 November 1996), Reports of Judgments and Decisions 1996-V.

Dodov v. Bulgaria, no. 59548/00 (ECtHR, 17 January 2008).

Dzeladinov and Others v. the Former Yugoslav Republic of Macedonia, no. 13252/02 (ECtHR, 10 April 2008).

El-Masri v. the Former Yugoslav Republic of Macedonia [GC], no. 39630/09 (ECHR, 2012).

"European Parliament Resolution of 5 October 2017 on Prison Systems and Conditions" (2015/2062(INI)) (Eur-lex.europa.eu, 2021), https://eur-lex.europa.eu /legal-content/EN/TXT/?uri=CELEX%3A52017IP0385, accessed 25 December 2020.

Gorgiev v. the Former Yugoslav Republic of Macedonia, no. 26984/05 (ECtHR, 19 April 2012).

Hajrulahu v. the Former Yugoslav Republic of Macedonia, no. 37537/07 (ECtHR, 29 October 2015).

Jasar v. the Former Yugoslav Republic of Macedonia, no. 69908/01 (ECtHR, 15 February 2007).

Kambovski, V., B. G. Lazetik, L. Nanev, O. Koshevaliska, B. Arifi, and Dz. Saiti. *Commentary on the Law on Justice for Children with Practicum* (Skopje: Juvenile Delinquency Prevention Council, 2018).

Kambovski, V., and T. E. Mujoska. *Legal Postulates on Criminal Justice Reform* (Skopje: Macedonian Academy of Sciences and Arts, 2020).

L.R. v. North Macedonia, no. 38067/15 (ECtHR, 23 January 2020).

Labita v. Italy [GC], no. 26772/95, ECHR 2000-IV.

Mowbray, A., *The Development of Positive Obligations under the European Convention on Human Rights by the European Court of Human Rights* (Hart Publishing, 2004)

"National Strategy for Development of the Penitentiary System, 2015–2019" (Pravda.gov.mk, 2015). https://www.pravda.gov.mk/Upload/Documents/ Nacionalna_strategijaMK_12_2014.pdf, accessed 27 November 2020.

"National Strategy for Development of the Penitentiary System, 2015–2019" (Pravda.gov.mk, 2015) https://www.pravda.gov.mk/Upload/Documents/ Nacionalna_strategijaMK_12_2014.pdf, accessed 27 November 2020.

"Nelson Mandela Rules" (Un.org, 2021) https://www.un.org/en/events/mandeladay /mandela_rules.shtml#:~:text=A%2FRES%2F70%2F175%20not%20only%20 adopted%20the%20revised,the%20course%20of%20his%20struggle, accessed 25 December 2020.

Okkalı v. Turkey, no. 52067/99, ECHR 2006-XII (extracts).

"Preventing Corruption and Promoting Integrity in Central Governments (Top Executive Functions) and Law Enforcement Agencies" (GrecoEval5Rep[2018]7, 2019) https://www.coe.int/en/web/greco/evaluations/north-macedonia, accessed 28 December 2020.

"Recommendations of the Senior Experts' Group: Urgent Reform Priorities" (Ec.europa.eu, 2015) https://ec.europa.eu/neighbourhood-enlargement/system/files/2016-12/20150619_recommendations_of_the_senior_experts_group.pdf, accessed 28 November 2020.

Refugees U, "Report to the Government of 'The Former Yugoslav Republic of Macedonia on the Visit' to 'The Former Yugoslav Republic of Macedonia' Carried out by the European Committee for the Prevention of Torture and Inhuman or Degrading Treatment or Punishment (CPT) from 6 to 9 December 2016" (Refworld, 2017) https://www.refworld.org/docid/59df47ae4.html, accessed 28 December 2020.

Reidy, A., *The Prohibition of Torture* (Directorate General of Human Rights, Council of Europe 2003).

Selami and Others v. the former Yugoslav Republic of Macedonia, no. 78241/13, (ECtHR, 1 March 2018).

Selmouni v. France [GC], no. 25803/94, ECHR 1999-V.

Sulejmanov v. the former Yugoslav Republic of Macedonia, no. 69875/01 (ECtHR, 24 April 2008).

"The Former Yugoslav Republic of Macedonia 2016 Report Communication on EU Enlargement Policy (COM (2016) 715 Final)" (Ec.europa.eu, 2016), https://ec.europa.eu/neighbourhood-enlargement/sites/near/files/pdf/key_documents/2016/20161109_report_the_former_yugoslav_republic_of_macedonia.pdf, accessed 28 December 2020.

Trajkoski v. the former Yugoslav Republic of Macedonia, no. 13191/02 (ECtHR, 7 February 2008).

Van Dijk, P., G. J. Hoof, and G. J. Van Hoof. *Theory and Practice of the European Convention on Human Rights* (Martinus Nijhoff Publishers, 1998).

NOTES

1. Criminal Code of the Republic of North Macedonia, Official Gazette, No. 37/1996; 80/1999; 48/2001; 4/2002; 16/2002; 43/2003; 19/2004; 40/2004; 81/2005; 50/2006; 60/2006; 73/2006; 87/2007; 7/2008; 139/2008; 114/2009; 51/2011; 51/2011; 135/2011; 185/2011; 142/2012; 143/2012; 166/2012; 55/2013; 82/2013; 14/2014; 27/2014; 28/2014; 41/2014; 41/2014; 115/2014; 132/2014; 160/2014; 199/2014; 196/2015; 226/2015; 97/2017; 170/2017; 248/2018; Link: https://pretsedatel.mk/wp-content/uploads/2020/03/Krivicen-zakonik.pdf, last accessed 28 November 2020. Another amendment to the law was prepared in December 2020. An expert group has been working on the new criminal code since 2019.

2. Official Gazette of R. Macedonia, No. 150/2010 dated 18 November 2010. Enters into force on 26 November 2010; Amendments, *Official Gazette of R. Macedonia*, No. 100/2012, 142/2016, 193/2016, and 198/2018.

3. Official Gazette of R. Macedonia, No. 99/2019 dated 21 May 2019. Enters into force on 29 May 2019; Amendments, *Official Gazette of R. Macedonia*, No. 220/2019.

4. Official Gazette of R. Macedonia, No. 96/2019 dated 17 May 2019. Enters into force on 25 May 2019.

5. Official Gazette of R. Macedonia, No. 148/2013 dated 29 October 2013. Enters into force on 6 November 2013; Amendments, *Official Gazette of R. Macedonia*, No. 152/2019; 275/2019.

6. Kambovski, V., et al., *Commentary on the Law on Justice for Children with Practicum* (Skopje: Juvenile Delinquency Prevention Council, 2018).

7. For more information, see Ljupco Arnaudovski and Aleksandra Gruevska Drakulevski, *Law on Execution of Sanctions: Integral Text with Preface, Brief Explanations and Register of Terms with Attachments* (1st ed., Studiorum Center for Regional Research and Cooperation, 2011), p. 10.

8. Available at https://www.un.org/en/events/mandeladay/mandela_rules.shtml -:~:text=A%2FRES%2F70%2F175 not only adopted the revised, the course of his struggle, accessed 30 December 2020.

9. Available at https://eur-lex.europa.eu/legal-content/EN/TXT/?uri=CELEX %3A52017IP0385/, accessed 30 December 2020.

10. National Strategy for Development of the Penitentiary System, 2015–2019.

11. The document was not made official at the time of submitting this chapter. The only published information was that one-day workshop for presentation of the new Strategy for Penitentiary System should be held by the end of December 2020. Source https://rm.coe.int/0900001680a03373/, accessed 30 December 2020.

12. The prison rules determines the manner of living and the organization of work in the institutions. Since June 2020, every penal and educational facility has a new prison rules.

13. On the surface area of 25.713 km^2, according to the official data from the State Statistical Office, on 31.12.2019 in the RNM, there were a total number of 2,076,255 inhabitants, which is 1.15% more compared to 2019 (Macedonia in figures, 2019). Source: State Statistical Office (*Stat.gov.mk*), http://www.stat.gov.mk/, accessed 30 December 2020.

14. Official Gazette of R. Macedonia, No. 233/2018 dated 20 December 2018. Enters into force on 20 December 2018.

15. Official Gazette of R. Macedonia, No. 226/2015 dated 2 January 2016. Enters into force on 1 November 2016.

16. Annual Reports on The Work of the Ombudsman (ombudsman.mk, 2021), http: //ombudsman.mk/%D0%9F%D0%BE%D1%87%D0%B5%D1%82%D0%BD%D0 %B0/%D0%93%D0%BE%D0%B4%D0%B8%D1%88%D0%BD%D0%B8_%D0 %B8%D0%B7%D0%B2%D0%B5%D1%88%D1%82%D0%B0%D0%B8.aspx, accessed 28 November 2021.

17. For the purposes of this paper, we requested information regarding the education process in all 12 penitentiary institutions, prisons, and CEF. We received 11 answers.

18. Official Gazette No.10/2020, dated 16 January 2020, enters into force on 17 January 2020.

19. For the purposes of this paper, we also requested information form the DES and prisons regarding the work for prisoners.

20. Link: (Pravda.gov.mk) https://www.pravda.gov.mk/zatvori, accessed 28 December 2020.

21. The construction of a new correctional facility was expected for more than 19 years and is a permanent solution to the long-term problem of accommodation of juveniles who have been sentenced to correctional measures. See more at "Macedonian Society of Penology" (Msp.org.mk, 2020), http://www.msp.org.mk/, accessed 24 November 2020; some activities were undertaken by children in the CEF in Volkovija before the New Year's holidays, as well: http://dspdp.com.mk/vesti/aktivnosti-vo-vpd-tetovo-vo-s-volkovija/, accessed 24 December 2020.

22. Source: "State Statistical Office" (Stat.gov.mk), http://www.stat.gov.mk/, accessed 28 November 2020.

23. The data refers to the period up to 31 December 2020.

24. Official Gazette No. 133/2020, dated 22 May 2020, enters into force on 23 May 2020.

25. *Boicenco v. Moldova* App no 41088/05 (ECtHR, 11 July 2006, §102), *Labita v. Italy* (App. no. 26772/95), § 119, ECtHR 2000-IV; *Selmouni v. France* (App. no. 25803/94, § 95), ECtHR 1999-V; *Assenov and Others v. Bulgaria* (ECtHR, 28 October 1998, § 93); *Chahal v. the United Kingdom* (ECtHR, 15 November 1996, § 79).

26. Aisling Reidy, *The Prohibition of Torture* (Directorate General of Human Rights, Council of Europe, 2003); Marten Breuer, *William A. Schabas: The European Convention on Human Rights: A Commentary Referent* (2015).

27. A. R. Mowbray, *The Development of Positive Obligations under the European Convention on Human Rights by the European Court of Human Rights* (Hart Publishing, 2004), p. 191–195.

28. Aisling Reidy, *The Prohibition of Torture* (Directorate General of Human Rights, Council of Europe, 2003).

29. *Dodov v. Bulgaria,* App. no. 59548/00 (ECtHR, 17 January 2008, § 83).

30. *Assenov and Others v. Bulgaria*, 28 October 1998, § 103, Reports of Judgments and Decisions 1998–VIII and *Boicenco v. Moldova,* App. no. 41088/05, § 123 (ECtHR, 11 July 2006).

31. *Jašar v. FYR Macedonia,* App. no. 69908/01 (ECtHR, 15 February 2007); *Trajkovski v. FYR Macedonia,* App. no. 13191/02 (ECtHR, 7 February 2008); *Sulejmanov v. FYR Macedonia,* App. no. 69875/01 (ECtHR, 24 April 2008); *Đeladinov and Others v. FYR Macedonia,* App. no. 13252/02 (ECtHR, 10 April 2008); *Selami and Others v. FYR Macedonia,* App. no. 78241/13 (ECtHR, 1 March 2018).

32. *Andonovski v. FYR Macedonia,* App. no. 24312/10 (ECtHR, 23 July 2015); *Asllani v. FYR Macedonia,* App. no. 24058/13 (ECtHR, 10 December 2015); *Hajrulahu v. FYR Macedonia,* App. no. 37537/07 (ECtHR, 29 October 2015).

33. *Gjorgiev v. FYR Macedonia,* App. no. 26984/05 (ECtHR, 19 April 2012).

34. See also *Okkalı v. Turkey,* App. no. 52067/99 § 65 ECHR, 2006–XII (extracts).

35. *El-Masri v. FYR Macedonia,* App. no. 39630/09 (ECtHR, 13 December 2012).

36. *L. R v. North Macedonia,* App. no. 38067/15 (ECtHR, 23 January 2020).

37. A. Nevin and Z. Wasserman, *Best Practices: Research Report, A Comparative Analysis of Prison Oversight Bodies* (Sonke Gender Justice, The Detention Justice Forum Open Society Foundation, 2019).

38. The Former Yugoslav Republic of Macedonia 2016 Report, Communication on EU Enlargement Policy (COM (2016) 715 final), Brussels, 9 November 2016.

39. The Former Yugoslav Republic of Macedonia 2016 Report, Communication on EU Enlargement Policy (COM (2016) 715 final), Brussels, 9 November 2016.

40.United Refugees, "Report to the Government of 'The Former Yugoslav Republic of Macedonia' on the Visit to 'The Former Yugoslav Republic of Macedonia' Carried out by the European Committee for the Prevention of Torture and Inhuman or Degrading Treatment or Punishment (CPT) from 6 to 9 December 2016" (Refworld, 2017)

41. Project *Support to the Establishment of an External Oversight Mechanism*, financed by the Council of Europe and the Ministry of Foreign Affairs of the Kingdom of the Netherlands, implemented by the Council of Europe in the period from 1 December 2015 until 30 April 2016.

42. *Official Gazette of R. Macedonia*, No. 150/2007, 111/2008, and 198/2018.

43. *Official Gazette of R. North Macedonia*, No. 42/2020.

44. "Preventing Corruption and Promoting Integrity in Central Governments (Top Executive Functions) and Law Enforcement Agencies" (GrecoEval5Rep[2018]7, 2019).

45. This term encompasses a police officer, authorized official for security and counterintelligence with police authorizations, members of the financial police and forest police, persons authorized by law of the Customs Administration who work on detecting crimes and authorized officials of the Ministry of Defense working on detecting and investigating crimes.

46. "Preventing Corruption and Promoting Integrity in Central Governments (Top Executive Functions) and Law Enforcement Agencies" (GrecoEval5Rep[2018]7, 2019).

47."ZKPKM" (Maclc.mk), http://www.maclc.mk/, accessed 28 November 2020.

48. "MYLA" (MYLA), http://myla.org.mk/, accessed 28 November 2020.

49. "MHC" (mhc.org.mk), https://mhc.org.mk/, accessed 28 November 2020.

Index

About the Contributors

Ed Johnston is an associate professor of Criminal Justice and Procedure at the University of Northampton, UK. Ed's research interest are in the areas of pre-trial disclosure, the role of the defense lawyer and the rise of managerialism in an adversarial setting. Ed's monograph *The Role of the Defense Lawyer* was published by Rowman & Littlefield in June 2021. Ed has published widely concerning issues within criminal justice. Ed runs the YouTube channel, *Criminal Justice Natters*.

Ed lives in Somerset in the southwest of England, with his partner, Wolfy, their two children, Erin and Jacob and cat, Harry.

Sophie Marsh is an associate lecturer in law and criminology at the University of the West of England. She is also a law PhD student at the University of the West of England. Her thesis will explore the extent to which rape myths are impacting the high levels of attrition in cases of rape. Sophie's interests include sexual offenses, criminal procedure, criminal law, and human rights. She runs an online blog, Soph Talks, and lives in Bristol with her partner, Charlie.

Raquel Borges Blázquez is an assistant professor in procedural law at the Faculty of Law, University of Valencia. Her lines of research are the protection of victims in criminal procedures, European criminal cooperation, and the use of artificial intelligence in the criminal justice system. She has carried out research stays in centers of recognized prestige, such as Max Planck Institute for the Study of Crime, Security and Law in Freiburg, the European Union Agency for Fundamental Rights (FRA) in Vienna and Max Planck Institute for Comparative Public Law and International Law in Heidelberg.

Zoran Burić is associate professor at the department of Criminal Procedural Law at the University of Zagreb Faculty of Law. He is the editor in chief of *Zagreb Law Review*. He wrote his PhD dissertation "Models of Cross-Border

Evidence Gathering in European Union Criminal Law" within the procedure for an international joint doctorate (University of Zagreb/University of Freiburg). Main fields of his professional interest are criminal procedural law, European Union criminal law, human rights in criminal proceedings, comparative criminal justice, rights of victims of crime, and psychiatry and law.

Toni Carr is an independent socio-legal researcher located in New Zealand. Her research focuses on problem solving courts, drug treatment courts, and sentencing. As part of her PhD, she conducted an ethnographic study of the Alcohol and Other Drug Treatment court pilot to investigate the impact of treatment policies and practices on offender health and wellbeing. From 2017–2020, she was a research fellow on a Marsden fellowship at the School of Law, Victoria University of Wellington

Mehzeb Chowdhury is an inventor, instructor, criminologist, and criminal law barrister based in the United Kingdom. He is the innovator of the MABMAT Crime Scene Imaging Rover, which has received acclaim from the American Bar Association (ABA) and the National Aeronautics and Space Administration (NASA). His work has been showcased by the Federal Bureau of Investigation (FBI) Scientific Program Committee at the National Institute of Standards and Technology (NIST), as well as the Chartered Society of Forensic Sciences (CSoFS). Chowdhury has been published in 20 countries, in eight languages, with headlining museum exhibits for his seminal work in forensic science at the National Science and Media Museum, Bradford, and the Museum of Science and Industry, Manchester. His research interests include criminology, criminalistics, forensic science, futures studies, criminal justice histories, science and technology studies, robotics, artificial intelligence, augmented and virtual reality technologies, and outer space studies. Chowdhury is also an award-winning filmmaker, with films screening in more than a hundred leading festivals around the world, and his contribution to science fiction has been exalted on three continents.

Freya Doughty is a doctoral candidate in the School of Law at Washington University in St. Louis, completing her JSD thesis on the intersection of international human rights law, environmental law, and children's rights. She is also an evaluation and assessment research assistant at the Gephardt Institute for Civic and Community Engagement, working toward boosting civic understanding and political involvement among Washington University's student population. Previously, Freya worked as a researcher for Mischon de Reya LLP in London on cases related to corruption and financial crime, and as a research assistant to Professor Charles Jalloh of the United Nations International Law Commission. She holds an LLB(Hons) from the University of the West of England in Bristol, and an LL.M in Public International Law from the London School of Economics and Political Science. She now lives in San Antonio, Texas, with her husband and their cat, George.

Richard Hester is a senior lecturer in social sciences at the University of Gloucestershire and is the academic course leader for BSc Criminology. He has an MSc in Criminology & Criminal Justice from the University of Portsmouth. His teaching expertise relates to policing, green criminology, research methods and restorative justice, and he has more than five years of teaching experience. Richard was a police officer with Thames Valley Police for 12 years, predominantly working in frontline policing roles before changing careers to work in Higher Education. In his police career, he specialized in football policing, working all across England and Wales policing football matches. He was also an experienced public order officer, working at a range of high-profile events, such as the London riots of 2011 and the Olympics in 2012. Richard has published research relating to improving policing of football matches. His ongoing research projects relate to Special Police Services for football policing, European eel trafficking, and comparative restorative justice.

Jack James is a lecturer in social sciences at the University of Gloucestershire. He predominantly teaches across the Professional Policing and Criminology degree programs, specializing in policing practice. Jack completed his BSc (Hons) in Criminology at the University of Gloucestershire in 2017, before working as a project coordinator for Gloucestershire Constabulary and Tewkesbury Borough Council. In this role, he worked in a multi-agency capacity to divert at-risk young people away from criminality and the criminal justice system. In 2019, he completed his master's degree at the University of Bath having studied International Security; he has worked as a lecturer full time since 2020. Jack has research interests in police use of force and TASER and was recently invited to speak at the National Police Chiefs' Council National Operational TASER conference. He is seeking to embark on his PhD studies in 2022, critically examining TASER use, representations, and perceptions. He has been a serving special constable for six years, reaching the substantive rank of special sergeant and recently the rank of temporary special inspector. Jack regularly completes upwards of 60 hours a month alongside his full-time lecturing role and was awarded Special Constable of the year for his force in 2019.

Eamon Keane is a lecturer in evidence and criminal procedure at the University of Glasgow. He holds degrees from the Universities of Dundee and Edinburgh. His academic work focuses broadly on the theoretical development and practical application of the Scots law of criminal evidence. His work often has an empirical component, and he is currently engaged on two funded projects concerning sexual history and character evidence, and the obtainment and disclosure of sensitive records in Scottish criminal trials. He has wider research interests in Scots criminal law generally. He is a member of the Law Society of Scotland's Criminal Law Committee and the Royal Society of Edinburgh's Young Academy of Scotland. Eamon is also a practicing solicitor who acts at a high-profile Scottish law firm on a consultancy basis. He has acted in various cases involving serious allegations of criminality and has been instructed by lawyers in other jurisdictions as an expert in respect of relevant legal matters pertaining to the Scots law of evidence, in extradition proceedings. Prior to entering academia, he spent two years at the Scottish Criminal Cases Review Commission, a non-departmental public body that investigates miscarriages of justice.

Elizabeta Ivičević Karas is professor at the Department of Criminal Procedural Law at Faculty of Law, University of Zagreb. She obtained her dual PhD at University Panthéon-Assas (Paris II) and University of Zagreb. She teaches Criminal Procedural Law, Penitentiary Law, and Human Rights and Criminal Justice. Her publications include four books, two manuals and numerous scientific papers. She is a member of Scientific Council for Government Administration, Judicature, and the Rule of Law of the Croatian Academy of Sciences and Art. She is also a member of Fair Trials–Legal Experts Advisory Panel (LEAP).

Gordana Lažetić has worked as a full-time professor of criminal procedural law at "Iustinianus Primus" Faculty of Law in Skopje since 2012. She served as vice dean of finance and vice dean of science from 2008 to 2014, and as a member of the University Senate from 2016 to 2020. She was a member of working groups for amending criminal legislation, witness protection, sanction execution, juvenile justice, and victim compensation, as well as working groups for drafting strategies for criminal law, judiciary, execution of sanctions, and financial investigation, among other issues. Prof. Lazetic was a member of the Governmental Council for judiciary reform, State Council for Prevention of Child Delinquency and National Council for higher education and scientific research. She was the manager of the South East European Law School Network (SEELS) and editor-in-chief of the *SEE Law Journal* from 2017 to 2021, as well as a member of the Balkan Criminology Network, which is part of the Max Planck Partner Group for Balkan Criminology in Freiburg, Germany. She has contributed to over 100 conferences, scientific and research projects, and has published more than 40 monographs, university textbooks, and brochures. She has also published over 100 articles in domestic and international journals.

Sarah Lloyd and I have always been interested in forensic psychology and legal psychology, particularly in the psychology of our Courts and how we can protect people from miscarriages of justice. I came back to academia in my 40s, which cemented my passion for learning and research in this field. I am currently a lecturer at Worcester University and I am also in the final year of my PhD. My PhD explores the group decision–making processes of juries. My work looks at how juries collectively reach a decision, using qualitative methodology to explore what they talk about, how they do this, and group factors that impact or influence these processes. It is so important to understand legal processes like these, in order to ensure our criminal justice system is as fair and informed as it possibly can be. At the moment, due to restrictions such as s.8 of the Contempt of Court Act, 1981, I use mock juries to explore these issues, but I hope one day to be able to research real jury deliberations as they happen, to increase our knowledge and understanding of these processes. I love goats and would love a small holding one day.

Eric Myles received his post-secondary education at the University of Toronto, Osgoode Hall Law School of York University and Oxford University and has been a visiting scholar at Harvard University. Since his admission to the Bar of Ontario in 1999, he has maintained an abiding interest in international law, publishing in the *Annuaire français de droit international*, the *Journal of the History of International Law,* and other fora. As legal counsel to the Ontario Regional Office of the Department of Justice Canada since 2000, he has focused his practice on Aboriginal law and tax law. His representation of Canada in multiple Indian residential school claims animated him to explore Aboriginal overrepresentation in Canadian correctional facilities—a phenomenon long eliciting commentary in Canada. He gained an opportunity to observe firsthand various circumstances that have contributed to the overrepresentation: to name several of the foremost circumstances, the intergenerational effects of the residential schools themselves on Canada's Aboriginals; racist attitudes within Euro-Canadian society; and Aboriginals' socio-economic marginalization. At the same time, his participation gave him insights into possible remedial measures: increased education of all parties to overrepresentation, reinforcement of Aboriginal identity and culture, and so forth.

Anna Pivaty is an assistant professor of criminal law and a researcher for the Institutions for Conflict Resolution research programme at Radboud University, Nijmegen, the Netherlands. Her research interests include alternatives to a criminal trial, pre-trial procedures, and digitalization of justice. She has also published extensively on criminal defense lawyering and procedural rights in criminal proceedings. Anna teaches courses on Dutch and European criminal (procedural) law, human rights, and socio-legal research methods.

Elena Mujoska-Trpevska PhD is a research fellow at the Center for Strategic Research at the Macedonian Academy of Sciences and Arts. She got her PhD degree in 2017. She was a lecturer in criminal law and criminal procedure at UACS' Faculty of Law in 2019 for undergraduate and master's students. In 2020, she passed the bar exam. Dr. Mujoska Trpevska was a member of the Ministry of Justice's working groups for drafting the Strategy for Judicial Sector Reform with an Action Plan (2017), amending the Law on Sanctions Execution (2018), and amending and codifying the Criminal Code in the Republic of North Macedonia (2019–2021). She is the author or co-author of a number of papers that have been published in a variety of domestic and international journals, and has participated in many national and international conferences. In her work, she has coordinated a number of scientific and research projects related to criminal law, penal law reform, penitentiary law, conditions in correctional institutions, human rights protection, hate crime and hate speech. Dr Elena Mujoska Trpevska is an NGO activist who has held the position of president of the Macedonian Society of Penology since 2017.

www.ingramcontent.com/pod-product-compliance
Ingram Content Group UK Ltd.
Pitfield, Milton Keynes, MK11 3LW, UK
UKHW041833031026
15587UKWH00002B/741